The World's Classics

CXV

ESSAYS AND SKETCHES

BY

LEIGH HUNT

OXFORD : HORACE HART
PRINTER TO THE UNIVERSITY

ESSAYS AND SKETCHES

BY

LEIGH HUNT

CHOSEN AND EDITED WITH AN INTRODUCTION

BY

R. BRIMLEY JOHNSON

HENRY FROWDE

OXFORD UNIVERSITY PRESS

LONDON, NEW YORK, TORONTO, MELBOURNE

JAMES HENRY LEIGH HUNT

Born, Southgate, Middlesex   .   .   October 19, 1784
Died, Putney .   .   .   .   .   August 28, 1859

This selection from Leigh Hunt's prose-writings
was first published in 'The World's Classics' in
1906 and reprinted in 1912.

INTRODUCTION

ALTHOUGH, perhaps, most generally known as the good friend of greater men, Leigh Hunt had an important influence on his generation, and cannot be summarily dismissed as a mere reflection of others. The occupation, and the purpose, of his life may be summed up in his own words of the paper he edited for so many years, to the permanent advantage of the Press—' to assist in producing a fusion of literary tastes into all subjects whatever.'

His politics were honest and enlightened ; his moral teaching, if somewhat sentimental, was courageously sincere ; he established theatrical criticism in England. But his greatest and most lasting contribution to literature was an *appreciation* of good books and great writers far more catholic and sympathetic than much of our brilliant or scholarly criticism. Lamb, Hazlitt, and Coleridge (among his contemporaries) worked with rare insight over certain fields ; but their limitations and prejudices are obvious. Leigh Hunt's distinction is universality. He never missed a good thing, ancient or modern. He insisted, again and again, on the beauty (then entirely neglected) of Chaucer and the old ballads, on the superiority of Shakespeare over the ' improvements ' of Dryden and his peers, on the forgotten music of Spenser's verse. He defended Keats, Shelley, and Wordsworth against the scurrilous attacks of ' established ' criticism, and many a less robust genius owed its birth and development to his generous encouragement. He lived to recommend Tennyson for the Laureateship, and to welcome, with rare insight, the *Paracelsus* and other ' difficult ' poems of Robert Browning.

In these days of the popular reprint and the Extension Lecturer, when even the half-penny papers have their literary columns, we may not recognize immediately the significance of this record. It should be remembered that Leigh Hunt was writing before the freedom of the Press had been thoroughly established, before we won political independence, before education. Admittedly he was non-academic. But it has been of incalculable benefit to his own, and to future, generations, that the most popular and most prolific journalist of the Dawn was inspired by almost matchless taste and almost universal sympathy.

The earlier essays here headed 'Books and Bookmen' reveal the man. They are obviously written in a well-stored library, its owner's familiar friend. He loved books of every age and fashion, had his own fancies about their writers, and was never weary of proclaiming their 'Beauties'. To-day, perhaps, we attach small value to signpost criticism; but even our superior knowledge and sound judgement may learn charity to the unfashionable, and discover the unexpected, under this genial guide. In fact, few of us are so steeped in literature as he; and an investigation into his allusions or, for example, into the sources of his 'Tales, Old and New,' would lead us by many a path yet untrodden for our fullest series of 'World's Classics'. Meanwhile, his enthusiasm over 'Cooke's Poets' and similar pioneers may serve to remind us of our own opportunities, and bear witness to the enthusiastic industry of those who paved the royal road.

Although typically Early Victorian, Leigh Hunt was also a born journalist. Many of the papers, 'About Town' and 'At Home', as well as those on 'The Weather', or on 'Dress and Manners', are the genuine 'holiday' article of to-day; based on keen and humorous observation of the commonplace. He anticipated the 'preservation of old buildings', and would have rejoiced in our tablets recording the homes of the famous. He is more emotional, and far more personal, than his grandchildren of the Press. His persistent cheerfulness may be resented as superficial and occasionally wearies the reader. But its foundations were sincerely erected on deep feeling and an experience of suffering that would have crushed a weaker man. It must be admitted further that 'the Country' he loved so well was frankly suburban; but we do not know the suburbs as he saw them. He travelled little, and—in his day—the gospel of Nature was new and commendable.

'The Characters' conform approximately to the special form best known among us through Samuel Butler, but never very popular in this country. Leigh Hunt's work, indeed, differs materially from the accepted models, and it is improbable he was consciously following any. I am inclined to think that 'the character' as a literary type must have escaped his notice, since he never alludes thereto, despite his enthusiasm for the 'Genuine Remains' of the author of *Hudibras.* Yet the form has been seldom, if ever, adopted with happier effect.

The essays as a whole resemble those of Lamb more nearly than any other (Hazlitt's being in the main deliberately scholastic and critical, dealing with set subjects). Yet Leigh Hunt was no Elia-monger. He does not, as he himself would have been the first to declare, ever reach the perfection of that prose-master. Technically speaking, he had no genius for style. But, on the other hand, his subjects are more varied, his views more extended; and the wider outlook nowhere lacks insight. The similarity between the two men consists in a rare gift for making literature by the light-handed but subtle treatment of apparent trivialities. Each in his manner, was a Prince of Miscellanists.

Personally, as in his work, Leigh Hunt never emerged from the shifts of journalism. Constitutionally incapable of settling down, he always faced new ventures with enthusiasm. He was born (October 19, 1784) in Southgate, then 'a scene of trees and meadows, of greenery and nestling cottages, . . . a place lying out of the way of innovation,' with ' the pure sweet air of antiquity about it.' The love of suburban scenery, acquired in childhood, never left him ; and, without regarding it as a term of reproach, he always avowed himself a true Cockney, though not so by descent. The *Autobiography* contains an amusing record of his ancestors, ' who, on the mother's side, seem all sailors and rough subjects, with a mitigation, on the female part, of quakerism ; as on the father's side they are all creoles and claret-drinkers, very polite and clerical.' His father and mother, indeed, only left America a little before his birth, driven thence by loyalty to the mother-country ; so that his sunny optimism and impressionableness may be fairly attributed to a strain of the Creole in the blood : tolerably evident, as we are told, in his complexion and general appearance. Although considerably spoiled as a child, he seems to have derived a good deal of enjoyment from the somewhat rough life at Christ Hospital, of which his recorded memories are still living,—with those of Lamb and Coleridge.

Immediately after his school-days, the injudicious father collected subscriptions for a volume of verse ' written between the ages of twelve and sixteen '; published in 1801 as *Juvenilia*, by J. H. L. Hunt. Though he acted for a time as clerk to an attorney, and served a few months in the War Office, the young Leigh never seriously entertained the idea of any profession outside letters. His first efforts were in imitation of *The Connoisseur*, itself copied from *The Spectator*; and he soon utilized his love of the theatre by boldly criticizing the reigning favourites in one of the numerous papers set up by John Hunt, the printer. In 1808 this same brother assisted him in the establishment of *The Examiner*, ' a Sunday paper on Politics, Domestic Economy, and Theatricals.' From that year until a week before his death, just over fifty years later, Leigh Hunt wrote continuously for the Press—as his own editor or under others ; and every one of the books subsequently issued by him was substantially a newspaper reprint. One can only marvel that, under such conditions, so much of his work is of permanent excellence.

Of his private habits, his wife, or his children, we know unexpectedly little; for like many other apparently frank and egotistical writers, he was reserved about personal affairs. The *Autobiography*, indeed, is a singularly honest confession of tastes and temperament; but most elusive and inconsequent as a record of facts. Probably there is little to be known; certainly nothing that should alter our estimate of the man's nature. A life devoted to literature and good-fellowship may be outwardly uneventful, though fertile in every kind of experience; and we cannot suppose his a weak personality who won and retained affection from the moody Hazlitt, the fastidious Lamb, that fine hater Thomas Carlyle and his sarcastic wife. His friends, indeed, great and little, were veritably legion; and their testimony is almost unanimous. His passionate devotion to Shelley never checked the mutual freedom of true comradeship, and *The Cenci* is dedicated as to an equal:—

Had I known a person more highly endowed than yourself with all that it becomes a man to possess, I had selected for this work the ornament of his name. One more gentle, honourable, innocent, and brave; one of more exalted toleration for all who do and think evil, and yet himself more free from evil; one who knows better how to receive and how to confer a benefit, though he must ever confer far more than he can receive; one of simpler, and, in the highest sense of the word, of purer life and manners, I never knew, and I had already been fortunate in friendships when your name was added to the list.

On two occasions, indeed, the busy monotony of his quiet, though struggling, existence was somewhat rudely disturbed. In February, 1812, *The Examiner* embarked on a crusade against the Prince Regent, which, however justifiable, was neither prudent nor generous. Our young editor had not yet conquered the delight in hard-hitting which marred his earliest theatrical criticism [1]; and his virtuous assumption of morality was ill calculated to edification. His statements, however, were true and libellous: the last of four attempted prosecutions was successful: Leigh Hunt was fined £500, and condemned to prison for two years. His own account of the experience is unique. He surrounded himself with book-cases and busts, with flowers and a pianoforte; till Lamb declared that 'there was no other such room except in a fairy tale.' His wife and children shared his captivity, and the friends of Liberty throughout the country made pilgrimages to his cell. He played 'martyr', indeed, with naïve enjoyment. But the reverse of the picture is not so pleasant. Confinement, and its surrounding incidents, permanently injured his health; while enforced idleness destroyed for ever the small seed of prudence and responsibility in affairs which principle had so recently implanted in the unfavourable soil of his mercurial temperament. The event brought him some valuable friends, but it increased his natural egoism and bodily indolence.

It was in prison that Leigh Hunt first met Lord Byron, with whom the other 'event' of his life was so unfortunately associated. Shortly after his release, when his health was poor and financial prospects discouraging, Shelley and Byron, then in Italy, invited the martyr-journalist to come out and edit for them a periodical in which no conventions or moral cowardice should be allowed to hamper the expression of advanced thought. Naturally Leigh Hunt welcomed the project with enthusiasm; and we, too, may dream over what might have been. But, only a few days after his arrival —Shelley was drowned! Byron and Hunt could neither mourn, nor work, in sympathy. We have recovered to-day from the blind enthusiasm which could see no fault in the 'noble poet'; and we find

---

[1] See the essay on 'Mr. Pope' below.

his character, in this episode, neither worse nor better than elsewhere. But to Leigh Hunt it was a crisis for which he was peculiarly unfitted, following immediately upon the tragedy of his life. He did not at first realize Byron's disloyalty to the enterprise he was still professing to support, and could not afford delay in the business on which he had been encouraged to depend. Byron haughtily doled out a miserable pittance to relieve the poverty he was himself creating—and paraded his generosity, while disowning a comrade. A few numbers of *The Liberal* ultimately appeared, far too reckless for an unfriendly public, and Leigh Hunt returned to England with bitter memories and only additional embarrassments in store. But, while recognizing his excuses, the world is yet unwilling to forgive him for accepting Byron's money and then venturing to criticize him in print. We forget that the literary patron (a pose by no means distasteful to Byron) was not quite out of date : we forget that Shelley had spoiled Leigh Hunt by princely generosity : we forget that Leigh Hunt himself was constitutionally incapable of understanding the ordinary British financial conventions. In all probability we are not aware that, in accepting the invitation of an enterprising publisher to write on the subject of the moment, he simply availed himself of the opportunity to tell the truth about matters in which he had been himself subjected to intolerable abuse. His own actions had been cruelly and wilfully misrepresented : his defence was dignified and moderate in comparison with the attack. Had *Lord Byron and his Contemporaries* never appeared we should have lost some valuable sidelights on genius which form a permanent contribution to literary biography. For his own sake, certainly, Leigh Hunt should have remained silent, but the indiscretion need not prejudice us to-day.

In later years his character suffered at the hands of a true friend ; but entirely without intention, and through no fault of his own. I fear there are those who still believe him to be the original Harold Skimpole.

Now Dickens had been, and remained, his intimate friend; while that hater of shams would never have tolerated Skimpole. His public and private denials are obviously sincere, and only the idle or ungenerous can ignore such evidence. The fact is that, with inexcusable carelessness, Dickens incorporated certain mannerisms of his friend into the portrait of a despicable, and quite different, type of character. The traits proved more generally recognizable than he had anticipated: men attempted to interpret the actual by the fictitious; and the mischief was done. Such calumnies die hard; but they should not be granted immortality.

Leigh Hunt's true character must live for us in his work; transparently generous, sympathetic, honourable, and courageous. 'He was poet, critic, essayist, and politician—sentimentalized. The affection for suburban detail, which limited his genuine nature-worship, may be recognized in his attitude towards life and art. He loved men more than man, and beautiful lines or phrases above great books. In every direction his judgement was led by sprightly feeling in submission to certain moral principles.

'By energy and fearless loyalty, involving the endurance of something like martyrdom, he achieved a solid service to the cause of Liberalism in one of its darkest periods; by persistent faithfulness to the "old masters" of literature he materially assisted, though to some extent on lines of his own, the popularization of taste and information, which may be said to have begun in his age; and by the exercise of independent critical judgement he encouraged new leaders. Gratitude, therefore, should teach us to forgive the undesirable shallowness of his intellect, and the serious faults in style, which are too frequently the result of his habitual indifference to the formal conventions. He may gain our affections, as he did those of his contemporaries, by the winning personality, so far removed from the strenuousness of to-day, that pervades every line he wrote, and finds its supreme utterance in a few admirable verses, many felicitous appreciations, and certain studies in the humorous-pathetic that defy definition [1].'

Leigh Hunt's work has never been adequately collected, though the enthusiastic labours of Mr. Alexander Ireland, Mr. Dykes Campbell, and others, enable one to trace the innumerable papers to which he contributed. With a few exceptions his published volumes are not particularly characteristic, and he never reprinted much of his best work. Though garrulous and irrelevant, he was a careful writer, and I have therefore concluded that his essays are best given complete from their original sources [2]. He certainly struck a number of critical epigrams; but even these are most forcible and suggestive in their own place. As the excellencies of his style were early developed, and he never conquered its limitations, a chronological arrangement would have no significance; and I venture to hope that the extent and the quality of his genius has been adequately presented by the grouping adopted herein.

Though an ardent reformer, Leigh Hunt always disliked writing on politics, and his contributions to this subject may be forgotten. *The Religion of the Heart* and *Sir Ralph Esher*, each in their own sphere, deserve popularity; but yield no extracts. Apart from these, all aspects of his work have been studied for selection.

R. BRIMLEY JOHNSON.

---

[1] *Leigh Hunt*. By R. Brimley Johnson, 1896. Swan Sonnenschein.
[2] From books like *The Autobiography* and *The Town* it has of course been necessary to 'cut' passages.

CONTENTS

'IN HEAVEN AND EARTH'

CHARACTERS

BOOKS AND BOOKMEN

CONTENTS

TALES, OLD AND NEW

KINGS AND PRINCES

ABOUT TOWN

THE THEATRES

THE COUNTRY

CONTENTS

OF DUMB ANIMALS

THE WEATHER

AT HOME

OF DRESS AND MANNERS

'IN HEAVEN AND EARTH'

THE ELEVEN COMMANDMENTS

[A Jar of Honey from Mount Hybla, 1848]

A CERTAIN bishop who lived some hundred years ago, and who was very unlike what is reported of her Majesty's new almoner; also very unlike the Christian bishops of old, before titles were invented for them; very unlike Fenelon too, who nevertheless had plenty of titles; very unlike St. Francis de Sales, who was for talking nothing but 'roses'; very unlike St. Vincent de Paul, who founded the Sisterhood of Charity; very unlike Rundle, who 'had a heart'; and Berkeley, who had 'every virtue under heaven'; and that other exquisite bishop (we blush to have forgotten his name), who was grieved to find that he had a hundred pounds at his banker's when the season had been so bad for the poor; this highly unresembling bishop, who, nevertheless, was like too many of his brethren—that is to say, in times past (for there is no bishop now, at least in any quarter of England, who is not remarkable for meekness, and does not make a point of turning his right cheek to be smitten, the moment you have smitten his left); this unepiscopal, and yet not impossible bishop, we say, was once accosted, during a severe Christmas, by a Parson Adams kind of inferior clergyman, and told a long story of the wants of certain poor people, of whose cases his lordship was unaware. What the dialogue was, which led to the remark we are about to mention, the reporters of the circumstance do not appear to have ascertained; but it seems that, the representations growing stronger and stronger on one side, and the determination to pay no attention to them acquiring proportionate vigour on

B

the other, the clergyman was moved to tell the bishop
that his lordship did not understand his 'eleven commandments.'

'Eleven commandments !' cried the bishop ; 'why,
fellow, you are drunk. Who ever heard of an eleventh
commandment ? Depart, or you shall be put in the
stocks.'

'Put thine own pride and cruelty in the stocks,' re-
torted the good priest, angered beyond his Christian
patience, and preparing to return to the sufferers for
whom he had pleaded in vain. 'I say there are *eleven*
commandments, *not* ten, and that it were well for such
flocks as you govern, if it were added, as it ought to be,
to the others over the tables in church. Does your lordship remember—do you in fact know anything at all of
Him who came on earth to do good to the poor and
woful, and who said, "Behold, I give unto you a *new
commandment*, LOVE ONE ANOTHER" ? '

AN EARTH UPON HEAVEN

[Companion, April 2, 1828]

SOMEBODY, a little while ago, wrote an excellent
article in the *New Monthly Magazine* on 'Persons one
would wish to have known.' He should write another
on 'Persons one could wish to have dined with.' There
is Rabelais, and Horace, and the Mermaid roysterers, and
Charles Cotton, and Andrew Marvell, and Sir Richard
Steele, *cum multis aliis* : and for the colloquial, if not
the festive part, Swift and Pope, and Dr. Johnson, and
Burke, and Horne Tooke. What a pity one cannot dine
with them all round ! People are accused of having
earthly notions of heaven. As it is difficult to have any
other, we may be pardoned for thinking that we could
spend a very pretty thousand years in dining and getting
acquainted with all the good fellows on record ; and
having got used to them, we think we could go very well
on, and be content to wait some other thousands for a

higher beatitude. Oh, to wear out one of the celestial lives of a triple century's duration, and exquisitely to grow old, in reciprocating dinners and teas with the immortals of old books! Will Fielding ' leave his card ' in the next world ? Will Berkeley (an angel in a wig and lawn sleeves !) come to ask how Utopia gets on ? Will Shakespeare (for the greater the man, the more the good-nature might be expected) know by intuition that one of his readers (knocked up with bliss) is dying to see him at the Angel and Turk's Head, and come lounging with his hands in his doublet-pockets accordingly ?

It is a pity that none of the great geniuses, to whose lot it has fallen to describe a future state, has given us his own notions of heaven. Their accounts are all modified by the national theology ; whereas the Apostle himself has told us, that we can have no conception of the blessings intended for us. ' Eye hath not seen, nor ear heard,' &c. After this, Dante's shining lights are poor. Milton's heaven, with the armed youth exercising themselves in military games, is worse. His best Paradise was on earth, and a very pretty heaven he made of it. For our parts, admitting and venerating as we do the notion of a heaven surpassing all human conception, we trust that it is no presumption to hope, that the state mentioned by the Apostle is the *final* heaven ; and that we may ascend and gradually accustom ourselves to the intensity of it, by others of a less superhuman nature. Familiar as we may be with poetry or calamity, and accustomed to surprises and strange sights of imagination, it is difficult to fancy even the delight of suddenly emerging into a new and boundless state of existence, where everything is marvellous, and opposed to our experience. We could wish to take gently to it : to be loosed not entirely at once. Our song desires to be ' a song of degrees.' Earth and its capabilities,—are these nothing ? And are they to come to nothing ? Is there no beautiful realization of the fleeting type that is shown us ? No body to this shadow ? No quenching to this taught and continued thirst ? No arrival at these natural homes and resting-places, which are so heavenly to our imaginations, even though they be built of clay, and are situate in the fields of our infancy ? We are becoming graver than we intended ; but to return to our proper style :—nothing shall persuade us, for the present, that Paradise Mount, in any pretty village in England, has not another Paradise Mount to correspond, in some less perishing region ; that is to say, provided anybody has set his heart upon it :—and that we shall not all be dining, and drinking tea, and complaining of the weather (we mean, for its not being perfectly blissful) three hundred years hence, in some snug interlunar spot, or perhaps in the moon itself, seeing that it is our next visible neighbour, and shrewdly suspected of being hill and dale.

It appears to us, that for a certain term of centuries, Heaven *must* consist of something of this kind. In a word, we cannot but persuade ourselves, that to realize everything that we have justly desired on earth, will *be* heaven,—we mean, for that period ; and that afterwards, if we behave ourselves in a proper pre-angelical manner, we shall go to another heaven, still better, where we shall realize all that we desired in our first. Of this latter we can as yet have no conception ; but of the former, we think some of the items may be as follows :—

Imprimis,—(not because friendship comes before love in point of degree, but because it precedes it in point of time, as at school we have a male companion before we are old enough to have a female one)—*Imprimis* then, a friend. He will have the same tastes and inclinations as ourselves, with just enough difference to furnish argument without sharpness ; and will be generous, just, entertaining, and no shirker of his nectar. In short, he will be the best friend we have had upon earth. We shall talk together ' of afternoons ' ; and when the *Earth* begins to rise (a great big moon, looking as happy as we know its inhabitants *will* be) other friends will join us, not so emphatically our friend as he, but excellent fellows all ; and we shall read the poets, and have some sphere-music (if we please), or renew one of our old earthly evenings, picked out of a dozen Christmasses.

Item, a mistress. In heaven (not to speak it profanely) we know, upon the best authority, that people are 'neither married nor given in marriage'; so that there is nothing illegal in the term. (By the way, there can be no clergyman there, if there are no official duties for them. We do not say, there will be nobody who has been a clergyman. Berkeley would refute that; and a hundred Welsh curates. But they would be no longer in orders. They would refuse to call themselves more Reverend than their neighbours.) Item then, a mistress; beautiful of course,—an angelical expression,—a Peri, or Houri, or whatever shape of perfection you choose to imagine her, and yet retaining the likeness of the woman you loved best on earth; in fact, she herself, but completed; all her good qualities made perfect, and all her defects taken away (with the exception of one or two charming little angelical peccadilloes, which she can only get rid of in a post-future state); good-tempered, laughing, serious, fond of everything about her without detriment to her special fondness for yourself, a great roamer in Elysian fields and forests, but not alone (they go in pairs there, as the jays and turtle-doves do with us); but above all things, true; oh, so true, that you take her word as you would a diamond, nothing being more transparent, or solid, or precious. Between writing some divine poem, and meeting our friends of an evening, we should walk with her, or fly (for we should have wings, of course) like a couple of human bees or doves, extracting delight from every flower, and with delight filling every shade. There is something too good in this to dwell upon; so we spare the fears (and hopes) of the prudish. We would lay her head upon our heart, and look more pleasure into her eyes, than the prudish or the profligate ever so much as fancied.

Item, books. Shakespeare and Spenser should write us *new ones*! Think of that. We should have another *Decameron*: and Walter Scott (for he will be there too; —we mean to beg Hume to introduce us) shall write us forty more novels, all as good as the Scotch ones; and

Radical as well as Tory shall love him.   It is true, we speak professionally, when we mention books.

> We think, admitted to that equal sky,
> The Arabian Nights must bear us company.

When Gainsborough died, he expired in a painter's enthusiasm, saying, 'We are all going to heaven, and Vandyke is of the party.'   He had a proper foretaste. Virgil had the same light, when he represented the old heroes enjoying in Elysium their favourite earthly pursuits ;   only one cannot help thinking, with the natural modesty of reformers, that the taste in this our interlunar heaven will be benefited from time to time by the knowledge of new-comers.   We cannot well fancy a celestial ancient Briton delighting himself with painting his skin, or a Chinese angel hobbling a mile up the Milky Way in order to show herself to advantage.

For breakfast, we must have a tea beyond anything Chinese.   Slaves will certainly not make the sugar ; but there will be cows for the milk.   One's landscapes cannot do without cows.

For horses we shall ride a Pegasus, or Ariosto's Hippogriff, or Sinbad's Roc.   We mean, for our parts, to ride them all, having a passion for fabulous animals.   Fable will be as fable then.   We shall have just as much of it as we like ;   and the Utilitarians will be astonished to find how much of that sort of thing will be in request. They will look very odd, by the by,—those gentlemen, when they first arrive ;   but will soon get used to the delight, and find there was more of it in their own doctrine than they imagined.

The weather will be extremely fine, but not without such varieties as shall hinder it from being tiresome. April will dress the whole country in diamonds ;   and there will be enough cold in winter to make a fire pleasant of an evening.   The fire will be made of sweet-smelling turf and sunbeams ;   but it will have a look of coal.   If we choose now and then, we shall even have inconveniences.

DEATHS OF LITTLE CHILDREN

[*Indicator*, April 5, 1820]

A GRECIAN philosopher being asked why he wept for the death of his son, since the sorrow was in vain, replied, ' I weep on that very account.' And his answer became his wisdom. It is only for sophists to pretend that we, whose eyes contain the fountains of tears, need never give way to them. It would be unwise not to do so on some occasions. Sorrow unlocks them in her balmy moods. The first bursts may be bitter and overwhelming ; but the soil, on which they pour, would be the worse without them. They refresh the fever of the soul,—the dry misery, which parches the countenance into furrows, and renders us liable to our most terrible ' flesh-quakes.'

There are sorrows, it is true, so great, that to give them some of the ordinary vents is to run a hazard of being overthrown. These we must rather strengthen ourselves to resist ; or bow quietly and dryly down in order to let them pass over us, as the traveller does the wind of the desert. But where we feel that tears would relieve us, it is false philosophy to deny ourselves at least that first refreshment ; and it is always false consolation to tell people that because they cannot help a thing, they are not to mind it. The true way is, to let them grapple with the unavoidable sorrow, and try to win it into gentleness by a reasonable yielding. There are griefs so gentle in their very nature, that it would be worse than false heroism to refuse them a tear. Of this kind are the deaths of infants. Particular circumstances may render it more or less advisable to indulge in grief for the loss of a little child ; but in general, parents should be no more advised to repress their first tears on such an occasion, than to repress their smiles towards a child surviving, or to indulge in any other sympathy. It is an appeal to the same gentle tenderness ; and such appeals are never made in vain. The end of them is an acquittal from the harsher bonds of affliction,—from the tying down of the spirit to one melancholy idea.

It is the nature of tears of this kind, however strongly they may gush forth, to run into quiet waters at last. We cannot easily, for the whole course of our lives, think with pain of any good and kind person whom we have lost. It is the divine nature of their qualities to conquer pain and death itself ; to turn the memory of them into pleasure ; to survive with a placid aspect in our imaginations. We are writing, at this moment, just opposite a spot which contains the grave of one inexpressibly dear to us. We see from our window the trees about it, and the church-spire. The green fields lie around. The clouds are travelling over head, alternately taking away the sunshine and restoring it. The vernal winds, piping of the flowery summer-time, are nevertheless calling to mind the far distant and dangerous ocean, which the heart that lies in that grave had many reasons to think of. And yet the sight of this spot does not give us pain. So far from it, it is the existence of that grave which doubles every charm of the spot ; which links the pleasures of our childhood and manhood together ; which puts a hushing tenderness in the winds, and a patient joy upon the landscape ; which seems to unite heaven and earth, mortality and immortality, the grass of the tomb and the grass of the green field, and gives a more maternal aspect to the whole kindness of nature. It does not hinder gaiety itself. Happiness was what its tenant, through all her troubles, would have diffused. To diffuse happiness, and to enjoy it, is not only carrying on her wishes, but realizing her hopes ; and gaiety, freed from its only pollutions, malignity and want of sympathy, is but a child playing about the knees of its mother.

The remembered innocence and endearments of a child stand us in stead of virtues that have died older. Children have not exercised the voluntary offices of friendship ; they have not chosen to be kind and good to us ; nor stood by us, from conscious will, in the hour of adversity. But they have shared their pleasures and pains with us as well as they could : the interchange of good offices between us has, of necessity, been less mingled with the troubles of the world ; the sorrow arising from their death is the only one which we can associate with their memories. These are happy thoughts that cannot die. Our loss may render them pensive ; but they will not always be painful. It is a part of the benignity of Nature, that pain does not survive like pleasure, at any time ; much less where the cause of it is an innocent one. The smile will remain reflected by memory ; as the moon reflects the light upon us, when the sun has gone into heaven.

When writers like ourselves quarrel with earthly pain (we mean writers of the same intentions, without implying, of course, anything about abilities or otherwise) they are misunderstood if they are supposed to quarrel with pains of every sort. This would be idle and effeminate. They do not pretend, indeed, that humanity might not wish, if it could, to be entirely free from pain ; for it endeavours at all times to turn pain into pleasure, or at least to set off the one with the other ; to make the former a zest, and the latter a refreshment. The most unaffected dignity of suffering does this ; and if wise, acknowledges it. The greatest benevolence towards others, the most unselfish relish of their pleasures, even at its own expense, does but look to increasing the general stock of happiness, though content, if it could, to have its identity swallowed up in that splendid contemplation. We are far from meaning that this is to be called selfishness. We are far indeed from thinking so, or of so confounding words. But neither is it to be called pain, when most unselfish ; if disinterestedness be truly understood. The pain that is in it softens into pleasure, as the darker hue of the rainbow melts into the brighter. Yet even if a harsher line is to be drawn between the pain and pleasure of the most unselfish mind (and ill health, for instance, may draw it), we should not quarrel with it, if it contributed to the general mass of comfort, and were of a nature which

general kindliness could not avoid. Made as we are,
there are certain pains, without which it would be difficult to conceive certain great and overbalancing pleasures. We may conceive it possible for beings to be
made entirely happy; but in our composition, something of pain seems to be a necessary ingredient, in order
that the materials may turn to as fine account as possible; though our clay, in the course of ages and experience, may be refined more and more. We may get rid
of the worst earth, though not of earth itself.

Now the liability to the loss of children,—or rather
what renders us sensible of it, the occasional loss itself,—
seems to be one of these necessary bitters thrown into
the cup of humanity. We do not mean that everybody
must lose one of his children, in order to enjoy the rest;
or that every individual loss afflicts us in the same proportion. We allude to the deaths of infants in general.
These might be as few as we could render them. But
if none at all ever took place, we should regard every
little child as a man or woman secured; and it will
easily be conceived, what a world of endearing cares and
hopes this security would endanger. The very idea of
infancy would lose its continuity with us. Girls and
boys would be future men and women, not present
children. They would have attained their full growth
in our imaginations, and might as well have been men
and women at once. On the other hand, those who
have lost an infant are never, as it were, without an
infant child. They are the only persons who, in one
sense, retain it always; and they furnish their neighbours with the same idea [1]. The other children grow up
to manhood and womanhood, and suffer all the changes
of mortality. This one alone is rendered an immortal
child. Death has arrested it with his kindly harshness,
and blessed it into an eternal image of youth and innocence.

[1] 'I sighed,' says old Captain Bolton, 'when I envied
you the two bonnie children, but I sigh not now to call
either the monk or the soldier mine own.'—*Monastery*,
vol. iii. p. 341.

Of such as these are the pleasantest shapes that visit our fancy and our hopes. They are the ever-smiling emblems of joy; the prettiest pages that wait upon imagination. Lastly, 'of these are the kingdom of heaven.' Wherever there is a province of that benevolent and all-accessible empire, whether on earth or elsewhere, such are the gentle spirits that must inhabit it. To such simplicity, or the resemblance of it, must they come. Such must be the ready confidence of their hearts, and creativeness of their fancy. And so ignorant must they be of the 'knowledge of good and evil,' losing their discernment of that self-created trouble, by enjoying the garden before them, and not being ashamed of what is kindly and innocent.

CRUELTY TO CHILDREN

[*Companion*, May 7, 1828]

READERS of newspapers are constantly being shocked with the unnatural conduct of parents towards their children. Some are detected in locking them up, and half-starving them: others tax them beyond their strength, and scourge them dreadfully for not bearing it: others take horrible dislikes to their children, and vex and torture them in every way they can think of, short of subjecting themselves to the gallows. In most cases the tryanny is of long duration before it is exposed. A whole neighbourhood are saddened by the cries of the poor victim, till they are obliged to rise up in self-defence, and bring the offender to justice. By this we may judge how many miseries are taking place, of which people have no suspicion; how many wretches have crimes of this sort, to account for the evil in their looks; and how many others, more criminal because more lying, go about in decent repute, while some oppressed and feeble relative, awfully patient, is awaiting in solitude the horror of the returning knock at the door.

It is sometimes alleged by offenders of this description, that the children have real faults, and are really provoking; that their conduct is very 'aggravating,' as the phrase is; and that 'nothing can mend them but blows,'—*which never do*. But whence come the faults of children? And how were they suffered to grow to such a height? Really,—setting aside these monsters of unpaternity,—parents are too apt to demand a great deal in their children, which they themselves do not possess. The child, on the mere will of the parents, and without any of their experience, is expected to have good sense, good temper, and heavens knows how many other good qualities; while the parents perhaps, notwithstanding all the lessons they have received from time and trouble, have little or nothing of any of them. Above all, they forget that, in originating the bodies of their children, they originate their minds and temperaments; that a child is but a continuation of his father and mother, or their fathers and mothers, and kindred; that it is further modified, and made what it is, by education and bringing up; and that on all these accounts the parents have no excuse for abusing and tormenting it, unless with equal wisdom and a glorious impartiality they should abuse and torment *themselves* in like manner —scourge their own flesh, and condemn themselves to a crust and a black hole. If a father were to give his own sore legs a good flogging for inheriting ill humours from his ancestors, he might with some show of reason proceed to punish the continuation of them in those of his child. If a cruel mother got into a handsome tub of cold water, of a winter morning, and edified the neighbours with the just and retributive shrieks which she thence poured forth for a couple of hours, crying out to her deceased 'mammy' that she would be a good elderly woman in future, and not a scold and a reprobate, then she might, like a proper madwoman (for she is but an improper one now), put her child into the tub after her, and make it shriek out 'mammy' in its turn.

But let us do justice to all one's fellow creatures, not forgetting these very 'aggravating' parents. To regard even them as something infernal, and forget that they as well as their children have become what they are from circumstances over which they had no control, is to fall into their own error, and forget our common humanity. We believe that the very worst of these domestic tyrants (and it is an awful lesson for the best of them) would have been shocked in early life, if they could have been shown, in a magic glass, what sort of beings they would become. Suppose one of them a young man, blooming with health, and not ill-natured, but subject to fits of sulkiness or passion, and not very wise; and suppose that in this glass he sees an old ill-looking fellow scowling, violent, outrageous, tormenting with a bloody scourge his own child, who is meagre, squalid, and half starved:—' Good God!' he would cry, ' can that be myself? Can that be my arm, and my face? And that my own poor little child? There *are* devils then, and I am doomed to be one of them.' And the tears would pour into his eyes.—No; not so, poor wretch: thou art no devil; there is no such thing as devilism, or pure malice for its own sake; the very cruellest actions are committed to relieve the cravings of their own want of excitement, more than to hurt another. But though no devil, you are very ignorant, and are not aware of this. The energies of the universe, being on a great scale, are liable, in their progress from worse to better, to great roughness in the working, and appalling sounds of discord. The wiser you become, the more you diminish this jarring, and tend to produce that amelioration. Learn this, and be neither appalled nor appalling; or if your reflections do not travel so far, and you are in no danger of continuing your evil course by the subtle desperations of superstition, be content to know, that nobody ill-treats another who is satisfied with his own conduct. If the case were otherwise, it would be worse; for you would not have the excuse, even of a necessity for relieving your own sensations. But it never *is* so, sophisticate about it as you may. The very pains you take to reconcile yourself *to* yourself, may show you how much need you have of doing so. It is nothing else which makes the silliest little child sulky;

and the same folly makes the grown man a tyrant. When you begin to ill-treat your child, you begin to punish in him your own faults; and you most likely do nothing but beat them in upon him with every stroke of the scourge: for why should he be wiser than you? Why should he be able to throw off the ill-humours, of which your greater energies cannot get rid?

These thoughts we address to those who are worthy of them; and who, not being tyrants, may yet become such, for want of reflection. Vulgar offenders can be mended only with the whole progress of society, and the advancement of education. There is one thing we must not omit to say; which is, that the best parents are apt to expect too much of their children, and to forget how much error they may have committed in the course of bringing them up. Nobody is in fault, in a criminal sense. Children have their excuses; and parents have their excuses; but the wiser any of us become, the less we exact from others, and the more we do to deserve their regard. The great art of being a good parent consists in setting a good example, and in maintaining that union of dispassionate firmness with habitual good-humour, which a child never *thinks* of treating with disrespect.

We have here been speaking principally of the behaviour of parents to *little children.* When violent disputes take place between parents and children grown up,—young men and women,—there are generally great faults on both sides; though, for an obvious reason, the parent, who has had the training and formation of the other, is likely to be most in the wrong. But unhappily, very excellent people may sometimes find themselves hampered in a calamity of this nature; and out of that sort of weakness, which is so confounded with strength, turn their very sense of being in the right to the same hostile and implacable purpose, as if it were the reverse. We can only say, that from all we have seen in the world, and indeed from the whole experience of mankind, they who are conscious of being right, are the first to make a movement towards reconciliation, let the cause of

quarrel be what it may ; and that there is no surer
method, in the eyes of any who know what human nature is, both to sustain the real dignity of the right side,
and to amend the wrong one. To kind-hearted fathers in
general, who have the misfortune to get into a dilemma
of this sort, we would recommend the pathetic story
of a French general, who was observed after the death
of his son in battle, never to hold up his head. He said
to a friend, ' My boy was used to think me severe ; and
he had too much reason to do so. He did not know how
I loved him at the bottom of my heart ; *and it is now
too late.*'

CHILD-BED

[Monthly Repository, November, 1835]

AND is child-bed among the graces, with its close
room, and its unwilling or idle visitors, and its jesting
nurse (the old and indecent stranger), and its un-
motherly, and unwifely, and unlovely lamentations ? Is
pain so unpleasant that love cannot reconcile it ?   And
can pleasures be repeated without shame, which are
regretted with hostile cries and resentment ?

No. But child-bed is among the graces, with the
handsome quiet of its preparation, and the smooth pillow
sustaining emotion, and the soft steps of love and respect, and the room in which the breath of the universe
is gratefully permitted to enter, and mild and venerable
aid, and the physician (the urbane security), and the
living treasure containing treasure about to live, who
looks in the eyes of him that caused it and seeks energy
in the grappling of his hand, and hides her face in
the pillow that she may save him a pain by stifling a
greater. There is a tear for what may have been done
wrong, ever ; and what may never be to be mutually
pardoned again ; but it is gone, for what needs it ?
Angelical are their whispers apart ; and Pleasure meets
Pain the seraph, and knows itself to be noble in the
smiling testimony of his severity.

It was on a May evening, in a cottage flowering with the greengage in the time of hyacinths and new hopes, when the hand that wrote this took the hand that had nine times laid thin and delicate on the bed of a mother's endurance; and he kissed it, like a bride's.

SWEARING

[Autobiography]

My mother set me an example of such excessive care and anxiety for those about us, that I remember I could not see her bite off the ends of her thread while at work without being in pain till I was sure she would not swallow them. She used to be so agitated at the sight of discord and quarrelling, particularly when it came to blows, and between the rudest or gayest combatants in the street, that, although it did not deprive her of courage and activity enough to interfere (which she would do if there was the slightest chance of effect, and which produced in myself a corresponding discrimination between sensibility and endeavour), it gave me an ultra-sympathy with the least show of pain and suffering; and she had produced in me such a horror, or rather such an intense idea of even violent words, and of the commonest trivial oath, that being led one day, perhaps by the very excess of it, to snatch a ' fearful joy ' in its utterance, it gave me so much remorse that for some time afterwards I could not receive a bit of praise, or a pat of encouragement on the head, without thinking to myself, ' Ah! they little suspect that I am the boy who said, " d—n it " '.

Dear mother! No one could surpass her in generosity; none be more willing to share, or to take the greatest portion of blame to themselves, of any evil consequences of mistake to a son; but if I have not swallowed very many camels in the course of my life, it has not been owing, perhaps, to this too great a straining at gnats. How happy shall I be (if I may) to laugh and compare

notes with her on the subject in any humble corner of
heaven ; to recall to her the filial tenderness with which
she was accustomed to speak of the mistakes of one of
her own parents, and to think that her grandchildren
will be as kind to the memory of their father.

I may here mention, as a ludicrous counterpart to
this story, and a sample of the fantastical nature of
scandal, that somebody having volunteered a defence
of my character on some occasion to Mr. Wordsworth,
as though the character had been questioned by him—
the latter said he had never heard anything against it,
except that I was ' given to swearing.'

I certainly think little of the habit of swearing, however idle, if it be carried no further than is done by many
gallant and very good men, wise and great ones not excepted. I wish I had no worse faults to answer for.
But the fact is, that however I may laugh at the puerile
conscience of the anecdote just mentioned, an oath has
not escaped my lips from that day to this.

I hope no ' good fellow ' will think ill of me for it. If
he did, I should certainly be tempted to begin swearing
immediately, purely to *vindicate* my character. But
there was no swearing in our family ; there was none in
our school (Christ's Hospital) ; and I seldom ever fell in
the way of it anywhere except in books ; so that the
practice was not put into my head. I look upon Tom
Jones, who swore, as an angel of light compared with
Blifil, who, I am afraid, swore no more than myself.
Steele, I suspect, occasionally rapped out an oath ;
which is not to be supposed of Addison. And this,
again, might tempt me into a grudge against my non-
juring turn of colloquy ; for I must own that I prefer
open-hearted Steele with all his faults, to Addison with
all his essays. But habit is habit, negative as well as
positive. Let him that is without one, cast the first
sarcasm.

ON THE RARE VICE CALLED LYING

[*Monthly Repository*, March, 1838]

THE great argument against the Ballot is, that it teaches people duplicity,—that the elector will promise his vote to one man, and give it to another. In short, that he will lie. Lying is a horrid vice,—*un*-English, and must not be suffered to pollute our shores. People lie in France. They lie in Italy. They lie in Spain and Portugal. They lie in Africa, in Asia, and America. But in England, who ever heard of such a thing ?

‘ What *is* lying ? ’ says the English courtier.

‘ Can’t say indeed, sir,’ says the footman.

‘ Never heard of it,’ says the tradesman.

‘ Never borough-mongered with it,’ says the peer.

‘ Never bribed with it,’ says the member of parliament.

‘ Never subscribed the thirty-nine articles with it,’ says the collegian.

‘ Never pretended to a call with it,’ says the clergyman.

‘ Never *nolo-episcopari’d* with it,’ says the bishop.

‘ Never played a *ruse de guerre* with it,’ says the general.

‘ Never told it to a woman,’ says the man of gallantry.

‘ Never argued for it,’ says the barrister.

‘ Never sent in a medicine with it,’ says the apothecary.

‘ Never jockeyed with it,’ says the turf-man.

‘ Never dealt with it,’ says the man at Crockford’s.

‘ Never wrote great A with it,’ says the underwriter.

‘ Never took in the custom-house with it,’ says the captain.

‘ Never doctor’d my port with it,’ says the wine merchant.

‘ Never praised or condemned with it,’ says the critic.

‘ Never concealed a motive with it,’ says the partisan.

‘ Never puff’d with it,’ says the bookseller.

‘ Nor I,’ says the manager.

' Nor I,' says the auctioneer.

' Nor I,' says the quack-doctor.

' Never used it in my bread,' says the baker.

' Nor in a bill,' says the tailor.

' Nor I in a measure,' says the coalman.

' Can't conceive how anybody ever thought of it,' says
the innkeeper.

' Never made an excuse with it,' says the fine lady.

' Nor I,' says the lady's-maid.

' Nor I,' says the milliner.

' Am a horrible sinner, but never went so far as that,'
says the Methodist.

' Never uttered one to my wife, pretty jealous soul,'
says the husband.

' Nor I to my husband, poor man,' says the wife.

' Nor I to my mother,' says the little boy.

' Nor I in one of my speeches,' says the king.

' Nor I in mine,' says the minister.

' Nor I at a foreign court,' says the diplomatist.

' Should never forgive myself such a thing,' says the
pickpocket.

' Couldn't live under it,' says the beggar.

' Never saved myself from starvation by it,' says the
Irishman.

' Nor I got a bawbee,' says the Scotchman.

' Nor I a penny,' says ALL ENGLAND.

O spirits of Lucian, of Rabelais, of Molière, of Henry
Fielding, of Sterne,—look down upon boroughmongers
and their anti-ballot men, in the shopkeeping nation of
England, and in the nineteenth century, protesting
against the horrible innovation of encouraging *the bribed
and misrepresented to say one thing in self-defence, and
intend another !*

Lying is the commonest and most conventional of all
the vices. It pervades, more or less, every class of the
community, and is fancied to be so necessary to the
carrying on of human affairs, that the practice is tacitly
agreed upon ; nay, in other terms, openly avowed. In
the monarch, it is *king-craft*. In the statesman, *expediency*. In the churchman, *mental reservation*. In

c 2

the lawyer, *the interest of his client*. In the merchant, manufacturer, and shopkeeper, *secrets of trade*. It was the opinion of King James, that without the art of lying a king was not worthy to reign. This was his boasted 'king-craft,' which brought his son to the block; for if poor Charles was a 'martyr,' it was certainly not to the spirit of truth. Lord Bacon was of opinion that lying, like alloy in metals, was a debasement, but good for the working. It worked him, great as he was, into a little and ruined man. Pleasant Sir Henry Wotton (himself an ambassador) defined an ambassador to be, 'An honest man sent to *lie* abroad for the good of his country.' Paley openly defends the 'mental reservation' of the churchman,—of the subscriber to the thirty-nine articles, &c.; and his is the great textbook of the universities. If you go into a shop for any article, you know very well that you cannot be secure of having it genuine; nor do you expect the shopkeeper to tell you the truth. The grocer notoriously sells Jamaica coffee for Mocha, the tobacconist his own snuff for Latakia and Macubau, the linen-draper cotton for thread, and British goods for India.

Well, granting all this,—says the boroughmonger,—don't you see that it overdoes your argument, and that if we all lie and cheat one another at this rate, we in reality do not cheat, and that the practice becomes comparatively innocent?

Excuse me—we answer—you *are* cheated, or how could you cheat? and what would be the use of the practice? You know the fact is general, and may often detect it in the particular; but still you are cheated in the gross. And supposing the case to be otherwise, or that the practice becomes comparatively innocent by its universality (which is to be granted), *why not make the duplicity charged against the Ballot equally innocent, by the same process, and for the same general accommodation?*

If it were understood that the elector had the same right and necessity to prevaricate for *his* convenience, as the candidate has to bribe or cajole for his,—if the thing were understood on both sides, and the voter's promise came to be of no more account than the great man's, or than the pretty thing said to the voter's wife and children, *where would be the harm of it*, ACCORDING TO YOUR OWN SHOWING ? or where the greater vice of it, than that of the famous ' king-craft,' or of the minister's ' expediency,' or of the thirty-nine article-man's ' mental reservation ' ?

The truth is, that such would and *will* be the result ; so much so, that candidates will at last cease to practise their tricks and tell *their* lies, out of a hopelessness of doing anything with the voters. But we will tell the anti-balloter what the harm will be in the meanwhile. The harm will be that *lies will no longer be told for his sake exclusively ;* AND THIS IS THE WHOLE REAL AMOUNT OF HIS GRIEVANCE. His grievance is precisely what the prince's is, who likes to have all the ' craft ' to himself, and not be deceived by his ministers ;—what the minister's is, who complains of want of truth in the opposition ; —what the opposition's is, when they cry ' Oh ! oh ! ' against the same things which they did when in place ;— what the wholesale dealer's cry is against the retail, and the master manufacturer's against the workman. The weapons of state and expediency will at length be turned against expediency itself,—against power and monopoly, —and used in behalf of the Many ; and this is what the virtuous indignation of the Few cannot bear.

But an insidious compliment may be paid to ' us youth ' of the press,—us ' philosophic radicals '; and it may be asked us, ' What ! do *you* advocate lying ? You advocate it under *any* circumstances ? *You* wish a man to say one thing and intend another ? Is the above *your* picture of society and of human nature ? We thought you had a better opinion of it ;—were believers in the goodness of the human heart, and did not take all your fellow creatures for such a parcel of hypocrites.'

' My dear sir,' we answer, ' we do not see you, and we know not who you may be. We know not whether you are one of the greatest liars under the sun, or only a conventional liar, like our friends the statesman and the

baker (good and true fellows perhaps out of the pale of
their offices and bakehouses). We are also totally ignorant whether you are a man who has a regard for
truth at the expense of conventionalities. Perhaps you
are. Perhaps you are even a martyr to those virtues,
with the possession of which you are pleased to compliment ourselves. But this we can tell you ; first, that
if you were the greatest liar that ever breathed, and
ourselves were lovers of the truth to an extent of which
you have no conception, and if you were to come to us
for help against a murderer, or a bailiff, or a tax-
gatherer, or a lying boroughmonger, we should make
no scruple to tell a lie for your sake ; and we can tell
you, secondly, that our above picture of society, and
our opinion of human nature, are two very different
things ; because we believe the vices of society to result
entirely from its imperfect knowledge, education, and
comfort; whereas we believe human nature to be capable
of all good and true things, and to be ever advancing in
them, the Ballot itself notwithstanding ; for the very
worst of the Ballot is, that it exchanges a lie for the sake
of an individual, into a lie for the sake of the country ;
and the best of it is, that it will ultimately do away the
necessity of either. With the Ballot must come extended suffrage (*that* is what you are afraid of). From
extended suffrage must come Universal Suffrage. And
from Universal Suffrage must come universal better
treatment of man by his fellows ;—universal *wiser* treatment ;—universal comforts ;—food for all, fire and cloth-
ing for all ; education for all, monopolies for *none* ;—
hence no necessity for lying ; which is only the resource
of the unequally treated against those whose lies, in
pretending a right so to treat them, are far greater and
more vicious.

O lover of truth ! believer in all good and beautiful
things ! believer even in one's self, and therefore believer in others, and such as are far better than one's
self ! putter of security into the heart, of solidity into
the ground we tread upon, of loveliness into the flowers, of
hope into the stars ! retainer of youth in age, and of

comfort in adversity ! bringer of tears into the eyes that
look upon these imperfect words, to think how large and
longing the mind of man is, compared with his frail
virtues and his transitory power, and what mornings of
light and abundance thou hast in store, nevertheless, for
the whole human race, preparing to ripen for them in
accordance with their belief in its possibility, and
their resolution to work for it in loving trust ! Oh !
shall they be thought guilty of deserting thee, because,
out of the very love of truth they feel themselves
bound to proclaim to what extent it does not exist ?
because, out of the very love of truth, they will not
suffer those who care nothing for it to pretend to a
religious zeal in its behalf, when the lie is to be turned
against themselves ?

One of the bitterest sights in the world to a lover of
equal dealing, is the selfish and conceited arrogance *with
which the rich demand virtues on the side of the poor, which
they do not exercise themselves.* The rich man lies through
his lawyer—through his dependant—through his footman ; lies when he makes ' *civil speeches* ' ;—lies when
he subscribes articles ;—lies when he goes to be married
(*vide* Marriage Service) ;—lies when he takes ' the oaths
and his seat ' ;—but that the *poor* man should lie ! that
he should give a false promise !—that he should risk the
direful, and unheard-of, and unparliamentary crime of
political perjury ! Oh, it is not to be thought of ! Think
of the example—think of the want of principle—think
of the harm done to the poor man's ' own mind '—to his
sense of right and wrong—to his eternal salvation. Nay,
not that either :—they have seldom the immodesty to
go as far as that. But what enormous want of modesty
to go so far as they do ! Why should the poor man be
expected to have scruples which the rich laugh at ? Why
deny him weapons which they make use of against himself ?—in this respect, as in too many others, resembling
their ' noble ' feudal ancestors, who had the nobleness
to fight in armour, while the common soldier was allowed
none.

Yet let us not be supposed to think ill of the rich or of

anybody, beyond the warrant of humanity—beyond all modesty of our own, or sense of the frailties which we possess plentifully in common with our fellow creatures. We think ill, in fact, of no one, in the only bad and deplorable sense of the term,—that sense which would make him out to be something wicked from sheer preference of evil to good, or of harm to others without impulse or excuse. We are of opinion, that all classes and descriptions of men are modified as they are by circumstances; and instead of lamenting that there is so much vice or mistake (for that is the word) during their advancement towards a wiser condition, we rejoice that there is so much virtue,—so much indelible and hopeful good. Nay, we can see a certain large and gallant healthiness of social constitution in man, in the very circumstance of vice's taking so gay or indifferent an air during what it supposes to be a necessity, or a condition of human nature; and the gayer it is, in some respects, the better; not only because of its having the less uneasy or mean conscience, but because it is the less given to cant and hypocrisy, and is ashamed of putting on a grave face of exaction upon others. The very worst of all vices (cruelty excepted)—that which seems to make the rich and prosperous hold their fellow creatures in such slight regard,—is often traceable only to a perverted sense of that identical importance in their eyes, which is grounded in a social feeling, and which, under a wiser education, would make them proud of sympathizing with the humblest. Those courtiers—those Whigs and Tories—those lawyers—those tradesmen we have been talking of,—how shocked would not many, perhaps most of them be, and what a right would they not have to resent it,—if you treated them as liars beyond the pale of their conventional duplicity? Take the grocer or the linendraper from behind his counter—apply to him in any concern but that of his shop,—and most likely he is as great a truth-teller as the rest. There is nothing you may not take his word for. And then see what affections all these people have; what lovers they are of their families; what anxious providers for their

children ; what ' good fellows ' as friends and helpers ;
and what a fool and coxcomb you ought to consider
yourself, if you dared to set yourself up, and pretend
that you were a bit better than any one of them, even
though circumstances might enable you to be free from
some of their errors,—perhaps with greater of your own.
Falsehood itself is sometimes almost pure virtue,—at
least it contemplates anything but the ordinary and unjust results of falsehood ; as in the case of a jury, who
deliberately tell a lie when, in order to save a man from
transportation, or a poor child from the jail, they bring
in a verdict of Not Guilty on the principal charge, knowing him to be otherwise.   Here the law is violated for
the sake of justice, and a lie told for the sake of the
beautiful truth that we ought to be humane to one
another.   But the law should be changed ?   True : and
so should ALL LAWS be changed which force just feelings
upon falsehood in self-defence ;—and as the rich advance in their notions of justice, and the poor get better
fed and taught, all such laws WILL be changed.

In short, dear anti-ballot people, whoever you are,
and granting for the sake of the argument, that all
which you say about the voter's prevarication will be
true (for in innumerable instances we deny that it will,
and in all it must eventually come to nothing in the
hopelessness of applying to him), but granting for the
sake of the argument, that all which you anticipate in
that respect will come to pass, we have two short things
to say to you, which appear to us to sum up all that is
necessary for the refutation of your reasoning : first,
that before you have a right to ask the voter not to be
false to you, you must get rid of your own falsehoods,
great and small ; and second, that when you do get rid
of them, *you will be such very conscientious men, that you
will not have the face to ask him to violate* HIS *conscience.*

CHARACTERS

THE OLD GENTLEMAN

[Indicator, Feb. 2, 1820]

OUR Old Gentleman, in order to be exclusively himself, must be either a widower or a bachelor. Suppose the former. We do not mention his precise age, which would be invidious ;—nor whether he wears his own hair or a wig ; which would be wanting in universality. If a wig, it is a compromise between the more modern scratch and the departed glory of the toupee. If his own hair, it is white, in spite of his favourite grandson, who used to get on the chair behind him, and pull the silver hairs out, ten years ago. If he is bald at top, the hairdresser, hovering and breathing about him like a second youth, takes care to give the bald place as much powder as the covered ; in order that he may convey to the sensorium within a pleasing indistinctness of idea respecting the exact limits of skin and hair. He is very clean and neat ; and in warm weather, is proud of opening his waistcoat half way down, and letting so much of his frill be seen ; in order to show his hardiness as well as taste. His watch and shirt-buttons are of the best ; and he does not care if he has two rings on a finger. If his watch ever failed him at the club or coffee-house, he would take a walk every day to the nearest clock of good character, purely to keep it right. He has a cane at home, but seldom uses it, on finding it out of fashion with his elderly juniors. He has a small cocked hat for gala days, which he lifts higher from his head than the round one, when made a bow to. In his pockets are two handkerchiefs (one for the neck at night-time), his spectacles, and his pocket-book. The pocket-book, among other things, contains a receipt for a cough, and

some verses cut out of an odd sheet of an old magazine,
on the lovely Duchess of A., beginning—

> When beauteous Mira walks the plain.

He intends this for a common-place book which he
keeps, consisting of passages in verse and prose cut out
of newspapers and magazines, and pasted in columns;
some of them rather gay. His principal other books
are Shakespeare's *Plays* and Milton's *Paradise Lost*:
the *Spectator*, the *History of England*; the works of
Lady M. W. Montague, Pope, and Churchill; Middleton's *Geography*, *The Gentleman's Magazine;* Sir John
Sinclair on Longevity; several plays with portraits in
character; *Account of Elizabeth Canning, Memoirs of
George Ann Bellamy, Poetical Amusements at Bath-
Easton*, Blair's *Works*, *Elegant Extracts; Junius* as
originally published; a few pamphlets on the American
War and Lord George Gordon, &c. and one on the
French Revolution. In his sitting rooms are some engravings from Hogarth and Sir Joshua; an engraved
portrait of the Marquis of Granby; ditto of M. le Comte
de Grasse surrendering to Admiral Rodney; a humorous piece after Penny; and a portrait of himself, painted
by Sir Joshua. His wife's portrait is in his chamber,
looking upon his bed. She is a little girl, stepping forward with a smile and a pointed toe, as if going to dance.
He lost her when she was sixty.

The Old Gentleman is an early riser, because he intends to live at least twenty years longer. He continues
to take tea for breakfast, in spite of what is said against
its nervous effects; having been satisfied on that point
some years ago by Dr. Johnson's criticism on Hanway,
and a great liking for tea previously. His china cups
and saucers have been broken since his wife's death, all
but one, which is religiously kept for his use. He passes
his morning in walking or riding, looking in at auctions,
looking after his India bonds or some such money
securities, furthering some subscription set on foot by
his excellent friend Sir John, or cheapening a new old
print for his portfolio. He also hears of the newspapers;

not caring to see them till after dinner at the coffee-house. He may also cheapen a fish or so; the fish-monger soliciting his doubting eye as he passes, with a profound bow of recognition. He eats a pear before dinner.

His dinner at the coffee-house is served up to him at the accustomed hour, in the old accustomed way, and by the accustomed waiter. If William did not bring it, the fish would be sure to be stale, and the flesh new. He eats no tart; or if he ventures on a little, takes cheese with it. You might as soon attempt to persuade him out of his senses, as that cheese is not good for digestion. He takes port; and if he has drank more than usual, and in a more private place, may be induced by some respectful inquiries respecting the old style of music, to sing a song composed by Mr. Oswald or Mr. Lampe, such as—

> Chloe, by that borrowed kiss,

or

> Come, gentle god of soft repose;

or his wife's favourite ballad beginning—

> At Upton on the Hill
> There lived a happy pair.

Of course, no such exploit can take place in the coffee-room; but he will canvass the theory of that matter there with you, or discuss the weather, or the markets, or the theatres, or the merits of 'my Lord North' or 'my Lord Rockingham'; for he rarely says simply, lord; it is generally 'my lord,' trippingly and genteelly off the tongue. If alone after dinner, his great delight is the newspaper; which he prepares to read by wiping his spectacles, carefully adjusting them on his eyes, and drawing the candle close to him, so as to stand sideways betwixt his ocular aim and the small type. He then holds the paper at arm's length, and dropping his eyelids half down and his mouth half open, takes cognizance of the day's information. If he leaves off, it is only when the door is opened by a new-comer, or when he suspects somebody is over-anxious to get the paper out of his hand. On these occasions, he gives an important hem! or so ; and resumes.

In the evening, our Old Gentleman is fond of going to the theatre, or of having a game of cards. If he enjoys the latter at his own house or lodgings, he likes to play with some friends whom he has known for many years : but an elderly stranger may be introduced, if quiet and scientific ; and the privilege is extended to younger men of letters ; who, if ill players, are good losers. Not that he is a miser ; but to win money at cards is like proving his victory by getting the baggage ; and to win of a younger man is a substitute for his not being able to beat him at rackets. He breaks up early, whether at home or abroad.

At the theatre, he likes a front row in the pit. He comes early, if he can do so without getting into a squeeze, and sits patiently waiting for the drawing up of the curtain, with his hands placidly lying one over the other on the top of his stick. He generously admires some of the best performers, but thinks them far inferior to Garrick, Woodward, and Clive. During splendid scenes, he is anxious that the little boy should see.

He has been induced to look in at Vauxhall again, but likes it still less than he did years back, and cannot bear it in comparison with Ranelagh. He thinks everything looks poor, flaring, and jaded. ' Ah ! ' says he, with a sort of triumphant sigh, ' Ranelagh was a noble place ! Such taste, such elegance, such beauty ! There was the Duchess of A., the finest woman in England, Sir ; and Mrs. L., a mighty fine creature ; and Lady Susan what 's her name, that had that unfortunate affair with Sir Charles. Sir, they came swimming by you like the swans.'

The Old Gentleman is very particular in having his slippers ready for him at the fire, when he comes home. He is also extremely choice in his snuff, and delights to get a fresh boxful in Tavistock Street, in his way to the theatre. His box is a curiosity from India. He calls

favourite young ladies by their Christian names, however
slightly acquainted with them ; and has a privilege also
of saluting all brides, mothers, and indeed every species
of lady on the least holiday occasion. If the husband,
for instance, has met with a piece of luck, he instantly
moves forward, and gravely kisses the wife on the cheek.
The wife then says, ' My niece, Sir, from the country ' ;
and he kisses the niece. The niece, seeing her cousin
biting her lips at the joke, says, 'My cousin Harriet, Sir ' ;
and he kisses the cousin. He never recollects such
weather, except during the Great Frost, or when he rode
down with Jack Skrimshire to Newmarket. He grows
young again in his little grandchildren, especially the
one which he thinks most like himself ; which is the
handsomest. Yet he likes best perhaps the one most
resembling his wife ; and will sit with him on his lap,
holding his hand in silence, for a quarter of an hour
together. He plays most tricks with the former, and
makes him sneeze. He asks little boys in general who
was the father of Zebedee's children. If his grandsons
are at school, he often goes to see them ; and makes
them blush by telling the master or the upper-scholars,
that they are fine boys, and of a precocious genius. He
is much struck when an old acquaintance dies, but adds
that he lived too fast ; and that poor Bob was a sad dog
in his youth ; ' a very sad dog, Sir, mightily set upon a
short life and a merry one.'

When he gets very old indeed, he will sit for whole
evenings, and say little or nothing ; but informs you,
that there is Mrs. Jones (the housekeeper),—' She'll
talk.'

THE OLD LADY

[Round Table No. 45, in *The Examiner*, Sept. 29, 1816]

IF the Old Lady is a widow and lives alone, the manners of her condition and time of life are so much the more apparent. She generally dresses in plain silks that make a gentle rustling as she moves about the silence of her room ; and she wears a nice cap with a lace border that comes under the chin. In a placket at her side is an old enamelled watch, unless it is locked up in a drawer of her toilet for fear of accidents. Her waist is rather tight and trim than otherwise, as she had a fine one when young ; and she is not sorry if you see a pair of her stockings on a table, that you may be aware of the neatness of her leg and foot. Contented with these and other evident indications of a good shape, and letting her young friends understand that she can afford to obscure it a little, she wears pockets, and uses them well too. In the one is her handkerchief, and any heavier matter that is not likely to come out with it, such as the change of a sixpence ;—in the other is a miscellaneous assortment consisting of a pocket-book, a bunch of keys, a needle-case, a spectacle-case, crumbs of biscuit, a nutmeg and grater, a smelling-bottle, and according to the season, an orange or apple, which after many days, she draws out, warm and glossy, to give to some little child that has well behaved itself. She generally occupies two rooms, in the neatest condition possible. In the chamber is a bed with a white coverlet, built up high and round to look well, and with curtains of a pastoral pattern, consisting alternately of large plants, and shepherds and shepherdesses. On the mantelpiece also are more shepherds and shepherdesses, with dot-eyed sheep at their feet, all in coloured ware, the man perhaps in a pink jacket and knots of ribbons at his knees and shoes, holding his crook lightly in one hand, and with the other at his breast turning his toes out and looking tenderly at the shepherdess :—the

woman, holding a crook also, and modestly returning his
look, with a gipsy-hat jerked up behind, a very slender
waist, with petticoat and hips to counteract, and the
petticoat pulled up through the pocket-holes in order to
show the trimness of her ankles. But these patterns, of
course, are various. The toilet is ancient, carved at the
edges, and tied about with a snow-white drapery of
muslin. Beside it are various boxes, mostly japan;
and the set of drawers are exquisite things for a little
girl to rummage, if ever little girl be so bold,—containing ribbons and laces of various kinds,—linen smelling
of lavender, of the flowers of which there is always dust
in the corners,—a heap of pocket-books for a series of
years,—and pieces of dress long gone by, such as head-
fronts, stomachers, and flowered satin shoes with enormous heels. The stock of letters are always under
especial lock and key. So much for the bed-room. In the
sitting-room, is rather a spare assortment of shining old
mahogany furniture, of carved arm-chairs equally old,
with chintz draperies down to the ground,—a folding or
other screen with Chinese figures, their round little-eyed
meek faces perking sideways;—a stuffed bird perhaps in
a glass case (a living one is too much for her);—a portrait
of her husband over the mantelpiece, in a coat with
frog-buttons, and a delicate frilled hand lightly inserted
in the waistcoat;—and opposite him, on the wall, is a
piece of embroidered literature, framed and glazed, containing some moral distich or maxim worked in angular
capital letters, with two trees or parrots below in their
proper colours, the whole concluding with an A B C and
numerals, and the name of the fair industrious, expressing it to be ' her work, Jan. 14, 1762.' The rest of the
furniture consists of a looking-glass with carved edges,
perhaps a settee, a hassock for the feet, a mat for the
little dog, and a small set of shelves, in which are the
Spectator and *Guardian*, the *Turkish Spy*, a Bible and
Prayer-book, *Young's Night Thoughts*, with a piece of
lace in it to flatten, Mrs. Rowe's *Devout Exercises of the
Heart*, Mrs. Glasse's *Cookery*, and perhaps *Sir Charles
Grandison*, and *Clarissa*. *John Buncle* is in the closet

among the pickles and preserves. The clock is on the landing-place between the two room-doors, where it ticks audibly but quietly ; and the landing-place, as well as the stairs, is carpeted to a nicety. The house is most in character, and properly coeval, if it is in a retired suburb, and strongly built, with wainscot rather than paper inside, and lockers in the windows. Before the windows also should be some quivering poplars. Here the Old Lady receives a few quiet visitors to tea and perhaps an early game at cards ; or you may sometimes see her going out on the same kind of visit herself, with a light umbrella turning up into a stick and crooked ivory handle, and her little dog equally famous for his love to her and captious antipathy to strangers. Her grandchildren dislike him on holidays; and the boldest sometimes ventures to give him a sly kick under the table. When she returns at night, she appears, if the weather happens to be doubtful, in a calash ; and her servant, in pattens, follows half behind and half at her side, with a lantern.

Her opinions are not many, nor new. She thinks the Clergyman a nice man. The Duke of Wellington, in her opinion, is a very great man ; but she has a secret preference for the Marquis of Granby. She thinks the young women of the present day too forward, and the men not respectful enough ; but hopes her grandchildren will be better ; though she differs with her daughter in several points respecting their management. She sets little value on the new accomplishments ; is a great though delicate connoisseur in butcher's meat and all sort of housewifery : and if you mention waltzes, expatiates on the grace and fine breeding of the minuet. She longs to have seen one danced by Sir Charles Grandison, whom she almost considers as a real person. She likes a walk of a summer's evening, but avoids the new streets, canals, &c., and sometimes goes through the churchyard where her other children and her husband lie buried, serious but not melancholy. She has had three great eras in her life,—her marriage —her having been at court to see the King and Queen and Royal

Family,—and a compliment on her figure she once received in passing from Mr. Wilkes, whom she describes as a sad loose man, but engaging. His plainness she thinks much exaggerated. If anything takes her at a distance from home, it is still the Court ; but she seldom stirs even for that. The last time but one that she went was to see the Duke of Wirtemberg : and she has lately been, most probably for the last time of all, to see the Princess Charlotte and Prince Leopold. From this beatific vision she returned with the same admiration as ever for the fine comely appearance of the Duke of York and the rest of the family, and great delight at having had a near view of the Princess, whom she speaks of with smiling pomp and lifted mittens, clasping them as passionately as she can together, and calling her, in a sort of transport of mixed loyalty and self-love, a fine royal young creature, and Daughter of England.

THE MAIDSERVANT

[Round Table No. 46, in *The Examiner*, Oct. 20, 1816]

MUST be considered as young, or else she has married the butcher, the butler, or her cousin, or has otherwise settled into a character distinct from her original one, so as to become what is properly called the domestic. The Maidservant, in her apparel, is either slovenly and fine by turns, and dirty always ; or she is at all times snug and neat and dressed according to her station. In the latter case, her ordinary dress is black stockings, a stuff gown, a cap, and a neck-handkerchief pinned corner-wise behind. If you want a pin, she just feels about her, and has always one to give you. On Sundays and holidays, and perhaps of afternoons, she changes her black stockings for white, puts on a gown of a better texture and fine pattern, sets her cap and her curls jauntily, and lays aside the neck-handkerchief for a high-body, which, by the way, is not half so pretty

There is something very warm and latent in the handkerchief,—something easy, vital, and genial. A woman in a high-bodied gown, made to fit her like a case, is by no means more modest, and is much less tempting. She looks like a figure at the head of a ship. We could almost see her chucked out of doors into a cart with as little remorse as a couple of sugar-loaves. The tucker is much better, as well as the handkerchief; and is to the other, what the young lady is to the servant. The one always reminds us of the Sparkler in Sir Richard Steele; the other of Fanny in *Joseph Andrews*.

But to return. The general furniture of her ordinary room the kitchen is not so much her own as her master's and mistress's, and need not be described: but in a drawer of the dresser or the table, in company with a duster, and a pair of snuffers, may be found some of her property, such as a brass thimble, a pair of scissors, a thread-case, a piece of wax candle much wrinkled with the thread, an odd volume of *Pamela*, and perhaps a sixpenny play, such as *George Barnwell* or Mrs. Behn's *Oroonoko*. There is a piece of looking-glass also in the window. The rest of her furniture is in the garret, where you may find a good looking-glass on the table; and in the window a Bible, a comb, and a piece of soap. Here stands also, under stout lock and key, the mighty mystery,—the box,—containing among other things her clothes, two or three song-books, consisting of nineteen for the penny; sundry Tragedies at a halfpenny the sheet; the Whole Nature of Dreams laid open, together with the Fortune Teller and the Account of the Ghost of Mrs. Veal; the Story of the Beautiful Zoa who was cast away on a desert island, showing how, &c.; some half-crowns in a purse, including pieces of country-money, with the good Countess of Coventry on one of them riding naked on the horse; a silver penny wrapped up in cotton by itself; a crooked sixpence, given her before she came to town, and the giver of which has either forgotten or been forgotten by her, she is not sure which;— two little enamel boxes, with looking-glass in the lids, one of them a fairing, the other ' a trifle from Margate ';

and lastly, various letters, square and ragged, and directed in all sorts of spellings, chiefly with little letters for capitals. One of them, written by a girl who went to a day-school, is directed 'miss.'

In her manners, the Maidservant sometimes imitates her young mistress ; she puts her hair in papers, cultivates a shape, and occasionally contrives to be out of spirits. But her own character and condition overcome all sophistications of this sort ; her shape, fortified by the mop and scrubbing-brush, will make its way : and exercise keeps her healthy and cheerful. From the same cause her temper is good ; though she gets into little heats when a stranger is over-saucy, or when she is told not to go so heavily downstairs, or when some unthinking person goes up her wet stairs with dirty shoes, —or when she is called away often from dinner ; neither does she much like to be seen scrubbing the street-door steps of a morning ; and sometimes she catches herself saying, 'drat that butcher,' but immediately adds, 'God forgive me.' The tradesmen indeed, with their compliments and arch looks, seldom give her cause to complain. The milkman bespeaks her good-humour for the day with 'Come, pretty maids.' Then follow the butcher, the baker, the oilman, &c., all with their several smirks and little loiterings ; and when she goes to the shops herself, it is for her the grocer pulls down his string from its roller with more than ordinary whirl, and tosses, as it were, his parcel into a tie,—for her, the cheesemonger weighs his butter with half a glance, cherishes it round about with his pattles, and dabs the little piece on it to make up, with a graceful jerk.

Thus pass the mornings between working, and singing, and giggling, and grumbling, and being flattered. If she takes any pleasure unconnected with her office before the afternoon, it is when she runs up the area-steps or to the door to hear and purchase a new song, or to see a troop of soldiers go by ; or when she happens to thrust her head out of a chamber window at the same time with a servant at the next house, when a dialogue infallibly ensues, stimulated by the imaginary obstacles between.

If the Maidservant is wise, the best part of her work is done by dinner-time ; and nothing else is necessary to give perfect zest to the meal. She tells us what she thinks of it, when she calls it ' a bit o' dinner.' There is the same sort of eloquence in her other phrase, ' a cup o' tea '; but the old ones, and the washerwomen, beat her at that. After tea in great houses, she goes with the other servants to hot cockles, or What-are-my-thoughts-like, and tells Mr. John to ' have done then ' ; or if there is a ball given that night, they throw open all the doors, and make use of the music upstairs to dance by. In smaller houses, she receives the visit of her aforesaid cousin ; and sits down alone, or with a fellow maidservant, to work ; talks of her young master or mistress and Mr. Ivins (Evans) ; or else she calls to mind her own friends in the country, where she thinks the cows and ' all that ' beautiful, now she is away. Meanwhile, if she is lazy, she snuffs the candle with her scissors ; or if she has eaten more heartily than usual, she sighs double the usual number of times, and thinks that tender hearts were born to be unhappy.

Such being the Maidservant's life indoors, she scorns when abroad to be anything but a creature of sheer enjoyment. The Maidservant, the sailor, and the schoolboy, are the three beings that enjoy a holiday beyond all the rest of the world ;—and all for the same reason,—because their inexperience, peculiarity of life, and habit of being with persons of circumstances or thoughts above them, give them all, in their way, a cast of the romantic. The most active of money getters is a vegetable compared with them. The Maidservant, when she first goes to Vauxhall, thinks she is in heaven. A theatre is all pleasure to her, whatever is going forward, whether the play, or the music, or the waiting which makes others impatient, or the munching of apples and gingerbread nuts which she and her party commence almost as soon as they have seated themselves. She prefers tragedy to comedy, because it is grander, and less like what she meets with in general ; and because she thinks it more in earnest also, especially in the love-scenes. Her favourite play is *Alexander the Great, or the Rival Queens.* Another great delight is in going a-shopping. She loves to look at the patterns in the windows, and the fine things labelled with those corpulent numerals of ' only 7s.'—' only 6s. 6d.' She has also, unless born and bred in London, been to see my Lord Mayor, the fine people coming out of Court, and the ' beasties ' in the Tower ; and at all events she has been to Astley's and the Circus, from which she comes away equally smitten with the rider and sore with laughing at the clown. But it is difficult to say what pleasure she enjoys most. One of the completest of all is the fair, where she walks through an endless round of noise, and toys, and gallant apprentices, and wonders. Here she is invited in by courteous well-dressed people as if she were the mistress. Here also is the conjurer's booth, where the operator himself, a most stately and genteel person all in white, calls her Ma'am ; and says to John by her side, in spite of his laced hat, ' Be good enough, Sir, to hand the card to the lady.'

Ah ! may her ' cousin ' turn out as true as he says he is ; or may she get home soon enough and smiling enough to be as happy again next time.

THE WAITER

[London Journal, June 13, 1835]

GOING into the City the other day upon business, we took a chop at a tavern, and renewed our acquaintance, after years of interruption, with that swift and untiring personage, yclept a waiter. We mention this long interval of acquaintance, in order to account for any deficiencies that may be found in our description of him. Our readers, perhaps, will favour us with a letter. He is a character before the public : thousands are acquainted with him, and can fill up the outline. But we felt irresistibly impelled to sketch him ; like a portrait-

painter who comes suddenly upon an old friend, or upon
an old servant of the family.

We speak of the waiter properly and generally so
called,—the representative of the whole, real, official
race,—and not of the humorist or other eccentric
genius occasionally to be found in it,—moving out of
the orbit of tranquil but fiery waiting,—not absorbed,—
not devout towards us,—not silent or monosyllabical;—
fellows that affect a character beyond that of waiter, and
get spoiled in club-rooms, and places of theatrical resort.

Your thorough waiter has no ideas out of the sphere
of his duty and the business; and yet he is not narrow-
minded either.   He sees too much variety of character
for that, and has to exercise too much consideration for
the 'drunken gentleman.'   But his world is the tavern,
and all mankind but its visitors.   His female sex are
the maidservants and his young mistress, or the widow.
If he is ambitious, he aspires to marry one of the latter:
if otherwise, and Molly is prudent, he does not know but
he may carry her off some day to be mistress of the
Golden Lion at Chinksford, where he will 'show off' in
the eyes of Betty Laxon who refused him.   He has no
feeling of noise itself but as the sound of dining, or of
silence but as a thing before dinner.   Even a loaf with
him is hardly a loaf; it is so many 'breads.'   His
longest speech is the making out of a bill *viva voce*—
'Two beefs—one potatoes—three ales—two wines—six
and twopence'—which he does with an indifferent
celerity, amusing to new-comers who have been relishing
their fare, and not considering it as a mere set of items.
He attributes all virtues to everybody, provided they
are civil and liberal; and of the existence of some vices
he has no notion.   Gluttony, for instance, with him, is
not only inconceivable, but looks very like a virtue.
He sees in it only so many more 'beefs,' and a generous
scorn of the bill.   As to wine, or almost any other liquor,
it is out of your power to astonish him with the quantity
you call for.   His 'Yes Sir' is as swift, indifferent, and
official, at the fifth bottle as at the first.   Reform and
other public events he looks upon purely as things in the

newspaper, and the newspaper as a thing taken in at
taverns, for gentlemen to read. His own reading is
confined to 'Accidents and Offences,' and the advertise-
ments for Butlers, which latter he peruses with an admiring fear, not choosing to give up 'a certainty.' When
young, he was always in a hurry, and exasperated his
mistress by running against the other waiters, and
breaking the 'neguses.' As he gets older, he learns to
unite swiftness with caution; declines wasting his breath
in immediate answers to calls; and knows, with a slight
turn of his face, and elevation of his voice, into what
precise corner of the room to pitch his 'Coming, Sir.'
If you told him that, in Shakespeare's time, waiters said
'Anon, anon, Sir,' he would be astonished at the repetition of the same word in one answer, and at the use
of three words instead of two; and he would justly infer,
that London could not have been so large, nor the chop-
houses so busy in those days. He would drop one of the
two syllables of his 'Yes, Sir,' if he could; but business
and civility will not allow it; and therefore he does
what he can by running them together in the swift
sufficiency of his 'Yezzir.'

Thomas!

Yezzir.

Is my steak coming?

Yezzir.

And the pint of port?

Yezzir.

You'll not forget the postman?

Yezzir.

For in the habit of his acquiescence Thomas not seldom
says 'Yes, Sir,' for 'No, Sir,' the habit itself rendering
him intelligible.

His morning dress is a waistcoat or jacket; his coat
is for afternoons. If the establishment is flourishing,
he likes to get into black as he grows elderly; by which
time also he is generally a little corpulent, and wears
hair-powder, dressing somewhat laxly about the waist
for convenience of movement. Not however that he
draws much upon that part of his body, except as a

poise to what he carries ; for you may observe that a waiter, in walking, uses only his lowest limbs, from his knees downwards. The movement of all the rest of him is negative, and modified solely by what he bears in his hands. At this period he has a little money in the funds, and his nieces look up to him. He still carries however a napkin under his arm, as well as a corkscrew in his pocket ; nor, for all his long habit, can he help feeling a satisfaction at the noise he makes in drawing a cork. He thinks that no man can do it better ; and that Mr. Smith, who understands wine, is thinking so too, though he does not take his eyes off the plate. In his right waistcoat pocket is a snuff-box, with which he supplies gentlemen late at night, after the shops are shut up, and when they are in desperate want of another fillip to their sensations, after the devil and toasted cheese. If particularly required, he will laugh at a joke, especially at that time of night, justly thinking that gentlemen towards one in the morning ' *will* be facetious.' He is of opinion it is in ' human nature ' to be a little fresh at that period, and to want to be put into a coach.

He announces his acquisition of property by a bunch of seals to his watch, and perhaps rings on his fingers ; one of them a mourning ring left him by his late master, the other a present, either from his nieces' father, or from some ultra-goodnatured old gentleman whom he helped into a coach one night, and who had no silver about him.

To see him dine, somehow, hardly seems natural. And he appears to do it as if he had no right. You catch him at his dinner in a corner,—huddled apart,— ' Thomas dining ! ' instead of helping dinner. One fancies that the stewed and hot meats and the constant smoke, ought to be too much for him, and that he should have neither appetite nor time for such a meal.

Once a year (for he has few holidays) a couple of pedestrians meet him on a Sunday in the fields, and cannot conceive for the life of them who it is ; till the startling recollection occurs—' Good God ! It's the waiter at the Grogram ! '

BUTLERS

[*Table Talk*]

TRAGEDY will break in upon one's dinner-table in spite of us. Mr. Wakley tells us that suicide is rife among *butlers*! The news is startling to people at dinner. How many faces must have been turned on butlers, the day on which the coroner made the remark; and how uncomfortable some of them must have felt! The teetotallers will not overlook it; for the cause appears obvious enough. The butler is always sipping. He is also the most sedentary of domestics, the house-keeper excepted; and wine-merchants accuse him of having a bad conscience. So he grows burly and un-easy; thinks he shall never retire into an inn or a public office; loses bits of his property in speculation; and when the antibilious pill fails him, there is an in-quest.

The poor butler should take to his legs, instead of his arm-chair. He should make himself easier in his mind, considering his temptations; and cultivate an interest in everything out of doors, except shares in railroads.

THE MONTHLY NURSE

[*Heads of the People*, 1846]

THE Monthly Nurse—taking the class in the lump, without such exceptions as will be noticed before we conclude—is a middle-aged, motherly sort of a gossip, hushing, flattering, dictatorial, knowing, ignorant, not very delicate, comfortable, uneasy, slip-slop kind of a blinking individual, between asleep and awake, whose business it is—under Providence and the doctor—to see that a child be not ushered with too little officious-ness into the world, nor brought up with too much good sense during the first month of its existence. All grown people, with her (excepting her own family), consist of wives who are brought to bed, and husbands who are bound to be extremely sensible of the supremacy of that event ; and all the rising generation are infants in laced caps, not five weeks old, with incessant thirst, screaming faces, thumpable backs, and red little minnikin hands tipped with buds of nails. She is the only maker of caudle in the world. She takes snuff ostentatiously, drams advisably, tea incessantly, advice indignantly, a nap when she can get it, cold whenever there is a crick in the door, and the remainder of whatsoever her mistress leaves to eat or drink, provided it is what somebody else would like to have. But she drinks rather than eats. She has not the relish for a ' bit o' dinner ' that the servant-maid has ; though nobody but the washerwoman beats her at a 'dish o' tea,' or at that which 'keeps cold out of the stomach,' and put weakness into it. If she is thin she is generally straight as a stick, being of a condition of body that not even drams will tumefy. If she is fat she is one of the fubsiest of the cosy ; though rheumatic withal, and requiring a complexional good-nature to settle the irritabilities of her position, and turn the balance in favour of comfort or hope. She is the victim of watching ; the arbitress of her superiors; the servant, yet rival, of doctors ; the opposer of innovations ; the regretter of all old household religions as to pap-boats, cradles, and swathes ; the inhabitant of a hundred bed-rooms ; the Juno Lucina of the ancients, or goddess of child-birth, in the likeness of a cook-maid. Her greatest consolation under a death (next to the corner cupboard, and the not having had her advice taken about a piece of flannel) is the handsomeness of the corpse ; and her greatest pleasure in life is when lady and baby are both gone to sleep, the fire bright, the kettle boiling, and her corns quiescent. She then first takes a piece of snuff, by way of pungent anticipation of bliss, or as a sort of concentrated essence of satisfaction ; then a glass of spirits—then puts the water in the tea-pot—then takes another glass of spirits (the last having been a small one, and the coming tea affording a

' counteraction ')—then smoothes down her apron, adjusts herself in her arm-chair, pours out the first cup of tea, and sits for a minute or two staring at the fire, with the solid complacency of an owl,—perhaps not without something of his snore, between wheeze and snuff-box.

Good and ill-nature, as in the case of every one else, make the great difference between the endurability, or otherwise, of this personage in your house ; and the same qualities, in the master and mistress, together with the amount of their good sense, or the want of it, have a like reaction. The good or ill, therefore, that is here said of the class in general, becomes applicable to the individual accordingly. But as all people will get what power they can, the pleasant by pleasant means, and the unpleasant by the reverse, so the office of the Monthly Nurse, be her temper and nature what it will, is one that emphatically exposes her to temptation that way ; and her first endeavour, when she comes into a house, is to see how far she can establish an undisputed authority on all points. In proportion to her success or otherwise in this object, she looks upon the lady as a charming, reasonable, fine, weak, cheatable creature, whose husband (as she tells him) ' can never be too grateful for her bearing such troubles on his account ' ; or as a Frenchified conceited madam, who will turn out a deplorable match for the poor gentleman, and assuredly be the death of the baby with her tantrums about ' natural living,' and her blasphemies against rum, pieces of fat, and Daffy's Elixir. The gentleman in like manner—or ' master,' as the humbler ones call him—is, according as he behaves himself, and receives her revelations for gospel, a ' sweet good man '—' quite a gentleman '—' just the very model of a husband for mistress,' &c. &c. ; or, on the other hand, he is a ' very strange gentleman '—' quite an oddity '—one that is ' not to be taught his own good '—that will ' neither be led or *druv* '—that will ' be the death of mistress with his constant *fidge-fidge* in and out of the room '—and his making her ' laugh in that dreadful manner,' and so forth ;—and, as to his ' pretending to hold the baby, it is like a cow with a candlestick.' 'Holding the baby,' indeed, is a science, which she reckons to belong exclusively to herself; she makes it the greatest favour to visitor or servant to let them venture upon a trial of it; and affable intimations are given to the oldest mothers of families, who come to see her mistress, how they will do well to receive a little instruction on that head, and not venture to substitute their fine-spun theories for her solid practice; for your Monthly Nurse (next to a positive grandson) is the greatest teacher of your grandmother how to suck eggs, in the world; and you may have been forty years in the habit of sticking a pin, and find your competency come to nothing before the explanatory pity of her information.

Respecting the 'doctor,' her thoughts cannot be so bold or even so patronizing. She is confessedly second to him, while he is present; and when he has left the room a spell remains upon her from his superior knowledge. Yet she has her hearty likes or dislikes of him too, and on the same grounds of self-reference. If she likes him, there 'never *was* such a beautiful doctor,' except perhaps Sir William, or Doctor Buttermouth (both dead), and always excepting the one that recommended herself. He is a 'fine man'—so patient—so without pride—and yet 'so firm, like';—nobody comes near him for a difficult case—for a fever case—for the management of a 'violent lady.' If she dislikes him, he is 'queer'—'odd'—'stubborn'—has the 'new ways,'—very proper, she has no doubt, but not what she has been used to, or seen practised by the doctors about court. And whether she likes him or not, she has always a saving grace for herself, of superiority to all other nurses, in point of experience and good luck. She has always seen a case of more difficulty than the one in hand, and knows what was done for it; and Doctor Gripps, who is 'always' called in to such cases, and who is a very pleasant though rough sort of gentleman, calls her his 'other right hand,' and 'the *jewel* that rhymes to *gruel*.'

Armed with these potential notions in general, and

the strongest possible sense of her vice-royalty over master and mistress for the time being, she takes possession of the new room and the new faces ; and the motto of her reign—the *Dieu et Mon Droit* of her escutcheon—is ' During the month.' This phrase she has always at hand, like a sceptre, wherewith to assert her privileges, and put down objection. ' During the month,' the lady is not to read a book. ' During the month,' nobody is to lay a finger on the bed for the purpose of making it, till her decree goes forth. ' During the month,' the muffler of the knocker is at her disposal. And ' During the month,' the husband is to be nobody, except as far as she thinks fit, not even (for the first week or so) to his putting his head in at the door. You would take him to be the last man who had anything to do with the business. However, for her own sake, she generally contrives to condescend to become friends with him, and he is then received into high favour—is invited to tea with his wife, at some ' unusually early ' period ; and Nurse makes a bit of buttered toast for ' master ' with her own hand, and not only repeats that ' baby is as like him as two peas ' (which it always is, the moment it is born, if the lady's inclination is supposed to set that way), but tells him that she fears he is ' a sad charming gentleman,' for that ' mistress talks of him in her sleep.' The phrases commonest in her mouth are mostly of an endearing or flattering sort, with an implication, in the tone, of her right to bestow them ; and she is very aristocratic in her ideas. She tells the lady in her hour of trial, as the highest encouragement to fortitude she can think of, that ' the Queen must suffer the same'; and the babies are always kings and queens, loves, darlings, jewels, and poppets. Beauties also, be sure :—and as all babies are beautiful, and the last always more beautiful than the one before it, and ' the child is father to the man,' mankind, according to Nurse, ought to be nothing but a multitude of Venuses and Adonises ; aldermen should be mere Cupids full grown ; and the passengers in Fleet Street, male and female, slay one another, as they go, with the unbearableness of their respective charms. But she has also modes of speech, simply pathetic or judicious. If the lady, when her health is inquired after, is in low spirits, she is described as ' taking *on so* '; if doing well, it must not be too well, for the honour of the importance of the case, and the general dignity of ailment; and hence the famous answer, ' as well as can be expected.' By the time the baby arrives at the robustness of a fortnight old, and appears to begin to smack its lips, it is manifestly the most ill-used of infant elegancies, if a series of random hits are not made at its mouth and cheeks with a piece of the fat of pig; and, when it is sleepy and yet 'will not go to sleep' (which is a phenomenon usually developed about the time the Nurse wants her tea), or when it is ' fractious ' for not having had *enough* pig, or from something else which has been counteracted, or anything but the sly sup of gin lately given it, or the pin which is now running into its back, it is equally clear, that if Daffy, or Godfrey, or rocking the chair, will not do, a perpetual thumping of the back, and jolting of its very soul out, will; and, accordingly, there lies the future lord or lady of the creation, prostrate across the nurse's knees, a lump in a laced cap and interminable clothes, getting redder and redder in the face, ejaculating such agonies between grunt and shout as each simultaneous thump will permit, and secretly saluted by its holder with ' brats,' and ' drat it,' and 'was there ever such an " obstropulous " little devil ! ' while her lips are loud in deprecation of the ' naughty milk,' or the ' naughty cot ' (which is to be beaten for its ill-behaviour); and ' Dordie' (Georgy) is told to ' go ' to a mysterious place, called ' Bye-Bye '; or the whole catechism of nursery interrogation is gone through, from the past tenses of the amenities of ' Was it a poppet then ? ' and ' Did it break its pretty heart ? ' up to the future glories of ' Shall it be a King then ? ' ' Shall it be a King Pepin ? ' ' Shall it be a Princy-wincy ? ' a ' Countess ? ' a ' Duchess ? ' ' Shall it break the fine gentlemen's hearts with those beautiful blue eyes ?' In the midst of tragicomic burlesque of this sort, have risen upon the world its future Marses and Apollos, its Napoleons, its Platos, and its Shakespeares.

Alas! that it should be made a question (ridiculed indeed by the shallow, the nurse among them, but very seriously mooted by philosophers) whether in that first and tenderest month of existence, the little bundle of already made organs, sensations, and passions, does not receive impressions from this frivolous elderly 'nobody,' which may affect the temper and disposition of the future man or woman! whether the 'beautiful fury'— though we confess we never saw such a phenomenon— whether the crash in the china closet, or the sacrifice of a daughter's happiness to a father's will and obstinacy, had not its first seeds sown in the lap of this poppet-dandling simpleton. Not its 'first,' we apprehend. Those, we take it, are of far earlier origin, the little creature being much older than is generally supposed, when it comes under the influence of this its third, and most transitory, and not always most foolish modifier. But we have no doubt that she contributes her portion of effect. This is, however, what she herself can by no means comprehend. 'As if any treatment' (she thinks) 'except in the article of rum and sugar, and the mode of holding, can be of consequence to one so young!' She is nevertheless very diligent in looking for 'marks' about its body, and tracing them to influences on the mother's mind; and yet she cannot see that the *then* impressible little creature is still impressible. Heaven and earth are to come together if the piece of fat is not supplied, or the clothes are not of the proper fashion: but the sudden affrightment, the secret blow, the deadening jolt to sleep, or the giving way to nothing but the last rage, these are to be of no importance. She has no doubt, nevertheless, that its brothers and sisters are all impressible, whatever the infant may be; and accordingly, with her usual instinct of the love of power, she generally contrives to do as much inconsiderate harm to them as possible, and lays the seeds of jealousy in their minds—if none be there already—by telling them that they must now cease to look upon themselves as the only important persons in the family, for that ' a little stranger has come to put their noses out of joint.' Pleasing and picturesque introduction to the fraternal affections !

Do not despise her ; no, not even when portrayed as in our artist's picture, under her worst aspect, for a warning. Engage not such a nurse as that if you can help it ; yet pity while you refuse her, for perhaps she would not have had the aspect, but for the unnatural sleeplessness to which her duties forced her, nor have been given to that poison by her side, but for some aggravation of care occasioned by domestic troubles of her own. Even she—even that wretched incontinent face and burly person—has once been an infant, as we all have,—perhaps flattered for her beauty (who would now think it ?), the darling and the spoil of some weak mother like herself. Thus are errors propagated, till we discover that personal reproach and satire are of little use, and that it is systems which are to be better taught, before individuals can improve. Poor old nurse ! Strange indeed would it be to begin with reprobating her ! Let us see that she does as little harm as may be, crown (or *half*-crown) her with fees for her caudle, and dismiss her as fast as possible, with a deprecation of her sciatica.

There is not only a good as well as a bad side in everything (and with the addition of a little good sense to good-nature, you may make a very pleasant nurse even out of such an one as we have described), but there are exceptions in all classes, better even than mere partakers of bad and good. The Monthly Nurse, as you ascend in society, is not seldom a highly respectable woman, who is nearly all that she should be—mild, firm, and well-meaning ; and we have known instances—or rather we should say, as far as our personal knowledge is concerned, one rare instance—in which the requisite qualifications were completed, and the precious individual (for when can a mother's luck be greater ?) was an intelligent gentlewoman ! This is what the assistant-moulder of the first month of the existence of a human being ought always to be, and what she always *would* be, if the world itself were older, and even the humblest and earliest form of education regarded as the important and sacred thing which it is.

The poets, who are the vindicators of beautiful and everlasting truths, in contradistinction to the fleeting deformities of mistakes and half-truths, made the greatest goddesses of antiquity preside over child-birth; and the reader, supposing him to be the worthy reader of whatsoever relates to humanity, and aware what small and indifferent things are its least dignified infirmities compared with its powers and affections, will not be sorry to have any ill-taste taken out of the mouth of his imagination on this subject by a passage from one of the earliest of them—supposed by some to have been Homer himself—in which the glorious old Greek, whoever he was, celebrates the birth of Apollo, and makes heaven and earth, the goddesses, the trees, the green meadows, and the incarnation of the spirit of sunshine, contribute to make it beautiful. We quote the version of Mr. Elton, as better even than Chapman's, only wishing that he had said 'prevailing,' or some more potent word of that sort, instead of 'valiant,' as the latter has come to mean a very ordinary sort of strength and heartiness, compared with that of the divine archer. As to apologizing for this final exaltation of our subject of the Monthly Nurse (which is a name that the 'sage and serious' Homer would not have scrupled to give to Diana herself, who was at once the *moon* and *midwife* of the ancient world), we shall no more think of doing it, than we should of blushing for the very moonlight when it sheds its beams on the bed of some newly-blessed mother, and combines thoughts of angels with her cradle.

—As the feet
Of the birth-speeding goddess touch'd the isle,
The labour seiz'd Latona, and the hour
Was come. Around a palm-tree's stem she threw
Her linked arms, and press'd her bowed knees
On the soft meadow. Earth beneath her smiled,
And Phoebus leap'd to light. The goddesses

E 2

Scream'd in their joy. There, oh thou archer god!
Those goddesses imbathed thee in fair streams
With chaste and pure immersion; swathing thee
With new-wove mantle, white, of delicate folds,
Clasp'd with a golden belt. His mother's milk
Fed not Apollo of the golden sword;
But Themis with immortal hands infused
Nectar and bland ambrosia. Then rejoiced
Latona, that her boy had sprung to light,
Valiant, and bearer of the bow; but when,
Oh Phoebus! thou hadst tasted with thy lips
Ambrosial food, the golden swathes no more
Withheld thee, panting; nor could bands restrain:
But every ligament was snapt in scorn.
Straight did Apollo stand in heaven, and face
Th' immortals. 'Give me,' cried the boy, 'a harp
And bending bow; and let me prophesy
To mortal man th' unerring will of Jove.'
 Far-darting Phoebus of the flowing hair
Down from the broad-track'd mountain pass'd, and all
Those goddesses look'd on in ravish'd awe,
And all the Delian Isle was heap'd with gold,
So gladden'd by his presence the fair son
Of Jove and of Latona. For he chose
That island as his home o'er every isle
Or continent, and lov'd it as his soul.
It flourish'd like a mountain, when its top
Is hid with flowering blossoms of a wood.

What a mixture of force and beauty is in these pictures!
How affecting is the graceful patience of the mother,
and the gentle beauty of the landscape! And how
noble, Apollo's suddenly ' standing in heaven '; and his
descent down the mountain, striking the goddesses with
awe, and showering golden light on the island, which
from that day forth flourishes out of the sea, like his own
luxuriant head of hair, or some woody *mountain top in
blossom!*

Yet the birth of the commonest human being is an
event hardly less divine, if we think of all that he is

destined to suffer and enjoy, and of his own immortal
hopes. Here is a charming passage from Beaumont,
which comes more home to us than these out-of-door
maternities of the Pagan heaven, with all their beauty.
A daughter is attended in child-birth by her mother,
who has warranted a betrothment not yet sanctioned by
the father :—

Violanta. Mother, I'd not offend you : might not
   Gerrard
Steal in, and see me in the evening ?
 Angelina.   Well,
Bid him do so.
 Viol.   Heaven's blessing on your heart.
Do you not call child-bearing *travel*, mother ?
 Angel. Yes.
 Viol. It may well be so. The bare-foot traveller
That's born a prince, and walks his pilgrimage,
Whose tender feet kiss the remorseless stones
Only, ne'er felt a travel like to it.
Alas, dear mother, you groan'd thus for me,
And yet how disobedient have I been !
 Angel. Peace, Violanta : thou hast always been
Gentle and good.
 Viol.   Gerrard is better, mother.
. . . . . I am now, methinks,
Even in the land of ease. I'll sleep.
 Angel. . . . . . Silken rest
Tie all thy cares up.

SEAMEN ON SHORE

[*Indicator*, March 15, 1820]

THE sole business of a seaman on shore, who has to go to sea again, is to take as much pleasure as he can. The moment he sets his foot on dry ground, he turns his back on all salt-beef and other salt-water restrictions. His long absence, and the impossibility of getting land pleasures at sea, put him upon a sort of desperate appetite. He lands, like a conqueror taking possession. He has been debarred so long, that he is resolved to have that matter out with the inhabitants. They must render an account to him of their treasures, their women, their victualling-stores, their entertainments, their every thing; and in return he will behave like a gentleman, and scatter his gold.

And first of the Common Sailor.—The moment the Common Sailor lands, he goes to see the watchmaker, or the old boy at the Ship.

READER. What, Sir? Before his mistress?

INDICATOR. Excuse me, Madam. His mistress, christened Elizabeth Monson, but more familiarly known by the appellation of Bet Monson, has been with him already. You remember the ballad—

When black-eyed Susan came on board.

LADY'S MAID [1]. I hope, Sir, you are not going to be vulgar in your remarks.

INDIC. Good God, Mrs. Jane, why should you think so! I am sure your lady does not expect it, or I should have had none but men for listeners on this subject.

[1] The great changes produced in people's fortunes by the nature of the times have unfortunately rendered this title but too common to a great variety of females; many of whom will not at all come under our present description. The Lady's Maid in the text is heiress to the Honours and Mrs. Slipslops of the last century.

LADY's M. Oh, Sir, if my lady does not think it vulgar, I'm sure I shan't; for there isn't a more delicater nor more genteeler person than my lady in all England, though I say it to her face who shouldn't. But you mentioned something about alehouses, or inns, or something; and you know they are rather vulgar.

INDIC. I'm sure, Mrs. Jane, I didn't think so, three years back, when you handed me that frothed glass of porter, with your pretty fingers, on a hot summer's day, under the great elm-tree there, at the door of the Jolly Miller.

LADY's M. Lard in heaven, Mr. Hindergaiter, why I vow you're a witch! Who'd have thought you'd have ever known that I kept my father-in-law's house for him, while my poor mother was laid up with the rheumatiz, all along of that vixen (God forgive me !) my own great aunt, who wouldn't let her come home one night in the shay, because she had married Tom Butts after being the wife of a Sergeant of Dragoons. And yet I must say for Mr. Butts, that for a landlord, and a man in a vulgarish situation, he was as well-behaved a man though a bold one, and might hold up his head as high, and was as kind and good-natured, and was as free from pride, and said as civil things to a body——

LADY. In short, Jane, he was not vulgar, and your dear old vixen of a great aunt was. There is no vulgarity, child, but impertinence and common cant; or being gross and ignorant, and proud of both; or having a feeling for all, and being ashamed of it. Remember the ragged sailor whom you kissed.

LADY's M. Lord, Ma'am, and did you see me kiss my poor brother William ? For it was my own brother, Ma'am, who you've heard me speak of—in the navy ; and he was so ragged then, because he had to cross the whole country to his home, and had spent all his money at Portsmouth ; and so I gave him my box of half-crowns, and he 's now captain's clerk's man, and it was he as sent me that live tortoise that made me scream so, and the cocoa-cup, and the shawl, and the purse made of grass, and the Hoty-hity feathers ; and I do think, if he was here, I could kiss him again, if he was as ragged as a rag-or-a-muffin, before all the world, aye, even before Sally Jones.

INDIC. Good. Now there you come round, Mrs. Jane, to the true point of politeness. I thought you better bred than you supposed, since I recollected how good-natured you looked at the Jolly Miller.

LADY'S M. Oh, Mr. Intricater, you're such another man !

INDIC. Nay, I assure you I do not think you even more genteel than you were then.

LADY'S M. Nay, now, Mr. Hingy-grater, I'm sure you flatter.

INDIC. But pray, Mrs. Jane, who is the awful presence of Sally Jones ?

LADY'S M. Presents, Sir ? She never gives no presents, lawful or unlawful, not she; nor for that matter never gets none, as I know of ; except mayhap a brass-thimble at Christmas, or a two-penny song-book, or a Trifle, as they very properly calls it, from Margate, with a piece of looking-glass in the inside, to see her proud, affected, niminy-piminy face in.

INDIC. But why should she object to your kissing your brother William ?

LADY'S M. Oh, forsooth, it 's vulgar, Sir ! So she said, when I kissed him before her once ; as if one's brother wasn't one's brother ; and as for that, she'd kiss her cousin fast enough before twenty people, if he'd make anything like an advantage. She is but a maid at boarding-school, where I was ; and never writes Miss on my letters ; and yet whenever she goes home to her father's, who is nothing but a little petty green-grocer in an alley, she insists, forsooth, on my Missing and Missing her, or she won't send me any news of the private theatre ; and she knows that vexes me, be-cause I really have a taste for the stage, and once played second part at school to Miss Gollogher. She was the Fair Penitent, Sir; a tall brown girl, HORN-BONE PINE, as the French say; and a great fortune, though her father did keep a dog-shop. But she called it a Managearee.

So, Sir, MISS SARAH JONES never condescends to write Miss to me, though she daredn't wear her hair without a cap at boarding-school, to save her head ; and my lady always permits me to wear my hair in a comb, to distinguish me from common helpers and such like. And besides that, though I have worn a cap, I never wore black worsted stockings as she does ; nor never set mop upon floor. As to sailors, she cannot abide 'en

INDIC. But you, Mrs. Jane, can : and let me tell you, that that is not the least advantage which you have over Miss Sarah Jones. So we will go on with our picture.

The first object of the seaman on landing is to spend his money : but his first sensation is the strange firmness of the earth, which he goes treading in a sort of heavy light way, half wagoner and half dancing-master, his shoulders rolling, and his feet touching and going ; the same way, in short, in which he keeps himself prepared for all the rolling chances of the vessel, when on deck. There is always, to us, this appearance of lightness of foot and heavy strength of upper works, in a sailor. And he feels it himself. He lets his jacket fly open, and his shoulders slouch, and his hair grow long to be gathered into a heavy pigtail ; but when full dressed, he prides himself on a certain gentility of toe ; on a white stocking and a natty shoe, issuing lightly out of the flowing blue trouser. His arms are neutral, hanging and swinging in a curve aloof ; his hands, half open, look as if they had just been handling ropes, and had no object in life but to handle them again. He is proud of appearing in a new hat and slops, with a Belcher handkerchief flowing loosely round his neck, and the corner of another out of his pocket. Thus equipped, with pinchbeck buckles in his shoes (which he bought for gold) he puts some tobacco in his mouth, not as if he were going to use it directly, but as if he stuffed it in a pouch on one side, as a pelican does fish, to employ it hereafter ; and so, with Bet Monson at his side, and perhaps a cane or whanghee twisted under his other arm, sallies forth to take possession of all Lubberland. He buys everything that he comes athwart,—nuts, gingerbread, apples, shoe-strings, beer, brandy, gin, buckles, knives, a watch (two, if he has money enough), gowns and handkerchiefs for Bet, and his mother and sisters, dozens of ' Superfine Best Men's Cotton Stockings,' dozens of ' Superfine Best Women's Cotton ditto,' best good Check for Shirts (though he has too much already), infinite needles and thread (to sew his trousers with some day), a footman's laced hat, Bear's Grease to make his hair grow (by way of joke), several sticks, all sorts of Jew articles, a flute (which he can't play, and never intends), a leg of mutton which he carries somewhere to roast, and for a piece of which the landlord of the Ship makes him pay twice what he gave for the whole ;—in short, all that money can be spent upon, which is everything but medicine gratis ; and this he would insist on paying for. He would buy all the painted parrots on an Italian's head, on purpose to break them, rather than not spend his money. He has fiddles and a dance at the Ship, with oceans of flip and grog ; and gives the blind fiddler tobacco for sweet-meats, and half a crown for treading on his toe. He asks the landlady, with a sigh, after her daughter Nance who first fired his heart with her silk-stockings ; and finding that she is married and in trouble, leaves five crowns for her ; which the old lady appropriates as part payment for a shilling in advance. He goes to the port playhouse with Bet Monson, and a great red hand-kerchief full of apples, gingerbread nuts, and fresh beef ; calls out for the fiddlers and Rule Britannia ; pelts Tom Sikes in the pit ; and compares Othello to the black ship's cook in his white night-cap. When he comes to London, he and some messmates take a hackney-coach, full of Bet Monsons and tobacco-pipes, and go through the streets smoking and lolling out of window. He has ever been cautious of venturing on horseback ; and among his other sights in foreign parts, relates with unfeigned astonishment how he has seen the Turks ride, —' Only,' says he, guarding against the hearer's incre-dulity, ' they have saddle-boxes to hold 'em in, fore and aft ; and shovels like for stirrups.' He will tell you how the Chinese drink, and the NEGROS dance, and the monkeys pelt you with coco-nuts; and how King Domy would have built him a mud hut and made him a Peer of the Realm, if he would have stopped with him and taught him to make trousers. He has a sister at a 'School for Young Ladies,' who blushes with a mixture of pleasure and shame at his appearance; and whose confusion he completes, by slipping fourpence into her hand, and saying out loud that he has 'no more copper' about him. His mother and elder sisters at home dote on all he says and does, telling him however that he is a great sea-fellow, and was always wild ever since he was a hop-o'-my-thumb no higher than the window-locker. He tells his mother that she would be a Duchess in Paranaboo; at which the good old portly dame laughs and looks proud. When his sisters complain of his romping, he says that they are only sorry it is not the baker. He frightens them with a mask made after the New Zealand fashion, and is forgiven for his learning. Their mantelpiece is filled by him with shells and shark's teeth; and when he goes to sea again, there is no end of tears, and God-bless yous, and home-made gingerbread.

His Officer on shore does much of all this, only, generally speaking, in a higher taste. The moment he lands he buys quantities of jewellery and other valuables, for all the females of his acquaintance; and is taken in for every article. He sends in a cart-load of fresh meat to the ship, though he is going to town next day; and calling in at a chandler's for some candles, is persuaded to buy a dozen of green wax, with which he lights up the ship at evening; regretting that the fine moonlight hinders the effect of the colour. A man, with a bundle beneath his arm, accosts him in an under-tone; and, with a look in which respect for his knowledge is mixed with an avowed zeal for his own interest, asks if his Honour will just step under the gangway here, and inspect some real India shawls. The gallant Lieutenant says to himself, 'This fellow knows what's what, by his face'; and so he proves it by being taken in on the spot. When he brings the shawls home, he says to his sister with an air of triumph, 'There, Poll, there's something for you; only cost me twelve, and is worth twenty, if it's worth a dollar.' She turns pale—'Twenty what, my dear George? Why, you haven't given twelve dollars for it, I hope?' 'Not I, by the Lord.'—'That's lucky; because you see, my dear George, that all together is not worth more than fourteen or fifteen shillings.' 'Fourteen or fifteen what! Why, it's real India, en't it? Why the fellow told me so; or I'm sure I'd as soon '—(here he tries to hide his blushes with a bluster) 'I'd as soon have given him twelve douses on the chaps as twelve guineas.' 'Twelve GUINEAS,' exclaims the sister; and then drawling forth 'Why—my—DEAR—George,' is proceeding to show him what the articles would have cost at Condell's, when he interrupts her by requesting her to go and choose for herself a tea-table service. He then makes his escape to some messmates at a coffee-house, and drowns his recollection of the shawls in the best wine, and a discussion on the comparative merits of the English and West Indian beauties and tables. At the theatre afterwards, where he has never been before, he takes a lady at the back of one of the boxes for a woman of quality; and when, after returning his long respectful gaze with a smile, she turns aside and puts her handkerchief to her mouth, he thinks it is in derision, till his friend undeceives him. He is introduced to the lady; and ever afterwards, at first sight of a woman of quality (without any disparagement either to those charming personages), expects her to give him a smile. He thinks the other ladies much better creatures than they are taken for; and for their parts, they tell him, that if all men were like himself, they would trust the sex again :—which, for aught we know, is the truth. He has, indeed, what he thinks a very liberal opinion of ladies in general; judging them all, in a manner, with the eye of a seaman's experience. Yet he will believe nevertheless in the 'true-love' of any given damsel whom he seeks in the way of marriage, let him roam as much, or remain as long at a distance, as he pleases. It is not that he wants feeling; but that he has read of it, time out of mind, in songs; and he looks upon constancy as a sort of exploit, answering to those which he performs at sea. He is nice in his watches and linen. He makes you presents of cornelians, antique seals, coconuts set in silver, and other valuables. When he shakes hands with you, it is like being caught in a windlass. He would not swagger about the streets in his uniform, for the world. He is generally modest in company, though liable to be irritated by what he thinks ungentlemanly behaviour. He is also liable to be rendered irritable by sickness ; partly because he has been used to command others, and to be served with all possible deference and alacrity ; and partly, because the idea of suffering pain, without any honour or profit to get by it, is unprofessional, and he is not accustomed to it. He treats talents unlike his own with great respect. He often perceives his own so little felt that it teaches him this feeling for that of others. Besides, he admires the quantity of information which people can get, without travelling like himself; especially when he sees how interesting his own becomes, to them as well as to everybody else. When he tells a story, particularly if full of wonders, he takes care to maintain his character for truth and simplicity, by qualifying it with all possible reservations, concessions, and anticipations of objection ; such as ' in case, at such times as, so to speak, as it were, at least, at any rate.' He seldom uses sea-terms but when jocosely provoked by something contrary to his habits of life; as for instance, if he is always meeting you on horseback, he asks if you never mean to walk the deck again; or if he finds you studying day after day, he says you are always overhauling your log-book. He makes more new acquaintances, and forgets his old ones less, than any other man in the busy world ; for he is so compelled to make his home everywhere, remembers his native one as such a place of enjoyment, has all his friendly recollections so fixed upon his mind at sea, and has so much to tell and to hear when he returns, that change and separation lose with him the most heartless part of their nature. He also sees such a variety of customs and manners, that he becomes charitable in his opinions altogether ; and charity, while it diffuses the affections, cannot let the old ones go. Half the secret of human intercourse is to make allowance for each other.

When the Officer is superannuated or retires, he becomes, if intelligent and inquiring, one of the most agreeable old men in the world, equally welcome to the silent for his card-playing, and to the conversational for his recollections. He is fond of astronomy and books of voyages, and is immortal with all who know him for having been round the world, or seen the Transit of Venus, or had one of his fingers carried off by a new Zealand hatchet, or a present of feathers from an Otaheitean beauty. If not elevated by his acquirements above some of his humbler tastes, he delights in a corner-cupboard holding his coco-nuts and punchbowl ; has his summer-house castellated and planted with wooden cannon ; and sets up the figure of his old ship, the Britannia or the Lovely Nancy, for a statue in the garden ; where it stares eternally with red cheeks and round black eyes, as if in astonishment at its situation.

Chaucer, who wrote his Canterbury Tales about four hundred and thirty years ago, has among his other characters in that work a Shipman, who is exactly of the same cast as the modern sailor,—the same robustness, courage, and rough-drawn virtue, doing its duty, without being very nice in helping itself to its recreations. There is the very dirk, the complexion, the jollity, the experience, and the bad horsemanship. The plain unaffected ending of the description has the air of a sailor's own speech ; while the line about the beard is exceedingly picturesque, poetical, and comprehensive. In copying it out, we shall merely alter the old spelling, where the words are still modern.

A Shipman was there, wonned far by west ;
For aught I wot, he was of Dartëmouth.
He rode upon a rouncie, as he couth [1],
All in a gown of falding to the knee.

[1] He rode upon a hack-horse, as well as he could.

A dagger hanging by a lace had he,
About his neck, under his arm adown.
The hot summer had made his hew all brown.
And certainly he was a good felaw.
Full many a draught of wine he haddë draw
From Bourdeaux ward, while that the chapman slep.
Of nice conscience took he no keep.
If that he fought and had the higher hand,
By water he sent 'em home to every land.
But of his craft, to reckon well his tides,
His streamës and his strandës him besides,
His harborough, his moon, and his lode manage,
There was not such from Hull unto Carthage.
Hardy he was, and wise, I undertake ;
With many a tempest had his beard been shake.
He knew well all the havens, as they were,
From Gothland to the Cape de Finisterre,
And every creek in Britain and in Spain.
His barge ycleped was the Magdelain.

When about to tell his Tale, he tells his fellow travellers
that he shall chink them so merry a bell,

That it shall waken all this company :
But it shall not be of philosophy,
Nor of physick, nor of terms quaint of law :
There is but little Latin in my maw.

The story he tells is a well-known one in the Italian novels,
of a monk who made love to a merchant's wife, and
borrowed a hundred francs of the husband to give her.
She accordingly admits his addresses during the absence
of her good man on a journey. When the latter returns,
he applies to the cunning monk for repayment, and is
referred to the lady ; who thus finds her mercenary
behaviour outwitted.

THE BUTCHER

[*London Journal, June 20, 1835*]

It was observed the other day in the *London Journal*, that 'butchers are wisely forbidden to be upon juries; not because they are not as good as other men by nature, and often as truly kind; but because the habit of taking away the lives of sheep and oxen inures them to the sight of blood, and violence, and mortal pangs.'

The *Times*, in noticing this passage, has corrected our error. There neither is, nor ever was, it seems, a law forbidding butchers to be upon juries; though the reverse opinion has so prevailed among all classes, that Locke takes it for granted in his *Treatise on Education*, and our own authority was the author of *Hudibras*, a man of very exact and universal knowledge. The passage that was in our mind is in his *Posthumous Works*, and is worth quoting on other accounts. He is speaking of those pedantic and would-be classical critics who judge the poets of one nation entirely by those of another. Butler's resistance of their pretensions is the more honourable to him, inasmuch as the prejudices of his own education, and even the propensity of his genius, lay on the learned and anti-impulsive side. But his judgement was thoroughgoing and candid. The style is of the off-hand careless order, after the fashion of the old satires and epistles, though not so rough :—

An English poet should be tried by his peers,
And not by pedants and philosophers,
Incompetent to judge poetic fury,
As butchers are forbid to be of a jury,
Besides the most intolerable wrong
To try their masters in a foreign tongue,

By foreign jurymen like Sophocles,
Or *tales* [1] falser than Euripides,
When not an English native dares appear
To be a witness for the prisoner,—
When all the laws they use to arraign and try
The innocent and wrong'd delinquent by,
Were made by a foreign lawyer and his pupils,
To put an end to all poetic scruples ;
And by the advice of virtuosi Tuscans,
Determin'd all the doubts of socks and buskins,—
Gave judgement on all past and *future plays*,
As is apparent by Speroni's case, [2]
Which Lope Vega first began to steal,
And after him the French *filou* [3] Corneille ;
And since, our English plagiaries *nim*
And steal their far-fetch'd criticisms from him,
And by an action, falsely laid, of *trover*, [4]
The lumber for their proper goods recover,
Enough to furnish all the lewd impeachers
Of witty Beaumont's poetry and Fletcher's,

[1] *Tales* (Latin) persons chosen to supply the place of men impannelled upon a jury or inquest, and not appearing when called. [We copy this from a very useful and pregnant volume, called the *Treasury of Knowledge*, full of such heaps of information as are looked for in lists and vocabularies, and occupying the very margins with proverbs. Mr. D'Israeli, sen., objects to this last overflow of contents, but not, we think, with his usual good sense and gratitude, as a lover of books. These proverbial sayings, which are the most universal things in the world, appear to us to have a particularly good effect in thus coming in to refresh one among the technicalities of knowledge.]

[2] Speroni, a celebrated critic in his day, and great plaguer, among others, of Tasso.

[3] *Filou*—pickpocket ! This irreverent epithet must have startled many of Butler's readers and brother-loyalists of the court of Charles the Second. But he suffered nothing to stand in the way of what seemed to him a just opinion.

[4] *Trover*—an action for goods found, and not delivered on demand.—*Treasury of Knowledge*. Butler's wit dragged every species of information into his net.

Who for a few *misprisions of wit,*
Are charg'd by those who ten times worse commit,
And for misjudging some unhappy scenes,
Are censured for it *with more unlucky sense:*

(How happily said!)

When all their worst miscarriages delight
And please more than the best that pedants write.

Having been guilty of this involuntary scandal against
the butchers, we would fain make them amends by
saying nothing but good of them and their trade; and
truly if we find the latter part of the proposition a little
difficult, they themselves are for the most part a jovial,
good-humoured race, and can afford the trade to be
handled as sharply as their beef on the block. There is
cut and come again in them. Your butcher breathes
an atmosphere of good living. The beef mingles kindly
with his animal nature. He grows fat with the best of
it, perhaps with inhaling its very essence; and has no
time to grow spare, theoretical, and hypochondriacal, like
those whose more thinking stomachs drive them upon
the apparently more innocent but less easy and analogous intercommunications of fruit and vegetables. For
our parts, like all persons who think at all,—nay, like the
butcher himself, when he catches himself in a strange
fit of meditation, after some doctor perhaps has 'kept
him low,' we confess to an abstract dislike of eating the
sheep and lamb that we see in the meadow; albeit our
concrete regard for mutton is considerable, particularly
Welsh mutton. But Nature has a beautiful way of re-
conciling all necessities that are unmalignant; and as
butchers at present must exist, and sheep and lambs
would not exist at all in civilized countries, and crop the
sweet grass so long, but for the brief pang at the end of
it, he is as comfortable a fellow as can be,—one of the
liveliest ministers of her mortal necessities,—of the
deaths by which she gives and diversifies life; and has
no more notion of doing any harm in his vocation, than
the lamb that swallows the lady-bird on the thyme. A
very pretty insect is she, and has had a pretty time of it;

a very calm, clear feeling, healthy, and, therefore, happy
little woollen giant, compared with her, is the lamb,—
her butcher; and an equally innocent and festive personage is the butcher himself, notwithstanding the
popular fallacy about juries, and the salutary misgiving
his beholders feel when they see him going to take the
lamb out of the meadow, or entering the more tragical
doors of the slaughter-house. His thoughts, while
knocking down the ox, are of skill and strength, and not
of cruelty. And the death, though it may not be the
very best of deaths, is, assuredly, none of the very worst.
Animals, that grow old in an artificial state, would have
a hard time of it in a lingering decay. Their mode of
life would not have prepared them for it. Their blood
would not run lively enough to the last. We doubt even
whether the John Bull of the herd, when about to be
killed, would change places with a very gouty, irritable
old gentleman; or be willing to endure a grievous being
of his own sort, with legs answering to the gout; much
less if Cow were to grow old with him, and plague him
with endless lowings, occasioned by the loss of her
beauty, and the increasing insipidity of the hay. A
human being who can survive those ulterior vaccina-
tions must indeed possess some great reliefs of his own,
and deserve them, and life may reasonably be a wonderfully precious thing in his eyes; nor shall excuse be
wanting to the vaccinators, and what made them such,
especially if they will but grow a little more quiet and
ruminating. But who would have the death of some
old, groaning, aching, effeminate, frightened, lingerer in
life, such as Maecenas for example, compared with a
good, jolly knock-down blow, at a reasonable period,
whether of hatchet or of apoplexy,—whether the bull's
death or the butcher's? Our own preference, it is true,
is for neither. We are for an excellent, healthy, happy
life, of the very best sort; and a death to match it, going
out calmly as a summer's evening. Our taste is not
particular. But we are for the knock-down blow,
rather than the death-in-life.

The butcher, when young, is famous for his health,

strength, and vivacity, and for his riding any kind of horse down any sort of hill, with a tray before him, the reins for a whip, and no hat on his head. It was a gallant of this sort that Robin Hood imitated, when he beguiled the poor Sheriff into the forest, and showed him his own deer to sell. The old ballads apostrophize him well as the ' butcher so bold,' or better—with the accent on the last syllable, ' thou bold butcher.' No syllable of his was to be trifled with. The butcher keeps up his health in middle life, not only with the food that seems so congenial to flesh, but with rising early in the morning, and going to market with his own or his master's cart. When more sedentary, and very jovial and good-humoured, he is apt to expand into a most analogous state of fat and smoothness, with silken tones and a short breath,—harbingers, we fear, of asthma and gout ; or the kindly apoplexy comes, and treats him as he treated the ox.

When rising in the world, he is indefatigable on Saturday nights, walking about in the front of those white-clothed and joint-abounding open shops, while the meat is being half-cooked beforehand with the gas-lights. The rapidity of his 'What-d'ye-buy?' on these occasions is famous ; and both he and the good housewives, distracted with the choice before them, pronounce the legs of veal ' *beautiful*—exceedingly.'

How he endures the meat against his head, as he carries it about on a tray, or how we endure that he should do it, or how he can handle the joints as he does with that habitual indifference, or with what floods of hot water he contrives to purify himself of the exoterical part of his philosophy on going to bed, we cannot say ; but take him all in all, he is a fine specimen of the triumph of the general over the particular.

The only poet that was the son of a butcher (and the trade may be proud of him) is Akenside, who naturally resorted to the ' Pleasures of Imagination.' As to Wolsey, we can never quite picture him to ourselves apart from the shop. He had the cardinal butcher's virtue of a love of good eating, as his picture shows ;

and he was foreman all his life to the butcher Henry the
Eighth. We beg pardon of the trade for this application of their name ; and exhort them to cut the cardinal
and stick to the poet.

WATCHMEN

[Companion, Feb. 6, 1820]

THE readers of these our fourpenny lucubrations need
not be informed that we keep no carriage. The consequence is, that being visitors of the theatre, and having
some inconsiderate friends who grow pleasanter and
pleasanter till one in the morning, we are great walkers
home by night ; and this has made us great acquaintances of watchmen, moonlight, *mud*-light, and other
accompaniments of that interesting hour. Luckily we
are fond of a walk by night. It does not always do us
good ; but that is not the fault of the hour, but our own,
who ought to be stouter; and therefore we extract what
good we can out of our necessity, with becoming temper.
It is a remarkable thing in nature, and one of the good-
naturedest things we know of her, that the mere fact of
looking about us, and being conscious of what is going
on, is its own reward, if we do but notice it in good-
humour. Nature is a great painter (and art and society
are among her works), to whose minutest touches the
mere fact of becoming alive is to enrich the stock of our
enjoyment.

We confess there are points liable to cavil in a walk
home by night in February. Old umbrellas have their
weak sides ; and the quantity of mud and rain may
surmount the picturesque. Mistaking a soft piece of
mud for hard, and so filling your shoe with it, especially
at setting out, must be acknowledged to be ' aggravating.' But then you ought to have boots. There are
sights, indeed, in the streets of London, which can be
rendered pleasant by no philosophy; things too grave

to be talked about in our present paper ; but we must premise, that our walk leads us out of town, and through streets and suburbs of by no means the worst description. Even there we may be grieved if we will. The farther the walk into the country, the more tiresome we may choose to find it ; and when we take it purely to oblige others, we must allow, as in the case of a friend of ours, that generosity itself on two sick legs may find limits to the notion of virtue being its own reward, and reasonably ' curse those comfortable people ' who, by the lights in their windows, are getting into their warm beds, and saying to one another—'Bad thing to be out of doors to-night.'

Supposing then that we are in a reasonable state of health and comfort in other respects, we say that a walk home at night has its merits, if you choose to meet with them. The worst part of it is the setting out,—the closing of the door upon the kind faces that part with you. But their words and looks on the other hand may set you well off. We have known a word last us all the way home, and a look make a dream of it. To a lover, for instance, no walk can be bad. He sees but one face in the rain and darkness ; the same that he saw by the light in the warm room. This ever accompanies him, looking in his eyes ; and if the most pitiable and spoilt face in the world should come between them, startling him with the saddest mockery of love, he would treat it kindly for her sake. But this is a begging of the question. A lover does not walk. He is sensible neither to the pleasures nor pains of walking. He treads on air ; and in the thick of all that seems inclement, has an avenue of light and velvet spread for him, like a sovereign prince.

To resume then, like men of this world. The advantage of a late hour is, that everything is silent, and the people fast in their beds. This gives the whole world a tranquil appearance. Inanimate objects are no calmer than passions and cares now seem to be, all laid asleep. The human being is motionless as the house or the tree ; sorrow is suspended ; and you endeavour to think, that

love only is awake. Let not readers of true delicacy be
alarmed, for we mean to touch profanely upon nothing
that ought to be sacred ; and as we are for thinking the
best on these occasions, it is of the best love we think ;
love, of no heartless order, legal or illegal ; and such
only as ought to be awake with the stars.

As to cares, and curtain-lectures, and such-like abuses
of the tranquillity of night, we call to mind, for their
sakes, all the sayings of the poets and others, about
' balmy sleep,' and the soothing of hurt minds, and the
weariness of sorrow, which drops into forgetfulness.
The great majority are certainly ' fast as a church ' by
the time we speak of ; and for the rest, we are among
the workers who have been sleepless for their advantage;
so we take out our licence to forget them for the time
being. The only thing that shall remind us of them, is
the red lamp, shining afar over the apothecary's door ;
which, while it does so, reminds us also that there is help
for them to be had. I see him now, the pale blinker,
suppressing the conscious injustice of his anger at being
roused by the apprentice, and fumbling himself out of
the house, in hoarseness and great coat, resolved to
make the sweetness of the Christmas bill indemnify him
for the bitterness of the moment.

But we shall be getting too much into the interior of
the houses. By this time the hackney-coaches have
left all the stands ; a good symptom of their having got
their day's money. Crickets are heard, here and there,
amidst the embers of some kitchen. A dog follows us.
Will nothing make him ' go along ' ? We dodge him
in vain ; we run ; we stand and ' hish ' at him ; accompanying the prohibition with dehortatory gestures, and
an imaginary picking up of a stone. We turn again,
and there he is, vexing our skirts. He even forces us
into an angry doubt whether he will not starve, if we
do not let him go home with us. Now if we could but
lame him without being cruel ; or if we were only an
overseer ; or a beadle ; or a dealer in dog-skin ; or a
political economist, to think dogs unnecessary. Oh,
come ; he has turned a corner ; he is gone ; we think

we see him trotting off at a distance, thin and muddy ; and our heart misgives us. But it was not our fault ; we were not ' hishing ' at the time. His departure was lucky, for he had got our enjoyments into a dilemma ; our ' article ' would not have known what to do with him. These are the perplexities to which your sympathizers are liable. We resume our way, independent and alone ; for we have no companion this time, except our never-to-be-forgotten and ethereal companion, the reader. A real arm within another's puts us out of the pale of walking that is to be made good. It is good already. A fellow pedestrian is company ; is the party you have left ; you talk and laugh, and there is no longer anything to be contended with. But alone, and in bad weather, and with a long way to go, here is something for the temper and spirits to grapple with and turn to account ; and accordingly we are booted and buttoned up, an umbrella over our heads, the rain pelting upon it, and the lamp-light shining in the gutters ; ' mud-shine,' as an artist of our acquaintance used to call it, with a gusto of reprobation. Now, walk cannot well be worse ; and yet it shall be nothing if you meet it heartily. There is a pleasure in overcoming any obstacle ; mere action is something ; imagination is more ; and the spinning of the blood, and vivacity of the mental endeavour, act well upon one another, and gradually put you in a state of robust consciousness and triumph. Every time you set down your leg, you have a respect for it. The umbrella is held in the hand, like a roaring trophy.

We are now reaching the country : the fog and rain are over ; and we meet our old friends the watchmen, staid, heavy, indifferent, more coat than man, pondering yet not pondering, old but not reverend, immensely useless. No ; useless they are not ; for the inmates of the houses think them otherwise, and in that imagination they do good. We do not pity the watchmen as we used. Old age often cares little for regular sleep. They could not be sleeping perhaps, if they were in their beds ; and certainly they would not be earning. What sleep they get, is perhaps sweeter in the watch-box,—a forbidden sweet; and they have a sense of importance, and a claim on the persons indoors, which together with the amplitude of their coating and the possession of the box itself, make them feel themselves, not without reason, to be 'somebody.' They are peculiar and official. Tomkins is a cobbler as well as they; but then he is no watchman. He cannot speak to 'things of night'; nor bid 'any man stand in the King's name.' He does not get fees and gratitude from the old, the infirm, and the drunken; nor 'let gentlemen go'; nor is he 'a parish-man.' The churchwardens don't speak to him. If he put himself ever so much in the way of 'the great plumber,' he would not say 'How do you find yourself, Tomkins?'—'An ancient and quiet watchman.' Such he was in the time of Shakespeare, and such he is now. Ancient, because he cannot help it; and quiet, because he will not help it, if possible; his object being to procure quiet on all sides, his own included. For this reason, he does not make too much noise in crying the hour, nor is offensively particular in his articulation. No man shall sleep the worse for him, out of a horrid sense of the word 'three.' The sound shall be three, four, or one, as suits their mutual convenience.

Yet characters are to be found even among watchmen. They are not all mere coat, and lump, and indifference. By the way, what do they think of in general? How do they vary the monotony of their ruminations from one to two, and from two to three, and so on? Are they comparing themselves with the unofficial cobbler; thinking of what they shall have for dinner to-morrow; or what they were about six years ago; or that their lot is the hardest in the world (as insipid old people are apt to think, for the pleasure of grumbling); or that it has some advantages nevertheless, besides fees; and that if they are not in bed, their wife is?

Of characters, or rather varieties among watchmen, we remember several. One was a Dandy Watchman, who used to ply at the top of Oxford Street, next the park. We called him the dandy, on account of his utter-

ance.   He had a mincing way with it, pronouncing the
a in the word 'past' as it is in *hat*,—making a little preparatory hem before he spoke, and then bringing out
his 'Păst ten' in a style of genteel indifference, as if,
upon the whole, he was of that opinion.

Another was the Metallic Watchman, who paced the
same street towards Hanover Square, and had a clang in
his voice like a trumpet.   He was a voice and nothing
else ; but any difference is something in a watchman.

A third, who cried the hour in Bedford Square, was
remarkable in his calling for being abrupt and loud.
There was a fashion among his tribe just come up at
that time, of omitting the words 'Past' and 'o'clock,'
and crying only the number of the hour.   I know not
whether a recollection I have of his performance one
night is entire matter of fact, or whether any subsequent
fancies of what might have taken place are mixed up
with it ; but my impression is, that as I was turning
the corner into the square with a friend, and was in the
midst of a discussion in which numbers were concerned,
we were suddenly startled, as if in solution of it, by a
brief and tremendous outcry of—ONE.   This paragraph
ought to have been at the bottom of the page, and the
word printed abruptly round the corner.

A fourth watchman was a very singular phenomenon,
a *Reading* Watchman.   He had a book, which he read
by the light of his lantern ; and instead of a pleasant,
gave you a very uncomfortable idea of him.   It seemed
cruel to pitch amidst so many discomforts and priva-
tions one who had imagination enough to wish to be
relieved from them. Nothing but a sluggish vacuity befits
a watchman.

But the oddest of all was the *Sliding* Watchman.
Think of walking up a street in the depth of a frosty
winter, with long ice in the gutters, and sleet over head,
and then figure to yourself a sort of bale of a man in
white, coming sliding towards you with a lantern in one
hand, and an umbrella over his head.   It was the oddest
mixture of luxury and hardship, of juvenility and old
age !   But this looked agreeable.   Animal spirits carry

everything before them; and our invincible friend seemed a watchman for Rabelais. Time was run at and butted by him like a goat. The slide seemed to bear him half through the night at once; he slipped from out of his box and his common-places at one rush of a merry thought, and seemed to say, 'Everything's in imagination;—here goes the whole weight of my office.'

But we approach our home. How still the trees! How deliciously asleep the country! How beautifully grim and nocturnal this wooded avenue of ascent, against the cold white sky! The watchmen and patrols, which the careful citizens have planted in abundance within a mile of their doors, salute us with their 'good mornings';—not so welcome as we pretend; for we ought not to be out so late; and it is one of the assumptions of these fatherly old fellows to remind us of it. Some fowls, who have made a strange roost in a tree, flutter as we pass them;—another pull up the hill, unyielding; a few strides on a level; and *there* is the light in the window, the eye of the warm soul of the house,—one's home. How particular, and yet how universal, is that word; and how surely does it deposit every one for himself in his own nest!

BOOKS AND BOOKMEN

MY BOOKS

[*Literary Examiner*, July 5 and 12, 1823]

SITTING, last winter, among my books, and walled round with all the comfort and protection which they and my fireside could afford me ; to wit, a table of high-piled books at my back, my writing-desk on one side of me, some shelves on the other, and the feeling of the warm fire at my feet ; I began to consider how I loved the authors of those books : how I loved them, too, not only for the imaginative pleasures they afforded me, but for their making me love the very books themselves, and delight to be in contact with them. I looked sideways at my Spenser, my Theocritus, and my *Arabian Nights;* then above them at my Italian poets ; then behind me at my Dryden and Pope, my romances, and my Boccaccio; then on my left side at my Chaucer, who lay on a writing-desk ; and thought how natural it was in C[harles] L[amb] to give a kiss to an old folio, as I once saw him do to Chapman's *Homer.* At the same time I wondered how he could sit in that front room of his with nothing but a few unfeeling tables and chairs, or at best a few engravings in trim frames, instead of putting a couple of arm-chairs into the back-room with the books in it, where there is but one window. Would I were there, with both the chairs properly filled, and one or two more besides ! ' We had talk, Sir,'—the only talk capable of making one forget the books.

Good God ! I could cry like one of the Children in the Wood to think how far I and mine are from home ; but this would not be ' decent or manly ' ; so I smile instead, and am philosophical enough to make your heart ache.

Besides, I shall love the country I am in more and more, and on the very account for which it angers me at present.

This is confessing great pain in the midst of my books. I own it; and yet I feel all the pleasure in them which I have expressed.

> Take me, my book-shelves, to your arms,
> And shield me from the ills of life.

No disparagement to the arms of Stella; but in neither case is pain a reason why we should not have a high enjoyment of the pleasure.

I entrench myself in my books equally against sorrow and the weather. If the wind comes through a passage I look about to see how I can fence it off by a better disposition of my movables; if a melancholy thought is importunate, I give another glance at my Spenser. When I speak of being in contact with my books, I mean it literally. I like to lean my head against them. Living in a southern climate, though in a part sufficiently northern to feel the winter, I was obliged, during that season, to take some of the books out of the study, and hang them up near the fireplace in the sitting-room, which is the only room that has such a convenience. I therefore walled myself in, as well as I could, in the manner above-mentioned. I took a walk every day, to the astonishment of the Genoese, who used to huddle against a bit of sunny wall, like flies on a chimney-piece; but I did this only that I might so much the more enjoy my *English* evening. The fire was a wood fire instead of a coal; but I imagined myself in the country. I remembered at the very worst, that one end of my native land was not nearer the other than England is to Italy.

While writing this article I am in my study again. Like the rooms in all houses in this country which are not hovels, it is handsome and ornamented. On one side it looks towards a garden and the mountains; on another, to the mountains and the sea. What signifies all this? I turn my back upon the sea; I shut up even one of the side windows looking upon the mountains, and retain no

prospect but that of the trees. On the right and left of
me are book-shelves; a bookcase is affectionately open
in front of me; and thus kindly enclosed with my books
and the green leaves, I write. If all this is too luxurious
and effeminate, of all luxuries it is the one that leaves
you the most strength. And this is to be said for
scholarship in general. It unfits a man for activity, for
his bodily part in the world; but it often doubles both
the power and the sense of his mental duties; and with
much indignation against his body, and more against
those who tyrannize over the intellectual claims of mankind, the man of letters, like the magician of old, is
prepared ' to play the devil ' with the great men of this
world, in a style that astonishes both the sword and the
toga.

I do not like this fine large study. I like elegance.
I like room to breathe in, and even walk about, when
I want to breathe and walk about. I like a great library
next my study; but for the study itself, give me a
small snug place, almost entirely walled with books.
There should be only one window in it, looking upon
trees. Some prefer a place with few, or no books at all
—nothing but a chair or a table, like Epictetus; but I
should say that these were philosophers, not lovers of
books, if I did not recollect that Montaigne was both.
He had a study in a round tower, walled as aforesaid.
It is true, one forgets one's books while writing—at
least they say so. For my part, I think I have them in
a sort of sidelong mind's eye; like a second thought,
which is none—like a waterfall, or a whispering wind.

I dislike a grand library to study in. I mean an immense apartment, with books all in Museum order,
especially wire-safed. I say nothing against the Museum itself, or public libraries. They are capital places
to go to, but not to sit in; and talking of this, I hate to
read in public, and in strange company. The jealous
silence; the dissatisfied looks of the messengers; the
inability to help yourself; the not knowing whether
you really ought to trouble the messengers, much less
the Gentleman in black, or brown, who is, perhaps, half

a trustee; with a variety of other jarrings between privacy and publicity, prevent one's settling heartily to work. They say 'they manage these things better in France'; and I dare say they do; but I think I should feel still more *distrait* in France, in spite of the benevolence of the servitors, and the generous profusion of pen, ink, and paper. I should feel as if I were doing nothing but interchanging amenities with polite writers.

A grand private library, which the master of the house also makes his study, never looks to me like a real place of books, much less of authorship. I cannot take kindly to it. It is certainly not out of envy; for three parts of the books are generally trash, and I can seldom think of the rest and the proprietor together. It reminds me of a fine gentleman, of a collector, of a patron, of Gil Blas and the Marquis of Marialva; of anything but genius and comfort. I have a particular hatred of a round table (not *the* Round Table, for that was a dining one) covered and irradiated with books, and never met with one in the house of a clever man but once. It is the reverse of Montaigne's Round Tower. Instead of bringing the books around you, they all seem turning another way, and eluding your hands.

Conscious of my propriety and comfort in these matters, I take an interest in the bookcases as well as the books of my friends. I long to meddle, and dispose them after my own notions. When they see this confession, they will acknowledge the virtue I have practised. I believe I did mention his book-room to C. L., and I think he told me that he often sat there when alone. It would be hard not to believe him. His library, though not abounding in Greek or Latin (which are the only things to help some persons to an idea of literature), is anything but superficial. The depths of philosophy and poetry are there, the innermost passages of the human heart. It has some Latin too. It has also a handsome contempt for appearance. It looks like what it is, a selection made at precious intervals from the book-stalls;—now a Chaucer at nine and twopence; now a Montaigne or a Sir Thomas Browne at two shil-

lings ; now a Jeremy Taylor ; a Spinoza ; an old
English Dramatist, Prior, and Sir Philip Sidney; and the
books are ' neat as imported.' The very perusal of the
backs is a ' discipline of humanity.' There Mr. Southey
takes his place again with an old Radical friend : there
Jeremy Collier is at peace with Dryden : there
the lion, Martin Luther, lies down with the Quaker
lamb, Sewell : there Guzman d'Alfarache thinks himself fit company for Sir Charles Grandison, and has his
claims admitted. Even the ' high fantastical ' Duchess
of Newcastle, with her laurel on her head, is received
with grave honours, and not the less for declining to
trouble herself with the constitutions of her maids.
There is an approach to this in the library of W. C., who
also includes Italian among his humanities. W[illiam]
H[azlitt], I believe, has no books, except mine ; but he
has Shakespeare and Rousseau by heart. [Vincent]
N[ovello], who though not a bookman by profession, is
fond of those who are, and who loves his volume enough
to read it across the fields, has his library in the common
sitting-room, which is hospitable. H. R.'s [1] books are
all too modern and finely bound, which however is not
his fault, for they were left him by will,—not the most
kindly act of the testator. Suppose a man were to be-
queath us a great japan chest three feet by four, with an
injunction that it was always to stand on the tea-table.
I remember borrowing a book of H. R. which, having
lost, I replaced with a copy equally well bound. I am
not sure I should have been in such haste, even to return the book, had it been a common-looking volume ;
but the splendour of the loss dazzled me into this ostentatious piece of propriety. I set about restoring it as if
I had diminished his fortunes, and waived the privilege
a friend has to use a man's things as his own. I may
venture upon this ultra-liberal theory, not only because
candour compels me to say that I hold it to a greater
extent, with Montaigne, but because I have been a meek

---

[1] Henry Robinson, the treasurer of Covent Garden
Theatre (A. Symons, p. 313).

son in the family of book-losers. I may affirm, upon a moderate calculation, that I have lent and lost in my time (and I am eight-and-thirty), half-a-dozen decent-sized libraries,—I mean books enough to fill so many ordinary bookcases. I have never complained; and self-love, as well as gratitude, makes me love those who do not complain of me.

But, like other patient people, I am inclined to burst out now that I grow less strong,—now that writing puts a hectic to my cheek. Publicity is nothing nowadays 'between friends.' There is R., not H. R., who in return for breaking my set of English Poets, makes a point of forgetting me, whenever he has poets in his eye; which is carrying his conscience too far. But W[illiam] H[azlitt] treated me worse; for not content with losing other of said English Poets, together with my Philip Sidney, (all in one volume) and divers pieces of Bacon, he vows I never lent them to him; which is ' the unkindest cut of all.' This comes of being magnanimous. It is a poor thing after all to be ' pushed from a level consideration ' of one's superiority in matters of provocation. But W[illiam] H[azlitt] is not angry on this occasion though he is forgetful; and in spite of his offences against me and mine (not to be done away with by his good word at intervals), I pardon the irritable patriot and metaphysician, who would give his last penny to an acquaintance, and his last pulse to the good of mankind. Why did he fire up at an idle word from one of the few men who thought as deeply as himself, and who ' died daily ' in the same awful cause ? But I forgive him, because *he* forgave him, and yet I know not if I can do it for that very reason.

Come, my best friends, my books, and lead me on:
'Tis time that I were gone.

I own I borrow books with as much facility as I lend. I cannot see a work that interests me on another person's shelf, without a wish to carry it off : but, I repeat, that I have been much more sinned against than sinning in the article of non-return ; and am scrupulous in the article of intention. I never had a felonious intent upon a book but once; and then I shall only say, it was under circumstances so peculiar, that I cannot but look upon the conscience that induced me to restore it, as having sacrificed the spirit of its very self to the letter; and I have a grudge against it accordingly. Some people are unwilling to lend their books. I have a special grudge against them, particularly those who accompany their unwillingness with uneasy professions to the contrary, and smiles like Sir Fretful Plagiary. The friend who helped to spoil my notions of property, or rather to make them too good for the world ' as it goes,' taught me also to undervalue my squeamishness in refusing to avail myself of the books of these gentlemen. He showed me how it was doing good to all parties to put an ordinary face on the matter; though I know his own blushed not a little sometimes in doing it, even when the good to be done was for another. (Dear S[helley], in all thy actions, small as well as great, how sure was the beauty of thy spirit to break forth.) I feel, in truth, that even when anger inclines me to exercise this privilege of philosophy, it is more out of revenge than contempt. I fear that in allowing myself to borrow books, I sometimes make extremes meet in a very sinful manner, and do it out of a refined revenge. It is like eating a miser's beef at him.

I yield to none in my love of bookstall urbanity. I have spent as happy moments over the stalls (until the woman looked out) as any literary apprentice boy who ought to be moving onwards. But I confess my weakness, in liking to see some of my favourite purchases neatly bound. The books I like to have about me most are, Spenser, Chaucer, the minor poems of Milton, the *Arabian Nights*, Theocritus, Ariosto, and such old good-natured speculations as Plutarch's *Morals*. For most of these I like a plain good old binding, never mind how old, provided it wears well; but my *Arabian Nights* may be bound in as fine and flowery a style as possible, and I should love an engraving to every dozen pages. Book-prints of all sorts, bad and good, take with me as

much as when I was a child : and.I think some books,
such as Prior's *Poems*, ought always to have portraits
of the authors. Prior's airy face with his cap on, is
like having his company. From early association, no
edition of Milton pleases me so much, as that in which
there are pictures of the Devil with brute ears, dressed
like a Roman General : nor of Bunyan, as the one containing the print of the Valley of the Shadow of Death,
with the Devil whispering in Christian's ear, or old Pope
by the wayside, and

Vanity Fair,
With the Pilgrims suffering there.

I delight in the recollection of the puzzle I used to have
with the frontispiece of the *Tale of a Tub*, of my real
horror at the sight of that crawling old man representing
Avarice, at the beginning of *Enfield's Speaker*, the *Looking Glass*, or some such book ; and even of the careless
schoolboy hats, and the prim stomachers and cottage
bonnets, of such golden-age antiquities as the *Village
School*. The oldest and most worn-out woodcut, representing King Pippin, Goody Two Shoes, or the grim
Soldan, sitting with three staring blots for his eyes and
mouth, his sceptre in one hand, and his other five fingers
raised and spread in admiration at the feats of the
Gallant London Prentice, cannot excite in me a feeling
of ingratitude. Cooke's edition of the *British Poets and
Novelists* came out when I was at school : for which
reason I never could put up with Suttaby's or Walker's
publications, except in the case of such works as the
Fairy Tales, which Mr. Cooke did not publish. Besides,
they are too cramped, thick, and mercenary ; and the
pictures are all frontispieces. They do not come in at
the proper places. Cooke realized the old woman's
beau idéal of a prayer-book,—' A little book, with a
great deal of matter, and a large type ' :—for the type
was really large for so small a volume. Shall I ever
forget his Collins and his Gray, books at once so ' su-
perbly ornamented ' and so inconceivably cheap ? Sixpence could procure much before ; but never could it

procure so much as then, or was at once so much respected, and so little cared for. His artist Kirk was the best artist, except Stothard, that ever designed for periodical works ; and I will venture to add (if his name rightly announces his country) the best artist Scotland ever produced, except Wilkie, but he unfortunately had not enough of his country in him to keep him from dying young. His designs for Milton and the *Arabian Nights,* his female extricated from the water in the *Tales of the Genii,* and his old hag issuing out of the chest of the Merchant Abadah in the same book, are before me now, as vividly as they were then. He possessed elegance and the sense of beauty in no ordinary degree ; though they sometimes played a trick or so of foppery. I shall never forget the gratitude with which I received an odd number of Akenside, value sixpence, one of the set of that poet, which a boarder distributed among three or four of us, ' with his mother's compliments.' The present might have been more lavish, but I hardly thought of that. I remember my number. It was the one in which there is a picture of the poet on a sofa, with Cupid coming to him, and the words underneath, ' Tempt me no more, insidious Love ! ' The picture and the number appeared to me equally divine. I cannot help thinking to this day, that it is right and natural in a gentleman to sit in a stage dress, on that particular kind of sofa, though on no other, with that exclusive hat and feathers on his head, telling Cupid to begone with a tragedy air. Cowley says that even when he was ' a very young boy at school, instead of his running about on holidays, and playing with his fellows, he was wont to steal from them and walk into the fields, either alone with a book, or with some one companion, if he could find one of the same temper.' When I was at school, I had no fields to run into, or I should certainly have gone there ; and I must own to having played a great deal ; but then I drew my sports as much as possible out of books, playing at Trojan wars, chivalrous encounters with coal-staves, and even at religious mysteries. When I was not at these games, I was either reading in a corner, or walking round the cloisters with a book under one arm and my friend linked with the other, or with my thoughts. It has since been my fate to realize all the romantic notions I had of a friend at that time, and just as I had embraced him in a distant country, to have him torn from me. This it is that sprinkles the most cheerful of my speculations now with tears, and that must obtain me the reader's pardon for a style unusually chequered and egotistical. No man was a greater lover of books than he. He was rarely to be seen, unless attending to other people's affairs, without a volume of some sort, generally of Plato or one of the Greek tragedians. Nor will those who understand the real spirit of his scepticism, be surprised to hear that one of his companions was the Bible. He valued it for the beauty of some of its contents, for the dignity of others, and the curiosity of all ; though the philosophy of Solomon he thought too *Epicurean*, and the inconsistencies of other parts afflicted him. His favourite part was the book of Job, which he thought the grandest of tragedies. He projected founding one of his own upon it ; and I will undertake to say, that Job would have sat in that tragedy with a patience and profundity of thought worthy of the original. Being asked on one occasion, what book he would save for himself if he could save no other? he answered, ' The oldest book, the Bible.' It was a monument to him of the earliest, most lasting, and most awful aspirations of humanity. But more of this on a fitter occasion.[1]

---

[1] I will mention, however, in this place, that an advantage of a very cunning and vindictive nature was taken of Mr. Shelley's known regard for the Bible, to represent him as having one with him at the time he was drowned. Nothing was more probable : and it is true that he had a book in his pocket, the remains of which, at the request of the author of this article, were buried with him, but it was the volume of Mr. Keats' poems, containing *Hyperion*, of which he was a great admirer. He borrowed it of me when I went away, and knowing how I valued it also, said that he would not let it quit him till he saw me again.

I love an author the more for having been himself a lover of books. The idea of an ancient library perplexes our sympathy by its map-like volumes, rolled upon cylinders. Our imagination cannot take kindly to a yard of wit, or to thirty inches of moral observation, rolled out like linen in a draper's shop. But we conceive of Plato as a lover of books; of Aristotle certainly; of Plutarch, Pliny, Horace, Julian, and Marcus Aurelius. Virgil, too, must have been one; and, after a fashion, Martial. May I confess, that the passage which I recollect with the greatest pleasure in Cicero, is where he says that books delight us at home, *and are no impediment abroad ;* travel with us, ruralize with us. His period is rounded off to some purpose : ' *Delectant domi, non impediunt foris ; peregrinantur rusticantur.*' I am so much of this opinion, that I do not care to be anywhere without having a book or books at hand, and like Dr. Orkborne, in the novel of *Camilla,* stuff the coach or post-chaise with them whenever I travel. As books, however, become ancient, the love of them becomes more unequivocal and conspicuous. The ancients had little of what we call learning. They made it. They were also no very eminent buyers of books—they made books for posterity. It is true, that it is not at all necessary to love many books, in order to love them much. The scholar, in Chaucer, who would rather have

> At his beddes head
> A twenty bokes, clothed, in black and red,
> Of Aristotle and his philosophy,
> Than robes rich, or fiddle, or psaltry—

doubtless beat all our modern collectors in his passion for reading ; but books must at least exist, and have acquired an eminence, before their lovers can make themselves known. There must be a possession, also, to perfect the communion ; and the mere contact is much, even when our mistress speaks an unknown language. Dante puts Homer, the great ancient, in his Elysium, upon trust ; but a few years afterwards, *Homer,* the book, made its appearance in Italy, and

Petrarch, in a transport, put it upon his bookshelves, where he adored it, like ' the unknown God.' Petrarch ought to be the god of the Bibliomaniacs, for he was a collector and a man of genius, which is an union that does not often happen. He copied out, with his own precious hand, the manuscripts he rescued from time, and then produced others for time to reverence. With his head upon a book he died. Boccaccio, his friend, was another ; nor can one look upon the longest and most tiresome works he wrote (for he did write some tiresome ones, in spite of the gaiety of his *Decameron*), without thinking, that in that resuscitation of the world of letters, it must have been natural to a man of genius to add to the existing stock of volumes, at whatsoever price. I always pitch my completest idea of a lover of books, either in these dark ages, as they are called,

(Cui cieco a torto il cieco volgo appella—)

or in the gay town days of Charles II., or a little afterwards. In both times the portrait comes out by the force of contrast. In the first, I imagine an age of iron warfare and energy, with solitary retreats, in which the monk or the hooded scholar walks forth to meditate, his precious volume under his arm. In the other, I have a triumphant example of the power of books and wit to contest the victory with sensual pleasure :—Rochester, staggering home to pen a satire in the style of Monsieur Boileau ; Butler, cramming his jolly duodecimo with all the learning that he laughed at ; and a new race of book poets come up, who, in spite of their periwigs and petit-maîtres, talk as romantically of ' the bays,' as if they were priests of Delphos. It was a victorious thing in books to beguile even the old French of their egotism, or at least to share it with them. Nature never pretended to do as much. And here is the difference between the two ages, or between any two ages in which genius and art predominate. In the one, books are loved because they are the records of nature and her energies; in the other, because they are the records of those records, or evidences of the importance of the individuals, and

proofs of our descent in the new and imperishable aristo-
cracy. This is the reason why rank (with few exceptions) is so jealous of literature, and loves to appropriate
or withhold the honours of it, as if they were so many
toys and ribbons, like its own. It has an instinct that
the two pretensions are incompatible. When Montaigne (a real lover of books) affected the order of St.
Michael, and pleased himself with possessing that fugitive little piece of importance, he did it because he would
pretend to be above nothing that he really felt, or that was
felt by men in general; but at the same time he vindicated his natural superiority over this weakness by
praising and loving all higher and lasting things, and by
placing his best glory in doing homage to the geniuses
that had gone before him. He did not endeavour to
think that an immortal renown was a fashion, like that
of the cut of his scarf; or that by undervaluing the one,
he should go shining down to posterity in the other,
perpetual lord of Montaigne and of the ascendant.

There is a period of modern times, at which the love of
books appears to have been of a more decided nature
than at either of these—I mean the age just before and
after the Reformation, or rather all that period when
book-writing was confined to the learned languages.
Erasmus is the god of it. Bacon, a mighty book-man,
saw, among his other sights, the great advantage of
loosening the vernacular tongue, and wrote both Latin
and English. I allow this is the greatest closeted age
of books; of old scholars sitting in dusty studies; of
heaps of 'illustrious obscure,' rendering themselves
more illustrious and more obscure by retreating from
the 'thorny queaches' of Dutch and German names
into the 'vacant interlunar caves' of appellations
latinized or translated. I think I see all their volumes
now, filling the shelves of a dozen German convents.
The authors are bearded men, sitting in old woodcuts,
in caps and gowns, and their books are dedicated to
princes and statesmen, as illustrious as themselves. My
old friend Wierus, who wrote a thick book, *De Praestigiis
Daemonum*, was one of them, and had a fancy worthy

of his sedentary stomach.   I will confess, once for all,
that I have a liking for them all.   It is my link with the
bibliomaniacs, whom I admit into our relationship, because my love is large, and my family pride nothing.
But still I take my idea of books read with a gusto, of
companions for bed and board, from the two ages before-
mentioned. The other is of too book-worm a description.
There must be both a judgement and a fervour ; a discrimination and a boyish eagerness ; and (with all due
humility) something of a point of contact between authors worth reading and the reader.   How can I take
Juvenal into the fields, or Valcarenghius *De Aortae
Aneurismate* to bed with me ?   How could I expect to
walk before the face of nature with the one ; to tire my
elbow properly with the other, before I put out my
candle, and turn round deliciously on the right side ?
Or how could I stick up *Coke upon Littleton* against
something on the dinner-table, and be divided between
a fresh paragraph and a mouthful of salad ?

I take our four great English poets to have all been
fond of reading.   Milton and Chaucer proclaim themselves for hard sitters at books.   Spenser's reading is
evident by his learning ; and if there were nothing else
to show for it in Shakespeare, his retiring to his native
town, long before old age, would be a proof of it.   It is
impossible for a man to live in solitude without such
assistance, unless he is a metaphysician or mathema-
tician, or the dullest of mankind ; and any country
town would be solitude to Shakespeare, after the bustle
of a metropolis and a theatre.   Doubtless he divided
his time between his books, and his bowling-green, and
his daughter Susanna.   It is pretty certain, also, that
he planted, and rode on horseback ; and there is evidence of all sorts to make it clear that he must have
occasionally joked with the blacksmith, and stood god-
father for his neighbours' children.   Chaucer's account
of himself must be quoted, for the delight and sympathy
of all true readers :—

> As for me, though that I can but lite,
>   On bookès for to rede I me delite,

And to hem yeve I faith and full credence,
And in mine herte have hem in reverence
So hertèly, that there is gamè none,
That fro my bookès maketh me to gone,
But it is seldome on the holy daie;
Save certainly whan that the month of May
Is comen, and that I hear the foulès sing,
And that the flourès ginnen for to spring.
Farewell my booke and my devociön.
The Legend of Good Women.

And again, in the second book of his *House of Fame,*
where *the eagle* addresses him :—

———Thou wilt make
At right full oft thine head to ake,
And in thy study as thou writest,
And evermore of Love enditest,
In honour of him and his praisings,
And in his folkès furtherings,
And in his matter all devisest,
And not him ne his folke despisest,
Although thou mayst go in the daunse
Of hem, that him list not advance;
Therefore as I said, ywis,
Jupiter consideth well this.
And also, beau sire, of other things;
That is, thou hast no tidings
Of Lovès folke, if they be glade,
Ne of nothing else that God made,
And not only fro ferre countree,
But no tidings commen to thee,
Not of thy very neighbouris,
That dwellen almost at thy dores;
Thou hearest neither that ne this,
For whan thy labour all done is,
And hast made all thy rekenings[1],
Instead of rest and of new things,

───

[1] Chaucer at this time had an office under the government.

Thou goest home to thine house anone,
And all so dombe as anie stone,
Thou sittest at another booke,
Till fully dazed is thy looke.

After I think of the bookishness of Chaucer and Milton, I always make a great leap to Prior and Fenton. Prior was first noticed, when a boy, by Lord Dorset, sitting in his uncle's tavern, and reading Horace. He describes himself, years after, when Secretary of Embassy at the Hague, as taking the same author with him in the Saturday's chaise, in which he and his mistress used to escape from town cares into the country, to the admiration of Dutch beholders. Fenton was a martyr to contented scholarship (including a sirloin and a bottle of wine), and died among his books, of inactivity. 'He rose late,' says Johnson, 'and when he had risen, sat down to his books and papers.' A woman that once waited on him in a lodging, told him, as she said, that he would 'lie a-bed and be fed with a spoon.' He must have had an enviable liver, if he was happy. I must own (if my conscience would let me), that I should like to lead, half the year, just such a life (woman included, though not that woman), the other half being passed in the fields and woods, with a cottage just big enough to hold us. Dacier and his wife had a pleasant time of it; both fond of books, both scholars, both amiable, both wrapt up in the ancient world, and helping one another at their tasks. If they were not happy, matrimony would be a rule even without an exception. Pope does not strike me as being a book-man; he was curious rather than enthusiastic; more nice than wise; he dabbled in modern Latin poetry, which is a bad symptom. Swift was decidedly a reader; the *Tale of a Tub*, in its fashion as well as substance, is the work of a scholarly wit; the *Battle of the Books* is the fancy of a lover of libraries. Addison and Steele were too much given up to Button's and the town. Periodical writing, though its demands seem otherwise, is not favourable to reading; it becomes too much a matter of business, and will either be attended to at the expense of the writer's books, or books, the very admonishers of his industry, will make him idle. Besides, a periodical work, to be suitable to its character, and warrant its regular recurrence, must involve something of a gossiping nature, and proceed upon experiences familiar to the existing community, or at least likely to be received by them in consequence of some previous tinge of inclination. You do not pay weekly visits to your friends to lecture them, whatever good you may do their minds. There will be something compulsory in reading the *Ramblers*, as there is in going to church. Addison and Steele undertook to regulate the minor morals of society, and effected a world of good, with which scholarship had little to do. Gray was a book-man; he wished to be always lying on sofas, reading ' eternal new novels of Crebillon and Marivaux.' This is a true hand. The elaborate and scientific look of the rest of his reading was owing to the necessity of employing himself : he had not health and spirits for the literary voluptuousness he desired. Collins, for the same reason, could not employ himself ; he was obliged to dream over Arabian tales, to let the light of the supernatural world half in upon his eyes. ' He loved,' as Johnson says (in that strain of music, inspired by tenderness), 'fairies, genii, giants, and monsters ; he delighted to rove through the meanders of enchantment, to gaze on the magnificence of golden palaces, to repose by the waterfalls of Elysian gardens.' If Collins had had a better constitution, I do not believe that he would have written his projected work upon the *Restoration of Literature*, fit as he was by scholarship for the task, but he would have been the greatest poet since the days of Milton. If his friend Thomas Warton had had a little more of his delicacy of organization, the love of books would almost have made him a poet. His edition of the minor poems of Milton is a wilderness of sweets. It is the only one in which a true lover of the original can pardon an exuberance of annotation ; though I confess I am inclined enough to pardon any notes that resemble it, however numerous. The 'builded rhyme' stands at the top of the page, like a fair edifice with all sorts of flowers and fresh waters at its foot. The young poet lives there, served by the nymphs and fauns.

Hinc atque hinc glomerantur Oreades.

Huc ades, o formose puer : tibi lilia plenis
Ecce ferunt Nymphae calathis : tibi candida Nais,
Pallentes violas et summa papavera carpens,
Narcissum et florem jungit bene olentis anethi.

Among the old writers I must not forget Ben Jonson and Donne. Cowley has been already mentioned. His boyish love of books, like all the other inclinations of his early life, stuck to him to the last ; which is the greatest reward of virtue. I would mention Izaak Walton, if I had not a grudge against him. His brother fishermen, the divines, were also great fishers of books. I have a grudge against them and their divinity. They talked much of the devil and divine right, and yet forgot what Shakespeare says of the devil's friend Nero, that he is 'an angler in the lake of darkness.' Selden was called 'the walking library of our nation.' It is not the pleasantest idea of him; but the library included poetry and wit, as well as heraldry and the Jewish doctors. His *Table Talk* is equally pithy and pleasant, and truly worthy of the name, for it implies other speakers. Indeed it was actually what it is called, and treasured up by his friends. Selden wrote complimentary verses to his friends the poets, and a commentary on Drayton's *Polyolbion.* Drayton was himself a reader, addicted to all the luxuries of scholarship. Chapman sat among his books, like an astrologer among his spheres and altitudes.

How pleasant it is to reflect, that all these lovers of books have themselves become books ! What better metamorphosis could Pythagoras have desired ! How Ovid and Horace exulted in anticipating theirs ! And how the world have justified their exultation ! They had a right to triumph over brass and marble. It is the

only visible change which changes no farther; which
generates and yet is not destroyed. Consider: mines
themselves are exhausted; cities perish; kingdoms are
swept away, and man weeps with indignation to think
that his own body is not immortal.

> Muoiono le città, muoiono i regni,
> E l' uom d' esser mortal par che si sdegni.

Yet this little body of thought, that lies before me in
the shape of a book, has existed thousands of years, nor
since the invention of the press can anything short of an
universal convulsion of nature abolish it. To a shape
like this, so small yet so comprehensive, so slight yet so
lasting, so insignificant yet so venerable, turns the
mighty activity of Homer, and so turning, is enabled to
live and warm us for ever. To a shape like this turns
the placid sage of Academus: to a shape like this the
grandeur of Milton, the exuberance of Spenser, the pungent elegance of Pope, and the volatility of Prior. In
one small room, like the compressed spirits of Milton,
can be gathered together

> The assembled souls of all that men held wise.

May I hope to become the meanest of these existences?
This is a question which every author who is a lover of
books, asks himself some time in his life; and which
must be pardoned, because it cannot be helped. I know
not. I cannot exclaim with the poet,

> Oh that my name were number'd among theirs,
> Then gladly would I end my mortal days.

For my mortal days, few and feeble as the rest of them
may be, are of consequence to others. But I should like
to remain visible in this shape. The little of myself that
pleases myself, I could wish to be accounted worth
pleasing others. I should like to survive so, were it only
for the sake of those who love me in private, knowing as
I do what a treasure is the possession of a friend's mind,
when he is no more. At all events, nothing while I live
and think, can deprive me of my value for such trea-

sures. I can help the appreciation of them while I last,
and love them till I die ; and perhaps, if fortune turns
her face once more in kindness upon me before I go, I
may chance, some quiet day, to lay my overbeating
temples on a book, and so have the death I most envy.

THE WORLD OF BOOKS

[Tait's Magazine, 1833]

To the Editor of Tait's Magazine.

Sir,—

To write in your Magazine makes me feel as if I, at
length, had the pleasure of being personally in Scotland,
a gratification which I have not yet enjoyed in any other
way. I dive into my channel of communication, like
another Alpheus, and reappear in the shop of Mr. Tait ;
not pursuing, I trust, anything *fugitive,* but behaving
very unlike a river-god, and helping to bring forth an
Edinburgh periodical.

Nor will you, sir, who enter so much into the interests
of your fellow creatures, and know so well of what their
faculties are capable, look upon this kind of presence as
a thing so purely unreal as it might be supposed. Our
strongest proofs of the existence of anything amounts
but to a proportionate belief to that effect ; and it would
puzzle a wise man, though not a fool, to prove to himself that I was not, in some spiritual measure, in any
place where I chose to pitch my imagination. I notice
this metaphysical subtlety merely, in the first place, to
baulk your friend the Pechler, should he think it a settled thing that a man cannot be in two places at once
(which would be a very green assumption of his) ; and
secondly, the better to impress a conviction which I
have,—that I know Scotland very well, and have been
there many times.

Whether we go to another country on these occasions,
in the manner of a thing spiritual, our souls being pitched

out of ourselves like rockets or meteors ; or whether the
country comes to us, and our large souls are inhabited
by it for the time being, upon the principle of the greater
including the less,—the mind of man being a far more
capacious thing than any set of square miles,—I shall
leave the curious to determine ; but if I am not intimate
with the very best parts of Scotland, and have not seen
them a thousand times, then do I know nothing of Burns,
or Allan Ramsay, or Walter Scott, or Smollett, or Ossian, or James the First or Fifth, or snoods, or cocker-
nonies, or gloamin', or birks and burnies, or plaids,
bonnets, and phillabegs, or John Knox, or Queen Mary,
or the Canongate, or the Calton Hill, or Hume and
Robertson, or Tweedside, or a haggis, or cakes, or
heather, or reels and strathspeys, or Glengarry, or all
the clans, or Auld Robin Gray, or a mist, or rappee, or
second sight, or the kirk, or the cutty-stool, or golf
and hurling, or the Border, or Bruce and Wallace, or
bagpipes, or bonnie lasses.

'A lover's plaid and a bed of heath,' says the right
poetical Allan Cunningham, ' are favourite topics with
the northern muse. When the heather is in bloom, it is
worthy of becoming the couch of beauty. *A sea of
brown blossom, undulating as far as the eye can reach, and
swarming with wild bees, is a fine sight.*' Sir, I have seen
it a million times, though I never set eyes on it.

Who that has ever read it, is not put into visual possession of the following scene in the *Gentle Shepherd* ?—

A flowrie howm between twa verdant braes,
Where lasses used to wash and spread their claes ;
A trotting burnie, wimpling through the ground,
Its channel pebbles shining smooth and round ;
Here view twa barefoot beauties, clean and clear.

Or this?—

The open field.—A cottage in a glen ;
An auld wife spinning at the sunny en'.

Or this other, a perfect domestic picture?—

While Peggy laces up her bosom fair,
Wi' a blue snood Jenny binds up her hair ;

Glaud by a morning ingle takes a beek,
The rising sun shines motty through the reek :
A pipe his mouth, the lasses please his een,
And now and then a joke maun intervene.

The globe we inhabit is divisible into two worlds ; one
hardly less tangible, and far more known than the other,
—the common geographical world, and the world of
books ; and the latter may be as geographically set
forth. A man of letters, conversant with poetry and
romance, might draw out a very curious map, in which
this world of books should be delineated and filled up,
to the delight of all genuine readers, as truly as that in
Guthrie or Pinkerton. To give a specimen, and begin
with Scotland,—Scotland would not be the mere territory it is, with a scale of so many miles to a degree, and
such and such a population. Who (except a patriot or
cosmopolite) cares for the miles or the men, or knows
that they exist, in any degree of consciousness with
which he cares for the never-dying population of books?
How many generations of men have passed away, and
will pass, in Ayrshire or Dumfries, and not all the
myriads be as interesting to us as a single Burns? What
have we known of them, or shall ever know, whether
lairds, lords, or ladies, in comparison with the inspired
ploughman? But we know of the bards and the lasses,
and the places which he has recorded in song ; we know
the scene of 'Tam o' Shanter's' exploit; we know the pastoral landscapes above quoted, and the scenes immor-
talized in Walter Scott and the old ballads ; and, therefore, the book-map of Scotland would present us with
the most prominent of these. We should have the
Border, with its banditti, towns, and woods ; Tweedside,
Melrose, and Roslin, 'Edina,' otherwise called Edinburgh
and Auld Reekie, or the town of Hume, Robertson, and
others ; Woodhouselee, and other classical and haunted
places ; the bower built by the fair hands of ' Bessie
Bell ' and ' Mary Gray'; the farm-houses of Burns's
friends ; the scenes of his loves and sorrows ; the land of
'Old Mortality,' of the 'Gentle Shepherd,' and of 'Ossian.'

The Highlands, and the great blue billowy domains of heather, would be distinctly marked out, in their most poetical regions ; and we should have the tracks of Ben Jonson to Hawthornden, of 'Rob Roy' to his hiding-places, and of 'Jeanie Deans' towards England. Ab-botsford, be sure, would not be left out ; nor the house of the 'Antiquary'—almost as real a man as his author. Nor is this all : for we should have older Scotland, the Scotland of James the First, and of 'Peeblis at the Play,' and Gawin Douglas, and Bruce, and Wallace ; we should have older Scotland still, the Scotland of Ariosto, with his tale of 'Ginevra,' and the new 'Andromeda,' delivered from the sea-monster at the Isle of Ebuda (the Hebrides) ; and there would be the residence of the famous 'Launcelot of the Lake,' at Berwick, called the Joyeuse Garde, and other ancient sites of chivalry and romance ; nor should the nightingale be left out in 'Ginevra's' bower, for Ariosto has put it there, and there, accordingly, it is and has been heard, let ornith-ology say what it will ; for what ornithologist knows so much of the nightingale as a poet ? We would have an inscription put on the spot—'Here the nightingale sings, contrary to what has been affirmed by White and others.'

This is the Scotland of books, and a beautiful place it is. I will venture to affirm, Sir, even to yourself, that it is a more beautiful place than the other Scotland, always excepting to an exile or a lover ; for the former is piqued to prefer what he must not touch ; and, to the latter, no spot is so charming as the ugliest place that contains his beauty. Not that Scotland has not many places literally as well as poetically beautiful : I know that well enough. But you see that young man there, turning down the corner of the dullest spot in Edinburgh, with a dead wall over against it, and delight in his eyes? He sees No. 4, the house where the girl lives he is in love with. Now what that place is to him, all places are, in their proportion, to the lover of books, for he has beheld them by the light of imagination and sympathy.

China, sir, is a very unknown place to us,—in one

sense of the word unknown ; but who is not intimate
with it as the land of tea, and *china*, and ko-tous, and
pagodas, and mandarins, and Confucius, and conical
caps, and people with little names, little eyes, and little
feet, who sit in little bowers, drinking little cups of tea,
and writing little odes? The Jesuits, and the teacups,
and the novel of Ju-Kiao-Li, have made us well acquainted with it ; better, a great deal, than millions of
its inhabitants are acquainted—fellows who think it in
the middle of the world, and know nothing of themselves. With *one* China they are totally unacquainted,
to wit, the great China of the poet and old travellers,
Cathay, ' seat of Cathian Can,' the country of which
Ariosto's ' Angelica ' was princess-royal ; yes, she was
a Chinese, ' the fairest of her sex, Angelica.' It shows
that the ladies in that country must have greatly de-
generated, for it is impossible to conceive that Ariosto,
and Orlando, and Rinaldo, and King Sacripant, who
was a Circassian, could have been in love with her for
having eyes and feet like a pig. I will deviate here into
a critical remark, which is, that the Italian poets seem
to have considered people the handsomer the farther
you went north. The old traveller, it is true, found a
good deal of the beauty that depends on red and white,
in Tartary and other western regions ; and a fine complexion is highly esteemed in the swarthy south. But
' Astolfo,' the Englishman, is celebrated for his beauty
by the Italian poets ; the unrivalled ' Angelica ' was a
Chinese ; and the handsomest of Ariosto's heroes,
' Zerbino,' of whom he writes the famous passage, ' that
nature made him, and then broke the mould,' was a
Scotchman. The poet had probably seen some very
handsome Scotchman in Romagna. With this piece of
' bribery and corruption ' to your national readers, I
return to my subject.

Book-England, on the map, would shine as the Albion
of the old Giants ; as the ' Logres ' of the Knights of the
Round Table ; as the scene of Amadis of Gaul, with its
island of Windsor ; as the abode of fairies, of the Druids,
of the divine Countess of Coventry, of Guy, Earl of War-

wick, of ' Alfred ' (whose reality was a romance), of the
Fair Rosamond, of the *Arcades* and *Comus*, of Chaucer
and Spenser, of the poets of the Globe and the Mermaid,
the wits of Twickenham and Hampton Court. Fleet
Street would be Johnson's Fleet Street ; the Tower
would belong to Julius Caesar; and Blackfriars to Suckling, Vandyke, and the *Dunciad*. Chronology and the
mixture of truth and fiction, that is to say, of one sort
of truth and another, would come to nothing in a work of
this kind ; for, as it has been before observed, things are
real in proportion as they are impressive. And who has
not as ' gross, open, and palpable ' an idea of ' Falstaff '
in Eastcheap, as of ' Captain Grose ' himself, beating up
his quarters? A map of fictitious, literary, and historical London, would, of itself, constitute a great curiosity.
So would one of Edinburgh, or of any other city in which
there have been great men and romantic events,
whether the latter were real or fictitious. Swift speaks
of maps, in which they

Place elephants for want of towns.

Here would be towns and elephants too, the popular and
the prodigious. How much would not Swift do for Ireland, in this geography of wit and talent ! What a
figure would not St. Patrick's Cathedral make ! The
other day, mention was made of a 'Dean of St. Patrick's'
now living ; as if there was, or ever could be, more than
one Dean of St. Patrick's ! In the Irish maps we should
have the Saint himself driving out all venomous creatures (what a pity that the most venomous retain a
property as absentees !); and there would be the old Irish
kings, and O'Donoghue with his White Horse, and the
lady of the ' gold wand ' who made the miraculous
virgin pilgrimage, and all the other marvels of lakes and
ladies, and the Round Towers still remaining to perplex
the antiquary, and Goldsmith's 'Deserted Village,' and
Goldsmith himself, and the birth-places of Steele and
Sterne, and the brief hour of poor Lord Edward Fitz-
gerald, and Carolan with his harp, and the schools of the
poor Latin boys under the hedges, and Castle Rackrent,

and Edgeworth's-town, and the Giant's Causeway, and
Ginleas and other classical poverties, and Spenser's
castle on the river Mulla, with the wood-gods whom his
pipe drew round him.　Ireland is wild ground still ; and
there are some that would fain keep it so, like a forest
to hunt in.

The French map would present us with the woods and
warriors of old Gaul, and Lucan's witch ; with Charle-
maine and his court at Tours ; with the siege of Paris
by the Saracens, and half the wonders of Italian poetry ;
with Angelica and Medoro ; with the castles of Orlando
and Rinaldo, and the traitor Gan ; with part of the
great forest of Ardenne (Rosalind being in it) ; with the
gentle territory of the Troubadours, and Navarre ; with
Love's Labour's Lost, and *Vaucluse* ; with Petrarch and
Laura, and the pastoral scenes of D'Urfé's romance, and
the ' Men-Wolves ' of Brittany, and the ' Fairy of Lusig-
nan.'　Napoleon, also (for he too was a romance),
should be drawn as a giant, meeting the allied forces in
the neighbourhood of Paris.

Italy would be covered with ancient and modern
romance ; with Homer, Virgil, Ovid, Dante, Boccaccio,
&c., with classical villas, and scenes Elysian and Infernal.　There would be the region of Saturn during his
Age of Gold, and the old Tuscan cities, and Phaeton in
the north, and the sirens and fairies at Naples, and
Polyphemus in Sicily, with the abodes of Boiardo and
Ariosto, and Horace's Mount Soracte, and the Cross of
St. Peter, and the city in the sea, and the golden
scenes of Titian and Raphael, and other names that
make us hear the music of their owners : Pythagoras
also with his philosophy, and Petrarch with his lute. A
circle of stars would tell us where Galileo lived ; and the
palace of Doria would look more than royal towards the
sea.

I dare not, in this hasty sketch, and with limited time
before me, indulge myself in other luxuries of recollection,
or do anything more than barely mention the names of
Spain, Fontarabia, and Cervantes ; of Greece ; of Per-
sia, and the *Arabian Nights* ; of Mount Caucasus, and

Turkey, and the Gothic north; of El Dorado and
Columbus; or the sea-snakes, floating islands, and other
marvels of the ocean; not forgetting the Atalantis of
Plato, and the regions of 'Gulliver' and 'Peter Wilkins.'
Neither can I have the pleasure of being suffocated with
contemplating, at proper length, the burning deserts of
Africa; or of hearing the ghastly sounds of its old
Satyrs and Aegipans in their woody hills at night-time,
described by Pomponius Mela; or of seeing the Stormy
Spirit of the Cape, stationed there for ever by Camoens,
and whose stature on the map would be like a mountain.
You will be good enough to take this paper as nothing
but a hint of what such a map might contain.

One word, however, respecting a heresy in fictitious
belief, which has been uttered by Rousseau, and repeated,
I am sorry to say, by our excellent poet Wordsworth,
the man of all men who ought not to reduce a matter of
fact to what might be supposed to be its poverty.
Rousseau, speaking of the banks of the Lignon, where
the scene of the old French romance is laid, expresses
his disappointment at finding there nothing like the
beautiful things he fancied in his childhood; and Mr.
Wordsworth in his poem of *Yarrow, Visited and Un-
visited*, utters a like regret, in speaking of the scene of
the 'bonny bride—the winsome marrow.' I know
there is such an opinion abroad, like many other errors;
but it does not become men of imagination to give in to
it; and I must protest against it, as a flat irreligion. I
do not pretend to be as romantic in my conduct as the
Genevese philosopher, or as poetical in my nature as the
bard of Rydal Mount; but I have, by nature, perhaps,
greater animal spirits than either; and a bit of health
is a fine prism to see fancies by. It may be granted, for
the sake of argument, that the book-Lignon and the
book-Yarrow are still finer things than the Lignon and
Yarrow geographical; but to be actually on the spot,
to look with one's own eyes upon the places in which our
favourite heroes or heroines underwent the circumstances that made us love them—this may surely make
up for an advantage on the side of the description in the

book ; and, in addition to this, we have the pleasure of seeing how much has been done for the place by love and poetry. I have seen various places in Europe, which have been rendered interesting by great men and their works ; and I never found myself the worse for seeing them, but the better. I seem to have made friends with them in their own houses ; to have walked, and talked, and suffered, and enjoyed with them ; and if their books have made the places better, *the books themselves were there which made them so*, and which *grew out of them.* The poet's hand was on the place, blessing it. I can no more separate this idea from the spot, than I can take away from it any other beauty. Even in London, I find the principle hold good in me, though I have lived there many years, and, of course, associated it with every commonplace the most unpoetical. The greater still includes the less : and I can no more pass through Westminster, without thinking of Milton ; or the Borough, without thinking of Chaucer and Shakespeare : or Gray's Inn, without calling Bacon to mind ; or Bloomsbury Square, without Steele and Akenside— than I can prefer brick and mortar to wit and poetry, or not see a beauty upon it beyond architecture, in the splendour of the recollection. I once had duties to perform, which kept me out late at night, and severely taxed my health and spirits. My path lay through a neighbourhood in which Dryden lived ; and though nothing could be more commonplace, and I used to be tired to the heart and soul of me, I never hesitated to go a little out of the way, purely that I might pass through Gerard Street, and so give myself the shadow of a pleasant thought.

　　　　　I am, Sir, your cordial well-wisher,

　　　　　　　　A Lover of Books.

WEDDED TO BOOKS

[*Indicator*, May 17, 1820]

BUT if people are to be wedded to their books, it is hard that under our present moral dispensations, they are not to be allowed the usual exclusive privileges of marriage. A friend thinks no more of borrowing a book nowadays, than a Roman did of borrowing a man's wife; and what is worse, we are so far gone in our immoral notions on this subject, that we even lend it as easily as Cato did his spouse. Now what a happy thing ought it not to be to have exclusive possession of a book, —one's Shakespeare for instance; for the finer the wedded work, the more anxious of course we should be, that it should give nobody happiness but ourselves. Think of the pleasure not only of being with it in general, of having by far the greater part of its company, but of having it entirely to oneself; of always saying internally, 'It is my property'; of seeing it well-dressed in ' black or red,' purely to please one's own eyes; of wondering how any fellow could be so impudent as to propose borrowing it for an evening; of being at once proud of his admiration, and pretty certain that it was in vain; of the excitement nevertheless of being a little uneasy whenever we saw him approach it too nearly; of wishing that it could give him a cuff of the cheek with one of its beautiful boards, for presuming to like its beauties as well as ourselves; of liking other people's books, but not at all thinking it proper that they should like ours; of getting perhaps indifferent to it, and then comforting ourselves with the reflection that others are not so, though to no purpose; in short, of all the mixed transport and anxiety to which the exclusiveness of the book-wedded state would be liable; not to mention the impossibility of other people's having any literary offspring from our fair unique, and consequently of the danger of loving any compilations but our own. Really if we could burn all other copies of our originals, as the

Roman Emperor once thought of destroying Homer, this system would be worth thinking of. If we had a good library, we should be in the situation of the Turks with their seraglios, which are a great improvement upon our petty exclusivenesses. Nobody could then touch our Shakespeare, our Spenser, our Chaucer, our Greek and Italian writers. People might say, ' Those are the walls of the library ! ' and ' sigh, and look, and sigh again ' ; but they should never get in. No Retrospective rake should anticipate our privileges of quotation. Our Mary Woolstonecrafts and our Madame de Staels,—no one should know how finely they were lettered,—what soul there was in their disquisitions. We once had a glimpse of the feelings which people would have on these occasions. It was in the library of Trinity College, Cambridge. The keeper of it was from home ; and not being able to get a sight of the manuscript of Milton's *Comus*, we were obliged to content ourselves with looking through a wire-work, a kind of safe, towards the shelf on which it reposed. How we winked, and yearned, and imagined we saw a corner of the all-precious sheets, to no purpose ! The feelings were not very pleasant, it is true ; but then as long as they were confined to others, they would of course only add to our satisfaction.

SOCIAL GENEALOGY

[*Indicator*, Nov. 17, 1819]

It is a curious and pleasant thing to consider, that a link of personal acquaintance can be traced up from the authors of our own times to those of Shakespeare, and to Shakespeare himself. Ovid, in recording with fondness his intimacy with Propertius and Horace, regrets that he had only seen Virgil (*Trist.* Book IV. v. 51). But still he thinks the sight of him worth remembering. And Pope, when a child, prevailed on some friends to take him to a coffee-house which Dryden frequented, merely to look at him ; which he did, to his great satisfaction. Now such of us as have shaken hands with a living poet might be able perhaps to reckon up a series of connecting shakes to the very hand that wrote of Hamlet, and of Falstaff, and of Desdemona.

With some living poets, it is certain. There is Thomas Moore, for instance, who knew Sheridan. Sheridan knew Johnson, who was the friend of Savage, who knew Steele, who knew Pope. Pope was intimate with Congreve, and Congreve with Dryden. Dryden is said to have visited Milton. Milton is said to have known Davenart ; and to have been saved by him from the revenge of the restored court, in return for having saved Davenant from the revenge of the Commonwealth. But if the link between Dryden and Milton, and Milton and Davenant is somewhat apocryphal, or rather dependent on tradition (for Richardson the painter tells us the latter from Pope, who had it from Betterton the actor, one of Davenant's company), it may be carried at once from Dryden to Davenant, with whom he was unquestionably intimate. Davenant then knew Hobbes, who knew Bacon, who knew Ben Jonson, who was intimate with Beaumont and Fletcher, Chapman, Donne, Drayton, Camden, Selden, Clarendon, Sidney, Raleigh, and perhaps all the great men of Elizabeth's and James's time, the greatest of them all undoubtedly. Thus have we a link of ' beamy hands ' from our own times up to Shakespeare.

In this friendly genealogy we have omitted the numerous side-branches or common friendships ; but of those we shall give an account by and by. It may be mentioned, however, in order not to omit Spenser, that Davenant resided some time in the family of Sir Fulke Greville Lord Brooke, the friend of Sir Philip Sidney. Spenser's intimacy with Sidney is mentioned by himself in a letter, still extant, to Gabriel Harvey.

We will now give the authorities for our intellectual pedigree. Sheridan is mentioned in Boswell as being admitted to the celebrated club of which Johnson, Goldsmith, and others were members. He had then, if we remember, just written his *School for Scandal*, which made him the more welcome. Of Johnson's friendship with Savage (we cannot help beginning the sentence with his favourite leading preposition), the well-known Life is an interesting and honourable record. It is said that in the commencement of their friendship they have sometimes wandered together about London for want of a lodging ;—more likely, for Savage's want of it, and Johnson's fear of offending him by offering a share of his own. But we do not remember how this circumstance is related by Boswell.

Savage's intimacy with Steele is recorded in a pleasant anecdote, which he told Johnson. Sir Richard once desired him, 'with an air of the utmost importance,' says his biographer, ' to come very early to his house the next morning.' Mr. Savage came as he had promised, found the chariot at the door, and Sir Richard waiting for him, and ready to go out. What was intended, and whither they were to go, Savage could not conjecture, and was not willing to inquire ; but immediately seated himself with Sir Richard. The coachman was ordered to drive, and they hurried with the utmost expedition to Hyde Park Corner, where they stopped at a petty tavern, and retired to a private room. Sir Richard then informed him that he intended to publish a pamphlet, and that he had desired him to come thither that he might write for him. They soon sat down to work, Sir Richard dictated, and Savage wrote, till the dinner that had been ordered was put upon the table. Savage was surprised at the meanness of the entertainment, and after some hesitation ventured to ask for wine, which Sir Richard, not without reluctance, ordered to be brought. They then finished their dinner, and proceeded in their pamphlet, which they concluded in the afternoon.

' Mr. Savage then imagined that his task was over, and expected that Sir Richard would call for the reckoning, and return home ; but his expectations deceived him, for Sir Richard told him that he was without money, and that the pamphlet must be sold before the dinner could be paid for, and Savage was therefore obliged to go and offer their new production for sale for two guineas, which with some difficulty he obtained. Sir Richard then returned home, having retired that day only to avoid his creditors, and composed the pamphlet only to discharge his reckoning.'

Steele's acquaintance with Pope, who wrote some papers for his *Guardian*, appears in the letters and other works of the wits of that time. Johnson supposes that it was his friendly interference, which attempted to bring Pope and Addison together after a jealous separation. Pope's friendship with Congreve appears also in his letters. He also dedicated the *Iliad* to him, over the heads of peers and patrons. Congreve, whose conversation most likely partook of the elegance and wit of his writings, and whose manners appear to have rendered him an universal favourite, had the honour in his youth of attracting singular respect and regard from Dryden. He was publicly hailed by him as his successor, and affectionately bequeathed the care of his laurels. Dryden did not know who had been looking at him in the coffee-house.

> Already I am worn with cares and age,
> And just abandoning th' ungrateful stage ;
> Unprofitably kept at Heaven's expense,
> I live a rent-charge on his providence.
> But you, whom every Muse and Grace adorn,
> Whom I foresee to better fortune born,
> Be kind to my remains ; and oh, defend,
> Against your judgement, your departed friend !
> Let not th' insulting foe my fame pursue,
> But shade those laurels which descend to you.

Congreve did so with great tenderness.

Dryden is reported to have asked Milton's permission to turn his *Paradise Lost* into a rhyming tragedy, which he called *The State of Innocence, or the Fall of Man*; a work, such as might be expected from such a mode of alteration. The venerable poet is said to have answered, ' Aye, young man, you may tag my verses, if you will.'

Be the connexion, however, of Dryden with Milton, or of Milton with Davenant, as it may, Dryden wrote the alteration of Shakespeare's *Tempest*, as it is now perpetrated, in conjunction with Davenant. They were great hands, but they should not have touched the pure grandeur of Shakespeare. The intimacy of Davenant with Hobbes is to be seen by their correspondence prefixed to *Gondibert*. Hobbes was at one time secretary to Lord Bacon, a singularly illustrious instance of servant and master. Bacon is also supposed to have had Ben Jonson for a retainer in some capacity; but it is certain that Jonson had his acquaintance, for he records it in his *Discoveries*. And had it been otherwise, his link with the preceding writers could be easily supplied through the medium of Greville and Sidney, and indeed of many others of his contemporaries. Here then we arrive at Shakspeare, and feel the electric virtue of his hand. Their intimacy, dashed a little, perhaps, with jealousy on the part of Jonson, but maintained to the last by dint of the nobler part of him and of Shakespeare's irresistible fineness of nature, is a thing as notorious as their fame. Fuller says, ' Many were the wit-combates betwixt (Shakespeare) and Ben Johnson, which two I behold like a Spanish great galleon and an English man of war : Master Johnson (like the former) was built far higher in learning : solid, but slow in his performances. Shakspeare, with the English man of war, lesser in bulk, but lighter in sailing, could turn with all tides, tack about, and take advantage of all winds, by the quickness of his wit and invention.' This is a happy simile, with the exception of what is insinuated about Jonson's greater ability. But let Jonson show for himself the affection with which he regarded one who did not irritate or trample down rivalry, but rose above it like the quiet and all-gladdening sun, and turned emulation to worship :—

Soul of the age !
Th' applause ! delight ! the wonder of our stage !
My Shakespeare, rise ! I will not lodge thee by
Chaucer or Spenser, or bid Beaumont lie

A little further, to make thee a room;
Thou art a monument without a tomb;
And art alive still, while thy book doth live,
And we have wits to read, and praise to give.

   .   .   .   .   .   .

He was not of an age, but for all time.

SHAKESPEARE'S BIRTHDAY

[*Indicator*, May 3, 1820]

NEXT Friday, making the proper allowance of twelve
days from the 23rd of April, according to the change of
the Style, is the birthday of Shakespeare. Pleasant
thoughts must be associated with him in everything.
If he is not to be born in April, he must be born in May.
Nature will have him with her on her blithest holidays,
like her favourite lover.

O thou divine human creature,—greater name than
even divine poet or divine philosopher,—and yet thou
wast all three,—a very spring and vernal abundance
of all fair and noble things is to be found in thy productions! They are truly a second nature. We walk in
them, with whatever society we please; either with
men, or fair women, or circling spirits, or with none
but the whispering airs and leaves. Thou makest
worlds of green trees and gentle natures for us, in thy
forests of Arden, and thy courtly retirements of Navarre.
Thou bringest us among the holiday lasses on the green
sward; layest us to sleep among fairies in the bowers
of midsummer; wakest us with the song of the lark
and the silver-sweet voices of lovers; bringest more
music to our ears both from earth and from the planets;
anon settest us upon enchanted islands, where it wel-
comes us again, from the touching of invisible instruments; and after all, restores us to our still desired
haven, the arms of humanity. Whether grieving us or
making us glad thou makest us kinder and happier

The tears which thou fetchest down are like the rains of April, softening the times that come after them. Thy smiles are those of the month of love, the more blessed and universal for the tears.

The birthdays of such men as Shakespeare ought to be kept, in common gratitude and affection, like those of relations whom we love. He has said, in a line full of him, that

One touch of nature makes the whole world kin.

How near does he become to us with his thousand touches! The lustre and utility of intellectual power is so increasing in the eyes of the world, that we do not despair of seeing the time when his birthday will be a subject of public rejoicing; when the regular feast will be served up in tavern and dwelling-house, the bust crowned with laurel, and the theatres sparkle with illuminations. The town is lucky enough once more to have a manager who is an enthusiast. If Mr. Elliston would light up the front of his theatre next Friday with the name of Shakespeare, we would warrant him a call from the pit, and whole shouts of acknowledgement.

In the meantime it is in the power of every admirer of Shakespeare to honour the day privately. Rich or poor, busy or at leisure, all may do it. The busiest finds time to eat his dinner, and may pitch one considerate glass of wine down his throat. The poorest may call him to mind, and drink his memory in honest water. We had mechanically written health, as if he were alive. So he is in spirit;—and the spirit of such a writer is so constantly with us, that it would be a good thing, a judicious extravagance, a contemplative piece of jollity, to drink his health instead of his memory. But this, we fear, should be an impulse. We must content ourselves with having felt it here, and drinking it in imagination. To act upon it, as a proposal of the day before yesterday, might be too much like getting up an extempore gesture, or practising an unspeakable satisfaction.

An outline, however, may be drawn of the manner in which such a birthday might be spent. The tone and colouring would be filled up, of course, according to the taste of the parties. If any of our readers, then, have leisure as well as inclination to devote a day to the memory of Shakespeare, we would advise them, in the first place, to walk out, whether alone or in company, and enjoy during the morning as much as possible of those beauties of nature of which he has left us such exquisite pictures. They would take a volume of him in their hands, the most suitable to the occasion; not to hold themselves bound to sit down and read it, nor even to refer to it, if the original work of nature should occupy them too much; but to read it, if they read anything; and to feel that Shakespeare was with them substantially as well as spiritually;— that they had him with them under their arm. There is another thought connected with his presence, which may render the Londoner's walk the more interesting. Shakespeare had neither the vanity which induces a man to be disgusted with what everybody can enjoy; nor on the other hand the involuntary self-degradation which renders us incapable of enjoying what is abased by our own familiarity of acquaintanceship. About the metropolis, therefore, there is perhaps not a single rural spot, any more than about Stratford-upon-Avon, which he has not himself enjoyed. The south side of London was the one nearest his theatre. Hyde Park was then, as it is now, one of the fashionable promenades. Richmond also was in high pride of estimation. At Greenwich Elizabeth held her court, and walked abroad amid the gallant service of the Sidneys and Raleighs. And Hampstead and Highgate, with the country about them, were as they have been ever since, the favourite resort of the lovers of natural productions. Nay, without repeating what we said in a former number about the Mermaid in Cornhill, the Devil Tavern in Fleet Street, the Boar's Head in Eastcheap, and other town associations with Shakespeare, the reader who cannot get out of London on his birthday, and who has the luck to be

hard at work in Chancery Lane or the Borough, may
be pretty certain that Shakespeare has admired the
fields and the May flowers there ; for the fields were
close to the latter, perhaps came up to the very walls
of the theatre ; and the suburban mansion and gardens
of his friend Lord Southampton occupied the spot now
called Southampton Buildings.   It was really a country
neighbourhood.   The Old Bourne (Holborn) ran by,
with a bridge over it ; and Gray's Inn was an academic
bower in the fields.

The dinner does not much signify.   The sparest or
the most abundant will equally suit the various fortunes
of the great poet ; only it will be as well for those who
can afford wine to pledge Falstaff in a cup of ' sherris
sack,' which seems to have been a sort of sherry negus.
After dinner Shakespeare's volumes will come well on
the table ; lying among the desert like laurels, where
there is one, and supplying it where there is not.   Instead of songs, the persons present may be called upon
for scenes.   But no stress need be laid on this proposition, if they do not like to read out loud.   The
pleasure of the day should be as much at liberty as
possible ; and if the company prefer conversation, it
will not be very easy for them to touch upon any subjects which Shakespeare shall not have touched upon
also.   If the enthusiasm is in high taste, the ladies
should be crowned with violets, which (next to the roses
of their lips) seem to have been his favourite flower.
After tea should come singing and music, especially the
songs which Arne set from his plays, and the ballad of
' Thou soft-flowing Avon.'   If an engraving or bust of
him could occupy the principal place in the room, it
would look like the ' present deity ' of the occasion ;
and we have known a very pleasant effect produced
by everybody's bringing some quotation applicable to
him from his works, and laying it before his image, to
be read in the course of the evening.

The Editor would have dilated on these matters, not
so much to recommend what the enthusiasm of the
moment will suggest, as to enjoy them with the reader,

and have his company, as it were, at an imaginary meeting. But he is too unwell now to write much, and should have taken the liberty of compiling almost the whole of his present number, could he have denied himself the pleasure of saying a few words on so happy an occasion.

A LAUREL FROM VAUCLUSE

[*Indicator*, July 12, 1820]

AND this piece of laurel is from Vaucluse! Perhaps Petrarch, perhaps Laura, sat under it! This is a true present. What an exquisite dry, old, vital, young-looking, everlasting twig it is! It has been plucked nine months, and looks as hale and as crisp as if it would last ninety years. It shall last at any rate as long as its owner, and longer, if care and love can preserve it. How beautifully it is turned! It was a happy pull from the tree. Its shape is the very line of beauty; it has berries upon it, as if resolved to show us in what fine condition the trees are; while the leaves issue from it, and swerve upwards with their elegant points, as though they had come from adorning the poet's head. Be thou among the best of one's keepsakes, thou gentle stem,—in *deliciis nostris*;—and may the very maidservant who wonders to see thy withered beauty in its frame, miss her lover the next five weeks, for not having the instinct to know that thou must have something to do with love.

Perhaps Petrarch has felt the old ancestral boughs of this branch, stretching over his head, and whispering to him of the name of Laura, of his love, and of their future glory; for all these ideas used to be entwined in one. (Sestina 2, Canzone 17, Sonetti 162, 163, 164, 207, 224, &c.) Perhaps it is of the very stock of that bough, which he describes as supplying his mistress with a leaning-stock when she sat in her favourite bower.

Giovane donna sotto un verde lauro
Vidi più bianca e più fredda che neve
Non percossa dal sol molti e molt' anni :
E 'l suo parlar, e 'l bel viso, e le chiome,
Mi piacquer sì, ch' i' l'ho agli occhi
Ed avrò sempre, ov' io sia in poggio o 'n riva.

Vol. I, Sestina 2.

A youthful lady under a green laurel
I saw, more fair and colder than white snows
Unshone upon for many and many a year ;
And her sweet looks, and hair, and way of speaking,
So pleased me, that I have her now before me,
And shall have, ever, whether on hill or lea.

The laurel seems more appropriated to Petrarch than
to any other poet.   He delighted to sit under its leaves ;
he loved it both for itself, and for the resemblance of
its name to that of his mistress ; he wrote of it continu-
ally ; and he was called from out of its shade to be
crowned with it in the Capitol.   It is a remarkable
instance of the fondness with which he cherished the
united ideas of Laura and the laurel, that he confesses it
to have been one of the greatest delights he experienced
in receiving the crown upon his head.

It was out of Vaucluse that he was called.   Vaucluse,
Valchiusa, the Shut Valley (from which the French, in
the modern enthusiasm for intellect, gave the name to
the department in which it lies), is a remarkable spot
in the old poetical region of Provence, consisting of a
little deep glen of green meadows surrounded with rocks,
and containing the fountain of the river Sorgue.
Petrarch, when a boy of eight or nine years of age, had
been struck with its beauty, and exclaimed that it was
the place of all others he should like to live in, better
than the most splendid cities.   He resided there afterwards for several years, and composed in it the greater
part of his poems.   Indeed, he says in his own account
of himself, that he either wrote or conceived in that
valley almost every work he produced.   He lived in a
little cottage with a small homestead, on the banks of

the river. Here he thought to forget his passion for Laura, and here he found it stronger than ever. We do not well see how it could have been otherwise; for Laura lived no great way off, at Chabrieres : and he appears to have seen her often in the very place. He paced along the river ; he sat under the trees ; he climbed the mountains ; but Love, he says, was ever by his side,

> Ragionando con meco, ed io con lui.
>
> He holding talk with me, and I with him.

We are supposing that all our readers are acquainted with Petrarch. Many of them doubtless know him intimately. Should any of them want an introduction to him, how should we speak of him in the gross ? We should say that he was one of the finest gentlemen and greatest scholars that ever lived ; that he was a writer who flourished in Italy in the fourteenth century at the time when Chaucer was young, during the reigns of our Edwards ; that he was the greatest light of his age ; that although so fine a writer himself, and the author of a multitude of works, or rather because he was both, he took the greatest pains to revive the knowledge of the ancient learning, recommending it everywhere, and copying out large manuscripts with his own hand ; that two great cities, Paris and Rome, contended which should have the honour of crowning him ; that he was crowned publicly, in the Metropolis of the World, with laurel and with myrtle ; that he was the friend of Boccaccio, the Father of Italian Prose ; and lastly, that his greatest renown nevertheless, as well as the predominant feelings of his existence, arose from the long love he bore for a lady of Avignon, the far-famed Laura, whom he fell in love with on the 6th of April, 1327, on a Good Friday ; whom he rendered illustrious in a multitude of sonnets, which have left a sweet sound and sentiment in the ear of all after lovers ; and who died, still passionately beloved, in the year 1348, on the same day and hour on which he first beheld her. Who she was, or why their connexion was not closer, remains a mystery. But that she was a real person, and that in spite of all her modesty she did not show an insensible countenance to his passion, is clear from his long-haunted imagination, from his own repeated accounts, from all that he wrote, uttered, and thought. One love, and one poet, sufficed to give the whole civilized world a sense of delicacy in desire, of the abundant riches to be found in one single idea, and of the going out of a man's self to dwell in the soul and happiness of another, which has served to refine the passion for all modern times ; and perhaps will do so, as long as love renews the world.

LOVERS OF ARCADY

[*Jar of Honey from Mount Hybla*, 1848]

How many other great and good men have there not been, with whom the humblest lover of Arcady may, in this respect, claim fellowship ?—men, nevertheless, fond of town also, and of the most active and busy life, when it was their duty to enter it. The most universal genius must of necessity include the green districts of the world in his circle, otherwise he would not run it a third part round. Shakespeare himself, prosperous manager as he was, retired to his native place before he was old. Do we think that, with all his sociality, his chief companions there were such as a country town afforded ? Depend upon it, they were the trees and the fields, and his daughter Susanna. Be assured that no gentleman of the place was seen so often pacing the banks of the Avon, sitting on the stiles in the meadows, looking with the thrush at the sunset, or finding

> Books in the running brooks,
> Sermons in stones, and good in everything.

Cervantes, the Shakespeare of Spain (for if his poetry answered but to one small portion of Shakespeare, his prose made up the rest), proclaims his truly pastoral heart, notwithstanding his satire, not only in his *Galatea*, but in a hundred passages of *Don Quixote*, particularly the episodes. He delighted equally in knowledge of the world and the most ideal poetic life. It is easy to see, by the stories of *Marcella* and *Leandra*, that this great writer wanted little to have become a Quixote himself, in the Arcadian line! Nothing but the extremest good sense supplied him a proper balance in this respect for his extreme romance.

Boccaccio was another of these great childlike minds, whose knowledge of the world is ignorantly confounded with a devotion to it. See, in his *Admetus*, and *Theseid*, and *Genealogia Deorum*, &c., and in the *Decameron* itself, how he revels in groves and gardens; and how, when he begins making a list of trees, he cannot leave off. Doubtless, he had been of a more sensual temperament than Cervantes; but his faith remained unshaken in the highest things. His veins might have contained an excess of the genial; but so did his heart. When the priest threatened him in advanced life with the displeasure of Heaven, he was shocked and alarmed, and obliged to go to Petrarch for comfort.

Chaucer was a courtier, and a companion of princes; nay, a reformer also, and a stirred out in the world. He understood that world, too, thoroughly, in the ordinary sense of such understanding; yet, as he was a true great poet in everything, so in nothing more was he so than in loving the country, and the trees and fields. It is as hard to get him out of a grove as his friend Boccaccio; and he tells us that, in May, he would often go out into the meadows to 'abide' there, solely in order to 'look upon the daisy.' Milton seems to have made a point of never living in a house that had not a garden to it.

GENIUS

[*Imagination and Fancy*]

O LOVELY and immortal privilege of genius! that can stretch its hand out of the wastes of time, thousands of years back, and touch our eyelids with tears. In these passages there is not a word which a man of the most matter-of-fact understanding might not have written, *if he had thought of it.* But in poetry, feeling and imagination are necessary to the perception and presentation even of matters of fact. They, and they only, see what is proper to be told, and what is to be kept back; what is pertinent, affecting, and essential. Without feeling, there is a want of delicacy and distinction; without imagination there is no true embodiment. In poets, even good of their kind, but without a genius for narration, the action would have been encumbered or diverted with ingenious mistakes. The over-contemplative would have given us too many remarks; the over-lyrical, a style too much carried away; the over-fanciful, conceits and too many similes; the unimaginative, the facts without the feeling, and not even those. We should have been told nothing of the ' grey chin,' of the house hearing them as they moaned, or of Achilles gently putting the old man aside; much less of that yearning for his father, which made the hero tremble in every limb. Writers without the greatest passion and power do not feel in this way, nor are capable of expressing the feeling; though there is enough sensibility and imagination all over the world to enable mankind to be moved by it, when the poet strikes his truth into their hearts.

VERSE

[*Imagination and Fancy*]

WITH regard to the principle of Variety in Uniformity by which verse ought to be modulated, and one-ness of impression diversely produced, it has been contended by some, that Poetry need not be written in verse at all ; that prose is as good a medium, provided poetry be conveyed through it ; and that to think otherwise is to confound letter with spirit, or form with essence. But the opinion is a prosaical mistake. Fitness and unfitness for *song*, or metrical excitement, just make all the difference between a poetical and prosaical subject ; and the reason why verse is necessary to the form of poetry is, that the perfection of poetical spirit demands it ;—that the circle of its enthusiasm, beauty, and power is incomplete without it. I do not mean to say that a poet can never show himself a poet in prose ; but that, being one, his desire and necessity will be to write in verse ; and that, if he were unable to do so, he would not, and could not, deserve his title. Verse to the true poet is no clog. It is idly called a trammel and a difficulty. It is a help. It springs from the same enthusiasm as the rest of his impulses, and is necessary to their satisfaction and effect. Verse is no more a clog than the condition of rushing upward is a clog to fire, or than the roundness and order of the globe we live on is a clog to the freedom and variety that abound within its sphere. Verse is no dominator over the poet, except inasmuch as the bond is reciprocal, and the poet dominates over the verse. They are lovers, playfully challenging each other's rule, and delighted equally to rule and to obey. Verse is the final proof to the poet that his mastery over his art is complete. It is the shutting up of his power in '*measureful* content' ; the answer of form to his spirit ; of strength and ease to his guidance. It is the willing action, the proud and fiery happiness, of the winged steed on whose back he has vaulted,

To witch the world with wondrous horsemanship.

Verse, in short, is that finishing, and rounding, and
'tuneful planetting' of the poet's creations, which is
produced of necessity by the smooth tendencies of their
energy or inward working, and the harmonious dance
into which they are attracted round the orb of the beautiful.   Poetry, in its complete sympathy with beauty,
must, of necessity, leave no sense of the beautiful, and
no power over its forms, unmanifested ; and verse flows
as inevitably from this condition of its integrity, as
other laws of proportion do from any other kind of
embodiment of beauty (say that of the human figure),
however free and various the movements may be that
play within their limits.   What great poet ever wrote
his poems in prose ? or where is a good prose poem, of
any length, to be found ?   The poetry of the Bible is
understood to be in verse, in the original.   Mr. Hazlitt
has said a good word for those prose enlargements of
some fine old song, which are known by the name of
Ossian ; and in passages they deserve what he said ;
but he judiciously abstained from saying anything
about the form.   Is Gesner's *Death of Abel* a poem ?
or Hervey's *Meditations* ?   The *Pilgrim's Progress* has
been called one ; and, undoubtedly, Bunyan had a
genius which tended to make him a poet, and one of
no mean order : and yet it was of as ungenerous and
low a sort as was compatible with so lofty an affinity ;
and this is the reason why it stopped where it did.   He
had a craving after the beautiful, but not enough of it
in himself to echo to its music.   On the other hand,
the possession of the beautiful will not be sufficient
without force to utter it.   The author of *Telemachus*
had a soul full of beauty and tenderness.   He was not
a man who, if he had had a wife and children, would
have run away from them, as Bunyan's hero did, to get
a place by himself in heaven.   He was 'a little lower
than the angels,' like our own Bishop Jewels and
Berkeleys ; and yet he was no poet.   He was too delicately, not to say feebly, absorbed in his devotions to
join in the energies of the seraphic choir.

LEVITY

[*Wit and Humour*]

I confess I felt this[1] so strongly when I began to reflect on the present subject, and found myself so perplexed with the demand, that I was forced to reject plan after plan, and feared I should never be able to give any tolerable account of the matter. I experienced no such difficulty with the concentrating seriousness and sweet attraction of the subject of ' Imagination and Fancy '; but this laughing jade of a topic, with her endless whims and faces, and the legions of indefinable shapes that she brought about me, seemed to do nothing but scatter my faculties, or bear them off deridingly into pastime. I felt as if I was undergoing a Saint Anthony's Temptation reversed,—a laughable instead of a frightful one. Thousands of merry devils poured in upon me from all sides,—doubles of Similes, buffooneries of Burlesques, stalkings of Mock-heroics, stings in the tails of Epigrams, glances of Innuendoes, dry looks of Ironies, corpulences of Exaggerations, ticklings of mad Fancies, claps on the back of Horse-plays, complacencies of *Unawarenesses*, flounderings of Absurdities, irresistibilities of Iterations, significancies of Jargons, wailings of Pretended Woes, roarings of Laughters, and hubbubs of Animal Spirits ;—all so general yet particular, so demanding distinct recognition, and yet so baffling the attempt with their numbers and their confusion, that a thousand masquerades in one would have seemed to threaten less torment to the pen of a reporter.

[1] That ' levity has as many tricks as the kitten.'—Ed.

TABLE-TALK

[*Table-Talk*]

Is so natural to man, that the mouth is the organ both of eating and speaking. The tongue is set flowing by the bottle. Johnson talked best when he dined ;— Addison could not talk at all till he drank. Table and conversation interchange their metaphors. We *devour* wit and argument, and *discuss* a turkey and chine. That man must be very much absorbed in reflection, or stupid, or sulky, or unhappy, or a mere hog at his trough, who is not moved to say something when he dines. The two men who lived with no other companions in the Eddystone Lighthouse, and who would not speak to one another during their six months, must have been hard put to it, when they tapped a fresh barrel. To be sure, the greater the temptation, the greater the sulk ; but the better-natured of the two must have found it a severe struggle on a very fine or very foggy day.

Table-talk, to be perfect, should be sincere without bigotry, differing without discord, sometimes grave, always agreeable, touching on deep points, dwelling most on seasonable ones, and letting everybody speak and be heard. During the wine after dinner, if the door of the room be opened, there sometimes comes bursting up the drawing-room stairs a noise like that of a tap-room. Everybody is shouting in order to make himself audible ; argument is tempted to confound itself with loudness ; and there is not one conversation going forward, but six, or a score. This is better than for-mality and want of spirits ; but it is no more the right thing, than a scramble is a dance, or the tap-room chorus a quartet of Rossini. The perfection of con-versational intercourse is when the breeding of high life is animated by the fervour of genius.

Nevertheless, the man who cannot be loud, or even vociferous, on occasion, is wanting on the jovial side of good-fellowship. Chesterfield, with all his sense and agreeableness, was but a solemn fop when he triumphantly asked whether anybody had ' ever seen him laugh ? ' It was as bad as the jealous lover in the play who says, ' Have *I* been the life of the company ? Have *I* made you all die with merriment ? ' And there were occasions, no doubt, when Chesterfield might have been answered as the lover was, ' No : to do you justice, you have been confoundedly stupid.'

Luckily for table-talkers in general, they need be neither such fine gentlemen as Chesterfield, nor such oracles as Johnson, no such wits as Addison and Swift, provided they have nature and sociability, and are not destitute of reading and observation.

CHEERFUL POETS

[Table-Talk]

CAST your eyes down any list of English writers, such, for instance, as that at the end of Mr. Craik's *History of our Literature*, and almost the only names that strike you as belonging to personally cheerful men are Beaumont and Fletcher, Suckling, Fielding, Farquhar, Steele, O'Keefe, Andrew Marvell, and Sterne. That Shakespeare was cheerful, I have no doubt, for he was almost everything ; but still it is not his predominant characteristic ; which is thought. Sheridan could ' set the table in a roar ' ; but it was a flustered one, at somebody's expense. His wit wanted good-nature. Prior has a smart air, like his cap. But he was a rake who became cynical. He wrote a poem in the character of Solomon, on the vanity of all things. Few writers make you laugh more than Peter Pindar : but there was a spice of the blackguard in him. You could not be sure of his truth or his good-will.

After all, it is not necessary to be cheerful in order to give a great deal of delight ; nor would the cheer-

fullest men interest us as they do, if they were incapable
of sympathizing with melancholy.   I am only speaking
of the rarity of a certain kind of sunshine in our literature, and expressing a little rainy-day wish that we had
a little more of it. It ought to be collected. There should
be a joyous set of elegant extracts—a *Literatura Hilaris*
or *Gaudens,*—in a score of volumes, that we could have
at hand, like a cellaret of good wine, against April or
November weather.   Fielding should be the port, and
Farquhar the champagne, and Sterne the malmsey ;
and whenever the possessor cast an eye on his stock
he should know that he had a choice draught for himself
after a disappointment, or for a friend after dinner,—
some cordial extract of Parson Adams, or Plume, or
Uncle Toby, generous as heart could desire, and as
wholesome for it as laughter for the lungs.

BOOKS FOR CHILDREN

[*The Town*]

But the most illustrious of all booksellers in our
boyish days, not for his great names, not for his dinners,
not for his riches that we know of, nor for any other full-
grown celebrity, but for certain little penny books,
radiant with gold and rich with bad pictures, was Mr.
Newberry, the famous children's bookseller, ' at the
corner of St. Paul's Churchyard,' next Ludgate Street.
The house is still occupied by a successor, and children
may have books there as formerly—but not the same.
The gilding, we confess, we regret : gold, somehow,
never looked so well as in adorning literature.   The
pictures also—may we own that we preferred the uncouth coats, the staring blotted eyes, and round pieces
of rope for hats, of our very badly drawn contemporaries, to all the proprieties of modern embellishment ?
We own the superiority of the latter, and would have
it proceed and prosper ; but a boy of our own time was

much, though his coat looked like his grandfather's.
The engravings probably were of that date. Enormous,
however, is the improvement upon the morals of these
little books ; and there we give them up, and with
unmitigated delight. The good little boy, the hero of the
infant literature in those days, stood, it must be acknowledged, the chance of being a very selfish man. His
virtue consisted in being different from some other little
boy, perhaps his brother ; and his reward was having
a fine coach to ride in, and being a King Pepin. Nowadays, since the world has had a great moral earthquake
that set it thinking, the little boy promises to be much
more of a man ; thinks of others, as well as works for
himself ; and looks for his reward to a character for
good sense and beneficence. In no respect is the progress of the age more visible, or more importantly so,
than in this apparently trifling matter. The most
bigoted opponents of a rational education are obliged
to adopt a portion of its spirit, in order to retain a hold
which their own teaching must accordingly undo : and
if the times were not full of hopes in other respects, we
should point to this evidence of their advancement,
and be content with it.

One of the most pernicious mistakes of the old children's books, was the inculcation of a spirit of revenge
and cruelty in the tragic examples which were intended
to deter their readers from idleness and disobedience.
One, if he did not behave himself, was to be shipwrecked
and eaten by lions ; another to become a criminal, who
was not to be taught better, but rendered a mere wicked
contrast to the luckier virtue ; and, above all, none
were to be poor but the vicious, and none to ride in their
coaches but little Sir Charles Grandisons, and all-perfect
Sheriffs. We need not say how contrary this was to
the real spirit of Christianity, which, at the same time,
they so much insisted on. The perplexity in after life,
when reading of poor philosophers and rich vicious men
was in proportion ; or rather virtue and merely worldly
success became confounded. In the present day the
profitableness of good conduct is still inculcated, but in

a sounder spirit. Charity makes the proper allowance for all ; and none are excluded from the hope of being wiser and happier. Men, in short, are not taught to love and labour for themselves alone or for their little dark corners of egotism ; but to take the world along with them into a brighter sky of improvement ; and to discern the want of success in success itself, if not accompanied by a liberal knowledge.

NOVELS

[Autobiography]

GOLDSMITH enchanted me. I knew no end of repeating passages out of the *Essays* and the *Citizen of the World*—such as the account of the Club, with its Babel of talk ; of Beau Tibbs, with his dinner of ox-cheek which ' his grace was so fond of ' ; and of the wooden-legged sailor, who regarded those that were lucky enough to have their ' legs shot off ' on board king's ships (which entitled them to a penny a day), as being ' born with golden spoons in their mouths.' Then there was his correct, sweet style ; the village-painting in his poems ; the *Retaliation*, which, though on an artificial subject, seemed to me (as it yet seems) a still more genuine effusion ; and, above all, the *Vicar of Wakefield* —with Burchell, whom I adored ; and Moses, whom I would rather have been cheated with, than prosper ; and the Vicar himself in his cassock, now presenting his ' Treatise against Polygamy ' (in the family picture) to his wife, habited as Venus ; and now distracted for the loss of his daughter Olivia, who is seduced by the villanous squire. I knew not whether to laugh at him, or cry with him most.

These, with Fielding and Smollett, Voltaire, Charlotte Smith, Bage, Mrs. Radcliffe, and Augustus La Fontaine, were my favourite prose authors. I had subscribed, while at school, to the famous circulating library in

Leadenhall Street, and I have continued to be such a glutton of novels ever since, that, except where they repel me in the outset with excessive wordiness, I can read their three-volume enormities to this day without skipping a syllable; though I guess pretty nearly all that is going to happen, from the mysterious gentleman who opens the work in the dress of a particular century, down to the distribution of punishments and the drying up of tears in the last chapter. I think the authors wonderfully clever people, particularly those who write most; and I should like the most contemptuous of their critics to try their hands at doing something half as engaging.

I READ EVERYTHING READABLE

[Autobiography]

I READ everything that was readable, old and new, particularly fiction, and philosophy, and natural history; was always returning to something Italian, or in Spenser, or in the themes of the East; lost no particle of Dickens, of Thackeray, of Mrs. Gaskell (whose *Mary Barton* gave me emotions that required, more and more, the consideration of the good which it must do); called out every week for my *Family Herald*, a little penny publication, at that time qualified to inform the best of its contemporaries; rejoiced in republications of wise and witty Mrs. Gore, especially seeing she only made us wait for something newer; delighted in the inexhaustible wit of Douglas Jerrold, Thackeray, and his coadjutors, Tom Taylor, Percival Leigh, and others, in *Punch*, the best-humoured and best-hearted satirical publication that ever existed; wondered when Bulwer Lytton would give us more of his potent romances and prospective philosophies; and hailed every fresh publication of James, though I knew half what he was going to do with his lady, and his gentleman, and his landscape, and his mystery, and his orthodoxy, and his criminal trial. But I was charmed with the new amusement which he brought out of old materials. I looked on him as I should look upon a musician, famous for 'variations.' I was grateful for his vein of cheerfulness, for his singularly varied and vivid landscapes, for his power of painting women at once lady-like and loving (a rare talent), for his making lovers to match, at once beautiful and well-bred, and for the solace which all this has afforded me, sometimes over and over again, in illness and in convalescence, when I required interest without violence, and entertainment at once animated and mild.

COOKE'S POETS

[Autobiography]

IN those times, Cooke's edition of the British poets came up. I had got an odd volume of Spenser; and I fell passionately in love with Collins and Gray. How I loved those little sixpenny numbers containing whole poets! I doted on their size; I doted on their type, on their ornaments, on their wrappers containing lists of other poets, and on the engravings from Kirk. I bought them over and over again, and used to get up select sets, which disappeared like buttered crumpets; for I could resist neither giving them away, nor possessing them. When the master tormented me—when I used to hate and loathe the sight of Homer, and Demosthenes, and Cicero—I would comfort myself with thinking of the sixpence in my pocket, with which I should go out to Paternoster Row, when school was over, and buy another number of an English poet.

UNCLE TOBY

[*Wit and Humour*]

But what sha l I say to thee, thou quintessence of the milk of human kindness, thou reconciler of war (as far as it was once necessary to reconcile it), thou returner to childhood during peace, thou lover of widows, thou master of the best of corporals, thou whistler at excommunications, thou high and only filial Christian gentleman, thou pitier of the devil himself, divine Uncle Toby! Why, this I will say, made bold by thy example, and caring nothing for what anybody may think of it who does not in some measure partake of thy nature, that he who created thee was the wisest man since the days of Shakespeare; and that Shakespeare himself, mighty reflector of things as they were, but no anticipator, never arrived at a character like thine. No master of *bonhomie* was he. No such thing, alas! did he find in the parson at Stratford-upon-Avon, or in the tap-rooms on his way to town, or in those of Eastcheap, or in the courts of Elizabeth and James, or even in the green-rooms of the Globe and Blackfriars, though he knew Decker himself, and probably had heard him speak of such a man as Signor Orlando Friscobaldo. Let him afford to lose the glory of this discovery; let Decker be enriched with it; and let Fielding and Sterne have the renown of finding the main treasure. As long as the character of Toby Shandy finds an echo in the heart of man, the heart of man is noble. It awaits the impress of all good things, and may prepare for as many surprises in the moral world, as science has brought about in the physical.

CHAUCER

[*Wit and Humour*]

CHAUCER'S comic genius is so perfect, that it may be said to include prophetic intimations of all that followed it. The liberal-thinking joviality of Rabelais is there; the portraiture of Cervantes, moral and external; the poetry of Shakespeare; the learning of Ben Jonson; the manners of the wits of Charles the Second; the *bonhomie* of Sterne; and the insidiousness, without the malice of Voltaire. One of its characteristics is a certain tranquil detection of particulars, expressive of generals; as in the instance just mentioned of the secret infirmity of the Cook. Thus the Prioress speaks French; but it is ' after the school of Stratford at Bow.' Her education was altogether more showy than substantial. The Lawyer was the busiest man in the world, and yet he 'seemed busier than he was.' He made something out of nothing, even in appearances.

SHAKESPEARE

[*Wit and Humour*]

SHAKESPEARE had as great a comic genius as tragic; and everybody would think so, were it possible for comedy to impress the mind as tragedy does. It is true, the times he lived in, as Hazlitt has remarked, were not so foppish and ridiculous as those of our prose comic dramatists, and therefore he had not so much to laugh at: and it is observed by the same critic, with equal truth, that his genius was of too large and magnanimous a description to delight in satire. But who doubts that had Shakespeare lived in those inferior times, the author of the character of Mercutio could have written that of Dorimant? of Benedick and Beatrice, the dialogues of Congreve? or of *Twelfth Night* and the *Taming of the Shrew,* the most uproarious farce ? I certainly cannot think with Dr. Johnson that he wrote comedy better than tragedy; that 'his tragedy seems to be skill, and his comedy instinct.' I could as soon believe that the instinct of Nature was confined to laughter, and that her tears were shed upon principles of criticism. Such may have been the Doctor's recipe for writing tragedy; but *Irene* is not *King Lear.* Laughter and tears are alike born with us, and so was the power of exciting them with Shakespeare; because it pleased Nature to make him a complete human being.

Shakespeare had wit and humour in perfection; and like every possessor of powers so happy, he rioted in their enjoyment. Molière was not fonder of running down a joke: Rabelais could not give loose to a more 'admirable fooling.' His mirth is commensurate with his melancholy; it is founded on the same knowledge and feeling, and it furnished him with a set-off to their oppression. When he had been too thoughtful with Hamlet, he 'took it out' with Falstaff and Sir Toby. Not that he was habitually melancholy. He had too healthy a brain for that, and too great animal spirits; but in running the whole circle of thought, he must of necessity have gone through its darkest as well as brightest phases; and the sunshine was welcome in proportion. Shakespeare is the inventor of the phrase, 'setting the table in a roar'; of the memory of Yorick; of the stomach of Falstaff, stuffed as full of wit as of sack. He 'wakes the night-owl with a catch'; draws 'three souls out of one weaver'; passes the 'equinoctial of Queubus' (some glorious torrid zone, lying beyond three o'clock in the morning); and reminds the 'unco righteous' for ever, that virtue, false or true, is not incompatible with the recreations of 'cakes and ale.' Shakespeare is said to have died of getting out of a sick-bed to entertain his friends Drayton and Ben Jonson, visitors from London. He might have died a later and a graver death, but he could not well have had one more genial, and therefore more poetical. Far was it from dishonouring the eulogizer of 'good men's feasts'; the recorder of the noble friends Antonio and Bassanio; the great thorough-going humanist, who did equal justice to the gravest and the gayest moments of life.

It is a remarkable proof of the geniality of Shakespeare's jesting, that even its abundance of ideas does not spoil it; for, in comedy as well as tragedy, he is the most reflective of writers. I know but of one that comes near him in this respect; and very near him (I dare to affirm) he does come, though he has none of his poetry, properly so-called. It is Sterne, in whose *Tristram Shandy* there is not a word without meaning— often of the profoundest as well as kindliest sort. The professed fools of Shakespeare are among the wisest of men. They talk Aesop and Solomon in every jest. Yet they amuse as much as they instruct us. The braggart Parolles, whose name signifies *words*, as though he spoke nothing else, scarcely utters a sentence that is not rich with ideas; yet his weakness and self-committals hang over them all like a sneaking infection, and hinder our laughter from becoming respectful. The scene in which he is taken blindfold among his old acquaintances, and so led to vilify their characters, under the impression that he is gratifying their enemies, is almost as good as the screen-scene in the *School for Scandal*.

BEN JONSON

[*Imagination and Fancy. Wit and Humour*]

IF Ben Jonson had not tried to do half what he did, he would have had a greater fame. His will and ambition hurt him, as they always hurt genius when set in front of it. Lasting reputation of power is only to be obtained by power itself; and this, in poetry, is the result not so much, if at all, of the love of the power, as of the power of love,—the love of truth and beauty,—great and potent things they,—not the love of self, which is generally a very little thing. The 'supposed rugged

old bard,' notwithstanding his huffing and arrogance,
had elegance, feeling, imagination, great fancy; but
by straining to make them all greater than they were,
bringing in the ancients to help him, and aiming to
include the lowest farce (perhaps by way of outdoing
the universality of Shakespeare), he became as gross
in his pretensions as drink had made him in person.
His jealous irritability and assumption tired out the
gentlest and most generous of his contemporaries—
men who otherwise really liked him (and he them),—
Decker for one; and he has ended in appearing to
posterity rather the usurper than the owner of a true
renown. He made such a fuss with his learning, that
he is now suspected to have had nothing else. Hazlitt
himself cannot give him credit for comic genius, so
grave and all-in-all does his pedantry appear to that
critic,—an erroneous judgement, as it seems to me,—
who cannot help thinking, that what altogether made
Ben what he was projected his ultra-jovial person
rather towards comedy than tragedy; and as a proof
of this, his tragedies are all borrowed, but his comedies
his own. *Twelfth Night* and other plays of Shakespeare
preceded and surpassed him in his boasted 'humour';
but his *Alchemist*, and especially his *Volpone*, seem to
me at the head of all severer English comedy. The
latter is a masterpiece of plot and treatment. Ben's
fancy, a power tending also rather to the comic than
tragic, was in far greater measure than his imagination;
and their strongest united efforts, as in the *Witches'
Meeting*, and the luxurious anticipations of Sir Epicure
Mammon, produce a smiling as well as a serious admiration. The three happiest of all his short effusions are
the *Epitaph on Lady Pembroke*, the address to *Cynthia*
(both of which are serious indeed, but not tragic), and
the *Catch of the Satyrs*, which is unique for its wild and
melodious mixture of the comic and the poetic. His
huge farces, to be sure (such as *Bartholomew Fair*), are
execrable. They seem to talk for talking sake, like
drunkards. And though his famous verses, beginning,
' Still to be neat, still to be drest,' are elegantly worded,

I never could admire them. There is a coarseness implied in their very refinement.

After all, perhaps it is idle to wish a writer had been otherwise than he was, especially if he is an original in his way, and worthy of admiration. His faults he may have been unable to mend, and they may not have been without their use, even to his merits. If Ben had not been Ben, Sir Epicure Mammon might not have talked in so high a tone. We should have missed, perhaps, something of the excess and altitude of his expressions—of his

Gums of Paradise and *eastern air*.

Let it not be omitted, that Milton went to the masques and odes of Ben Jonson for some of his elegancies even of his dignified muse.

. . . .

Ben Jonson's famous humour is as pampered, jovial, and dictatorial as he was in his own person. He always gives one the idea of a man sitting at the head of a table and a coterie. He carves up a subject as he would a dish ; talks all the while to show off both the dish and himself ; and woe betide difference of opinion, or his ' favourite aversion,' envy. He was not an envious man himself, provided you allowed him his claims. He praised his contemporaries all round, chiefly in return for praises. He had too much hearty blood in his veins to withhold eulogy where it was not denied him ; but he was somewhat too willing to cancel it on offence. He complains that he had given heaps of praises undeserved ; tells Drayton that it had been doubted whether he was a friend to anybody (owing, doubtless, partly to this caprice): and in the collection of epigrams, printed under his own care, there are three consecutive copies of verse, two of them addressed to Lord Salisbury in the highest style of panegyric, and the third to the writer's muse, consisting of a recantation, apparently of the same panegyric, and worth repeating here for its scorn and spleen.

TO MY MUSE

Away, and leave me, *thou thing most abhorr'd,*
That hast betray'd me to a worthless lord ;
Made me commit *most fierce idolatry*
To a great image through thy luxury.
Be thy next master's *more* unlucky Muse,
And, as thou'st mine, his hours and youth abuse.
Get him the time's long grudge, the court's ill will,
And, reconcil'd, keep him suspected still.
Make him lose all his friends ; and, which is worse,
Almost all ways to any better course.

(This is melancholy.)

With me thou leav'st an happier Muse than thee,
And which thou brought'st me, welcome Poverty.
She shall instruct my after thoughts to write
Things manly, and not smelling parasite.
But I repent me :—stay. Whoe'er is rais'd
For worth he has not, he is tax'd, not prais'd.

This is ingenious and true ; but from a lord so
' worthless,' it hardly became the poet to withdraw the
alms of his panegyric. He should have left posterity
to do him justice, or have reposed on the magnanimity
of a silent disdain. Lord Salisbury was the famous
Robert Cecil, son of Burleigh. Ben Jonson had probably found his panegyric treated with neglect, perhaps
contempt ; and it was bold in him to return it ; but it
was proclaiming his own gratuitous flattery.

It has been objected to Ben Jonson's humours, and
with truth, that they are too exclusive of other qualities ;
that the characters are too much absorbed in the peculiarity, so as to become personifications of an abstrac-
tion. They have also, I think, an amount of turbulence
which hurts their entire reality ; gives them an air of
conscious falsehood and pretension, as if they were
rather acting the thing than being it. But this, as
before intimated, arose from the character of the
author, and his own wilful and flustered temperament.

If they are not thoroughly what they might be, or such as Shakespeare would have made them, they are admirable Jonsonian presentations, and overflowing with wit, fancy, and scholarship.

BEAUMONT AND FLETCHER

[Imagination and Fancy. Wit and Humour]

POETRY of the highest order and of the loveliest character abounds in Beaumont and Fletcher, but so mixed up with inconsistent, and too often, alas! revolting matter, that, apart from passages which do not enter into the plan of this book [1], I had no alternative but either to confine the extracts to the small number which ensue, or to bring together a heap of the smallest quotations,— two or three lines at a time. I thought to have got a good deal more out of the *Faithful Shepherdess*, which I had not read for many years; but on renewing my acquaintance with it, I found that the same unaccountable fascination with the evil times which had spoilt these two fine poets in their other plays, had followed its author, beyond what I had supposed, even into the regions of Arcadia.

Mr. Hazlitt, who loved sometimes to relieve his mistrust by a fit of pastoral worship, pronounces the *Faithful Shepherdess* to be 'a perpetual feast of nectar'd sweets, where no crude surfeit reigns.' I wish I could think so. There are both hot and cold dishes in it, which I would quit at any time to go and dine with the honest lovers of Allan Ramsay, whose *Gentle Shepherd*, though of another and far inferior class of poetry, I take upon the whole to be the completest pastoral drama that ever was written.

[1] *Imagination and Fancy* and *Wit and Humour* were two volumes of Selections for family reading, to which Leigh Hunt prefixed critical notes on each author.—ED.

It is a pity that Beaumont and Fletcher had not been born earlier, and in the neighbourhood of Shakespeare, and become his playmates. The wholesome company of the juvenile yeoman (like a greater Sandford) might have rectified the refined spirits of the young gentlemen, and saved their Hippocrene from becoming ditch-water. Even as it is, they seem different men when writing in their own persons, and following the taste of the town. Compare, for example, Beaumont's exquisite verses on *Melancholy* with any one of their plays; or Fletcher's lines entitled *An Honest Man's Fortune*, with the play of the same name, to which it is appended. The difference is so great, and indeed is discernible to such an equal degree in the poetry which startles you in the plays themselves (as if two different souls were writing one passage), that it appears unaccountable, except on some principle anterior to their town life, and to education itself. Little is known of either of their families, except that there were numerous poets in both; but Fletcher's father was that Dean of Peterborough (afterwards Bishop of London) who behaved with such unfeeling impertinence to the Queen of Scots in her last moments, and who is said (as became such a man) to have died of chagrin because Elizabeth was angry at his marrying a second time. Was poetry such a 'drug' with 'both their houses' that the friends lost their respect for it? or was Fletcher's mother some angel of a woman—some sequestered Miranda of the day—with whose spirit the 'earth' of the Dean her husband but ill accorded?

Every devout lover of poetry must have experienced the wish of Coleridge, that Beaumont and Fletcher had written 'poems instead of tragedies.' Imagine as voluminous a set of the one as they have given us of the other! It would have been to sequestered real life what Spenser was to the land of Faery,—a retreat beyond all groves and gardens, a region of medicinal sweets of thought and feeling. Nor would plenty of fable have been wanting. What a loss! And this,—their birthright with posterity—these extraordinary men sold for the mess of the loathsome pottage of the praise and profligacy of the court of James I.

But let us blush to find fault with them, even for such a descent from their height, while listening to their diviner moods.

.   .   .   .

Since expressing in the above volume [*Imagination and Fancy*] the surprise which everybody feels at the astounding mixture of licence and refinement displayed by these poets (for the grossness of earlier writers is but a simplicity compared with it), I have come to the conclusion that it was an excess of animal spirits, encouraged by the demands of the times, and the intoxication of applause. They were the sons of men of rank : they had been thrown upon the town in the heyday of their blood, probably with a turn for lavish expenditure ; they certainly wanted money as they advanced, and were glad to get it of gross audiences ; they had been taught to confound loyalty with servility, which subjected them to the dissolute influence of the court of James the First ; they came among the actors and the playwrights, with advantages of position, perhaps of education and accomplishments, superior to them all : their confidence, their wit, their enjoyment was unbounded ; everybody was glad to hear what the gay gentlemen had to say ; and forth they poured it accordingly, without stint or conscience. Beaumont died young ; but Fletcher, who went writing on, appears to have taken a still greater licence than his friend. The son of the bishop had probably been tempted to go farther out of bounds than the son of the judge ; for Dr. Fletcher was not such a bishop as Grindal or Jewel. The poet might have been taught hypocrisy by his father ; and, in despising it as he grew up, had gone to another extreme.

The reader of [these plays] will observe the difference between the fierce weight of the satire of *Volpone*, in which poison and suffocation are brought in to aggravate, and the gayer caricature of Beaumont and

Fletcher. It is equally founded on truth—equally wilful and superabundant in the treatment of it, but more light and happy. You feel that the writers enjoyed it with a gayer laugh. The pretended self-deception with which a coward lies to his own thoughts —the necessity for support which induces him to apply to others as cowardly as himself for the warrant of their good opinion, and the fascination of vanity which impels such men into the exposure which they fancy they have taken the subtlest steps to guard against— are most entertainingly set forth in the interview of Bassus with the two Bullies, and the subsequent catastrophe of all three in the hands of Bacurius. The nice balance of distinction and difference in which the bullies pretend to weigh the merits of kicks and beatings, and the impossibility which they affect of a shadow of imputation against their valours, or even of the power to assume it hypothetically, are masterly plays of wit of the first order.

MIDDLETON, DECKER, AND WEBSTER

[Imagination and Fancy]

WHEN about to speak of these and other extra-ordinary men of the days of Shakespeare, the Marstons, Rowleys, Massingers, Draytons, &c., including those noticed already, I wasted a good deal of time in trying to find out how it was that, possessing, as most of them did, such a pure vein of poetry, and sometimes saying as fine things as himself, they wrote so much that is not worth reading, sometimes not fit to be read. I might have considered that, either from self-love, or necessity, or both, too much writing is the fault of all ages and of every author. Even Homer, says Horace, sometimes nods. How many odes might not Horace himself have spared us! How many of his latter books, Virgil! What theology, Dante and Milton! What romances, Cervantes! What comedies, Ariosto! What tragedies, Dryden ! What heaps of words, Chaucer and Spenser ! What *Iliads*, Pope !

Shakespeare's contemporaries, however, appear to have been a singularly careless race of men, compared with himself. Could they have been rendered so by that very superiority of birth and education which threw them upon the town, in the first instance, with greater confidence, his humbler prospects rendering him more cautious ? Or did their excess of wit and fancy require a counter-perfection of judgement, such as he only possessed ? Chapman and Drayton, though their pens were among the profusest and most unequal, seem to have been prudent men in conduct ; so in all probability were Ford and Webster ; but none of these had the animal spirits of the others. Shakespeare had animal spirits, wit, fancy, judgement, prudence in money matters, understanding like Bacon, feeling like Chaucer, mirth like Rabelais, dignity like Milton ! What a man ! Has anybody discovered the reason why he never noticed a living contemporary, and but one who was dead ? and this, too, in an age of great men, and when they were in the habit of acknowledging the pretensions of one another. It could not have been jealousy, or formality, or inability to perceive merits which his own included ; and one can almost as little believe it possible to have been owing to a fear of disconcerting his aristocratic friends, for they too were among the eulogizers : neither can it be attributed to his having so mooted all points, as to end in caring for none ; for in so great and wise a nature, *good* nature must surely survive everything, both as a pleasure and a duty. I have made up my mind to think that his theatrical *managership* was the cause. It naturally produced a dislike of pronouncing judgements and incurring responsibilities. And yet he was not always a manager ; nor were all his literary friends playwrights. I think it probable, from the style, that he wrote the sonnet in which Spenser is eulogized :—

If music and sweet poetry agree, &c.,

but this is doubtful; and Spenser was not one of his dramatic fellows. Did he see too many faults in them *all* to praise them!! Certainly the one great difference between him and them, next to superiority of genius, is the prevailing relevancy of all he wrote; its freedom, however superabundant, from inconsistency and caprice. But could he find nothing to praise? Nothing in the whole contemporary drama? Nothing in all the effusions of his friends and brother clubbists of the 'Mermaid' and the 'Triple Tun'?

I take Webster and Decker to have been the two greatest of the Shakespeare men, for unstudied genius, next after Beaumont and Fletcher; and in some respects they surpassed them. Beaumont and Fletcher have no such terror as Webster, nor any such piece of hearty, good, affecting human clay as Decker's 'Old Signior Orlando Friscobaldo.' Is there any such man even in Shakespeare?—any such exaltation of that most delightful of all things, *bonhomie*? Webster sometimes overdoes his terror; nay, often. He not only riots, he debauches in it; and Decker, full of heart and delicacy as he is, and qualified to teach refinement to the refined, condescends to an astounding coarseness. Beaumont and Fletcher's good company saved them from that, in words. In spirit they are full of it. But Decker never mixes up (at least not as far as I can remember) any such revolting and impossible contradictions in the same character as they do. Neither does he bring a doubt on his virtues by exaggerating them. He believes heartily in what he does believe, and you love him in consequence. It was he that wrote that character, the piety of which has been pronounced equal to its boldness:—

> The best of men
> That e'er wore earth about him was a sufferer;
> A soft, meek, patient, humble, tranquil spirit;
> The first true gentleman that ever breath'd.

His universal sympathy enabled him to strike out that audacious and happy simile, 'untameable as *flies*,' which Homer would have admired, though it is fit to make poetasters shudder. The poetaster, had Decker offered to make him a present of it, would have been afraid of being taken for a fly himself. Images are either grand in themselves, or for the thought and feeling that accompany them. This has all the greatness of Nature's 'equal eye.' You may see how truly Decker felt it to be of this kind, by the company in which he has placed it ; and there is a consummation of propriety in its wildness, for he is speaking of lunatics :—

> There are of mad men, as there are of tame,
> All humour'd not alike. We have here some
> So apish and fantastic, will play with a feather ;
> And though 't would grieve a soul to see God's image
> So blemish'd and defaced, yet do they act
> Such antic and such pretty lunacies,
> That, spite of sorrow, they will make you smile.
> Others again we have *like hungry lions,*
> *Fierce as wild bulls,* untameable as flies.

Middleton partakes of the poetry and sweetness of Decker, but not to the same height : and he talks more at random. You hardly know what to make of the dialogue or stories of some of his plays. But he has more fancy : and there is one character of his (De Flores in the *Changeling*) which, for effect at once tragical, probable, and poetical, surpasses anything I know of in the drama of domestic life. Middleton has the honour of having furnished part of the witch poetry to Macbeth, and of being conjoined with it also in the powerful and beautiful music of Locke.

BUTLER

[*Wit and Humour*]

BUTLER is the wittiest of English poets, and at the same time he is one of the most learned, and what is more, one of the wisest. His *Hudibras*, though naturally the most popular of his works from its size, subject, and witty excess, was an accident of birth and party compared with his Miscellaneous Poems ; yet both abound in thoughts as great and deep as the surface is sparkling ; and his genius altogether, having the additional recommendation of verse, might have given him a fame greater than Rabelais, had his animal spirits been equal to the rest of his qualifications for a universalist. At the same time, though not abounding in poetic sensibility, he was not without it. He is author of the touching simile,

> *True as the dial to the sun,*
> *Although it be not shin'd upon.*

The following is as elegant as anything in Lovelace or Waller :—

> —*What security's too strong*
> *To guard that gentle heart from wrong,*
> *That to its friend is glad to pass*
> *Itself away, and all it has,*
> *And like an anchorite, gives over*
> *This world, for the heaven of a lover ?*

And *this*, if read with the seriousness and singleness of feeling that become it, is, I think, a comparison full of as much grandeur as cordiality,—

> *Like Indian widows, gone to bed*
> *In flaming curtains to the dead.*

You would sooner have looked for it in one of Marvel's poems, than in *Hudibras*.

Butler has little humour. His two heroes, Hudibras and Ralph, are not so much humorists as pedants. They are as little like their prototypes, Don Quixote and Sancho, as two dreary puppets are unlike excesses of humanity. They are not even consistent with their other prototypes, the Puritans, or with themselves, for they are dull fellows, unaccountably gifted with the author's wit. In this respect, and as a narrative, the poem is a failure. Nobody ever thinks of the story, except to wonder at its inefficiency; or of Hudibras himself, except as described at his outset. He is nothing but a ludicrous figure. But considered as a banter issuing from the author's own lips, on the wrong side of Puritanism, and indeed on all the pedantic and hypocritical abuses of human reason, the whole production is a marvellous compound of wit, learning, and felicitous execution. The wit is pure and incessant; the learning as quaint and out-of-the-way as the subject; the very rhymes are echoing scourges, made of the peremptory and the incongruous. This is one of the reasons why the rhymes have been so much admired. They are laughable, not merely in themselves, but from the masterly will and violence with which they are made to correspond to the absurdities they lash. The most extraordinary licence is assumed as a matter of course; the accentuation jerked out of its place with all the indifference and effrontery of a reason ' sufficing unto itself.' The poem is so peculiar in this respect, the laughing delight of the reader so well founded, and the passages so sure to be accompanied with a full measure of wit and knowledge, that I have retained its best rhymes throughout, and thus brought them together for the first time.

Butler, like the great wit of the opposite party, Marvel, was an honest man, fonder of his books than of worldly success, and superior to party itself in regard to final principles. He wrote a satire on the follies and vices of the court, which is most likely the reason why it is doubted whether he ever got anything by *Hudibras*; and he was so little prejudiced in favour of the scholarship he possessed, that he vindicated the born poet above the poet of books, and would not have Shakespeare tried by a Grecian standard.

CONGREVE

[*The Town*]

CONGREVE'S bequest created a good deal of gossip. Curll, the principal scandal-monger of those times, got up a catch-penny life of him, professing to be written by 'Charles Wilson, Esq.,' but supposed to be the work of Oldmixon. There is no relying upon Charles Wilson; but, from internal evidence, we may take his word occasionally; and we may believe him when he says that the duchess and her friends were alarmed at the threatened book. The picture which he draws of her manner has also an air like a woman of quality. She had demanded a sight of the documents on which the book was founded; and being refused, asked what authority they had, and what pieces contained in it were genuine. 'Upon being civilly told there would be found several essays, letters, and characters of that gentleman's writing,' says Mr. Wilson, 'she, with a most affected, extraordinary, dramatic drawl, cried out, "Not one single sheet of paper, I dare to swear."' [1] Mr. Wilson's own grand air in return is very amusing. He speaks of Arbuthnot's coming with 'expresses,' probably to Curll's; and adds, that if he be dispatched with any more, 'he may, if he please, come to me, who am as easily to be found in Great Russell Street, Bloomsbury, *when in town*, as he is in Burlington Gardens.—Cha. Wilson.'

Mr. Wilson's book opens with a copy of the will, in which £500 are left among the Congreves; about £500 more to the friends and domestics, &c. (not omitting £200 to Mrs. Bracegirdle); and all the rest (with power to

---

[1] *Memoirs of the Life, Writings, &c., of William Congreve, Esq.,* 1730, p. xi. Curll discreetly omits his name in the title-page. [On reconsidering the interview (though we have no longer the book by us, and therefore speak from memory) we are doubtful whether the lady was not Mrs. Bracegirdle, instead of the duchess.]

annul or increase the complimentary part of the legacies)
to the Duchess of Marlborough. We know not that
anybody could have brought forward grounds for
objecting to this will, had the duchess been poor herself ;
for his relations may or may not have had claims upon
him—relations, as such, not being of necessity friends,
though it is generally fit that they should partake of
the family prosperity. We except, of course, a man's
immediate kindred, particularly those whom he has
brought into the world. But here was a woman, rolling
in wealth, and relatives neither entirely forgotten, nor
yet, it seems, properly assisted. The bequest must,
therefore, either have been a mere piece of vanity, or
the consequence of habitual subjection to a woman's
humours. The duchess was not ungrateful to his
memory. She raised him, as we have seen, a monument ; and it is related in Cibber's *Lives of the Poets*,
we know not on what authority, that she missed his
company so much, as to cause ' an image of him to be
placed every day on her toilet-table, to which she
would talk as to the living Mr. Congreve, with all the
freedom of the most *polite* and *unreserved* conversation.'
There is something very ludicrous in this way of putting
a case, which might otherwise be affecting. It is as if
there had been a sort of polite mania on both sides.

Congreve's plays are exquisite of their kind, and the
excessive heartlessness and duplicity of some of his characters are not to be taken without allowance for the *ugly
ideal*. There is something not natural, both in his
characters and wit ; and we read him rather to see
how entertaining he can make his superfine ladies and
gentlemen, and what a pack of sensual busybodies they
are, like insects over a pool, than from any true sense
of them as ' men and women.' As a companion he
must have been exquisite to a woman of fashion. We
can believe that the duchess, in ignorance of any tragic
emotion but what was mixed with his loss, would really
talk with a waxen image of him in a peruke, and think
the universe contained nothing better. It was carrying
wit and politeness beyond the grave. Queen Constance

in Shakespeare makes grief put on the pretty looks of her lost child : the Duchess of Marlborough made it put on a wig and jaunty air, such as she had given her friend in his monument in Westminster Abbey. No criticism on his plays could be more perfect. Congreve's serious poetry is a refreshment, from its extreme insipidity and common-place. Everybody is innocent in some corner of the mind, and has faith in something. Congreve had no faith in his fellow creatures, but he had a scholar's (not a poet's) belief in nymphs and weeping fauns ; and he wrote elegies full of them, upon queens and marquisses. If it be true that he wrote the character of Aspasia (Lady Elizabeth Hastings), in the *Tatler* (No. 42), he had indeed faith in something better ; for in that paper is not only given an admiring account of a person of very exalted excellence, but the author has said of her one of the finest things that a sincere heart could utter ; namely, that ' to love her was a liberal education.' We cannot help thinking, however, that the generous and trusting hand of Steele is very visible throughout this portrait ; and in the touch just mentioned in particular.

SMOLLETT

[Table-Talk]

THOUGH Smollett sometimes vexes us with the malicious boy's-play of his heroes, and sometimes disgusts with his coarseness, he is still the Smollett whom now, as in one's boyhood, it is impossible not to heartily laugh with. He is an accomplished writer, and a masterly observer, and may be called the finest of caricaturists. His caricatures are always substantially true : it is only the complexional vehemence of his gusto that leads him to toss them up as he does, and tumble them on our plates. Then as to the objections against his morality, nobody will be hurt by it.

The delicate and sentimental will look on the whole matter as a joke; the accessories of the characters will deter *them*: while readers of a coarser taste, for whom their friends might fear most, because they are most likely to be conversant with the scenes described, are, in our opinion, to be seriously benefited by the perusal; for it will show them that heroes of their description are expected to have virtues as well as faults, and that they seldom get anything by being positively disagreeable or bad. Our author's lovers, it must be owned, are not of the most sentimental or flattering description. One of their common modes of paying their court, even to those they best love and esteem, is by writing lampoons on other women! Smollett had a strong spice of pride and malice in him (greatly owing, we doubt not, to some scenes of unjust treatment he witnessed in early youth), which he imparts to his heroes; all of whom, probably, are caricatures of himself, as Fielding's brawny, good-natured, idle fellows are of *him*. There is no serious evil intention, however. It is all out of resentment of some evil, real or imaginary; or is made up of pure animal spirit and the love of venting a complexional sense of power. It is energy, humour, and movement, not particularly amiable, but clever, entertaining, and interesting, and without an atom of hypocrisy in it. No man will learn to be shabby by reading Smollett's writings.

SWIFT

[Wit and Humour]

FOR the qualities of sheer wit and humour, Swift had no superior, ancient or modern. He had not the poetry of Aristophanes, or the animal spirits of Rabelais; he was not so incessantly witty as Butler; nor did he possess the delicacy of Addison, or the good nature of Steele or Fielding, or the pathos and depth of Sterne: but his wit was perfect, as such; a sheer meeting of the extremes of difference and likeness; and his knowledge of character was unbounded. He knew the humour of great and small, from the king down to the cook-maid. Unfortunately, he was not a healthy man; his entrance into the Church put him into a false position; mysterious circumstances in his personal history conspired with worldly disappointment to aggravate it; and that hypochondriacal insight into things, which might have taught him a doubt of his conclusions and the wisdom of patience, ended in making him the victim of a diseased blood and angry passions. Probably there was something morbid even in his excessive coarseness. Most of his contemporaries were coarse, but not so outrageously as he.

When Swift, however, was at his best, who was so lively, so entertaining, so original? He has been said to be indebted to this and that classic, and this and that Frenchman; to Lucian, to Rabelais, and to Cyrano de Bergerac; but though he was acquainted with all these writers, their thoughts had been evidently thought by himself; their quaint fancies of things had passed through his own mind; and they ended in results quite masterly, and his own. A great fanciful wit like his wanted no helps to the discovery of Brobdingnag and Laputa. The Big and Little Endians were close to him every day, at court and at church.

Swift took his principal measure from Butler, and he emulated his rhymes; yet his manner is his own.

There is a mixture of care and precision in it, announcing at once power and fastidiousness, like Mr. Dean going with his verger before him, in flowing gown and five-times washed face, with his nails pared to the quick. His long irregular prose verses, with rhymes at the end, are an invention of his own ; and a similar mixture is discernible even in those, not excepting a feeling of musical proportion. Swift had more music in him than he loved to let ' fiddlers ' suppose ; and throughout all his writings there may be observed a jealous sense of power, modifying the most familiar of his impulses.

After all, however, Swift's verse, compared with Pope's or with Butler's, is but a kind of smart prose. It wants their pregnancy of expression. His greatest works are *Gulliver's Travels* and the *Tale of a Tub.*

POPE

[*Wit and Humour*]

BESIDES being an admirable wit and satirist, and a man of the most exquisite good sense, Pope was a true poet ; and though in all probability his entire nature could never have made him a great one (since the whole man contributes to form the genius, and the very weakness of his organization was in the way of it), yet in a different age the boy who wrote the beautiful verses

Blest be the man whose wish and care

would have turned out, I think, a greater poet than he was. He had more sensibility, thought, and fancy, than was necessary for the purposes of his school ; and he led a sequestered life with his books and his grotto, caring little for the manners he drew, and capable of higher impulses than had been given him by the wits of the time of Charles the Second. It was unlucky for him (if indeed it did not produce a lucky variety for the reading world) that Dryden came immediately before him. Dryden, a robuster nature, was just great enough to mislead Pope; and French ascendancy completed his fate. Perhaps, after all, nothing better than such a honey and such a sting as this exquisite writer developed, could have been got out of his little delicate pungent nature; and we have every reason to be grateful for what they have done for us. Hundreds of greater pretensions in poetry have not attained to half his fame, nor did they deserve it; for they did not take half his pains. Perhaps they were unable to take them, for want of as good a balance of qualities. Success is generally commensurate with its grounds.

Pope, though a genius of a less masculine order than Dryden, and not possessed of his numbers or his impulsiveness, had more delicacy and fancy, has left more passages that have become proverbial, and was less confined to the region of matter of fact. Dryden never soared above earth, however nobly he walked it. The little fragile creature had wings; and he could expand them at will, and ascend, if to no great imaginative height, yet to charming fairy circles just above those of the world about him, disclosing enchanting visions at the top of drawing-rooms, and enabling us to see the spirits that wait on coffee-cups and hoop-petticoats.

RICHARDSON

[The Town]

IN a house, 'in the centre of Salisbury Square or Salisbury Court, as it was then called,' Richardson spent the greater part of his town life, and wrote his earliest work, *Pamela*. Probably a good part of all his works were composed there, as well as at Fulham, for the pen was never out of his hand. He removed from this house in 1755, after he had written all his works; and taking eight old tenements in the same quarter, pulled them down, and built a large and commodious range of warehouses and printing offices. 'The dwelling-house,' says Mrs. Barbauld, 'was neither so large nor

so airy as the one he quitted, and therefore the reader
will not be so ready, probably, as Mr. Richardson seems
to have been, in accusing his wife of perverseness in not
liking the new habitation as well as the old.'[1] This
was the second Mrs. Richardson. He calls her in other
places his ' worthy-hearted wife ' ; but complains that
she used to get her way by seeming to submit, and then
returning to the point, when the heat of objection
was over. She was a formal woman. His own manners
were strict and formal with regard to his family, probably because he had formed his notions of life from old
books, and also because he did not well know how to
begin to do otherwise (for he was naturally bashful), and
so the habit continued through life. His daughters
addressed him in their letters by the title of ' Honoured
Sir,' and are always designating themselves as ' ever
dutiful.' Sedentary living, eternal writing, and perhaps
that indulgence in the table, which, however moderate,
affects a sedentary man twenty times as much as an
active one, conspired to hurt his temper (for we may
see by his picture that he grew fat, and his philosophy
was in no respect as profound as he thought it) ; but
he was a most kind-hearted generous man ; kept his
pocket full of plums for children, like another Mr.
Burchell ; gave a great deal of money away in charity,
very handsomely too ; and was so fond of inviting
friends to stay with him, that when they were ill, he
and his family must needs have them to be nursed.
Several actually died at his house at Fulham, as at an
hospital for sick friends.

It is a fact not generally known (none of his biographers seem to have known it) that Richardson was
the son of a joiner, received what education he had
(which was very little, and did not go beyond English),
at Christ's Hospital.[2] It may be wondered how he
could come no better taught from a school which had

---

[1] *Correspondence of Samuel Richardson*, &c., by Anna
Letitia Barbauld, vol. i. p. 97.

[2] Our authority (one of the highest in this way) is Mr.

sent forth so many good scholars; but in his time, and indeed till very lately, that foundation was divided into several schools, none of which partook of the lessons of the others; and Richardson, agreeably to his father's intention of bringing him up to trade, was most probably confined to the writing-school, where all that was taught was writing and arithmetic. It was most likely here that he intimated his future career, first by writing a letter, at eleven years of age, to a censorious woman of fifty, who pretended a zeal for religion; and afterwards, at thirteen, by composing love-letters to their sweethearts for three young women in the neighbourhood, who made him their confidant. To these and others he also used to read books, their mothers being of the party; and they encouraged him to make remarks; which is exactly the sort of life he led with Mrs. Chapone, Miss Fielding, and others, when in the height of his celebrity. 'One of the young women,' he informs us, 'highly gratified with her lover's fervour, and vows of everlasting love, has said, when I have asked her direction, "I cannot tell you what to write, but (her heart on her lips) you cannot write too kindly"; all her fear was that she should incur a slight for her kindness.' This passage, with its pretty breathless parenthesis, is in the style of his books. If the writers among his female coterie in after-life owed their inspiration to him, he only returned to them what they had done for himself. Women seem to have been always about him, both in town and country; which made Mrs. Barbauld say, very agreeably, that he ' lived in a kind of flower-garden of ladies.' This has been grudged him, and thought effeminate; but we must make allowance for early circumstances, and recollect what the garden produced for us. Richardson did not pretend to be able to do without female society. Perhaps, however, they did not quiet his sensibility so much as they charmed it. We think, in his Correspondence, a tendency is observable to indulge

Nichols, in his *Literary Anecdotes of the Eighteenth Century*. vol. iv. p. 579.

in fancies, not always so paternal as they agree to call
them ; though doubtless all was said in honour, and
the ladies never found reason to diminish their reverence. A great deal has been said of his vanity and the
weakness of it. Vain he undoubtedly was, and vanity
is no strength ; but it is worth bearing in mind, that a
man is often saved from vanity, not because he is
stronger than another, but because he is less amiable,
and did not begin, as Richardson did, with being a
favourite so early. Few men are surrounded, as he
was, from his very childhood, with females ; and few
people think so well of their species or with so much
reason. In all probability, too, he was handsome when
young, which is another excuse for him. His vanity
is more easily excused than his genius accounted for
considering the way in which he lived. The tone of
Lovelace's manners and language, which has created
so much surprise in an author who was a city printer,[1]
and passed his life among a few friends between Fleet
Street and a suburb, was caught, probably, not merely
from Cibber, but from the famous profligate Duke of
Wharton, with whom he became acquainted in the
course of his business. But the unwearied vivacity
with which he has supported it is wonderful. His
pathos is more easily accounted for by his nerves, which
for many years were in a constant state of excitement,
particularly towards the close of his life, which terminated in 1761, at the age of seventy-two, with the death
most common to sedentary men of letters, a stroke of
apoplexy.[2] He was latterly unable to lift a glass of
wine to his mouth without assistance.

[1] 'Richardson, with all his moral punctilio, and his in-
culcations to young ladies to keep at home, was a great
walker in public places, and observer of pretty ankles.
He says that, in looking at a lady, he always began " with
the feet." This seems odd in a worshipper of Clarissa
Harlowe. It helps, however, to account for Lovelace.'—
Old Court Suburb, p. 235.

[2] ——Apoplexy cramm'd intemperance knocks
Down to the ground at once, as butcher felleth ox ;—

At Fulham and Parson's Green (at which latter place he lived for the last five or six years), Richardson used to sit with his guests about him, in a parlour or summer-house, reading, or communicating his manuscripts as he wrote them. The ladies made their remarks; and alterations or vindications ensued. His characters, agreeably to what we feel when we read of them (for we know them all as intimately as if we occupied a room in their house), interested his acquaintances so far that they sympathized with them as if they were real; and it is well known that one of his correspondents, Lady Bradshaigh, implored him to reform Lovelace, in order 'to save a soul.' In Salisbury Court, Richardson, of course, had the same visitors about him; but the 'flower-garden' is not talked of so much there as at Fulham. In the evening the ladies read and worked by themselves, and Richardson retired to his study; a most pernicious habit for a man of his bad nerves. He should have written early in the morning, taken good exercise in the day, and amused himself in the evening. When he walked in town it was in the park, where he describes himself (to a fair correspondent who wished to have an interview with him, and who recognized him from the description) as ' short, rather plump, about five feet five inches, fair wig, one hand generally in his bosom, the other a cane in it, which he leans upon under the skirts of his coat, that it may imperceptibly serve him as a support when attacked by

says Thomson, in his *Castle of Indolence*. It was the death which the good-natured, indolent poet probably expected for himself, and which he would have had, if a cold and fever had not interfered; for there is an apoplexy of the head alone, as well as of the whole body; and men of letters who either exercise little, or work overmuch, seem almost sure to die of it, or of palsy; which is a disease analogous. It is the last stroke, given in the kind resentment of nature, to the brains which should have known better than bring themselves to such a pass. In the biography of Italian literati, ' Mori d' apoplessia '—(he died of apoplexy)—is a common verdict.

sudden tremors or dizziness, of a light brown complexion, teeth not yet failing.' 'What follows,' observes Mrs. Barbauld, ' is very descriptive of the struggle in his character, between innate bashfulness and a turn for observation ' :—' Looking directly forwards, as passengers would imagine, but observing all that stirs on either hand of him, without moving his short neck ; a regular even pace, stealing away ground rather than seeming to rid it ; a grey eye, too often overclouded by mistiness from the head, by chance lively, very lively if he sees any he loves ; if he approaches a lady, his eye is never fixed first on her face, but on her feet, and rears it up by degrees, seeming to set her down as so and so.' [1]

Latterly Richardson attended little to business. He used even to give his orders to his workmen in writing ; a practice which Sir John Hawkins is inclined to attribute to stateliness and bad temper, but for which Mrs. Barbauld finds a better reason in his bad nerves. His principal foreman also was deaf, as the knight himself acknowledges. Richardson encouraged his men to be industrious, sometimes by putting half-a-crown among the types as a prize to him who came first in the morning, at others by sending fruit for the same purpose from the country. Agreeably to his natural bashfulness, he was apt to be reserved with strangers. Sir John Hawkins tells us, that he once happened to get into the Fulham stage when Richardson was in it (most likely he got in on purpose) ; and he endeavoured to bring the novelist into conversation, but could not succeed, and was vexed at it. But Sir John was one of that numerous class of persons who, for reasons better known to others than to themselves,

Deemen gladly to the badder end,

as the old poet says ; and Richardson probably knew this pragmatical person, and did not want his acquaintance.

Johnson was among the visitors of Richardson in Salisbury Court. He confessed to Boswell, that al-

---

[1] *Correspondence*, as above, vol. i. p. 177.

though he had never much sought after anybody,
Richardson was an exception. He had so much respect
for him, that he took part with him in a preposterous
undervaluing of Fielding, whom he described in the
comparison as a mere writer of manners, and sometimes
as hardly any writer at all. And yet he told Boswell
that he had read his *Amelia* through 'without stopping':
and according to Mrs. Piozzi she was his favourite
heroine. In the comparison of Richardson with
Fielding, he was in the habit of opposing the nature of
one to the manners of the other; but Fielding's manners
are only superadded to his nature, not opposed to it,
which makes all the difference. As to Richardson, he
was so far gone upon this point, in a mixture of pique
and want of sympathy, that he said, if he had not known
who Fielding was, ' he should have taken him for an
ostler.' Fielding, it is true, must have vexed him
greatly by detecting the pettiness in the character of
Pamela. Richardson, as a romancer, did not like to
have the truth forced upon him, and thus was inclined
to see nothing but vulgarity in the novelist. This must
have been unpleasant to the Misses Fielding, the sisters,
who were among the most intimate of Richardson's
friends. Another of our author's visitors was Hogarth.
It must not be forgotten that Richardson was kind to
Johnson in money matters; and to use Mrs. Barbauld's
phrase, had once ' the honour ' to be bail for him.

We conclude our notice, which, on the subject of so
original a man, has naturally beguiled us into some
length, with an interesting account of his manners and
way of life, communicated by one of his female
friends to Mrs. Barbauld. ' My first recollection of
him,' says she, ' was in his house in the centre of Salisbury Square, or Salisbury Court as it was then called ;
and of being admitted as a playful child into his study,
where I have often seen Dr. Young and others; and where
I was generally caressed and rewarded with biscuits or
bonbons of some kind or other ; and sometimes with
books, for which he, and some more of my friends,
kindly encouraged a taste, even at that early age, which

has adhered to me all my long life, and continues to be the solace of many a painful hour. I recollect that he used to drop in at my father's, for we lived nearly opposite, late in the evening to supper; when, as he would say, he had worked as long as his eyes and nerves would let him, and was come to relax with a little friendly and domestic chat. I even then used to creep to his knee and hang upon his words, for my whole family doted on him; and once, I recollect that at one of these evening visits, probably about the year 1753, I was standing by his knee when my mother's maid came to summon me to bed; upon which, being unwilling to part from him and manifesting some reluctance, he begged I might be permitted to stay a little longer; and, on my mother's objecting that the servant would be wanted to wait at supper (for, in those days of friendly intercourse and *real* hospitality, a decent maid-servant was the only attendant at *his own* and many creditable tables, where, nevertheless, much company was received), Mr. Richardson said, " I am sure Miss P. is now so much a woman, that she does not want any one to attend her to bed, but will conduct herself with so much propriety, and put out her own candle so carefully, that she may henceforward be indulged with remaining with us till supper is served.' This hint and the confidence it implied, had such a good effect upon me that I believe I never required the attendance of a servant afterwards while my mother lived; and by such sort of ingenious and gentle devices did he use to encourage and draw in young people to do what was right. I also well remember the happy days I passed at his house at North End; sometimes with my mother, but often for weeks without her, domesticated as one of his own children. He used to pass the greatest part of the week in town; but when he came down, he used to like to have his family flock around him, when we all first asked and received his blessing, together with some small boon from his paternal kindness and attention, for he seldom met us empty-handed, and was by nature most generous and liberal.'

ALLAN RAMSAY

[Jar of Honey from Mount Hybla, 1848]

ALLAN RAMSAY is the prince of the homely pastoral drama. Burns wrote in this class of poetry at no such length as Ramsay; but he was pastoral poetry itself, in the shape of an actual, glorious peasant, vigorous as if Homer had written him, and tender as generous strength, or as memories of the grave. Ramsay and he have helped Scotland for ever to take pride in its heather, and its braes, and its bonny rivers, and be ashamed of no beauty or honest truth, in high estate or in low—an incalculable blessing. Ramsay, to be sure, with all his genius, and though he wrote an entire and excellent dramatic pastoral, in five legitimate acts, is but a small part of Burns—is but a field in a corner compared with the whole Scots pastoral region. He has none of Burns's pathos; none of his grandeur; none of his burning energy; none of his craving after universal good. How universal is Burns! What mirth in his cups! What softness in his tears! What sympathy in his very satire! What manhood in everything! If Theocritus, the inventor of a loving and affectionate Polyphemus, could have foreseen the verses on the 'Mouse' and the 'Daisy' turned up with the plough, the 'Tam o' Shanter,' ' O Willie brew'd a peck o' maut,' ' Ye banks and braes o' bonnie Doon,' &c. (not to mention a hundred others, which have less to do with our subject), tears of admiration would have rushed into his eyes.

COLERIDGE

[Imagination and Fancy. Autobiography]

COLERIDGE lived in the most extraordinary and agitated period of modern history ; and to a certain extent he was so mixed up with its controversies, that he was at one time taken for nothing but an apostate republican, and at another for a dreaming theosophist. The truth is, that both his politics and theosophy were at the mercy of a discursive genius, intellectually bold but educationally timid, which, anxious, or rather willing, to bring conviction and speculation together, mooting all points as it went, and throwing the subtlest glancing lights on many, ended in satisfying nobody, and concluding nothing. Charles Lamb said of him, that he had 'the art of making the unintelligible appear intelligible.' He was the finest dreamer, the most eloquent talker, and the most original thinker of his day ; but for want of complexional energy, did nothing with all the vast *prose* part of his mind but help the Germans to give a subtler tone to criticism, and sow a few valuable seeds of thought in minds worthy to receive them. Nine-tenths of his theology would apply equally well to their own creeds in the mouths of a Brahmin or a Mussulman.

His poetry is another matter. It is so beautiful, and was so quietly content with its beauty, making no call on the critics, and receiving hardly any notice, that people are but now beginning to awake to a full sense of its merits. Of pure poetry, strictly so called, that is to say, consisting of nothing but its essential self, without conventional and perishing helps, he was the greatest master of his time. If you could see it in a phial, like a distillation of roses (taking it, I mean, at its best), it would be found without a speck. The poet is happy with so good a gift, and the reader is ' happy in his happiness.' Yet so little, sometimes, are a man's contemporaries and personal acquaintances able or disposed to estimate him properly, that while Coleridge, unlike Shakespeare, lavished praises on his poetic friends, he had all the merit of the generosity to himself ; and even Hazlitt, owing perhaps to causes of political alienation, could see nothing to admire in the exquisite poem of *Christabel*, but the description of the quarrel between the friends ! After speaking, too, of the *Ancient Mariner* as the only one of his poems that he could point out to any one as giving an adequate idea of his great natural powers, he adds, ' It is High German, however, and in it he seems to conceive of poetry but as a drunken dream, reckless, careless, and heedless of past, present, and to come.' This is said of a poem, with which fault has been found for the exceeding conscientiousness of its moral ! O ye critics, the best of ye, what havoc does personal difference play with your judgements ! It was not Mr. Hazlitt's only or most unwarrantable censure, or one which friendship found hardest to forgive. But peace, and honour too, be with his memory ! If he was a splenetic and sometimes jealous man, he was a disinterested politician and an admirable critic : and lucky were those whose natures gave them the right and the power to pardon him.

Coleridge, though a born poet, was in his style and general musical feeling the disciple partly of Spenser, and partly of the fine old English ballad-writers in the collection of Bishop Percy. But if he could not improve on them in some things, how he did in others, especially in the art of being thoroughly musical ! Of all our writers of the briefer narrative poetry, Coleridge is the finest since Chaucer ; and assuredly he is the sweetest of all our poets. Waller's music is but a court-flourish in comparison ; and though Beaumont and Fletcher, Collins, Gray, Keats, Shelley, and others, have several as sweet passages, and Spenser is in a certain sense musical throughout, yet no man has written whole poems, of equal length, so perfect in the sentiment of music, so varied with it, and yet leaving on the ear so unbroken and single an effect.

> A damsel with a dulcimer
> In a vision once I saw ;
> It was an Abyssinian maid,
> And on her dulcimer she play'd,
> Singing of Mount Abora.

That is but one note of music ever sweet, yet never cloying.

Coleridge was fat, and began to lament, in very delightful verses, that he was getting infirm. There was no old age in his verses. I heard him one day, under the Grove at Highgate, repeat one of his melodious lamentations, as he walked up and down, his voice undulating in a stream of music, and his regrets of youth sparkling with visions ever young. At the same time, he did me the honour to show me that he did not think so ill of all modern liberalism as some might suppose, denouncing the pretensions of the money-getting in a style which I should hardly venture upon, and never could equal ; and asking with a triumphant eloquence what chastity itself were worth, if it were a casket, not to keep love in, but hate, and strife, and worldliness ? On the same occasion, he built up a metaphor out of a flower, in a style surpassing the famous passage in Milton ; deducing it from its root in religious mystery, and carrying it up into the bright, consummate flower, 'the bridal chamber of reproductiveness.' Of all 'the Muse's mysteries,' he was as great a high-priest as Spenser ; and Spenser himself might have gone to Highgate to hear him talk, and thank him for his *Ancient Mariner*. His voice did not always sound very sincere ; but perhaps the humble and deprecating tone of it, on those occasions, was out of consideration for the infirmities of his hearers, rather than produced by his own. He recited his *Kubla Khan* one morning to Lord Byron, in his lordship's house in Piccadilly, when I happened to be in another room.

I remember the other's coming away from him, highly struck with his poem, and saying how wonderfully he talked. This was the impression of everybody who heard him.

WORDSWORTH

[Autobiography]

MR. WORDSWORTH, whom Mr. Hazlitt designated as one that would have had the wide circle of his humanities made still wider, and a good deal more pleasant, by dividing a little more of his time between his lakes in Westmoreland and the hotels of the metropolis, had a dignified manner, with a deep and roughish but not unpleasing voice, and an exalted mode of speaking. He had a habit of keeping his left hand in the bosom of his waistcoat ; and in this attitude, except when he turned round to take one of the subjects of his criticism from the shelves (for his contemporaries were there also), he sat dealing forth his eloquent but hardly catholic judgements. In his 'father's house' there were not 'many mansions.' He was as sceptical on the merits of all kinds of poetry but one, as Richardson was on those of the novels of Fielding.

Under the study in which my visitor and I were sitting was an archway, leading to a nursery-ground ; a cart happened to go through it while I was inquiring whether he would take any refreshment ; and he uttered, in so lofty a voice, the words, 'Anything which is *going forward*,' that I felt inclined to ask him whether he would take a piece of the cart. Lamb would certainly have done it. But this was a levity which would neither have been so proper on my part, after so short an acquaintance, nor very intelligible, perhaps, in any sense of the word, to the serious poet. There are good-humoured warrants for smiling, which lie deeper even than Mr. Wordsworth's thoughts for tears.

I did not see this distinguished person again till

thirty years afterwards; when, I should venture to say, his manner was greatly superior to what it was in the former instance; indeed, quite natural and noble, with a cheerful air of animal as well as spiritual confidence; a gallant bearing, curiously reminding me of the Duke of Wellington, as I saw him walking some eighteen years ago by a lady's side, with no unbecoming oblivion of his time of life. I observed, also, that the poet no longer committed himself in scornful criticisms, or, indeed, in any criticisms whatever, at least as far as I knew. He had found out that he could, at least, afford to be silent. Indeed, he spoke very little of anything. The conversation turned upon Milton, and I fancied I had opened a subject that would have 'brought him out,' by remarking, that the most diabolical thing in all *Paradise Lost* was a feeling attributed to the angels. 'Aye!' said Mr. Wordsworth, and inquired what it was. I said it was the passage in which the angels, when they observed Satan journeying through the empyrean, let down a set of steps out of heaven, on purpose to add to his misery—to his despair of ever being able to re-ascend them; they being angels in a state of bliss, and he a fallen spirit doomed to eternal punishment. The passage is as follows:—

Each stair was meant mysteriously, nor stood
There always, but, drawn up to heaven, sometimes
Viewless; and underneath a bright sea flow'd
Of jasper, or of liquid pearl, whereon
Who after came from earth sailing arriv'd
Wafted by angels, or flew o'er the lake
Rapt in a chariot drawn by fiery steeds.
The stairs were then let down, whether to dare
The fiend by easy ascent, *or aggravate*
His sad exclusion from the doors of bliss.

Mr. Wordsworth pondered, and said nothing. I thought to myself, what pity for the poor devil would not good Uncle Toby have expressed! Into what indignation would not Burns have exploded! What knowledge of themselves would not have been forced upon those same coxcombical and malignant angels by Fielding or Shakespeare !

Walter Scott said that the eyes of Burns were the finest he ever saw. I cannot say the same of Mr. Wordsworth's; that is, not in the sense of the beautiful, or even of the profound. But certainly I never beheld eyes that looked so inspired or supernatural. They were like fires half burning, half smouldering, with a sort of acrid fixture of regard, and seated at the further end of two caverns. One might imagine Ezekiel or Isaiah to have had such eyes. The finest eyes, in every sense of the word, which I have ever seen in a man's head (and I have seen many fine ones) are those of Thomas Carlyle.

LORD BYRON

[*Autobiography*]

It is a credit to my noble friend that he was by far the pleasantest when he had got a little wine in his head. The only time I invited myself to dine with him, I told him I did it on that account, and that I meant to push the bottle so that he should intoxicate me with his good company. He said he would have a set-to ; but he never did. It was a little before he left Italy; and there was a point in contest between us (not regarding myself) which he thought perhaps I should persuade him to give up. When in his cups, which was not often more immoderately, he was inclined to be tender ; but not weakly so, nor lachrymose. I know not how it might have been with everybody, but he paid me the compliment of being excited to his very best feelings ; and when I rose late to go away, he would hold me down, and say with a look of entreaty, ' Not yet.' Then it was that I seemed to talk with the proper natural Byron as he ought to have been ; and I used to think there was not a sacrifice which I could not have made to keep him in that temper, and see his friends love him as much as the world admired. But I ought to have made

the sacrifice at once. I should have broken the ice
between us which had been generated on points of
literary predilection ; and admired, and shown that
I admired, as I ought to have done, his admirable
genius. It was not only an oversight in me ; it was
a want of friendship. Friendship ought to have made
me discover what less cordial feelings had kept me blind
to. Next morning the happy moment had gone, and
nothing remained but to despair and joke.

In his wine he would volunteer an imitation of somebody, generally of Incledon. He was not a good mimic
in the detail, but he could give a lively broad sketch ;
and over his cups his imitations were good-natured,
which was not always the case at other times. His
Incledon was vocal. I made pretensions to the ora-
torical part ; and between us we boasted that we made
up the entire phenomenon. He would sometimes, however, give a happy comprehensive idea of a person's
manner and turn of mind by the utterance of a single
phrase, or even word. Thus he would pleasantly pretend that Braham called 'enthusiasm' *entoozymoozy* ;
and in the extraordinary combination of lightness,
haste, indifference, and fervour with which he would
pitch out that single word from his lips, accompanied
with a gesture to correspond, he would really set before
you the admirable singer in one of his (then) characteristic passages of stage dialogue. He did not live to see
Braham become an exception in his dialogue as in his
singing.

MOORE

[*Autobiography*]

MOORE's forehead was bony and full of character, with ' bumps' of wit, large and radiant enough to transport a phrenologist; Sterne had such another. His eyes were as dark and fine as you would wish to see under a set of vine-leaves; his mouth generous and good-humoured, with dimples; and his manner as bright as his talk, full of the wish to please and be pleased. He sang, and played with great taste on the pianoforte, as might be supposed from his musical compositions. His voice, which was a little hoarse in speaking (at least I used to think so), softened into a breath, like that of the flute, when singing. In speaking, he was emphatic in rolling the letter *r*, perhaps out of a despair of being able to get rid of the national peculiarity. The structure of his versification, when I knew him, was more artificial than it was afterwards; and in his serious compositions it suited him better. He had hardly faith enough in the sentiments of which he treated to give way to his impulses in writing, except when they were festive and witty; and artificial thoughts demand a similar embodiment. Both patriotism and personal experience, however, occasionally inspired him with lyric pathos; and in his naturally musical perception of the right principles of versification, he contemplated the fine, easy-playing, muscular style of Dryden, with a sort of perilous pleasure. I remember his quoting with delight a couplet of Dryden's, which came with a particular grace from his lips :—

Let honour and preferment go for gold ;
But glorious beauty isn't to be sold.

Beside the pleasure I took in Moore's society as a man of wit, I had a great esteem for him as a man of candour and independence. His letters were full of all that was pleasant in him. As I was a critic at that

time, and in the habit of giving my opinion of his works
in the *Examiner*, he would write me his *opinion* of the
opinion, with a mixture of good humour, admission, and
deprecation, so truly delightful, and a sincerity of criticism on my own writings so extraordinary for so
courteous a man, though with abundance of balm and
eulogy, that never any subtlety of compliment could
surpass it; and with all my self-confidence I never ceased
to think that the honour was on my side, and that I
could only deserve such candour of intercourse by being
as ingenuous as himself.   This admiring regard for him
he completed by his behaviour to an old patron of his,
who, not thinking it politic to retain him openly by his
side, proposed to facilitate his acceptance of a place
under the Tories ; an accommodation which Moore
rejected as an indignity.   I thought, afterwards, that
a man of such a spirit should not have condescended to
attack Rousseau and poor foolish Madame de Warens,
out of a desire to right himself with polite life, and with
the memory of some thoughtless productions of his own.
Polite life was only too happy to possess him in his graver
days ; and the thoughtless productions, however to be
regretted on reflection, were reconcilable to reflection
itself on the same grounds on which Nature herself and
all her exuberance is to be reconciled.   At least, without
presuming to judge Nature in the abstract, an ultra-
sensitive and enjoying poet is himself a production of
Nature; and we may rest assured, that she will no more
judge him with harshness ultimately, than she will
condemn the excess of her own vines and fig-trees.

LAMB

[*Autobiography. Table Talk. Indicator*, Jan. 31, 1821]

CHARLES LAMB has a head worthy of Aristotle, with
as fine a heart as ever beat in human bosom, and limbs
very fragile to sustain it.   There was a caricature of
him sold in the shops, which pretended to be a likeness.
P[rocte]r went into the shop in a passion, and asked
the man what he meant by putting forth such a libel.
The man apologized, and said that the artist meant no
offence.   Mr. Lamb's features are strongly yet delicately cut : he has a fine eye as well as forehead ; and no
face carried in it greater marks of thought and feeling.
It resembles that of Bacon, with less worldly vigour and
more sensibility.

As for his frame, so is his genius. It is as fit for thought
as can be, and equally as unfit for action ; and this
renders him melancholy, apprehensive, humorous, and
willing to make the best of everything as it is, both from
tenderness of heart and abhorrence of alteration.   His
understanding was too great to admit an absurdity ;
his frame is not strong enough to deliver it from a fear.
His sensibility to strong contrasts is the foundation of
his humour, which is that of a wit at once melancholy
and willing to be pleased.   He will beard a superstition,
and shudder at the old phantasm while he does it.   One
could imagine him cracking a jest in the teeth of a
ghost, and then melting into thin air himself, out of
sympathy with the awful.   His humour and his knowledge both, are those of Hamlet, of Molière, of Carlin,
who shook a city with laughter, and, in order to divert
his melancholy, was recommended to go and hear himself. Yet he extracts a real pleasure out of his jokes,
because good-heartedness retains that privilege when it
fails in everything else.   I should say he condescended
to be a punster, if condescension were a word befitting
wisdom like his. Being told that somebody had lam-
pooned him, he said, ' Very well, I'll Lamb-pun him.'

His puns are admirable, and often contain as deep
things as the wisdom of some who have greater names.
Such a man, for instance, as Nicole, the Frenchman, who
was a baby to him. He would have cracked a score of
jokes at him, worth his whole book of sentences ; pelted
his head with pearls. Nicole would not have understood him, but Rouchefoucauld would, and Pascal too ;
and some of our old Englishmen would have understood him still better. He would have been worthy of
hearing Shakespeare read one of his scenes to him, hot
from the brain. Commonplace finds a great comforter
in him, as long as it is good-natured ; it is to the ill-
natured or the dictatorial only that he was startling.
Willing to see society go on as it does, because he despairs
of seeing it otherwise, but not at all agreeing in his
interior with the common notions of crime and punishment, he 'dumbfounded' a long tirade against vice one
evening, by taking the pipe out of his mouth, and asking
the speaker, 'Whether he meant to say that a thief was
not a good man ?' To a person abusing Voltaire, and
indiscreetly opposing his character to that of Jesus
Christ, he said admirably well (though he by no means
overrated Voltaire, nor wanted reverence in the other
quarter), that 'Voltaire was a very good Jesus Christ
for the French.' He likes to see church-goers continue
to go to church, and has written a tale in his sister's
admirable little book (Mrs. Leicester's School) to encourage the rising generation to do so ; but to a conscientious deist he had nothing to object; and if an
atheist found every other door shut against him, he
would assuredly not find his. I believe he would have
had the world remain precisely as it is, provided it
innovated no farther ; but this spirit in him was anything but a worldly one, or for his own interests. He
hardly contemplates with patience the fine new buildings in the Regent's Park : and, privately speaking, he
has a grudge against official heaven-expounders, or
clergymen. He would rather, however, be with a
crowd that he disliked, than feel himself alone. He
said to me one day, with a face of great solemnity,

' What must have been that man's feelings, who thought himself *the first deist* ? ' Finding no footing in certainty, he delights to confound the borders of theoretical truth and falsehood. He is fond of telling wild stories to children, engrafted on things about them; writes letters to people abroad, telling them that a friend of theirs [Mr. Alsager, the commercial editor of the *Times*] has come out in genteel comedy; and persuaded G[eorge] D[yer] that *Lord Castlereagh* was the author of *Waverley* ! The same excellent person walking one evening out of his friend's house into the New River, Mr. Lamb (who was from at home at the time) wrote a paper under his signature of Elia (now no longer anonymous), stating that common friends would have stood dallying on the bank, have sent for neighbours, &c., but that *he*, in his magnanimity, jumped in, and rescued his friend after the old noble fashion. He wrote in the same magazine two lives of Liston and Munden, which the public took for serious, and which exhibit an extraordinary jumble of imaginary facts and truth of by-painting. Munden he made born at ' Stoke Pogis ': the very sound of which is like the actor speaking and digging his words. He knows how many false conclusions and pretensions are made by men who profess to be guided by facts only, as if facts could not be misconceived, or figments taken for them; and therefore, one day, when somebody was speaking of a person who valued himself on being a matter-of-fact man, ' Now,' said he, ' I value myself on being a matter-of-lie man.' This did not hinder his being a man of the greatest veracity, in the ordinary sense of the word ; but ' truth,' he said, ' was precious, and not to be wasted on everybody.' Those who wish to have a genuine taste of him, and an insight into his modes of life, should read his essays on *Hogarth* and *King Lear*, his *Letters*, his article on the *London Streets*, on *Whist-Playing*, which he loves, and on *Saying Grace before Meat*, which he thinks a strange moment to *select* for being grateful. He said once to a brother whist-player, whose hand was more clever than clean, and who had enough in him to afford a joke, ' M., if dirt were trumps, what hands you would hold.'

Rosamund Gray is the story of a lovely young girl, a perfect picture of intelligent innocence, whose family have been brought low in the world, and who grows up with a blind old grandmother, that dotes and rests all her being upon her. There grows a love between her and a frank-hearted youth, Allan Clare, which is described, or rather constantly implied and felt, with a world of delicacy and young devotedness. Allan had a sister, who learned to love Rosamund as he did ; and one night, after the two friends had had a happy long walk about the fields and green places near the village, Rosamund, unable to get out of her head the scenes which were now endeared to her by Allan's sister as well as himself, played her grandmother for the first time in her life a little trick, and in the irrepressible and innocent enthusiasm of her heart stole out of the cottage to go over them again. Matravis, a villain, met her— ' Late at night he met her, a lonely, unprotected virgin —no friend at hand—no place near of refuge.'—We thank the author for making this scoundrel sallow and ugly. It looks as if his physical faculties were perturbed and bad by nature, like a mistake; and that these had infected the humanity common to us all. Rosamund, 'polluted and disgraced, wandered, an abandoned thing, about the fields and meadows till daybreak.' She then did not go home, but laid herself down stupefied at Elinor Clare's gate ; and in her friend's house she soon died, having first heard that her grandmother had died in the meanwhile. The blind old woman—her death is thus related :—

' An old man, that lay sick in a small house adjoining to Margaret's, testified the next morning, that he had plainly heard the old creature calling for her grand-daughter. All the night long she made her moan, and ceased not to call upon the name of Rosamund. But no Rosamund was there—*the voice died away, but not till near day-break.*

'When the neighbours came to search in the morning Margaret was missing! She had *straggled* out of bed, and made her way into Rosamund's room—worn out with fatigue and fright, when she found the girl not there, she had laid herself down to die—and, it is thought, she died *praying*—for she was discovered in a kneeling posture, her arms and face extended on the pillow, where Rosamund had slept the night before— a smile was on her face in death.'

As to Rosamund, she scarcely uttered a word thenceforward. 'She expired in the arms of Elinor—quiet, gentle, as she lived—thankful that she died not among strangers—and expressing by signs rather than words, a gratitude for the most trifling services, the common offices of humanity. She died uncomplaining.'

Allan's sister, to whom Matravis had once paid his addresses, though *in vain*, died of a frenzy-fever; and the young blighted lover himself is missed for a long while afterwards, till recognized sitting on his sister's tombstone in the village by his friend the surgeon, who is the supposed author of the book. His goodness, his sympathy with his fellow creatures, had survived his happiness; and he was still the same gentle yet manly creature as ever. His great enjoyment, his 'wayward pleasure, *for he refused to name it a virtue*,' was in visiting hospitals, and unostentatiously contriving to do personal and pecuniary services to the most wretched. The surgeon was called one night to attend the dying bed of a man of the name of Matravis. Allan went with him, to give the miserable wretch what comfort he could: but he talked deliriously, bidding them 'not tell Allan Clare,' who stood shedding over him his long-repressed tears.—The paper before us glimmers through our own.

Lamb was a humanist, in the most universal sense of the term. His imagination was not great, and he also wanted sufficient heat and music to render his poetry as good as his prose; but as a prose writer, and within the wide circuit of humanity, no man ever took a more complete range than he. He had felt, thought, and suffered so much, that he literally had intolerance for nothing; and he never seemed to have it, but when he supposed the sympathies of men, who might have known better, to be imperfect. He was a wit and an observer of the first order, as far as the world around him was concerned, and society in its existing state; for as to anything theoretical or transcendental, no man ever had less care for it, or less power. To take him out of habit and convention, however tolerant he was to those who could speculate beyond them, was to put him into an exhausted receiver, or to send him naked, shivering, and driven to shatters, through the regions of space and time. He was only at his ease in the old arms of humanity; and humanity loved and comforted him like one of its wisest, though weakest children. His life had experienced great and peculiar sorrows; but he kept up a balance between those and his consolations, by the goodness of his heart, and the ever-willing sociality of his humour; though, now and then, as if he would cram into one moment the spleen of years, he would throw out a startling and morbid subject for reflection, perhaps in no better shape than a pun; for he was a great punster. It was a levity that relieved the gravity of his thoughts and kept them from falling too heavily earthwards.

Lamb was under the middle size, and of fragile make; but with a head as fine as if it had been carved on purpose. He had a very weak stomach. Three glasses of wine would put him in as lively a condition as can only be wrought in some men by as many bottles; which subjected him to mistakes on the part of the inconsiderate.

Lamb's essays, especially those collected under the signature of ELIA, will take their place among the daintiest productions of English *wit-melancholy*,—an amiable melancholy being the groundwork of them, and serving to throw out their delicate flowers of wit and character with the greater nicety. Nor will they be liked the less for a sprinkle of old language, which was natural in him by reason of his great love of the old English writers. Shakespeare himself might have read them, and Hamlet have quoted them.

JOHN KEATS

[*Indicator*, Sept. 20, 1820]

AH, dear friend, as valued a one as thou art a poet,— John Keats,—we cannot, after all, find it in our hearts to be glad, now thou art gone away with the swallows to seek a kindlier clime. The rains began to fall heavily the moment thou wast to go ;—we do not say, poet-like, for thy departure. One tear in an honest eye is more precious to thy sight than all the metaphorical weepings in the universe ; and thou didst leave many starting to think how many months it would be till they saw thee again. And yet thou didst love meta-phorical tears too, in their way ; and couldst always liken everything in nature to something great or small ; and the rains that beat against thy cabin-window will set, we fear, thy over-working wits upon many com-parisons that ought to be much more painful to others than thyself ;—Heaven mend their envious and ignorant numskulls. But thou hast ' a mighty soul in a little body ' ; and the kind cares of the former for all about thee shall no longer subject the latter to the chance of impressions which it scorns ; and the soft skies of Italy shall breathe balm upon it ; and thou shalt return with thy friend the nightingale, and make all thy other friends as happy with thy voice as they are sorrowful to miss it. The little cage thou didst sometime share with us looks as deficient without thee, as thy present one may do without us ; but—farewell for awhile : thy heart is in our fields : and thou wilt soon be back to rejoin it.

L. HUNT

N

CARLYLE

[Autobiography]

HERE, also, I became acquainted with Thomas
Carlyle, one of the kindest and best, as well as most
eloquent of men ; though in his zeal for what is best he
sometimes thinks it incumbent on him to take not the
kindest tone, and in his eloquent demands of some
hearty uncompromising creed on our parts, he does not
quite set the example of telling us the amount of his
own.   Mr. Carlyle sees that there is a good deal of rough
work in the operations of Nature : he seems to think
himself bound to consider a good deal of it devilish,
after the old Covenanter fashion, in order that he may
find something angelical in giving it the proper quantity
of vituperation and blows ; and he calls upon us to
prove our energies and our benevolence by acting the
part of the wind rather than the sun, of warring rather
than peace-making, of frightening and forcing rather
than conciliating and persuading.   Others regard this
view of the one thing needful, however strikingly set
forth, as an old and obsolete story, fit only to be finally
done with, and not worth the repetition of the old
series of reactions, even for the sake of those analogies
with the physical economy of the world, which, in the
impulse which Nature herself gives us towards pro-
gression, we are not bound to suppose everlastingly
applicable to its moral and spiritual development.   If
mankind are destined never to arrive at years of dis-
cretion, the admonition is equally well-founded and
unnecessary ; for the old strifes will be continued at
all events, the admonition (at best) being a part of
them.   And even then, I should say that the world is still
a fine, rich, strenuous, beautiful, and desirable thing,
always excepting the poverty that starves, and one or
two other evils which on no account must we consent
to suppose irremediable.   But if the case be otherwise,
if the hopes which Nature herself has put into our hearts

be something better than incitements to hopeless action, merely for the action's sake, and this beautiful planet be destined to work itself into such a condition as we feel to be the only fit condition for that beauty, then, I say, with every possible respect for my admirable friend, who can never speak but he is worth hearing, that the tale which he condescends to tell is no better than our old nursery figment of the *Black Man and the Coal-hole,* and that the growing desire of mankind for the cessation of bitterness, and for the prevalence of the sweets of gentleness and persuasion, is an evidence that the time has arrived for dropping the thorns and husks of the old sourness and austerity, and showing ourselves worthy of ' the goods the gods provide us.'

Mr. Carlyle's antipathy to 'shams' is highly estimable and salutary. I wish Heaven may prosper his denouncements of them, wherever they exist. But the danger of the habit of denouncing—of looking at things from the antipathetic instead of the sympathetic side— is, that a man gets such a love for the pleasure and exaltation of fault-finding, as tempts him, in spite of himself, to make what he finds ; till at length he is himself charged with being a 'sham' ; that is to say, a pretender to perceptions and virtues which he does not prove, or at best a willing confounder of what differs from modes and appearances of his own, with violations of intrinsical wisdom and goodness. Upon this principle of judgement, Nature herself and the universe might be found fault with ; and the sun and the stars denounced for appearing no bigger than they do, or for not confining the measure of their operation to that of the taper we read by. Mr. Carlyle adopted a peculiar semi-German style, from the desire of putting thoughts on his paper instead of words, and perhaps of saving himself some trouble in the process. I feel certain that he does it from no other motive ; and I am sure he has a right to help himself to every diminution of trouble, seeing how many thoughts and feelings he undergoes. He also strikes an additional blow with the peculiarity, rouses men's attention by it and helps his rare and powerful understanding to produce double its effect. It would be hard not to dispense with a few verbs and nominative cases, in consideration of so great a result. Yet, if we were to judge him by one of his own summary processes, and deny him the benefit of his notions of what is expedient and advisable, how could he exculpate this style, in which he denounces so many ' shams,' of being itself a sham ? of being affected, unnecessary, and ostentatious ? a jargon got up to confound pretension with performance, and reproduce endless German talk under the guise of novelty ?

Thus much in behalf of us dulcet signors of philanthropy, and conceders of good intention, whom Mr. Carlyle is always girding at, and who beg leave to say that they have not confined their lives to words, any more than the utterers of words more potential, but have had their ' actions ' too, and their sufferings, and even their thoughts, and have seen the faces of the gods of wonder and melancholy ; albeit they end with believing them to be phantoms (however useful) of bad health, and think nothing finally potential but gentleness and persuasion.

It has been well said, that love money as people may, there is generally something which they love better : some whim, or hobby-horse ; some enjoyment or recreation ; some personal, or political, or poetical predilection ; some good opinion of this or that class of men ; some club of one's fellows, or dictum of one's own ;—with a thousand other *somes* and probabilities. I believe that what Mr. Carlyle loves better than his fault-finding, with all its eloquence, is the face of any human creature that looks suffering, and loving, and sincere; and I believe further, that if the fellow creature were suffering only, and neither loving nor sincere, but had come to a pass of agony in this life, which put him at the mercies of some good man for some last help and consolation towards his grave, even at the risk of loss to repute, and a sure amount of pain and vexation, that man, if the groan reached him in its forlornness, would be Thomas Carlyle.

MADAME DE SÉVIGNÉ

[From an essay on this writer, *Edinburgh Review*, October, 1842]

THAT is the great charm of Madame de Sévigné— *truth*. Truth, wit, and animal spirits compose the secret of her delightfulness ; but truth above all, for it is that which shows all the rest to be true. If she had not more natural virtues than most other good people, she had more natural *manners* ; and the universality of her taste, and the vivacity of her spirits, giving her the widest range of enjoyment, she expressed herself naturally on all subjects, and did not disdain the simplest and most familiar phraseology, when the truth required it. Familiarities of style, taken by themselves, have been common more or less to all wits, from the days of Aristophanes to those of Byron ; and, in general, so have animal spirits. Rabelais was full of both. The followers of Pulci and Berni, in Italy, abound in them. What distinguishes Madame de Sévigné is, first, that she was a woman so writing, which till her time had been a thing unknown, and has not been since witnessed in any such charming degree ; and second, and above all, that she writes ' the truth, the whole truth, and nothing but the truth ' ; never giving us falsehood of any kind, not even a single false metaphor, or only half-true simile or description ; nor writing for any purpose on earth, but to say what she felt, and please those who could feel with her. If we consider how few writers there are, even among the best, to whom this praise, in its integrity, can apply, we shall be struck, perhaps, with a little surprise and sorrow for the craft of authors in general ; but certainly with double admiration for Madame de Sévigné. We do not mean to say that she is always right in opinion, or that she had no party or conventional feelings. She entertained, for some years, some strong prejudices. She was bred up in so ex-

clusive an admiration for the poetry of Corneille, that
she thought Racine would go out of fashion. Her
loyalty made her astonished to find that Louis was not
invincible ; and her connexion with Count de Grignan,
who was employed in the *dragonades* against the Hu-
guenots, led her but negatively to disapprove those
inhuman absurdities. But these were accidents of
friendship or education : her understanding outlived
them ; nor did they hinder her, meantime, from describing
truthfully what she felt, and from being right, as well
as true, in nine-tenths of it all. Her sincerity made
even her errors a part of her truth. She never pretended to be above what she felt ; never assumed a
profound knowledge ; never disguised an ignorance.
Her mirth, and her descriptions, may sometimes appear
exaggerated ; but the spirit of truth, not of contradiction, is in them ; and excess in such cases is not falsehood, but enjoyment—not the wine adulterated, but
the cup running over. All her wit is healthy ; all its
images entire and applicable throughout—not palsy-
stricken with irrelevance ; not forced in, and then found
wanting, like Walpole's conceit about the trees, in the
passage above quoted. Madame de Sévigné never
wrote such a passage in her life. All her lightest and
most fanciful images, all her most daring expressions,
have the strictest propriety, the most genuine feeling,
a home in the heart of truth ;—as when, for example,
she says, amidst continual feasting, that she is 'famished
for want of hunger' ; that there were no ' interlinea-
tions ' in the conversation of a lady, who spoke from
the heart ; that she went to vespers one evening out
of pure opposition, which taught her to comprehend the
' sacred obstinacy of martyrdom'; that she did not
keep a ' philosopher's shop ' ; that it is difficult for
people in trouble to ' bear thunder-claps of bliss in
others.' It is the same from the first letter we have
quoted to the last ; from the proud and merry boasting
of the young mother with a boy, to the candid shudder
about the approach of old age, and the refusal of death
to grant a moment to the dying statesman—' no, not

a single moment.' She loved nature and truth without misgiving; and nature and truth loved her in return, and have crowned her with glory and honour.

BOCCACCIO

[Autobiography]

[At Maiano] I passed a very disconsolate time[1]; yet the greatest comfort I experienced in Italy was living in that neighbourhood, and thinking, as I went about, of Boccaccio. Boccaccio's father had a house at Maiano, supposed to have been situated at the Fiesolan extremity of the hamlet. That divine writer (whose sentiment outweighed his levity a hundredfold, as a fine face is oftener serious than it is merry) was so fond of the place, that he has not only laid the two scenes of the *Decameron* on each side of it, with the valley his company resorted to in the middle, but has made the two little streams that embrace Maiano, the Affrico and the Mensola, the hero and heroine of his *Nimphale Fiesolano*. A lover and his mistress are changed into them, after the fashion of Ovid. The scene of another of his works is on the banks of the Mugnone, a river a little distant; and the *Decameron* is full of the neighbouring villages. Out of the windows of one side of our house we saw the turret of the Villa Gherardi, to which, according to his biographers, his 'joyous company' resorted in the first instance. A house belonging to Macchiavelli was nearer a little to the left; and farther to the left, among the blue hills, was the white village of Settignano, where Michael Angelo was born. The house is still remaining in possession of the family. From our windows on the other side we saw, close to us, the Fiesole of antiquity and of Milton, the site of the Boccaccio-house before mentioned still closer, the Valley

---

[1] It was after the break-up of *The Liberal* and the death of Shelley, and when Hunt's health was poor.—Ed.

of Ladies at our feet ; and we looked over towards the
quarter of the Mugnone and of a house of Dante, and
in the distance beheld the mountains of Pistoia. Lastly,
from the terrace in front, Florence lay clear and
cathedralled before us, with the scene of Redi's *Bacchus*
rising on the other side of it, and the Villa of Arcetri,
illustrious for Galileo.

But I stuck to my Boccaccio haunts, as to an old
home. I lived with the divine human being, with his
friends of the *Falcon* and the *Basil*, and my own not
unworthy melancholy ; and went about the flowering
lanes and hills, solitary indeed, and sick to heart, but
not unsustained. In looking back to such periods of
one's existence, one is surprised to find how much they
surpass many seasons of mirth, and what a rich tone of
colour their very darkness assumes, as in some fine old
painting. My almost daily walk was to Fiesole,
through a path skirted with wild myrtle and cyclamen ;
and I stopped at the cloister of the Doccia, and sat on
the pretty melancholy platform behind it, reading or
looking through the pines down to Florence. In the
Valley of Ladies I found some English trees (trees, not
vine and olive), and even a meadow ; and these, while
I made them furnish me with a bit of my old home in
the north, did no injury to the memory of Boccaccio,
who is of all countries, and who finds his home wherever
we do ourselves—in love, in the grave, in a desert
island.

ISAAC WALTON

[*Indicator*, Nov. 17, 1819]

THE anglers are a race of men who puzzle us. We do not mean for their patience, which is laudable ; nor for the infinite non-success of some of them, which is desirable. Neither do we agree with the good joke attributed to Swift, that angling is always to be considered as ' a stick and a string, with a fly at one end and a fool at the other.' Nay, if he had books with him and a pleasant day, we can even account for the joyousness of that prince of all punters, who having been seen in the same identical spot one morning and evening, and asked both times whether he had had any success, said No ; but in the course of the day he had had a ' glorious nibble.'

But the anglers boast of the innocence of their pastime ; yet it puts fellow creatures to the torture. They pique themselves on their meditative faculties ; and yet their only excuse is a want of thought. It is this that puzzles us. Old Isaac Walton, their patriarch, speaking of his inquisitorial abstractions on the banks of a river, says :—

> Here we may
> Think and pray,
> Before death
> Stops our breath.
> Other joys
> Are but toys,
> And to be lamented.

So saying, he ' stops the breath ' of a trout, by plucking him up into an element too thin to respire, with a hook and a tortured worm in his jaws.

> Other joys
> Are but toys.

If you ride, walk, or skate, or play at cricket, or at rackets, or enjoy a ball or a concert, it is 'to be lamented.' To put pleasure into the faces of half a dozen agreeable women is a toy unworthy of the manliness of a worm-sticker. But to put a hook into the gills of a carp,—there you attain the end of a reasonable being; there you show yourself truly a lord of the creation. To plant your feet occasionally in the mud is also a pleasing step. So is cutting your ankles with weeds and stones.

> Other joys
> Are but toys.

The book of Isaac Walton upon angling is undoubtedly a delightful performance in some respects. It smells of the country air, and of the flowers in cottage windows. Its pictures of rural scenery, its simplicity, its snatches of old songs, are all good and refreshing; and his prodigious relish of a dressed fish would not be grudged him, if he had killed it a little more decently. He really seems to have a respect for a piece of salmon; to approach it, like the grace, with his hat off. But what are we to think of a man, who, in the midst of his tortures of other animals, is always valuing himself on his wonderful harmlessness; and who actually follows up one of his most complacent passages of this kind with an injunction to impale a certain worm twice upon the hook, because it is lively, and might get off? All that can be said of such an extraordinary inconsistency is, that having been bred up in an opinion of the innocence of his amusement, and possessing a healthy power of exercising voluntary thoughts (as far as he had any), he must have dozed over the opposite side of the question, so as to become almost, perhaps quite, insensible to it. And angling does indeed seem the next thing to dreaming. It dispenses with locomotion, reconciles contradictions, and renders the very countenance null and void. A friend of ours, who is an admirer of Walton, was struck, just as we were, with the likeness of the old angler's face to a fish. It is hard, angular, and of no expression. It seems to have been 'subdued to what it worked in '; to have become native to the watery element. One might have said to Walton, ' O flesh, how art thou fishified ! ' He looks like a pike, dressed in broad cloth instead of butter.

The face of his pupil and follower, or, as he fondly called himself, son, Charles Cotton, a poet and a man of wit, is more good-natured and uneasy.[1] Cotton's pleasures had not been confined to fishing. His sympathies, indeed, had been a little superabundant ; and left him perhaps not so great a power of thinking as he pleased. Accordingly, we find more symptoms of scrupulousness upon the subject of angling in his writings, than in those of his father.

Walton says that an angler does no hurt but to fish ; and this he counts as nothing. Cotton argues, that the slaughter of them is not to be ' repented '; and he says to his father (which looks as if the old gentleman some-times thought upon the subject too):

> There whils behind some bush we wait
> The scaly people to betray,
> We'll prove it just with treacherous bait
> To make the preying trout our prey.

This argument, and another about fishes being made for ' man's pleasure and diet,' are all that anglers have to say for the innocence of their sport. But they are both as rank sophistications as can be ; mere beggings of the question. To kill fish outright is a different matter. Death is common to all ; and a trout, speedily killed by a man, may suffer no worse fate than from the jaws of a pike. It is the mode, the lingering cat-like cruelty of the angler's sport, that renders it unworthy. If fish were made to be so treated, then men were also made to be racked and throttled by Inquisitors. Indeed, among other advantages of angling, Cotton reckons up a tame fish-like acquiescence to whatever the powerful choose to inflict.

---

[1] The reader may see both the portraits in the late editions of Walton [1819].

> We scratch not our pates,
> Nor repine at the rates
> Our superiors impose on our living ;
> But do frankly submit,
> Knowing they have more wit
> In demanding, than we have in giving.

> Whilst quiet we sit,
> We conclude all things fit,
> Acquiescing with hearty submission, &c.

And this was no pastoral fiction. The anglers of those times, whose pastimes became famous from the celebrity of their names, chiefly in divinity, were great fallers in with passive obedience. They seemed to think (whatever they found it necessary to say now and then upon that point) that the great had as much right to prey upon men, as the small had upon fishes : only the men luckily had not hooks put into their jaws, and the sides of their cheeks torn to pieces. The two most famous anglers in history are Antony and Cleopatra. These extremes of the angling character are very edifying.

We should like to know what these grave divines would have said to the heavenly maxim of ' Do as you would be done by.' Let us imagine ourselves, for instance, a sort of human fish. Air is but a rarer fluid ; and at present, in this November weather, a supernatural being who should look down upon us from a higher atmosphere would have some reason to regard us as a kind of pedestrian carp. Now fancy a Genius fishing for us. Fancy him baiting a great hook with pickled salmon, and twitching up old Isaac Walton from the banks of the River Lee, with the hook through his ear. How he would go uproaring and screaming, and thinking the devil had got him !

> Other joys
> Are but toys.

We repeat, that if fish were made to be so treated, then we were just as much made to be racked and suffocated ; and a footpad might have argued that old Isaac was made to have his pocket picked, and then tumbled into the river. There is no end of these idle and selfish beggings of the question, which at last argue quite as much against us as for us. And granting them, for the sake of argument, it is still obvious, on the very same ground, that men were also made to be taught better. We do not say that all anglers are of a cruel nature. Many of them, doubtless, are amiable men in other matters. They have only never thought, perhaps, on that side of the question, or been accustomed from childhood to blink it. But once thinking, their amiableness and their practice become incompatible; and if they should wish, on that account, never to have thought upon the subject, they would only show that they cared for their own exemption from suffering and not for its diminution in general.

TALES, OLD AND NEW

THE SHOEMAKER OF VEYROS

[*Indicator*, Dec. 1, 1819]

IN the time of the old kings of Portugal, Don John, a natural son of the reigning prince, was governor of the town of Veyros, in the province of Alentejo. The town was situate (perhaps is there still) upon a mountain, at the foot of which runs a river; and at a little distance there was a ford over it, under another eminence. The bed of the river thereabouts was so high as to form a shallow sandy place; and in that clear spot of water the maidens of Veyros, both of high rank and humble, used to wash their clothes.

It happened one day that Don John, riding out with a company, came to the spot at the time the young women were so employed: and being, says our author, 'a young and lusty gallant,' he fell to jesting with his followers upon the bare legs of the busy girls, who had tucked up their clothes, as usual, to their work. He passed along the river; and all his company had not yet gone by, when a lass in a red petticoat, while tucking it up, showed her legs somewhat high; and clapping her hand on her right calf, said loud enough to be heard by the riders, ' Here's a white leg, girls, for the Master of Avis.' [1]

These words, spoken probably out of a little lively bravado, upon the strength of the governor's having gone by, were repeated to him when he got home, together with the action that accompanied them: upon which the young lord felt the eloquence of the speech so

---

[1] An order of knighthood, of which Don John was Master.

deeply, that he contrived to have the fair speaker brought to him in private; and the consequence was, that our lively natural son, and his sprightly challenger, had another natural son.

Ines (for that was the girl's name) was the daughter of a shoemaker in Veyros; a man of very good account, and wealthy. Hearing how his daughter had been sent for to the young governor's house, and that it was her own light behaviour which subjected her to what he was assured she willingly consented to, he took it so to heart, that at her return home she was driven by him from the house, with every species of contumely and spurning. After this he never saw her more. And to prove to the world and to himself that his severity was a matter of principle, and not a mere indulgence of his own passions, he never afterwards lay in a bed, nor eat at a table, nor changed his linen, nor cut his hair, nails, or beard; which latter grew to such a length, reaching below his knees, that the people used to call him Barbadon, or Old Beardy.

In the meantime his grandson, called Don Alphonso, not only grew to a man, but was created Duke of Braganza; his father Don John having been elected to the crown of Portugal; which he wore after such noble fashion, to the great good of his country, as to be surnamed the Memorable. Now the town of Veyros stood in the middle of seven or eight others, all belonging to the young Duke, from whose place at Villa Viciosa it was but four leagues distant. He therefore had good intelligence of the shoemaker his grandfather; and being of a humane and truly generous spirit, the account he received of the old man's way of life made him at last extremely desirous of paying him a visit. He accordingly went with a retinue to Veyros; and meeting Barbadon in the streets, he alighted from his horse, bareheaded; and in the presence of that stately company and the people, asked the old man his blessing. The shoemaker, astonished at this sudden spectacle, and at the strange contrast which it furnished to his humble rank, stared in a bewildered manner upon the unknown

personage, who thus knelt to him in the public way,
and said, 'Sir, do you mock me?' 'No,' answered
the Duke; 'may God so help me, as I do not: but in
earnest I crave I may kiss your hand and receive your
blessing, for I am your grandson, and son to Ines your
daughter, conceived by the king, my lord and father.'
No sooner had the shoemaker heard these words, than
he clapped his hands before his eyes, and said,
'God bless me from ever beholding the son of so wicked
a daughter as mine was! And yet, forasmuch as you
are not guilty of her offence, hold; take my hand and
my blessing, in the name of the Father, and of the Son,
and of the Holy Ghost.' So saying, he laid one of his
old hands upon the young man's head, blessing him;
but neither the Duke nor his followers could persuade
him to take the other away from his eyes, neither would
he talk with him a word more. In this spirit, shortly
after, he died: and just before his death, he directed
a tomb to be made for him, on which were sculptured
the tools belonging to his trade, with this epitaph:—

This sepulchre Barbadon caused to be made,
(Being of Veyros, a shoemaker by his trade)
For himself and the rest of his race,
Excepting his daughter Ines in any case.[1]

The author says that he has 'heard it reported by
the ancientest persons, that the fourth Duke of Braganza, Don James, son to Donna Isabel, sister to the
King Don Emanuel, caused that tomb to be defaced,
being the sepulchre of his fourth grandfather.'[2]

[1] We have retained the homely translation of our in-
formant as most likely to resemble the cast of the original.
His account of the story is to be found in the Supplement
to the Adventures of Don Sebastion, *Harleian Miscellany*,
vol. ii.

[2] It appears by this that the Don John of the tradition
is John the First, who was elected King of Portugal, and
became famous for his great qualities; and that his son
by the alleged shoemaker's daughter was his successor,
Alphonso the Fifth.

As for the daughter, the conclusion of whose story comes lagging in like a penitent, ' she continued,' says the writer, ' after she was delivered of that son, a very chaste and virtuous woman ; and the king made her commandress of Santos, a most honourable place, and very plentiful, to the which none but princesses were admitted, living, as it were, abbesses and princesses of a monastery built without the walls of Lisbon, called Santos, that is, Saints, founded by reason of some martyrs that were martyred there. And the religious women of that place have liberty to marry with the knights of their order before they enter into that holy profession.'

The rest of our author's remarks are in too curious a spirit to be omitted. ' In this monastery,' he says, ' the same Donna Ines died, leaving behind her a glorious reputation for her virtue and holiness. Observe, gentle reader, the constancy that this Portuguese, a shoemaker, continued in, loathing to behold the honourable estate of his grandchild, nor would any more acknowledge his daughter, having been a lewd woman, for purchasing advancement with dishonour. This considered, you will not wonder at the Count Julian, that plagued Spain, and executed the king Roderigo for forcing his daughter la Cava. The example of this shoemaker is especially worthy the noting, and deeply to be considered, for, besides that it makes good our assertion, it teaches the higher not to disdain the lower, as long as they be virtuous and lovers of honour. It may be, that this old man for his integrity, rising from a virtuous zeal, merited that a daughter coming by descent from his grandchild, should be made Queen of Castile, and the mother of great Isabel, grandmother to the Emperor Charles the Fifth, and Ferdinando.'

Alas ! a pretty posterity our shoemaker had, in Philip the Second and his successors,—a race more suitable to his severity against his child, than his blessing upon his grandchild. Old Barbadon was a fine fellow too, after his fashion. We do not know how he reconciled his unforgiving conduct with his Christianity ; but he had enough precedents on that point. What we admire in him is his showing that he acted out of principle, and did not mistake passion for it. His crepidarian sculptures indeed are not so well; but a little vanity may be allowed to mingle with and soften such edge-tools of self-denial as he chose to handle. His treatment of his daughter was ignorant, and in wiser times would have been brutal; especially when it is considered how much the conduct of children is modified by education and other circumstances: but then a brutal man would not have accompanied it with such voluntary suffering of his own. Neither did Barbadon leave his daughter to take her chance in the wide world, thinking of the evils she might be enduring, only to give a greater zest of fancied pity to the contentedness of his cruelty. He knew she was well taken care of; and if she was not to have the enjoyment of his society, he was determined that it should be a very uncomfortable one to himself. He knew that she lay on a princely bed, while he would have none at all. He knew that she was served upon gold and silver, while he renounced his old chestnut table,—the table at which she used to sit. He knew while he sat looking at his old beard and the wilful sordidness of his hands, that her locks and fair limbs were objects of worship to the gallant and the great. And so he set off his destitutions against her over-possession; and took out the punishment he gave her, in revenge upon himself. This was the instinct of a man who loved a principle, but hated nobody:—of a man who in a wiser time would have felt the wisdom of kindness. Thus his blessing upon his grandchild becomes consistent with his cruelty to his child: and his living stock was a fine one in spite of him. His daughter showed a sense of the wound she had given such a father, by relinquishing the sympathies she loved, because they had hurt him: and her son, worthy of such a grandfather and such a daughter, and refined into a gracefulness of knowledge by education, thought it no mean thing or vulgar to kneel to the grey-headed artisan in the street, and beg the blessing of his honest hand.

THE HAMADRYAD[1]

[*Indicator*, Sept. 13, 1820]

An Assyrian of the name of Rhoecus observing a fine old oak tree ready to fall with age, ordered it to be sustained with props. He was continuing his way through the solitary skirts of the place, when a Nymph of more than human look appeared before him, with gladness in her eyes. 'Rhoecus,' she said, 'I am the Nymph of the tree you have saved from perishing. My life is, of course, implicated in its own. But for you, my existence must have terminated. But for you, the sap would have ceased to flow through its boughs, and the godlike essence I received from it to animate these veins. No more should I have felt the wind in my hair, the sun upon my cheeks, or the balmy rain upon my body. Now I shall feel them many years to come. Many years also will your fellow creatures sit under my shade, and hear the benignity of my whispers, and repay me with their honey and their thanks. Ask what I can give you, Rhoecus, and you shall have it.'

The young man, who had done a graceful action but had not thought of its containing so many kindly things, received the praises of the Nymph with a due mixture of surprise and homage. He did not want courage, however; and emboldened by her tone and manner, and still more by a beauty which had all the buxom bloom of humanity in it, with a preternatural gracefulness besides, he requested that she would receive him as a lover. There was a look in her face at this request, answering to modesty, but something still finer. Having no guilt, she seemed to have none of the common infirmities either of shame or impudence. In fine, she consented to reward Rhoecus as he wished; and said she would send a bee to inform him of the hour of their meeting.

[1] See the Scholiast upon Apollonius Rhodius, or the Mythology of Natalis Comes.

Who now was so delighted as Rhoecus ? for he was a great admirer of the fair sex, and not a little proud of their admiring him in return ; and no human beauty whom he had known could compare with the Hamadryad. It must be owned at the same time that his taste for love and beauty was not of quite so exalted a description as he took it for. If he was fond of the fair sex, he was pretty nearly as fond of dice, and feasting, and any other excitement which came in his way ; and unluckily he was throwing the dice that very noon when the bee came to summon him.

He was at a very interesting part of the game,—so much so, that he did not at first recognize the object of the bee's humming. ' Confound this bee !' said he, ' it seems plaguily fond of me.' He brushed it away two or three times, but the busy messenger returned, and only hummed the louder. At last he bethought him of the Nymph ; but his impatience seemed to increase with his pride, and he gave the poor insect such a brush as sent him away crippled in both his thighs.

The bee returned to his mistress as well as he could ; and shortly afterwards was followed by his joyous assailant, who came triumphing in the success of his dice and his passion. ' I am here,' said the Hamadryad. Rhoecus looked among the trees, but could see nobody. ' I am here,' said a grave sweet voice, ' right before you.' Rhoecus saw nothing. ' Alas,' said she, ' Rhoecus, you cannot see me, nor will you see me more. I had thought better of your discernment and your kindness ; but you were but gifted with a momentary sight of me. You will see nothing in future but common things, and those sadly. You are struck blind to everything else. The hand that could strike my bee with a lingering death, and prefer the embracing of the dice-box to that of affectionate beauty, is not worthy of love and the green trees.'

The wind sighed off to a distance; and Rhoecus felt that he was alone.

THE MOUNTAIN OF THE TWO LOVERS

[Companion, Feb. 20, 1828]

WE forget in what book it was, many years ago, that
we read the story of a lover who was to win his mistress
by carrying her to the top of a mountain, and how he did
win her, and how they ended their days on the same spot.

We think the scene was in Switzerland; but the mountain, though high enough to tax his stout heart to the
uttermost, must have been among the lowest. Let us
fancy it a good lofty hill in the summer-time. It was,
at any rate, so high, that the father of the lady, a proud
noble, thought it impossible for a young man so bur-
dened to scale it. For this reason alone, in scorn, he
bade him do it, and his daughter should be his.

The peasantry assembled in the valley to witness so
extraordinary a sight. They measured the mountain
with their eyes; they communed with one another, and
shook their heads; but all admired the young man;
and some of his fellows, looking at their mistresses,
thought they could do as much. The father was on
horseback, apart and sullen, repenting that he had
subjected his daughter even to the show of such a
hazard; but he thought it would teach his inferiors
a lesson. The young man (the son of a small land-pro-
prietor, who had some pretensions to wealth, though
none to nobility) stood, respectful-looking but confident,
rejoicing in his heart that he should win his mistress,
though at the cost of a noble pain, which he could
hardly think of as a pain, considering who it was that
he was to carry. If he died for it, he should at least
have had her in his arms, and have looked her in the
face. To clasp her person in that manner was a pleasure which he contemplated with such transport, as is
known only to real lovers; for none others know how
respect heightens the joy of dispensing with formality,
and how the dispensing with the formality ennobles
and makes grateful the respect.

The lady stood by the side of her father, pale, desirous, and dreading. She thought her lover would succeed, but only because she thought him in every respect the noblest of his sex, and that nothing was too much for his strength and valour. Great fears came over her nevertheless. She knew not what might happen in the chances common to all. She felt the bitterness of being herself the burden to him and the task; and dared neither to look at her father nor the mountain. She fixed her eyes now on the crowd (which nevertheless she beheld not) and now on her hand and her fingers' ends, which she doubled up towards her with a pretty pretence,—the only deception she had ever used. Once or twice a daughter or a mother slipped out of the crowd, and coming up to her, notwithstanding their fears of the lord baron, kissed that hand which she knew not what to do with.

The father said, 'Now, Sir, to put an end to this mummery'; and the lover, turning pale for the first time, took up the lady.

The spectators rejoice to see the manner in which he moves off, slow but secure, and as if encouraging his mistress. They mount the hill; they proceed well; he halts an instant before he gets midway, and seems refusing something; then ascends at a quicker rate; and now being at the midway point, shifts the lady from one side to the other. The spectators give a great shout. The baron, with an air of indifference, bites the tip of his gauntlet, and then casts on them an eye of rebuke. At the shout the lover resumes his way. Slow but not feeble in his step, yet it gets slower. He stops again, and they think they see the lady kiss him on the forehead. The women begin to tremble, but the men say he will be victorious. He resumes again; he is half-way between the middle and the top; he rushes, he stops, he staggers; but he does not fall. Another shout from the men, and he resumes once more; two-thirds of the remaining part of the way are conquered. They are certain the lady kisses him on the forehead and on the eyes. The women burst into tears, and the stoutest men look pale. He ascends slowlier than ever, but seeming to be more sure. He halts, but it is only to plant his foot to go on again ; and thus he picks his way, planting his foot at every step, and then gaining ground with an effort. The lady lifts up her arms, as if to lighten him. See : he is almost at the top ; he stops, he struggles, he moves sideways, taking very little steps, and bringing one foot every time close to the other. Now—he is all but on the top : he halts again ; he is fixed ; he staggers. A groan goes through the multitude. Suddenly, he turns full front towards the top ; it is luckily almost a level ; he staggers, but it is forward :—Yes :—every limb in the multitude makes a movement as if it would assist him :—see at last : he is *on* the top ; and down he falls flat with his burden. An enormous shout ! He has won : he has won. Now he has a right to caress his mistress, and she is caressing him, for neither of them gets up. If he has fainted, it is with joy, and it is in her arms.

The baron puts spurs to his horse, the crowd following him. Half way he is obliged to dismount ; they ascend the rest of the hill together, the crowd silent and happy, the baron ready to burst with shame and impatience. They reach the top. The lovers are face to face on the ground, the lady clasping him with both arms, his lying on each side.

'Traitor !' exclaimed the baron, 'thou hast practised this feat before on purpose to deceive me. Arise !' 'You cannot expect it, Sir,' said a worthy man, who was rich enough to speak his mind : 'Samson himself might take his rest after such a deed.'

'Part them !' said the baron.

Several persons went up, not to part them, but to congratulate and keep them together. These people look close ; they kneel down ; they bend an ear ; they bury their faces upon them. 'God forbid they should ever be parted more,' said a venerable man ; 'they never can be.' He turned his old face streaming with tears, and looked up at the baron :—'Sir, they are dead.'

GELLIAS

[*A Jar of Honey from Mount Hybla*, 1848]

THIS individual we have kept to the last, though he was little more than a private person, and is not at all famous. But we have a special regard for him ; far more, indeed, than for most of those that have been mentioned; and we think that such of our readers as are not already acquainted with him, will have one too ; for he was of that tip-top class of human beings called ' good fellows,' and a very prince of the race. What renders him a still better fellow than he might otherwise have been, and doubles his heroical qualities in discerning eyes, is, that he was but an insignificant little body to look at, and not very well shaped ; a mannikin, in short, that Sir Godfrey Kneller's nephew, the slave-trader, who rated the painter and his friend Pope at less than ' ten guineas' ' worth ' the pair,' would probably not have valued at more than two pounds five.

The name of this great unknown was Gellias, and you must search into by-corners, even of Sicilian history, to find anything about him ; but he was just the man for our Jar ; sweet as the honey that Samson found in the jaws of the lion.

Gellias was the richest man in the rich city of Agrigentum. The Agrigentines, according to a saying of their countryman Empedocles, were famous for ' building as if they were to live for ever, and feasting as if they were to die next day.' But they were as good-natured and hospitable as they were festive ; and Gellias, in accordance with the superiority of his circumstances, was the most good-natured and hospitable of them all. His magnificence resembled that of a Barmecide. Slaves were stationed at the gates of his noble mansion to invite strangers to enter. His cellar had three hundred reservoirs cut in the solid rock, each containing seven hundred gallons of wine at their service. One day five hundred horsemen halted at his door, who had been overtaken by a storm. He lodged and entertained them all; and, by way of dry clothes, made each man a present of a new tunic and robe.

His wit appears to have been as ready as it was pungent. He was sent ambassador on some occasion to the people of Centauripa, a place at the foot of Mount Aetna. When he rose in the assembly to address them, his poor little figure made so ridiculous a contrast with his mission, that they burst into fits of laughter. Gellias waited his time, and then requested them not to be astonished; 'for,' said he, 'it is the custom with Agrigentum to suit the ambassador to his locality —to send noble-looking persons to great cities, and insignificant ones to the insignificant.'

The combined magnanimity and address of this sarcasm are not to be surpassed. Ambassadors are privileged people; but they have not always been spared by irritated multitudes; yet our hero did not hesitate to turn the ridicule of the Centauripans on themselves. He 'showed up' the smallness of their pretensions, both as a community and as observers. He did not blink the fact of his own bodily insignificance—too sore a point with little people in general, notwithstanding that many of the greatest spirits of the world have resided in frames as petty. He made it the very ground for exposing the still smaller pretensions of the souls and understandings of his deriders. Or, supposing that he said it with a good-humoured smile—with an air of rebuke to their better sense—still the address was as great, and the magnanimity as candid. He not only took the 'bull by the horns,' but turned it with his mighty little hands into a weapon of triumph. Such a man, insignificant as his general exterior may have been, must, after all, have had something fine in some part of it—something great in some part of its expression; probably fine eyes, and a smile full of benignity.

Gellias proved that his soul was of the noblest order, not only by a princely life, but by the heroical nature of his death. Agrigentum lay on the coast opposite Carthage. It had been a flourishing place, partly by

reason of its commerce with that city ; but was at last
insulted by it and subdued. Most of the inhabitants
fled. Among those who remained was Gellias. He
fancied that his great wealth, and his renown for hospitality, would procure him decent treatment. Finding,
however, that the least to be expected of the enemy
was captivity, he set fire to a temple into which he had
conveyed his wealth, and perished with it in the flames ;
thus, says Stolberg, at once preventing ' the profanation
of the place, the enriching of the foe, and the disgrace
of slavery.'

There ought to be a book devoted to the history of
those whose reputations have not received their due.
It would make a curious volume. It would be old in
the materials, novel in the interest, and of equal delight
and use. It is a startling reflection, that while men such
as this Gellias must be dug up from the byways of
history, its high-road is three-parts full of people who
would never have been heard of but for accidents of
time and place. Take, for instance, the majority of the
Roman emperors, of those of Germany, of the turbulent
old French noblesse, and indeed of three-fourths, perhaps nine-tenths, of historical names all over the world.

THE TRUE ENJOYMENT OF SPLENDOUR

A CHINESE APOLOGUE

[*Reflector*, No. III, Art. xix, 1812]

DOUBTLESS, saith the illustrious Me, he that gaineth
much possession hath need of the wrists of Hong and
the sericusness of Shan-Fee, since palaces are not built
with a tea-spoon, nor are to be kept by one who runneth
after butterflies. But above all it is necessary that he
who carrieth a great burden, whether of gold or silver,
should hold his head as lowly as is necessary, lest in
lifting it on high he bring his treasure to nought, and
lose with the spectators the glory of true gravity, which
is meekness.

Quo, who was the son of Quee, who was the son of Quee-Fong, who was the five hundred and fiftieth in lineal descent from the ever-to-be-remembered Fing, chief minister of the Emperor Yau, one day walked out into the streets of Pekin in all the lustre of his rank. Quo, besides the greatness of his birth and the multitude of his accomplishments, was a courtier of the first order, and his pigtail was proportionate to his merits, for it hung down to the ground and kissed the dust as it went with its bunch of artificial roses. Ten huge and sparkling rings, which encrusted his hands with diamonds, and almost rivalled the sun that struck on them, led the ravished eyes of the beholders to the more precious enormity of his nails, which were each an inch long, and by proper nibbing might have taught the barbarians of the West to look with just scorn on their many-writing machines. But even these were nothing to the precious stones that covered him from head to foot. His bonnet, in which a peacock's feather was stuck in a most engaging manner, was surmounted by a sapphire of at least the size of a pigeon's egg ; his shoulders and sides sustained a real burden of treasure ; and he was one of the handsomest men at court, being exceedingly corpulent, and indeed, as his flatterers gave out, hardly able to walk, it may be imagined that he proceeded at no undignified pace. He would have ridden in his sedan, had he been lighter of body, but so much unaffected corpulence was not to be concealed, and he went on foot that nobody might suspect him of pretending to a dignity he did not possess. Behind him, three servants attended, clad in the most gorgeous silks ; the middle one held his umbrella over his head ; he on the right bore a fan of ivory, whereon were carved the exploits of Whay-Quang ; and he on the left sustained a purple bag on each arm, one containing opium and Areca-nut, the other the ravishing preparation of Gin-Seng, which possesses the Five Relishes. All the servants looked the same way as their master, that is to say, straight forward, with their eyes majestically half-shut, only they cried every now and then with a loud voice,—' Vanish from before the illustrious Quo, favourite of the mighty Brother of the Sun and Moon.'

Though the favourite looked neither to the right nor to the left, he could not but perceive the great homage that was paid him as well by the faces as the voices of the multitude. But one person, a Bonze, seemed transported beyond all the rest with an enthusiasm of admiration, and followed at a respectful distance from his side, bowing to the earth at every ten paces and exclaiming, ' Thanks to my lord for his jewels ! ' After repeating this for about six times, he increased the expressions of his gratitude and said, ' Thanks to my illustrious lord from his poor servant for his glorious jewels,'—and then again, ' Thanks to my illustrious lord, whose eye knoweth not degradation, from his poor servant, who is not fit to exist before him, for his jewels that make the rays of the sun look like ink.'   In short, the man's gratitude was so great, and its language delivered in phrases so choice, that Quo could contain his curiosity no longer, and turning aside, demanded to know his meaning :   ' I have not given you the jewels,' said the favourite, ' and why should you thank me for them ? '

' Refulgent Quo ! ' answered the Bonze, again bowing to the earth, ' what you say is as true as the five maxims of Fo, who was born without a father :—but your slave repeats his thanks, and is indeed infinitely obliged. You must know, O dazzling son of Quee, that of all my sect I have perhaps the greatest taste for enjoying myself. Seeing my lord therefore go by, I could not but be transported at having so great a pleasure, and said to myself, " The great Quo is very kind to me and my fellow citizens : he has taken infinite labour to acquire his magnificence, he takes still greater pains to preserve it, and all the while, I, who am lying under a shed, enjoy it for nothing ".'

A hundred years after, when the Emperor Wang heard this story, he diminished the expenditure of his household one half, and ordered the dead Bonze to be raised to the rank of a Colao.

A FABLE

[Table-Talk]

Want of Imagination plays strange tricks with most people. I will tell you a fable.

A traveller came into an unknown country where the people were more like birds than men, and twice as tall as the largest ostriches. They had beaks and wings, and lived in gigantic nests, upon trees of a proportionate size. The traveller, who was unfortunately a capital singer, happened to be indulging in one of his favourite songs, when he was overheard by a party of this monstrous people, who caught him and carried him home. Here he led such a life as made him a thousand times wish for death. The bird family did not seem to be cruel to one another, or even intentionally so to him ; for they soon found out what he liked to eat, and gave him plenty of it. They also flattened him a corner of the nest for a bed ; and were very particular in keeping out of his way a pet tiger which threw him into the most dreadful agitations. But in all other respects, whether out of cruelty or fondness, or want of thought, they teased him to death. His habitation, at best, was totally unfit for him. His health depended upon exercise, particularly as he was a traveller ; but he could not take any in the nest because it was hollow like a basin ; and had he attempted to step out of it he would have broken his neck. Sometimes they would handle him in their great claws, till his heart beat as if it would come through his ribs. Sometimes they kissed and fondled him with their horrid beaks. Sometimes they pulled his nose this way and that, till he gaped and cried out for anguish ; upon which they would grin from ear to ear, and stroke back his head, till the hairs came out by the roots. If he did not sing they would pull his arms about, and cruelly spread out his fingers, as if to discover what was the matter with him ; and when he did sing to beguile his sorrows, he had the mortification of finding that they looked upon it as a mark of his contentment and happiness. They would sing themselves (for some of them were pretty good singing-birds for so coarse a species), to challenge him, as it were, to new efforts. At length our poor traveller fell sick of a mortal distemper, the termination of which was luckily hastened by the modes they took to cure it. 'Wretch that I am!' cried he, in his last moments, 'I used to think it unmanly to care about keeping a goldfinch, or even a lark; but all my manliness, in a like situation, cannot prevent me from dying of torture.'

AN APOLOGUE

[From an essay called ' Fiction and Matter of Fact,' in Wishing Cap Papers, *Examiner*, 1824]

DURING a wonderful period of the world, the kings of the earth leagued themselves together to destroy all opposition; to root out, if they could, the very thoughts of mankind. Inquisition was made for blood. The ears of the grovelling lay in wait for every murmur. On a sudden, during this great hour of danger, there arose in a hundred parts of the world a cry, to which the cry of the Blatant Beast was a whisper. It proceeded from the wonderful multiplication of an extraordinary creature, which had already turned the cheeks of the tyrants pallid. It groaned and it grew loud: it spoke with a hundred tongues; it grew fervidly on the ear, like the noise of millions of wheels. And the sound of millions of wheels was in it, together with other marvellous and awful noises. There was the sharpening of swords, the braying of trumpets, the neighing of warhorses, the laughter of solemn voices, the rushing by of lights, the movement of impatient feet, a tread as if the world were coming. And ever and anon there were pauses with ' a still small voice,' which made a trembling in the night-time. But still the glowing sound of the wheels renewed itself; gathering early towards the morning. And when you came up to one of these creatures, you saw with fear and reverence its mighty confirmation, being like wheels indeed, and a great vapour. And ever and anon the vapour boiled, and the wheels went rolling, and the creature threw out of its mouth visible words, that fell into the air by millions, and spoke to the uttermost parts of the earth. And the nations (for it was a loving though a fearful creature) fed upon its words like the air they breathed : and the monarchs paused, for they knew their masters.

This is Printing by Steam.—It will be said that it is an allegory, and that all allegories are but fiction, and flat ones. I am far from producing it as a specimen of the poetical power now in existence. Allegory itself is out of fashion, though it was a favourite exercise of our old poets when the public were familiar with shows and spectacles. But allegory is the readiest shape into which imagination can turn a thing mechanical; and in the one before us is contained the mechanical truth and the spiritual truth of that very matter-of-fact thing called a Printing Press : each of them as true as the other, or neither could take place. A business of screws and iron wheels is, or appears to be, a very commonplace matter; but not so the will of the hand that sets them in motion; not so the operations of the mind that directs them what to utter. We are satisfied respecting the one by science; but what is it that renders us sensible of the wonders of the other, and their connexion with the greatest mysteries of nature ? Thought—Fancy—*Imagination*.

KINGS AND PRINCES

WOLSEY

[The Town]

WE have always thought the epithet of 'full-blown,' as applied to Wolsey, the happiest poetical hit ever made by Dr. Johnson :

> In full-blown dignity see Wolsey stand,
> Law in his voice, and fortune in his hand.

His ostentation, his clerical robes, his very corpulence, and his subsequent *fading*, all conspire to render the image felicitous. Wolsey is the very flower of priestly prosperity—fat, full-blown, gorgeous, called into life by sunshine ; the very odours he was fond of carrying in his hand became a part of his efflorescence ; one imagines his cheek florid, and his huge silken vestments expanding about him, like bloated petals. Anon, the blast blows from the horrid royal mouth : the round flower hangs its head ; it lays its dead neck on the earth ; and in its room is a loathed weed.

Wolsey, however, did not grow to be what he was with the indolence of a flower. He began his career with as much personal as mental activity, rendered himself necessary to the indolence of a young and luxurious sovereign,—in fact, became his sovereign's will in another shape, relieving the royal person of all trouble, and at the same time securing all his wishes, from a treaty down to a mistress ; and hence, as he himself intimated, the whole secret of his prosperity. He had industry, address, eloquence, the power of pleasing, the art (till success spoilt him) of avoiding whatever was unpleasant. He could set his master at ease with himself, in the smallest points of discourse, as well as on greater occasions. Henry felt no misgiving in his presence. He beheld in his lordly and luxurious agent a second self, with a superior intellect, artfully subjected to his own, so as to imply intellectual as well as royal superiority ; and he loved the priestly splendour of Wolsey, because, in setting the Church so high, and at the same time carrying himself so loyally, the churchman only the more elevated the prince. The moment the great servant appeared as if he could do without the greater master, by a fortune superior to failure in his projects, Henry's favour began to give way ; and when the princely churchman, partly in the heedlessness arising from long habits of security, and partly in the natural resentment of a superior mind, expressed a doubt whether this sovereign was acting with perfect justice towards him, his doom was sealed. Kings never forgive a wound to their self-love. They have been set so high above fellowship by their fellow creatures, that they feel, and in some measure they have a right to feel, the least intimation of equality, much more of superiority, as an offence, especially when it is aggravated by a secret sense of the justice of the pretension ; and all Wolsey's subsequent self-abasements could not do away with that stinging recollection, pleased as Henry was to widen the distance between them, and recover his own attitude of self-possession by airs of princely pity. Wolsey was a sort of Henry, himself—wilful, worldly, and fat, but with more talents and good-nature ; for he appears to have been a man of rare colloquial abilities, and, where he was not opposed in large matters, of a considerate kindliness. He was an attached as well as affable master ; and his consciousness of greater merit in himself would never have suffered him to send a couple of poor light-hearted girls to the scaffold, for bringing the royal marriage-bed into some shadow of a doubt of its sacredness. He would have sent them to a nunnery, and had a new marriage, without a tragedy in it, like a proper Christian Sultan ! Had Henry been in Wolsey's place, he would have proposed to set up the Inquisition; and King Thomas would have reproved him, and told him that such severities did not become two such fat and jolly believers as they.

The people appear to have liked Wolsey much. They enjoyed his pomp as a spectacle, and pitied his fall. They did not grudge his pomp to one who was so generous. Besides, they had a secret complacency in the humbleness of his origin, seeing that he rose from it by real merit. Those that quarrelled with him for his pride, were proud nobles and grudging fellow divines. It is pretty clear that Shakespeare, who was such a 'good fellow' himself, had a regard for Wolsey as another. He takes opportunities for echoing his praises, and dresses his fall in robes of pathos and eloquence. As to a true feeling of religion, it is out of the question in considering Wolsey's history and times. It was not expected of him. It was not the fashion or the morality of the day. It was sufficient that the Church made its way in the world, and secretly elevated the interests of literature and scholarship along with it. A king in those times was regarded as a visible God upon earth, not thoroughly well-behaved, but much to be believed in; and if the Church could compete with the State, it was hoped that more perfect times would somehow or other ensue. A good deal of licence was allowed it on behalf of the interests of better things—a singular arrangement, and, as the event turned out, not likely to better itself so peaceably as was hoped for; but it was making the best, under the circumstances, of the old perplexity between 'the shows of things, and the desires of the mind.' Wolsey (as the prosperous and the upper classes are apt to do in all ages) probably worshipped success itself as the final proof of all which the divine Governor of the world intended, in his dealings with individuals or society. Hence his proud swelling while possessed of it, and his undisguised tears and lamentations during his decline. He talks with his confidants about the King and good fortune, like a boy crying for a cake, and they respectfully echo his groans,

and evidently think them not at all inconsistent, either
with manliness or wisdom.

There was a breadth of character in all that Wolsey
thought, did, and suffered—in his strength and in his
weakness. In his prosperity he set no bounds to his
pomp : in adversity he cries out and calls upon the
gods, not affecting to be a philosopher. When he was
angry he huffed and used big words, like his master ;
when in good humour, he loaded people with praise ;
and he loved a large measure of it himself. He issued
forth, with his goodly bulk and huge garments, and
expected a worship analogous to his amplitudes. There
is a passage written with great humour by Sir Thomas
More, which, according to Dr. Wordsworth (the poet's
brother), is intended, 'no doubt, to represent the
Cardinal at the head of his table.' What reasons the
doctor has for not doubting the application, we cannot
say, and therefore do not think ourselves any more
justified than inclined to dispute them. The supposition
is highly probable. Wolsey must have offered a fine
dramatic spectacle to the eyes of a genius like More.

But if Wolsey set store by his fine speaking, he knew
also what belonged to his *hat* ; he was quite alive to the
effect produced by his office, and knew how to *get up*
and pamper a ceremony—to cook up a raw material
of dignity for the public relish. It should be no fault of
his, that any toy of his rank should not be looked up to
with awe. Accordingly, a most curious story is told of the
way in which he contrived that the Cardinal's hat,
which was sent him during his residence in York Place,
should make its first appearance in public. Cavendish
says, that the hat having been sent by the Pope through
the hands of an ordinary messenger, without any state,
Wolsey caused him to be 'stayed by the way,' newly
dressed in rich apparel, and met by a gorgeous cavalcade
of prelates and gentry. But a note in Mr. Singer's
edition, referring to Tindal and Fox, tells us that the
messenger actually reached him in York Place, was
clothed by him as aforesaid, *and sent back with the hat
to Dover*, from whence the cavalcade went and fetched

him. The hat was then set on a sideboard full of plate, with tapers round about it, 'and the greatest Duke in the lande must make curtsie thereto.'

HENRY THE EIGHTH

[*The Town*]

We have said more about Wolsey than we intend to say of Henry the Eighth; for the son of a butcher was a great man, and his master was only a king. Henry, born a prince, became a butcher; Wolsey, a butcher, became a prince. And we are not playing upon the word as applied to the king; for Henry was not only a butcher of his wives, he resembled a brother of the trade in its better and more ordinary course. His pleasures were of the same order; his language was coarse and jovial; he had the very straddle of a fat butcher, as he stands in his doorway. Take any picture or statue of Henry the Eighth—fancy its cap off, and a knife in its girdle, and it seems in the very act of saying 'What d'ye buy? What d'ye buy?' There is even the petty complacency in the mouth, after the phrase is uttered.

And how formidable is that petty unfeeling mouth, in the midst of those wide and wilful cheeks! Disturb the self-satisfaction of that man, derange his bile for an instant, make him suppose that you do not quite think him

Wisest, virtuousest, discreetest, best,

and what hope have you from the sentence of that mass of pampered egotism?

Let us not do injustice, however, even to the doers of it. What better was to be looked for, in those times, from the circumstances under which Henry was born and bred—from the son of a wilful father, and an unfeeling State marriage—from the educated combiner of Church and State, instinctively led to entertain the worldliest notions of both, and of heaven itself—from the inheritor of the greatest wealth, and power, and irresponsibility, ever yet concentrated in an English sovereign ? It has been attempted of late by various writers (and the attempt is a good symptom, being on the charitable side) to make out a case for Henry the Eighth, as if he were a sort of rough but honest fellow, a kind of John Bull of that age, who meant well upon the whole, and thought himself bound to keep up the conventionalities of his country. We know not what compliment is intended to be implied by this, either to Henry or his countrymen ; but really when a man sends his wives, one after the other, to the scaffold, evidently as much to enable him to marry another as to vindicate any propriety—when he ' cuts ' and sacrifices his best friends and servants, and pounces upon their goods—when he takes every licence himself, though he will not allow others even to be suspected of it— when he grows a brute beast in size as well as in habits, and dies shedding superfluous blood to the last—we cannot, for our parts, as Englishmen, but be glad of some better excuses for him of the kind above stated, than such as are to be found in the roots of the national character, however jovial. Imagine only the endearments that must have passed between this man and Anne Bullen, and then fancy the heart that could have sent the poor little, hysterical, half-laughing, half-crying thing to the scaffold ! The man was *mad* with power and vanity. That is his real excuse.

It has been said, that all which he did was done by law, or at least under the forms of it, and by the consent, sometimes by the recommendation, of his statesmen. The assertion is not true in all instances ; and where it is, what does it prove but that his tyrannical spirit had helped to make his statesmen slaves ? They knew what he wished, and notoriously played the game into his hands. When they did not, their heads went off. That circumstances had spoilt them altogether, and that society, with all its gaudiness, was but in a half-barbarous state, is granted ; but it is no less true, that his office, his breeding, and his natural temper, conspired to make Henry the worst and most insolent of a violent set of men ; and he stands straddling out accordingly in history, as he does in his pictures, an image of sovereign brutality.

Excessive vanity, aggravated by all the habits of despotism and luxury, and accompanied, nevertheless, by that unconscious misgiving which is natural to inequalities between a man's own powers and those which he derives from his position, is the clue to the character of Henry the Eighth. Accordingly no man gave greater ear to tale-bearers and sowers of suspicion, nor resented more cruelly or meanly the wounds inflicted on his self-love, even by those who least intended them, or to whom he had shown the greatest fondness. The latter, indeed, he treated the worst, out of a frenzy of egotistical disappointment : for his love arose, not from any real regard for their merits, but from what he had taken for a flattery to his own. Sir Thomas More knew him well, when, in observation to some one who had congratulated him on the King's having walked up and down with his arm around his neck, he said that he would have that neck cut in two next day, if the head belonging to it opposed his will. He not only took back without scruple all that he had given to Wolsey, but he went to live in the houses of his fallen friend and servant—places which a man of any feeling and kindly remembrance would have avoided. He was very near picking a murderous quarrel with his last wife, Catherine Parr, on one of his theological questions. And how did he conduct himself to the memory of poor Anne Bullen, even on the day of her execution ?

ELIZABETH

[The Town]

It was under Elizabeth that Whitehall shone out in all its romantic splendour. It was no longer the splendour of Wolsey alone, nor of Henry alone, or with a great name by his side now and then; but of a Queen, surrounded and worshipped through a long reign by a galaxy of the brightest minds and most chivalrous persons ever assembled in English history.

Here she comes, turning round the corner from the Strand, under a canopy of state, leaving the noisier, huzzaing multitude behind the barriers that mark the precincts of the palace, and bending her eyes hither and thither, in acknowledgement of the kneeling obeisances of the courtiers. Beside her are Cecil and Knolles, and Northampton, and Bacon's father; or, later in life, Leicester, and Burleigh, and Sir Philip Sidney, and Greville, and Sir Francis Drake (and Spenser is looking on); or, later still, Essex and Raleigh, and Bacon himself, and Southampton, Shakespeare's friend, with Shakespeare among the spectators. We shall see her by and by, at that period, as brought to life to us in the description of Heutzner the traveller. At present (as we have her at this moment in our eye) she is younger, of a large and tall, but well-made figure, with fine eyes, and finer hands, which she is fond of displaying. We are too apt to think of Elizabeth as thin and elderly, and patched up; but for a good period of her life she was plump and personable, warranting the history of the robust romps of the Lord Admiral, Seymour; and till her latter days (and even then, as far as her powers went), we are always to fancy her at once spirited and stately of carriage, impulsive (except on occasions of ordinary ceremony), and ready to manifest her emotions in look and voice, whether as woman or Queen; in a word, a sort of Henry the Eighth corrected by a female nature and a better understanding—or perhaps an Anne Bullen, enlarged, and made less feminine, by the father's grossness. The Protestants have represented her as too staid, and the Catholics as too violent and sensual. According to the latter, Whitehall was a mere sink of iniquity. It was not likely to be so, for many reasons; but neither, on the other hand, do we take it to have been anything like the pattern of self-denial which some fond writers have supposed. Where there is power, and leisure, and luxury, though of the most legitimate kind, and refinement, though of the most intellectual, self-denial on the side of enjoyment is not apt to be the reigning philosophy; nor would it reasonably be looked for in any court, at all living in wealth and splendour.

Imagine the sensations of Elizabeth, when she first set down in the palace at Whitehall, after escaping the perils of imputed illegitimacy, of confinement for party's sake and for religion's, and all the other terrors of her father's reign and of Mary's, danger of death itself not excepted. She was a young Queen of twenty-five years of age, healthy, sprightly, good-looking, with plenty of will, power, and imagination; and the gallantest spirits of the age were at her feet. How pitiable, and how respectable, become almost all sovereigns, when we consider them as human beings put in possession of almost superhuman power; and when we reflect in general how they have been brought up, and what a provocative to abuse at all events becomes the possession of a throne! We in general spoil them first;—we always tempt them to take every advantage, by worshipping them as if they were different creatures from ourselves;—and then we are astonished that they should take us at our word. How much better would it be to be astonished at the likeness they retain to us, even in the kindlier part of our weaknesses.

By a very natural process, considering the great and chivalrous men of that day, Elizabeth became at once one of the greatest of Queens and one of the most flattered and vain of women. Nor were the courtiers so entirely insincere as they are supposed to have been, when they worshipped her as they did, and gave her

credit for all the beauty and virtue under heaven. On
the contrary, the power to benefit them went hand-in-
hand with their self-love to give them a sincere though
extravagant notion of their mistress ; and the romantic
turn of the age and its literature, its exploits, its poetry,
all conspired to warm and sanction the enthusiasm on
both sides, and to blind the admiration to those little
outward defects, and inward defects too, which love at
all periods is famous for overlooking—nay, for convert-
ing into noble grounds of denial, and of subjection to
a sentiment. Thus Elizabeth's hook nose, her red hair,
nay, her very age and crookedness at last, did not stand
in the way of raptures at her ' beauty ' and ' divine
perfections,' any more than a flaw in the casket that
held a jewel. The spirit of love and beauty was there :
the appreciation of the soul of both ; the glory of
exciting, and of giving, the glorification ;—and all the
rest was a trifle, an accident, a mortal show of things,
which no gentleman and lady can help. The Queen
might even swear a good round oath or so occasionally ;
and what did it signify ? It was a pleasant ebullition
of the authority which is above taxation ; the Queen
swore, and not the woman ; or if the woman did, it was
only an excess of feeling proper to balance the account,
and to bring her royalty down to a level with good hearty
human nature.

It has been said, that as Elizabeth advanced in life,
the courtiers dropped the mention of her beauty; but
this is a mistake. They were more sparing in the
mention of it, but when they spoke they were conscious
that the matter was not to be minced. When her Majesty
was in her sixty-second year, the famous Earl of Essex
gave her an entertainment, in the course of which she
was complimented on her ' *beauty* ' and *dazzling outside*,
in speeches written for the occasion by Lord, then
' Mr. Francis, Bacon.' [1] Sir John Davies, another

---

[1] Nichols's *Progresses and Public Processions of Queen
Elizabeth*, year 1595, pp. 4-8. ' He will ever bear in his
heart the picture of her beauty.' ' He now looks on his

lawyer, who was not born till she was near forty, and could not have written his acrostical 'Hymns' upon her till she was elderly, celebrates her as awakening 'thoughts of young love,' and being 'beauty's rose indeed'[1]; and it is well known that she was at a reverend time of life when Sir Walter Raleigh wrote upon her like a despairing lover, calling her 'Venus' and 'Diana,' and saying he could not exist out of her presence. . . . .

Of one thing, it surprises us that there could ever have been a question; namely, that Elizabeth was a great as well as fortunate sovereign,—a woman of extraordinary intellect. To the undervaluing remark that she had wise ministers, it was well answered that she chose them; and if, like most other people, she was less wise and less correct in her conduct than she had the reputation of being, nothing, on that very account, can surely be thought too highly of the wonderful address with which she succeeded in sitting upon the top of the Protestant world as she did throughout her whole reign, supreme over her favourites as well as her ministers—the refuge of struggling opinion, and the idol of romance.

GEORGE THE SECOND

[Old Court Suburb]

GEORGE THE FIRST would seldom be visible in these promenades. George the Second, a man shorter than his short father, but smart, strutting, decided-looking, with higher features and an under-hanging jaw, was fond of being seen; and in all probability not seldom paraded the gardens, amidst avenues of bows and curtseys. Though by no means the conjuror for which he

mistress's outside with the eyes of sense, which are dazzled and amazed.'

[1] See the poems in Anderson's edition, vol. ii. p. 706.

took himself, he was a less dull, though hardly better informed man than his father ; had the same instinctive wisdom of self-security, which led to the putting and maintaining the government in the hands of Sir Robert Walpole ; was nevertheless the same petty German autocrat, ruling, as far as he ruled at all, like a martinet and a barrack-master ; thought men and women (according to the report of Lady Mary) born for nothing else but to be 'kicked or kissed for his diversion' ; and whenever one of the ladies gave him to understand that she differed with him on that point, he fancied that she only wanted an excuse for getting out of him a little of what he valued above all things—money. He one day counted his guineas so often for this purpose, in the presence of Miss Bellenden, that she told him 'if he did it again, she should go out of the room.' He appears, on a subsequent occasion, to have done it again ; upon which the disgusted beauty gave a jerk to the rouleau that scattered the guineas about the floor, and ran off while he was picking them up.

George's strutting airs of dignity were but disguises of the want of it. Lady Deloraine, who was governess of his children, and at the same time supposed to be one of his mistresses, had her chair pulled from under her one evening at Kensington by the Princess Emily, as she was going to sit down to cards. Her ladyship sprawled on the floor ; and his dignified Majesty did not scruple to be very much diverted, and laugh. The Countess, in return, contrived without more ado to play him the same trick ; and his dignity was so offended that a rupture ensued between them, and she was forbidden the Court.

George the Second, like his father, had two chief mistresses ; one of them a German, of the name of Walmoden, whom he made Countess of Yarmouth ; the other, the Countess of Suffolk before-mentioned ; both of them well-tempered, discreet women, who appear to have been as much the favourites of his sober hours, or more so, than of the impassioned moments for which credit was given them. His chief passion had been for

his wife ; and Sir Robert Walpole showed a rare knowledge of a little-suspected, but no less certain corner in
human nature, by discovering that the wife retained an
ascendancy over the mistresses by setting her husband's
pleasure above every other consideration, and so possessing his unbounded confidence.   It was a curious instance
of the sentiments of those times ; at least, in courts ;
but Caroline of Anspach had been bred up in them, and
she carried their toleration to an amount that was
perhaps unequalled, especially among those who most
availed themselves of the licence. This was the reverse
of her own case, for she seems to have been as faithful
as she was devoted ; and her husband passionately said
of her, after her death, that he had never loved any
woman as he did her.

GEORGE THE THIRD

[Autobiography]

GEORGE THE THIRD was a very brave and honest man.
He feared nothing on earth, and he acted according to
his convictions.   But, unfortunately, his convictions
were at the mercy of a will far greater than his understanding ;   and hence his courage became obstinacy,
and his honesty the dupe of his inclinations.   He was
the son of a father with little brain, and of a mother
who had a diseased blood : indeed, neither of his parents
was healthy.   He was brought up in rigid principles
of morality on certain points, by persons who are
supposed to have evaded them in their own conduct ;
he was taught undue notions of kingly prerogative ;
he was suffered to grow up, nevertheless, in homely as
well as shy and moody habits ; and while acquiring a
love of power tending to the violent and uncontrollable,
he was not permitted to have a taste of it till he became
his own master. The consequences of this training were
an extraordinary mixture of domestic virtue with official

duplicity ; of rustical, mechanical tastes and popular
manners, with the most exalted ideas of authority ;
of a childish and self-betraying cunning, with the most
stubborn reserves ; of fearlessness with sordidness ;
good-nature with unforgivingness ; and of the health
and strength of temperance and self-denial, with the
last weaknesses of understanding, and passions that
exasperated it out of its reason. The English nation
were pleased to see in him a crowning specimen of themselves—a royal John Bull. They did not discover till
too late (perhaps have not yet discovered) how much
of the objectionable, as well as the respectable, lies
hidden in the sturdy nickname invented for them by
Arbuthnot ; how much the animal predominates in it
over the intellectual ; and how terribly the bearer of it
may be overridden, whether in a royal or a national
shape. They had much better get some new name for
themselves, worthy of the days of Queen Victoria and
of the hopes of the world.

A LITTLE PRINCE

[Old Court Suburb]

THE history of this poor little personage[1] is painfully
curious. There is a common saying, ' As happy as a
prince ' ; and if ever prince was thought happy by those
who were not in the secret of courts, this premature
victim of his birth and breeding was probably held to
be supremely so, especially by all the little boys of
England. He was heir to a throne ; he lived apart
from its troubles in the house of his father and mother ;
and, what must have appeared a stupendous felicity in
the eyes of the little boys, he not only possessed a real,
right earnest, steel sword, instead of one made of lath

---

[1] [William, Duke of Gloucester, the infant son of Queen
Anne and Prince George of Denmark.]

and paint, and besides that, a suit of real soldiers'
clothes—absolute, right earnest regimentals, all red
and gold—but, amazing to think! he was colonel of
a positive regiment of boys, all dressed in soldiers'
clothes too. He rode at the head of them ; he sat
opposite them during parade on a live horse, his own
pony ; could order them about, and cry March ! and
look grand and manly ; and all the while music would
play—real proper fifes, and drums, and trumpets, not
at all ' penny ' ; and he had cannon too, and castles,
and a wooden horse to put his soldiers on, when they
did wrong ; and they stood sentinels at his door-ways,
and were the terror of the neighbouring cake-shops and
apple-stalls, like any proper full-grown gentlemen
soldiers. They even had field-days on Wormwood
Scrubs, and reviews in Kensington Gardens, and King
William was there to see. In short, Campden House was
Little Boy's Paradise.

Alas ! the god of this paradise was a sickly big-headed
child, the victim of his very birth and breeding, and
doomed to an early death. He was the only survivor
of seventeen children, not one of whom ought to have
been born ; for Anne had destroyed her person and
constitution by gross living—a propensity derived from
her mother, Anne Hyde, perhaps from her grandfather
Clarendon; and as the most important of all physiologies
was not studied in those days, nobody seems to have
suspected (indeed few people still suspect) what disas-
trous liabilities are entailed upon offspring by habits of
this or of any other injurious kind in parents. The poor
little prince was afflicted with water on the brain. He
had a head large enough for a grown person, with all
the sickly tendencies that accompany such a warning
symptom; yet his dull, though anxious, and not naturally
unkind parents so little knew how to treat him, or
attended so little to the advice of those who knew better,
that after making him weak in body and obstinate in
mind with wrong indulgences, they tried to force him
into health and good temper by severe treatment. The
poor child was flogged to make him take his medicine ;

flogged to make him walk when he needed help; flogged to make him go up and down stairs. At the age of eleven he was no more.

THE PRINCE REGENT

[Autobiography]

THIS article[1], no doubt, was very bitter and contemptuous; therefore, in the legal sense of the term, very libellous; the more so, inasmuch as it was very true. There will be no question about the truth of it, at this distance of time, with any class of persons, unless, possibly, with some few of the old Tories, who may think it was a patriotic action in the Prince to displace the Whigs for their opponents. But I believe that, under all the circumstances, there are few persons indeed nowadays, of any class, who will not be of opinion that, bitter as the article was, it was more than sufficiently avenged by two years' imprisonment and a fine of a thousand pounds. For it did but express what all the world were feeling, with the exception of the Prince's once bitterest enemies, the Tories themselves, then newly become his friends; and its very sincerity and rashness, had the Prince possessed greatness of mind to think so, might have furnished him such a ground for pardoning it, as would have been the best proof he could have given us of our having mistaken him, and turned us into blushing and grateful friends. An attempt to bribe us on the side of fear did but further disgust us. A free and noble waiving of the punishment would have bowed our hearts into regret. We should have found in it the evidence of that true generosity of nature paramount to whatsoever was frivolous or appeared to be mean, which his flatterers claimed for him, and which would have made us doubly blush for the formal virtues to which we seemed to be

[1] [*Examiner*, 1812. See Introduction, pp. ix, x.]

attached, when, in reality, nothing would have better pleased us than such a combination of the gay and the magnanimous. I say doubly blush, for I now blush at ever having been considered, or rather been willing to be considered, an advocate of any sort of conventionality, unqualified by liberal exceptions and prospective enlargement; and I am sure that my brother, had he been living, who was one of the best-natured and most indulgent of men, would have joined with me in making the same concession; though I am bound to add that, with all his indulgence of others, I have no reason to believe that he had ever stood in need of that pardon for even conventional licence, from the necessity of which I cannot pretend to have been exempt....

Neither have I any quarrel, at this distance of time, with the Prince Regent; for though his frivolity, his tergiversation, and his treatment of his wife, will not allow me to respect his memory, I am bound to pardon it as I do my own faults, in consideration of the circumstances which mould the character of every human being. Could I meet him in some odd corner of the Elysian fields, where charity had room for both of us, I should first apologize to him for having been the instrument in the hand of events for attacking a fellow creature, and then expect to hear him avow as hearty a regret for having injured myself, and unjustly treated his wife.

VICTORIA

[*Old Court Suburb*]

WE remember well the peculiar kind of personal
pleasure which it gave us to see the future Queen, the
first time we ever did see her, coming up a cross path
from the Bayswater gate, with a girl of her own age by
her side, whose hand she was holding, as if she loved her.
It brought to our mind the warmth of our own juvenile
friendships ; and made us fancy that she loved everything else that we had loved in like measure,—books,
trees, verses, Arabian tales, and the good mother who
had helped to make her so affectionate.

A magnificent footman, in scarlet, came behind her,
with the splendidest pair of calves in white stockings
that we ever beheld.   He looked somehow like a
gigantic fairy, personating, for his little lady's sake,
the grandest kind of footman he could think of ; and
his calves he seemed to have made out of a couple of the
biggest chaise-lamps in the possession of the godmother
of Cinderella.   As the princess grew up, the world
seemed never to hear of her, except as it wished to hear,
—that is to say, in connexion with her mother ; and
now it never hears of her, but in connexion with
children of her own, and with her husband, and her
mother still, and all good household pleasures and
hospitalities, and public virtues of a piece with them.
May life ever continue to appear to her what, indeed,
it really is to all who have eyes for seeing beyond the
surface ; namely, a wondrous fairy scene, strange,
beautiful, mournful too, yet hopeful of being ' happy
ever after,' when its story is over ; and wise, meantime,
in seeing much where others see nothing, in shedding
its tears patiently, and in doing its best to diminish the
tears around it.

ABOUT TOWN

STATIONERS' HALL

[The Town]

BETWEEN Amen Corner and Ludgate Street, at the end of a passage from Ave-Maria Lane, ' stood a great house of stone and wood, belonging in old time to John, Duke of Bretagne, and Earl of Richmond, cotemporary with Edward II and III. After him it was possessed by the Earls of Pembroke, in the time of Richard II and Henry IV, and was called Pembroke's Inn, near Ludgate. It then fell into the possession of the Earl of Abergavenny, and was called Burgavenny House, under which circumstances it remained in the time of Elizabeth. To finish the anti-climax,' says Pennant, ' it was finally possessed by the Company of Stationers, who rebuilt it of wood, and made it their Hall. It was destroyed by the Great Fire, and was succeeded by the present plain building.' [1] Of the once powerful possessors of the old mansion nothing now is remembered, or cared for ; but in the interior of the modern building are to be seen, looking almost as if they were alive, and as if we knew them personally, the immortal faces of Steele and Richardson, Prior in his cap, and Dr. Hoadley, a liberal bishop. There is also Mrs. Richardson, the wife of the novelist, looking as prim and particular as if she had been just chucked under the chin; and Robert Nelson, Esq., supposed author of the *Whole Duty of Man,* and prototype of Sir Charles Grandison, as regular and passionless in his face as if he had been made only to wear his wig. The same is not to be said of the face of Steele, with his black eyes and social aspect ; and

---

[1] Pennant's *London,* p. 377.

Q 2

still less of Richardson, who, instead of being the smooth, satisfied-looking personage he is represented in some engravings of him (which makes his heartrending romance appear unaccountable and cruel), has a face as uneasy as can well be conceived—flushed and shattered with emotion. We recognize the sensitive, enduring man, such as he really was—a heap of bad nerves. It is worth anybody's while to go to Stationers' Hall on purpose to see these portraits. They are not of the first order as portraits, but evident likenesses. Hoadley looks at once jovial and decided, like a good-natured controversialist. Prior is not so pleasant in his prints: his nose is a little aquiline, instead of turned up; and his features, though delicate, not so liberal. But if he has not the best look of his poetry, he has the worst. He seems as if he had been sitting up all night; his eyelids droop: and his whole face is *used* with rakery.

It is impossible to see Prior and Steele together without regretting that they quarrelled: but as they did quarrel, it was fit that Prior should be in the wrong. From a Whig he had become a Tory, and showed that his change was not quite what it ought to have been, by avoiding the men with whom he had associated, and writing contemptuously of his fellow wits. All the men of letters, whose portraits are in this hall, were, doubtless, intimate with the premises, and partakers of Stationers' dinners. Richardson was Master of the Company. Morphew, a bookseller in the neighbourhood, was one of the publishers of the *Tatler*; and concerts as well as festive dinners used to take place in the great room, of both of which entertainments Steele was fond. It was here, if we mistake not, that one of the inferior officers of the Company, a humorist on sufferance, came in, one day, on his knees, at an anniversary dinner when Bishop Hoadley was present, in order to drink to the 'Glorious Memory [1].' The company, Steele included, were pretty far gone; Hoadley had remained as long as he well could; and the genuflector was drunk.

[1] Of William III.

Steele, seeing the Bishop a little disconcerted, whispered him, 'Do laugh, my lord ; pray laugh :—'tis *humanity* to laugh.' The good-natured prelate acquiesced. Next day, Steele sent him a penitential letter, with the following couplet :—

> Virtue with so much ease on Bangor sits,
> All faults he pardons, though he none commits.

The most illustrious musical performance that ever took place in the hall was that of Dryden's Ode. A society for the annual commemoration of St. Cecilia, the patroness of music, was instituted in the year 1680, not without an eye perhaps to the religious opinions of the heir presumptive who was shortly to ascend the throne as James the Second. An ode was written every year for the occasion, and set to music by some eminent composer ; and the performance of it was followed by a grand dinner. In 1687, Dryden contributed his first ode, entitled 'A Song for Saint Cecilia's Day,' in which there are finer things than in any part of the other, though as a whole it is not so striking. Ten years afterwards it was followed by 'Alexander's Feast,' the dinner, perhaps, being a part of the inspiration. Poor Jeremiah Clarke, who shot himself for love, was the composer. This is the ode with the composition of which Bolingbroke is said to have found Dryden in a state of emotion one morning, the whole night having been passed, *agitante deo*, under the fever of inspiration.

From Stationers' Hall once issued all the almanacs that were published, with all the trash and superstition they kept alive. Francis Moore is still among their 'living dead men.' Francis must now be a posthumous old gentleman, of at least one hundred and fifty years of age. The first blunder the writers of these books committed, in their cunning, was the having to do with the state of the weather ; their next was to think that the grandmothers of the last century were as immortal as their title-pages, and that nobody was getting wiser than themselves. The mysterious solemnity of their hiero-glyphics, bringing heaven and earth together, like a vision in the Apocalypse, was imposing to the nurse and the child; and the bashfulness of their bodily sympathies no less attractive. We remember the astonishment of a worthy seaman, some years ago, at the claim which they put into the mouth of the sign Virgo. The monopoly is now gone; almanacs have been forced into improvement by emulation; and the Stationers (naturally enough at the moment) are angry about it. This fit of ill-humour will pass; and a body of men, interested by their very trade in the progress of liberal knowledge, will by and by join the laugh at the tenderness they evinced in behalf of old wives' fables. It is observable that their friend Bickerstaff (Steele's assumed name in the *Tatler*) was the first to begin the joke against them.

COVENT GARDEN MARKET

[The Town]

COVENT GARDEN market has always been the most agreeable in the metropolis, because it is devoted exclusively to fruit, flowers, and vegetables. A few crockery-ware shops make no exceptions to this 'bloodless' character. The seasons here regularly present themselves in their most gifted looks,—with evergreens in winter, the fresh verdure of spring, all the hues of summer, and whole loads of desserts in autumn. The country girls who bring the things to market at early dawn are a sight themselves worthy of the apples and roses; the good-natured Irish women who attend to carry baskets for purchasers are not to be despised, with the half humorous, half pathetic tone of their petitions to be employed; and the ladies who come to purchase crown all. No walk in London, on a fine summer's day, is more agreeable than the passage through the flowers here at noon, when the roses and green leaves are newly watered, and blooming faces come to look at them in those cool and shady avenues, while the hot sun is basking in the streets. On these occasions we were very well satisfied with the market in its old state. The old sheds and irregular avenues, when dry, assorted well with the presence of leaves and fruits. They had a careless picturesque look, as if a bit of an old suburban garden had survived from ancient times.

Nothing, however, but approbation can be bestowed on the convenient and elegant state into which the market has been raised by the magnificence of the noble proprietor, whose arms we are glad to see on the side next James Street. They are a real grace to the building and to the owner, for they are a stamp of liberality. In time we hope to see the roofs of the new market covered with shrubs and flowers, nodding over the balustrades, and fruits and red berries sparkling in the sun. As an ornament, nothing is more beautiful in combination than the fluctuating grace of foliage and the stability of architecture. And, as a utility, the more air and sun the better. There is never too much sun in this country, and every occasion should be seized to take advantage of it.

CHRIST HOSPITAL

[*Autobiography*]

PERHAPS there is not a foundation in the country so truly English, taking that word to mean what Englishmen wish it to mean—something solid, unpretending, of good character, and free to all. More boys are to be found in it who issue from a greater variety of ranks than in any school in the kingdom ; and as it is the most various so it is the largest of all the free schools. Nobility do not go there, except as boarders. Now and then a boy of a noble family may be met with, and he is reckoned an interloper, and against the charter ; but the sons of poor gentry and London citizens abound ; and with them an equal share is given to the sons of tradesmen of the very humblest description, not omitting servants. I would not take my oath—but I have

a strong recollection, that in my time there were two
boys, one of whom went up into the drawing-room to his
father, the master of the house; and the other down
into the kitchen to *his* father, the coachman. One
thing, however, I know to be certain, and it is the noblest
of all, namely, that the boys themselves (at least it was
so in my time) had no sort of feeling of the difference of
one another's ranks out of doors. The cleverest boy
was the noblest, let his father be who he might.
Christ Hospital is a nursery of tradesmen, of merchants,
of naval officers, of scholars; it has produced some of
the greatest ornaments of their time; and the feeling
among the boys themselves is, that it is a medium
between the patrician pretension of such schools as
Eton and Westminster, and the plebeian submission of
the charity schools. In point of university honours it
claims to be equal with the best; and though other
schools can show a greater abundance of eminent names,
I know not where many will be found who are a greater
host in themselves. One original author is worth a
hundred transmitters of elegance: and such a one is
to be found in Richardson, who here received what
education he possessed. Here Camden also received the
rudiments of his. Bishop Stillingfleet, according to the
Memoirs of Pepys, was brought up in the school. We
have had many eminent scholars, two of them Greek pro-
fessors, to wit, Barnes and the present Mr. Scholefield,
the latter of whom attained an extraordinary succession
of university honours. The rest are Markland; Middleton, late Bishop of Calcutta; and Mitchell, the translator of *Aristophanes*. Christ Hospital, I believe, towards
the close of the last century and the beginning of
the present, sent out more living writers, in its proportion, than any other school. There was Dr. Richards,
author of the *Aboriginal Britons*; Dyer, whose life was
one unbroken dream of learning and goodness, and
who used to make us wonder with passing through the
school-room (where no other person in 'town clothes'
ever appeared) to consult books in the library; Le
Grice, the translator of *Longus*; Horne, author of some

well-known productions in controversial divinity ; Surr,
the novelist (not in the Grammar School); James White,
the friend of Charles Lamb, and not unworthy of him,
author of *Falstaff's Letters* (this was he who used to give
an anniversary dinner to the chimney-sweepers, merrier
than, though not so magnificent as, Mrs. Montague's);
Pitman, a celebrated preacher, editor of some school-
books and religious classics (also a veritable man of wit) ;
Mitchell, before mentioned ; myself, who stood next
him ; Barnes, who came next, the Editor of the *Times*,
than whom no man (if he had cared for it) could have
been more certain of attaining celebrity for wit and
literature ; Townsend, a prebendary of Durham, author
of *Armageddon*, and several theological works ; Gilly,
another of the Durham prebendaries, an amiable man,
who wrote the *Narrative of the Waldenses* ; Scargill, a
Unitarian minister, author of some tracts on Peace and
War, &c. ; and lastly, whom I have kept by way of
climax, Coleridge and Charles Lamb, two of the most
original geniuses, not only of the day, but of the country.
We have had an ambassador among us ; but as he,
I understand, is ashamed of us, we are hardly more
ashamed of him, and accordingly omit him.

In the time of Henry the Eighth Christ Hospital was
a monastery of Franciscan friars. Being dissolved
among the others, Edward the Sixth, moved by a sermon
of Bishop Ridley's, assigned the revenues of it to the
maintenance and education of a certain number of poor
orphan children, born of citizens of London. I believe
there has been no law passed to alter the letter of this
intention ; which is a pity, since the alteration has taken
place. An extension of it was probably very good, and
even demanded by circumstances. I have reason, for
one, to be grateful for it. But tampering with matters-
of-fact among children is dangerous. They soon learn
to distinguish between allowed poetical fiction and
that which they are told, under severe penalties, never
to be guilty of ; and this early sample of contradiction
between the thing asserted and the obvious fact can
do no good even in an establishment so plain-dealing in

other respects as Christ Hospital. The place is not only designated as an orphan-house in its Latin title, but the boys, in the prayers which they repeat every day, implore the pity of heaven upon ' us poor orphans.' I remember the perplexity this caused me at a very early period. It is true, the word orphan may be used in a sense implying destitution of any sort; but this was not its Christ Hospital intention; nor do the younger boys give it the benefit of that scholarly interpretation. There was another thing (now, I believe, done away) which existed in my time, and perplexed me still more. It seemed a glaring instance of the practice likely to result from the other assumption, and made me prepare for a hundred falsehoods and deceptions, which, mixed up with contradiction, as most things in society are, I sometimes did find, and oftener dreaded. I allude to a foolish custom they had in the ward which I first entered, and which was the only one that the company at the public suppers were in the habit of going into, of hanging up, by the side of each bed, a clean white napkin, which was supposed to be the one used by the occupiers. Now these napkins were only for show, the real towels being of the largest and coarsest kind. If the masters had been asked about them, they would doubtless have told the truth; perhaps the nurses would have done so. But the boys were not aware of this. They saw these ' white lies' hanging before them, a conscious imposition; and I well remember how alarmed I used to feel, lest any of the company should direct their inquiries to me.

Christ Hospital (for this is its proper name, and not Christ's Hospital) occupies a considerable portion of ground between Newgate Street, Giltspur Street, St. Bartholomew's, and Little Britain. There is a quadrangle with cloisters; and the square inside the cloisters is called the Garden, and most likely was the monastery garden. Its only delicious crop, for many years, has been pavement. Another large area, presenting the Grammar and Navigation Schools, is also misnomered the Ditch; the town-ditch having formerly run that way. In

Newgate Street is seen the Hall, or eating-room, one of the noblest in England, adorned with enormously long paintings by Verrio and others, and with an organ. A portion of the old quadrangle once contained the library of the monks, and was built or repaired by the famous Whittington, whose arms were to be seen outside; but alterations of late years have done it away.

In the cloisters a number of persons lie buried, besides the officers of the house. Among them is Isabella, wife of Edward the Second, the 'She-wolf of France.' I was not aware of this circumstance then; but many a time, with a recollection of some lines in 'Blair's Grave' upon me, have I run as hard as I could at night-time from my ward to another, in order to borrow the next volume of some ghostly romance. In one of the cloisters was an impression resembling a gigantic foot, which was attributed by some to the angry stamping of the ghost of a beadle's wife! A beadle was a higher sound to us than to most, as it involved ideas of detected apples in church-time, 'skulking' (as it was called) out of bounds, and a power of reporting us to the masters. But fear does not stand upon rank and ceremony.

The wards, or sleeping-rooms, are twelve, and contained, in my time, rows of beds on each side, partitioned off, but connected with one another, and each having two boys to sleep in it. Down the middle ran the binns for holding bread and other things, and serving for a table when the meal was not taken in the hall; and over the binns hung a great homely chandelier.

To each of these wards a nurse was assigned, who was the widow of some decent liveryman of London, and who had the charge of looking after us at night-time, seeing to our washing, &c., and carving for us at dinner: all of which gave her a good deal of power, more than her name warranted. The nurses, however, were almost invariably very decent people, and performed their duty; which was not always the case with the young ladies, their daughters. There were five schools: a grammar school, a mathematical or navigation school (added by

Charles the Second, through the zeal of Mr. Pepys), a
writing, a drawing, and a reading school. Those who
could not read when they came on the foundation went
into the last. There were few in the last-but-one, and I
scarcely know what they did, or for what object. The
writing school was for those who were intended for trade
and commerce; the mathematical, for boys who went
as midshipmen into the naval and East India service;
and the grammar school for such as were designed for
the Church, and to go to the University. The writing
school was by far the largest; and, what is very curious
(which is not the case now), all the schools were kept
quite distinct; so that a boy might arrive at the age of
fifteen in the grammar school and not know his multiplication table; which was the case with myself. Nor
do I know it to this day! Shades of Horace Walpole
and Lord Lyttelton! come to my assistance, and enable
me to bear the confession: but so it is. The fault was
not my fault at the time; but I ought to have repaired
it when I went out in the world; and great is the mischief which it has done me.

Our dress was of the coarsest and quaintest kind,
but was respected out of doors, and is so. It consisted
of a blue drugget gown, or body, with ample skirts to
it; a yellow vest underneath in winter-time; small-
clothes of Russia duck; worsted yellow stockings; a
leathern girdle; and a little black worsted cap, usually
carried in the hand. I believe it was the ordinary dress
of children in humble life during the reign of the Tudors.
We used to flatter ourselves that it was taken from the
monks; and there went a monstrous tradition that at
one period it consisted of blue velvet with silver buttons.
It was said, also, that during the blissful era of the blue
velvet, we had roast mutton for supper; but that the
small-clothes not being then in existence, and the mutton
suppers too luxurious, the eatables were given up for
the ineffables.

Our routine of life was this. We rose to the call of a
bell, at six in summer and seven in winter; and after
combing ourselves, and washing our hands and faces,

went, at the call of another bell, to breakfast. All this took up about an hour. From breakfast we proceeded to school, where we remained till eleven, winter and summer, and then had an hour's play. Dinner took place at twelve. Afterwards was a little play till one, when we again went to school, and remained till five in summer and four in winter. At six was the supper. We used to play after it in summer till eight. In winter, we proceeded from supper to bed. On Sundays, the school-time of the other days was occupied in church, both morning and evening ; and as the Bible was read to us every day before every meal, and on going to bed, besides prayers and graces, we rivalled the monks in the religious part of our duties.

Being able to read, and knowing a little Latin, I was put at once into the Under Grammar School. How much time I wasted there in learning the accidence and syntax I cannot say ; but it seems to me a long while. My grammar seemed always to open at the same place. Things are managed differently now, I believe, in this as well as in many other respects. Great improvements have been made in the whole establishment. The boys feed better, learn better, and have longer holidays in the country. In my time, they never slept out of the school, but on one occasion, during the whole of their stay ; this was for three weeks in summer-time, which they were bound to pass at a certain distance from London. They now have these holidays with a reasonable frequency ; and they all go to the different schools, instead of being confined, as they were then, some to nothing but writing and cyphering, and some to the languages. It has been doubted by some of us elders whether this system will beget such temperate, proper students, with pale faces, as the other did. I dare say our successors are not afraid of us. I had the pleasure, some years since, of dining in company with a Deputy Grecian, who, with a stout rosy-faced person, had not failed to acquire the scholarly turn for joking which is common to a classical education ; as well as those simple, becoming manners, made up of modesty and proper confidence, which have been often remarked as distinguishing the boys of this foundation.

' But what is a Deputy Grecian ? ' Ah, reader ! to ask that question, and at the same time to know anything at all worth knowing, would at one time, according to our notion of things, have been impossible. When I entered the school, I was shown three gigantic boys, young men rather (for the eldest was between seventeen and eighteen), who, I was told, were going to the University. These were the Grecians. They were the three head boys of the grammar school, and were understood to have their destiny fixed for the Church. The next class to these, like a College of Cardinals to those three Popes (for every Grecian was in our eyes infallible), were the Deputy Grecians. The former were supposed to have completed their Greek studies, and were deep in Sophocles and Euripides. The latter were thought equally competent to tell you anything respecting Homer and Demosthenes. These two classes, and the head boys of the navigation school, held a certain rank over the whole place, both in school and out. Indeed, the whole of the navigation school, upon the strength of cultivating their valour for the navy, and being called King's boys, had succeeded in establishing an extraordinary pretension to respect. This they sustained in a manner as laughable to call to mind as it was grave in its reception. It was an etiquette among them never to move out of a right line as they walked, whoever stood in their way. I believe there was a secret understanding with Grecians and Deputy Grecians, the former of whom were unquestionably lords paramount in point of fact, and stood and walked aloof when all the rest of the school were marshalled in bodies. I do not remember any clashing between these civil and naval powers ; but I remember well my astonishment when I first beheld some of my little comrades overthrown by the progress of one of these very straightforward marine personages, who walked on with as tranquil and unconscious a face as if nothing had happened. It was not a fierce-looking push ; there seemed to be no intention in it. The insolence lay in the boy not appearing to know that such inferior creatures existed. It was always thus wherever he came. If aware, the boys got out of his way; if not, down they went, one or more; away rolled the top or the marbles, and on walked the future captain—

In maiden navigation, frank and free.

These boys wore a badge on the shoulder, of which they were very proud; though in the streets it must have helped to confound them with charity boys. For charity boys, I must own, we all had a great contempt, or thought so. We did not dare to know that there might have been a little jealousy of our own position in it, placed as we were midway between the homeliness of the common charity school and the dignity of the foundations. We called them ' *chizzy-wags*,' and had a particular scorn and hatred of their nasal tone in singing.

KENSINGTON

[*Old Court Suburb*]

THE overflowing of the Thames, to which Chelsea and Hammersmith were subject, stopped short of the higher ground of Kensington; there was no great road through it till comparatively modern times, the only highway for travellers westward being the old Roman, or present Uxbridge Road, then bending southerly (as it still branches) to Turnham Green; and thus are we to picture to ourselves the future royal suburb, as consisting of half a dozen rustical tenements of swineherds and other foresters clustering about the homestead of the chieftain or speculator, whoever he was, that first cleared away a spot in that corner. By degrees dairymen came, and ploughmen; then vine-growers; and the first Norman proprietor we hear of is a bishop.

' Albericus de Ver tenet de episcopo Constantiensi
  Chenesit(um).'

Aubrey de Vere holds Kensington of the Bishop of
  Constance.

So writes Doomsday Book. Constance is Coutances
in Normandy; and the bishop, who was probably
anything but a reverend personage, in the modern sense
of the epithet, but a stalwart, jolly fellow, clad in arms
cap-à-pie, was also Grand Justiciary of England; that
is to say, one whose business it was to do injustice to
Englishmen, and see their goods and chattels delivered
over to his countrymen, the Normans. Accordingly,
to set a good legal example, the Justiciary seizes upon
this manor of Kensington, which belonged, it seems,
to one ' Edward ': a name which signifies Happy Keeper.
So Happy Keeper (unless detained to keep the pigs)
makes the best of his way off, blessing this delightful
bishop and judge, whose office it is to oust proprietors;
and he is, perhaps, stripped and murdered, somewhere
about Notting Hill, by his lordship's chaplain.[1]

KENSINGTON PALACE

[*Old Court Suburb*]

IT is not improbable that Kensington Palace and
Gardens originated in the royal nursery to which allusion has been made as having been established in this
district, for the benefit of his children, by King Henry
the Eighth. If so, here Queen Elizabeth grew up awhile,
as well as Queen Victoria; and here health was in vain
attempted to be given to the sicklier temperaments of
Edward the Sixth, who died young, and his sister,
Queen Mary, who lived only to be an unhappy bigot.

As the circumstance, however, does not appear ascer-

---

[1] For the crimes and iniquities of the military church-
men who came over with William of Normandy, see
Thierry's *History of the Conquest*, passim.

tainable, antiquaries must put up with the later and
less illustrious origin which has been found for these
distinguished premises, in the house and grounds belonging to the family of the Finches, Earls of Notting-
ham. Whether the tenement which they occupied had
once been royal or not, it seems to have been but a small
mansion in their time; probably consisting of nothing
more than the now least-visible portion of it north-west;
and indeed, though it was subsequently enlarged under
almost every one of the sovereigns by whom it was
occupied, it was never, in one respect, anything but
what it still is, namely, one of the plainest and least-
pretending of princely abodes.

In vain we are told that Wren is supposed to have
built the south front, and Kent (a man famous in his
time) the east front. We can no more get up any
enthusiasm about it as a building, than if it were a box
or a piece of cheese. But it possesses a Dutch solidity;
it can be imagined full of English comfort; it is quiet;
in a good air; and though it is a palace, no tragical
history is connected with it; all which considerations
give it a sort of homely, fireside character, which seems
to represent the domestic side of royalty itself, and thus
renders an interesting service to what is not always so
well recommended by cost and splendour. Windsor
Castle is a place to receive monarchs in; Buckingham
Palace to see fashion in; Kensington Palace seems a place
to drink tea in; and this is by no means a state of things
in which the idea of royalty comes least home to the
good wishes of its subjects. The reigns that flourished
here, appositely enough to the notion of the building,
were all tea-drinking reigns—at least, on the part of the
ladies; and if the present queen does not reign there,
she was born and bred there, growing up quietly under
the care of a domestic mother; during which time the
pedestrian, as he now goes quietly along the gardens,
fancies no harsher sound to have been heard from the
Palace windows than the 'tuning of the tea-things,'
or the sound of a pianoforte.

THE PARK (ST. JAMES'S)

[*The Town*]

ONE of the most popular aspects of St. James's Park is that of a military and music-playing and milk-drinking spot. The milk-drinkings, and the bands of music, and the parades, are the same as they used to be in our boyish days ; and, we were going to add, may they be immortal. But though it is good to make the best of war as long as war cannot be helped, and though music and gold lace, &c., are wonderful helps to that end, yet conscience will not allow us to blink all we know of a very different sort respecting battlefields and days after the battle. We say, therefore, may war turn out to be as mortal, and speedily so, as railroads and growing good sense can make it ; though in the meantime, and the more for that hope, we may be allowed to indulge ourselves as we did when children, in admiring the pretty figures which it cuts in this place—the harmlessness of its glitter and the transports of its beholders. Will anybody who has beheld it when a boy ever forget how his heart leaped within him when, having heard the music before he saw the musicians, he issued hastily from Whitehall on to the parade, and beheld the serene and stately regiment assembled before the colonel, the band playing some noble march, and the officers stepping forwards to the measure with their saluting swords ? Will he ever forget the mystical dignity of the bandmajor, who made signs with his staff ; the barbaric, and as it were, Othello-like height and lustre of the turbaned black who tossed the cymbals ; the dapper juvenility of the drummers and fifers ; and the astounding prematureness of the little boy who played on the triangle ? Is it in the nature of human self-respect to forget how this little boy, dressed in a ' right earnest ' suit of regimentals, and with his hair as veritably powdered and plastered as the best, fetched those amazing strides by the side of Othello, which absolutely

' kept up ' with his lofty shanks, and made the schoolboy think the higher of his own nature for the possibility ?

Furthermore, will he ever forget how some regiment of horse used to come over the Park to Whitehall, in the midst of this parade, and pass the foot-soldiers with a sound of clustering magnificence and dancing trumpets ? Will he ever forget how the foot then divided itself into companies, and turning about and deploying before the colonel, marched off in the opposite direction, carrying away the schoolboy himself and the crowd of spectators with it; and so, now with the brisk drums and fifes, and now with the deeper glories of the band, marched gallantly off for the courtyard of the palace, where it again set up its music-book, and enchanted the crowd with Haydn or Mozart ?   What a strange mixture, too, was the crowd itself—boys and grown men, gentlemen, vagabonds, maid-servants—there they all went listening, idling, gazing on the ensign or the band-major, keeping pace with the march, and all of them more or less, particularly the maid-servants, doting on the ' sogers.'   We, for one, confess to having drunk deep of the attraction, or the infection, or the balmy reconcilement (whichever the reader pleases to call it).   Many a holiday morning have we hastened from our cloisters in the city to go and hear ' the music in the Park,' delighted to make one in the motley crowd, and attending upon the last flourish of the hautboys and clarionets. There we first became acquainted with feelings which we afterwards put into verse (if the recollection be not thought an impertinence); and there, without knowing what it was called, or who it was that wrote it, we carried back with us to school the theme of a glorious composition, which afterwards became a favourite with operagoers under the title of *Non più andrai*, the delightful march in *Figaro*.   We suppose it is now, and has ever since, been played there, to the martialization of hundreds of little boys, and the puzzlement of philosophy.   Everything in respect to military parade takes place, we believe, in the Park just as it used to do, or with little variation.   The objects also which you

behold, if you look at the parade and its edifices, are
the same. The Admiralty, the Treasury, the back of
the Minister's house in Downing Street, and the back-
front of the solid and not inappropriate building called
the Horse Guards, look as they did fifty years ago;
and there also continue to stand the slender Egyptian
piece of cannon and the dumpy Spanish mortar,
trophies of the late war with France. The inscriptions,
however, on those triumphant memorials contain no
account of the sums we are still paying for having
waged it.

'The soldiers' and the 'milk from the cow' do not
at all clash in the minds of boyhood. The juvenile
imagination ignores what it pleases, especially as its
knowledge is not very great. It no more connects the
idea of village massacre with guns and trumpets than
it supposes the fine scarlet coat capable of being ragged
and dirty. Virgil may say something about ruined
fields, and people compelled to fly for their lives; but
this is only part of a 'lesson,' and the calamities but
so many nouns and verbs. The maid-servants, and
indeed the fair sex in general, till they become wives
and mothers, enjoy the like happy exemption from ugly
associations of ideas; and the syllabub is taken under
the trees, with a delighted eye to the milk on one side
and the military show on the other.

IN PRISON

[*Autobiography*]

THE doctor then proposed that I should be removed into the prison infirmary; and this proposal was granted. Infirmary had, I confess, an awkward sound, even to my ears. I fancied a room shared with other sick persons, not the best fitted for companions; but the good-natured doctor (his name was Dixon) undeceived me. The infirmary was divided into four wards, with as many small rooms attached to them. The two upper wards were occupied, but the two on the floor had never been used: and one of these, not very providently (for I had not yet learned to think of money), I turned into a noble room. I papered the walls with a trellis of roses; I had the ceiling coloured with clouds and sky; the barred windows I screened with Venetian blinds; and when my bookcases were set up with their busts, and flowers and a pianoforte made their appearance, perhaps there was not a handsomer room on that side the water. I took a pleasure, when a stranger knocked at the door, to see him come in and stare about him. The surprise on issuing from the Borough, and passing through the avenues of a gaol, was dramatic. Charles Lamb declared there was no other such room, except in a fairy tale.

But I possessed another surprise; which was a garden. There was a little yard outside the room, railed off from another belonging to the neighbouring ward. This yard I shut in with green palings, adorned it with a trellis, bordered it with a thick bed of earth from a nursery, and even contrived to have a grass-plot. The earth I filled with flowers and young trees. There was an apple-tree, from which we managed to get a pudding the second year. As to my flowers, they were allowed to be perfect. Thomas Moore, who came to see me with Lord Byron, told me he had seen no such heart's-ease. I bought the *Parnaso Italiano* while in

prison, and used often to think of a passage in it, while
looking at this miniature piece of horticulture :—

Mio picciol orto,
A me sei vigna, e campo, e selva, e prato.—BALDI.

My little garden,
To me thou'rt vineyard, field, and meadow, and
wood.

Here I wrote and read in fine weather, sometimes under
an awning. In autumn, my trellises were hung with
scarlet-runners, which added to the flowery investment.
I used to shut my eyes in my arm-chair, and affect to
think myself hundreds of miles off.

But my triumph was in issuing forth of a morning.
A wicket out of the garden led into the large one
belonging to the prison. The latter was only for vegetables ; but it contained a cherry-tree, which I saw
twice in blossom. I parcelled out the ground in my
imagination into favourite districts. I made a point of
dressing myself as if for a long walk ; and then, putting
on my gloves, and taking my book under my arm,
stepped forth, requesting my wife not to wait dinner if
I was too late. My eldest little boy, to whom Lamb
addressed some charming verses on the occasion, was
my constant companion, and we used to play all sorts
of juvenile games together. It was, probably, in dreaming of one of these games (but the words had a more
touching effect on my ear) that he exclaimed one
night in his sleep, ' No : I'm not lost ; I'm found.'
Neither he nor I were very strong at that time ; but I
have lived to see him a man of eight and forty ; and
wherever he is found, a generous hand and a great
understanding will be found together.

TREES

[*The Town*]

As a link of a very pleasing description between old times and new not unconnected with what we have been speaking of, we shall conclude our introduction by observing, that there is scarcely a street in the *city* of London, perhaps not one, nor many out of the pale of it, from some part of which the passenger may not discern a *tree*. Most persons to whom this has been mentioned have doubted the accuracy of our information, nor do we profess hitherto to have ascertained it; though since we heard the assertion, we have made a point of endeavouring to do so whenever we could, and have not been disappointed. The mention of the circumstance generally creates a laughing astonishment, and a cry of 'impossible!' Two persons who successively heard of it the other day, not only thought it incredible as a general fact, but doubted whether half a dozen streets could be found with a twig in them; and they triumphantly instanced 'Cheapside' as a place in which it was 'out of the question.' Yet in Cheapside is an actual, visible, and even ostentatiously visible tree, to all who have eyes to look about them. It stands at the corner of Wood Street, and occupies the space of a house. There was a solitary one the other day in St. Paul's Churchyard which has now got a multitude of young companions. A little child was shown us a few years back, who was said never to have beheld a tree but that single one in St. Paul's Churchyard. Whenever a tree was mentioned, she thought it was that and no other. She had no conception even of the remote tree in Cheapside! This appears incredible; but there would seem to be no bounds, either to imagination or to the want of it. We were told the other day, on good authority, of a man who had resided six-and-thirty years in the square of St. Peter's at Rome, and then for the first time went inside the Cathedral.

There is a little garden in *Watling Street!* It lies completely open to the eye, being divided from the footway by a railing only.

In the body of our work will be found notices of other trees and green spots, that surprise the observer in the thick of the noise and smoke. Many of them are in churchyards. Others have disappeared during the progress of building. Many courts and passages are named from trees that once stood in them, as Vine and Elm Court, Fig-tree Court, Green-arbour Court, &c. It is not surprising that *garden-houses,* as they were called, should have formerly abounded in Holborn, in Bunhill Row, and other (at that time) suburban places. We notice the fact, in order to observe how fond the poets were of occupying houses of this description. Milton seems to have made a point of having one. The only London residence of Chapman which is known, was in Old Street Road ; doubtless at that time a rural suburb. Beaumont and Fletcher's house, on the Surrey side of the Thames (for they lived as well as wrote together), most probably had a garden : and Dryden's house in Gerard Street looked into the garden of the mansion built by the Earls of Leicester. A tree, or even a flower, put in a window in the streets of a great city (and the London citizens, to their credit, are fond of flowers) affects the eye something in the same way as the hand-organs, which bring unexpected music to the ear. They refresh the common-places of life, shed a harmony through the busy discord, and appeal to those first sources of emotion, which are associated with the remembrance of all that is young and innocent. They seem also to present to us a portion of the tranquillity we think we are labouring for, and the desire of which is felt as an earnest that we shall realize it somewhere, either in this world or in the next. Above all, they render us more cheerful for the performance of present duties ; and the smallest seed of this kind, dropt into the heart of man, is worth more, and may terminate in better fruits, than anybody but a great poet could tell us.

CHURCHYARDS

[Old Court Suburb]

RETURNING out of Kensington Square by the way we
entered it, we come, in the most open part of the High
Street, to the parish church and churchyard ; the
former, a small and homely building for so distinguished
a suburb ; the latter suggesting a doubt whether a
burial ground ought to abut so closely on a public way.

In some moods of the mind, the juxtaposition is very
painful. It looks as if death itself were no escape from
the turmoils of life. We feel as if the noise of carts and
cries were never to be out of one's hearing ; as if the
tears, however hidden, of those who stood mournfully
looking at our graves were to be mocked by the passing
crowd of indifferent spectators ; as if the dead might be
sensible of the very market going on, with all its night-
lights and bustle (as it does here on Saturdays), and of
the noise of drunken husbands and wives, persisting in
bringing a sense of misery into one's last home.

On the other hand, the sociable man may sometimes
be disposed to regard with complacency this kind of
posthumous intercourse with the living. He may feel
as if the dead were hardly the departed—as if they were
still abiding among their friends and fellow creatures,
not displeased even to hear the noise and the bustle ;
or, at least, as if in ceasing to hear our voices they were
still, so to speak, reposing in our arms. Morning, somehow, in this view of the case, would seem to be still
theirs, though they choose to lie in bed ; cheerful noon
is with them, without their having any of the trouble
of it. The names made be read on their tombstones as
familiarly as they used to be on their doors ; children
play about their graves, unthinkingly indeed, but joy-
ously, and with as little thought of irreverence as butterflies ; and the good fellow going home at night from his
party breathes a jovial, instead of a mournful, blessing
on their memories. Perhaps he knew them. Perhaps

he has been joining in one of their old favourite glees by Callcott or Spofforth, the former of whom was a Kensington man, and the latter of whom lies buried here, and is recorded at the church door. And assuredly the dead Spofforth would find no fault with his living remembrancer.

In quiet country places there is, in fact, a sort of compromise in this instance between the two feelings of privacy and publicity, which we have often thought very pleasing. The dead in a small, sequestered village, seem hardly removed from their own houses. The last home seems almost a portion of the first. The clergyman's house often has the churchyard as close to it as the garden ; and when he goes into his grave he seems but removed into another room ; gone to bed, and to his sleep. He has not 'left.' He lies there with his family, still ready to waken with them all on the heavenly morning.

This, however, is a feeling upon the matter which we find it difficult to realize in a bustling town. We are there convinced, upon the whole, that, whether near to houses or away from them, the sense of quiet is requisite to the proper idea of the churchyard. The dead being actually severed from us, no longer having voices, all sights and sounds, but of the gentlest and quietest kind, seem to be impertinences towards them ; not to belong to them. Quiet, being the thing farthest removed from cities, and what we imagine to pervade all space, and the gulfs between the stars, is requisite to make us feel that we are standing on the threshold of heaven.

Upon the whole, therefore, we cannot approve of churchyards in the living thoroughfares, and thus must needs object to the one in the place before us ; though there are portions of it to the north and west of the church more sequestered (for a small remove in these cases makes a great difference) ; and in those portions the most noticeable of the graves are situate. They are not many ; nor have we much to say of persons lying in the church itself, or in the church vaults. What notices we have to give, whether in church or churchyard, we shall put in chronological order, as not only being most convenient, but having a certain mortal propriety.

COACHES

[*Indicator*, Aug. 23 and 30, 1820]

ACCORDING to the opinion commonly entertained respecting an author's want of ready money, it may be allowed us to say that we retain from childhood a considerable notion of 'a ride in a coach.' Nor do we hesitate to confess that by coach we especially mean a hired one; from the equivocal rank of the post-chaise, down to that despised old castaway, the hackney.

It is true that the carriage, as it is indifferently called (as if nothing less genteel could carry any one) is a more decided thing than the chaise; it may be swifter even than the mail, leaves the stage at a still greater distance in every respect, and (forgetting what it may come to itself) darts by the poor old lumbering hackney with immeasurable contempt. It rolls with a prouder ease than any other vehicle. It is full of cushions and comfort; elegantly coloured inside and out; rich, yet neat; light and rapid, yet substantial. The horses seem proud to draw it. The fat and fair-wigged coachman 'lends his sounding lash,' his arm only in action and that little, his body well set with its own weight. The footman, in the pride of his nonchalance, holding by the straps behind, and glancing down sideways betwixt his cocked hat and neckcloth, stands swinging from east to west upon his springy toes. The horses rush along amidst their glancing harness. Spotted dogs leap about them, barking with a princely superfluity of noise. The hammercloth trembles through all its fringe. The paint flashes in the sun. We, contemptuous of everything less convenient, bow backwards and forwards with a certain indifferent air of gentility, infinitely predominant. Suddenly, with a happy mixture of turbulence and truth, the carriage dashes up by the curb-stone to the very point desired, and stops with a lordly wilfulness of decision. The coachman looks as if nothing had happened. The footman is down in an instant ; the knocker reverberates into the farthest corner of the house ; doors, both carriage and house, are open ;—we descend, casting a matter-of-course eye at the bystanders ; and the moment we touch the pavement the vehicle, as if conscious of what it has carried, and relieved from the weight of our importance, recovers from its sidelong inclination with a jerk, tossing and panting, as it were, for very breath, like the proud heads of the horses.

All this, it must be owned, is very pretty ; but it is also gouty and superfluous. It is too convenient,—too exacting,—too exclusive. We must get too much for it, and lose too much by it. Its plenty, as Ovid says, makes us poor. We neither have it in the republic of letters, nor would desire it in any less jacobinical state. Horses, as many as you please, provided men have enough to eat:—hired coaches, a reasonable number :—but health and good-humour at all events.

Gigs and curricles are things less objectionable, because they cannot be so relied upon as substitutes for exercise. Our taste in them, we must confess, is not genuine. How shall we own it ? We like to be driven, instead of drive ;—to read or look about us, instead of keeping watch on a horse's head. We have no relish even for vehicles of this description, that are not safe. Danger is a good thing for giving a fillip to a man's ideas ; but even danger, to us, must come recommended by something useful. We have no ambition to have TANDEM written on our tombstone.

The prettiest of these vehicles is undoubtedly the curricle, which is also the safest. There is something worth looking at in the pair of horses, with that sparkling pole of steel laid across them. It is like a bar of music, comprising their harmonious course. But to us even gigs are but a sort of unsuccessful run at gentility. The driver, to all intents and purposes, had better be on the horse. Horseback is the noblest way of being carried in the world. It is cheaper than any other constant mode of riding; it is common to all ranks; and it is manly, graceful, and healthy. The handsomest mixture of danger with dignity, in the shape of a carriage, was the tall phaeton with its yellow wings. We remember looking up to it with respect in our childhood, partly for its own loftiness, partly for its name, and partly perhaps for the figure it makes in the prints to novels of that period. The most gallant figure which mere modern driving ever cut, was in the person of a late Duke of Hamilton; of whom we have read or heard somewhere, that he used to dash round the streets of Rome, with his horses panting, and his hounds barking about his phaeton, to the equal fright and admiration of the Masters of the World, who were accustomed to witness nothing higher than a lumbering old coach or a cardinal on a mule.

A post-chaise involves the idea of travelling, which in the company of those we love is home in motion. The smooth running along the road, the fresh air, the variety of scene, the leafy roads, the bursting prospects, the clatter through a town, the gaping gaze of a village, the hearty appetite, the leisure (your chaise waiting only upon your own movements), even the little contradictions to home comfort and the expedients upon which they set us, all put the animal spirits at work, and throw a novelty over the road of life. If anything could grind us young again, it would be the wheels of a post-chaise. The only monotonous sight is the perpetual up-and-down movement of the postilion, who, we wish exceedingly, could take a chair. His occasional retreat to the bar which occupies the place of a box, and his affecting to sit upon it, only reminds us of its exquisite want of accommodation. But some have given the bar, lately, a surreptitious squeeze in the middle; and flattened it a little into something obliquely resembling an inconvenient seat.

If we are to believe the merry Columbus of Down-Hall, calashes, now almost obsolete for any purpose, used to be hired for travelling occasions a hundred years back;

but he preferred a chariot; and neither was good.
But see how pleasantly good-humour rides over its
inconveniences.

Then answered 'Squire Morley, ' Pray get a calash,
That in summer may burn, and in winter may splash;
I love dirt and dust; and 'tis always my pleasure
To take with me much of the soil that I measure.'

But Matthew thought better; for Matthew thought
    right,
And hired a chariot so trim and so tight,
That extremes both of winter and summer might pass;
For one window was canvas, the other was glass.

' Draw up,' quoth friend Matthew; ' Pull down,' quoth
    friend John,
' We shall be both hotter and colder anon.'
Thus, talking and scolding, they forward did speed;
And Ralpho paced by under Newman the Swede.

Into an old inn did this equipage roll,
At a town they called Hodson, the sign of the Bull;
Near a nymph with an urn that divides the highway,
And into a puddle throws mother of tea.

' Come here, my sweet landlady, pray how d'ye do?
Where is Cicely so cleanly, and Prudence, and Sue?
And where is the widow that dwelt here below?
And the hostler that sung about eight years ago?

And where is your sister, so mild and so dear,
Whose voice to her maids like a trumpet was clear?'
' By my troth,' she replies, ' you grow younger, I think:
And pray, sir, what wine does the gentleman drink?

Why now let me die, sir, or live upon trust,
If I know to which question to answer you first:
Why things, since I saw you, most strangely have
    varied,
The hostler is hanged, and the widow is married.

And Prue left a child for the parish to nurse,
And Cicely went off with a gentleman's purse;

And as to my sister, so mild and so dear,
She has lain in the churchyard full many a year.'

' Well ; peace to her ashes !   What signifies grief ?
She roasted red veal, and she powdered lean beef :
Full nicely she knew to cook up a fine dish ;
Nor tough were her pullets, and tender her fish.'

PRIOR.

This quotation reminds us of a little poem by the same
author, entitled ' The Secretary,' which, as it is short,
and runs upon chaise-wheels, and seems to have slipped
the notice it deserves, we will do ourselves the pleasure
of extracting also.   It was written when he was Secretary of Embassy at the Hague, where he seems to have
edified the Dutch with his insisting upon enjoying
himself.   The astonishment with which the good
Hollander and his wife look up to him as he rides, and
the touch of yawning dialect at the end, are extremely
pleasant.

While with labour assiduous due pleasure I mix,
And in one day atone for the business of six,
In a little Dutch chaise on a Saturday night,
On my left hand my Horace, a nymph on my right :
No memoirs to compose, and no post-boy to move,
That on Sunday may hinder the softness of love ;
For her, neither visits, nor parties at tea,
Nor the long-winded cant of a dull refugee :
This night and the next shall be hers, shall be mine,
To good or ill-fortune the third we resign :
Thus scorning the world and superior to fate,
I drive on my car in processional state.
So with Phia through Athens Pisistratus rode ;
Men thought her Minerva, and him a new god.
But why should I stories of Athens rehearse,
Where people knew love, and were partial to verse
Since none can with justice my pleasures oppose,
In Holland half drowned in interest and prose ?
By Greece and past ages what need I be tried,
When the Hague and the present are both on my side ?

And is it enough for the joys of the day,
To think what Anacreon or Sappho would say ?
When good Vandergoes, and his provident *vrow*,
As they gaze on my triumph, do freely allow,
That, search all the province, you'll find no man *dàr* is
So blest as the *Englishen Heer Secretar'* is.

If Prior had been living now, he would have found the
want of travelling accommodation flourishing most in
a country, for whose graver wants we have to answer,
without having her wit to help us. There is a story
told of an Irish post-chaise, the occupier of which,
without quitting it, had to take to his heels. It was
going down hill, as fast as wind and the impossibility
of stopping could make it, when the foot passengers
observed a couple of legs underneath, emulating, with
all their might, the rapidity of the wheels. The bottom
had come out ; and the gentleman was obliged to run
for his life.

We must relate another anecdote of an Irish post-
chaise, merely to show the natural tendencies of the
people to be lawless in self-defence. A friend of ours
who was travelling among them, used to have this
proposition put to him by the postilion, whenever he
approached a turnpike. 'Plase your honour, will I
drive at the pike ?' The pike hung loosely across the
road. Luckily, the rider happened to be of as lawless
a turn for justice as the driver, so the answer was always
a cordial one—' Oh, yes—drive at the pike.' The pike
made way accordingly ; and in a minute or two, the
gate people were heard and seen, screaming in vain
after the illegal charioteers.

Fertur equis auriga, neque audit currus.

VIRGIL.

The driver's borne beyond their swearing,
And the post-chaise is hard of hearing.

As to following them, nobody in Ireland thinks of moving
too much, legal or illegal.

The pleasure to be had in a Mail-coach is not so much

at one's command as that in a post-chaise. There is
generally too little room in it, and too much hurry
out of it. The company must not lounge over their
breakfast, even if they are all agreed. It is an
understood thing, that they are bound to be uncom-
fortably punctual. They must get in at seven o'clock,
though they are all going upon business they do not
like or care about, or will have to wait till nine before
they can do anything. Some persons know how to
manage this haste, and breakfast and dine in the cracking of a whip. They stick with their fork, they joint,
they sliver, they bolt. Legs and wings vanish before
them, like a dragon's before a knight-errant. But if one
is not a clergyman or a regular jolly fellow, one has no
chance this way. To be diffident or polite, is fatal.
It is a merit eagerly acknowledged, and as quickly set
aside. At last you begin upon a leg, and are called off.
A very troublesome degree of science is necessary for
being well settled in the coach. We remember travelling in our youth, upon the north road, with an orthodox
elderly gentleman of very venerable peruke, who talked
much with a grave-looking young man about universities, and won our inexperienced heart with a notion
that he was deep in Horace and Virgil. He was much
deeper in his wig. Towards evening, as he seemed
restless, we asked with much diffidence whether a change
even for the worse might not relieve him ; for we were
riding backwards, and thought that all elderly people
disliked that way. He insinuated the very objection ;
so we recoiled from asking him again. In a minute or
two, however, he insisted that we were uneasy ourselves,
and that he must relieve us for our own sake. We pro-
tested as filially as possible against this ; but at last,
out of mere shame of disputing the point with so benevolent an elder, we changed seats with him. After an
interval of bland meditation, we found the evening sun
full in our face. His new comfort set him dozing ; and
every now and then he jerked his wig in our eyes, till we
had the pleasure to see him take out a nightcap and
look extremely ghastly.—The same person, and his

serious young companion, tricked us out of a good bed
we happened to get at the inn.

The greatest peculiarity attending a Mail-coach arises
from its travelling at night. The gradual decline of talk,
the incipient snore, the rustling and alteration of legs
and nightcaps, the cessation of other noises on the road,
the sound of the wind or rain, of the moist circuit of
the wheels, and of the time-beating tread of the horses,
—all dispose the traveller, who cannot sleep, to a double
sense of the little that is left him to observe. The coach
stops, the door opens; a rush of cold air announces
at once the demands and merits of the guard, who is
taking his leave, and is anxious to remember us. The
door is clapped to again; the sound of everything outside becomes dim; and voices are heard knocking up
the people of the inn, and answered by issuing yawns
and excuses. Wooden shoes clog heavily about. The
horses' mouths are heard swilling up the water out of
tubs. All is still again; and some one in the coach
takes a long breath. The driver mounts, and we resume our way. It happens that we can sleep anywhere
except in a mail-coach; so that we hate to see a prudent
warm old fellow, who has been eating our fowls and
intercepting our toast, put on his night-cap in order to
settle himself till morning. We rejoice in the digs that
his neighbour's elbow gives him, and hail the long-
legged traveller that sits opposite. A passenger of our
wakeful description must try to content himself with
listening to the sounds above-mentioned; or thinking
of his friends; or turning verses, as Sir Richard Black-
more did, ' to the rumbling of his coach's wheels ';
or chatting with the servant-girl who is going to place
(may nobody get her dismissed nine months hence !);
or protecting her against the Methodist in the corner;
or if alone with her, and she has a kind face, protecting
her against a much more difficult person,—himself.
Really, we must say, that enough credit is not given to
us lawless persons who say all we think, and would have
the world enjoy all it could. There is the author of the
Mail-coach Adventure, for instance. With all his

amorous verses, his yearnings after the pleasant laws of the Golden Age, and even his very hymns (which, we confess, are a little mystic), we would rather trust a fair traveller to his keeping, than some much graver writers we have heard of. If he forgot himself, he would not think it a part of virtue to forget her. But his absolution is not ready at hand, as for graver sinners. The very intensity of the sense of pleasure will often keep a man from destroying its after-thoughts in another, when harsher systems will forget themselves, only to confound brutality with repentance.

The Stage-coach is a very great and unpretending accommodation. It is a cheap substitute, notwithstanding all its eighteen-penny and two and sixpenny temptations, for keeping a carriage or a horse; and we really think, in spite of its gossiping, is no mean help to village liberality; for its passengers are so mixed, so often varied, so little yet so much together, so compelled to accommodate, so willing to pass a short time pleasantly, and so liable to the criticism of strangers, that it is hard if they do not get a habit of speaking or even thinking more kindly of one another, than if they mingled less often or under other circumstances. The old and infirm are treated with reverence; the ailing sympathized with; the healthy congratulated; the rich not distinguished; the poor well met; the young, with their faces conscious of pride, patronized and allowed to be extra. Even the fiery, nay the fat, learn to bear each other: and if some high-thoughted persons will talk now and then of their great acquaintances, or their preference of a carriage, there is an instinct which tells the rest that they would not make such appeals to their good opinion, if they valued it so little as might be supposed. Stoppings and dust are not pleasant; but the latter may be had on much grander occasions; and if any one is so unlucky as never to keep another stopping himself, he must be content with the superiority of his virtue. The mail or stage-coachman, upon the whole, is no inhuman mass of great coat, gruffness, civility, and old boots. The latter is the politer, from the smaller range of acquaintance, and his necessity for preserving them. His face is red, and his voice rough, by the same process of drink and catarrh. He has a silver watch with a steel chain, and plenty of loose silver in his pocket mixed with halfpence. He serves the houses he goes by for a clock. He takes a glass at every ale-house; for thirst, when it is dry, and for warmth when it is wet. He likes to show the judicious reach of his whip, by twigging a dog or goose on the road, or children that get in the way. His tenderness to descending old ladies is particular. He touches his hat to Mrs. Smith. He gives 'the young woman' a ride; and lends her his box-coat in the rain. His liberality in imparting his knowledge to any one that has the good fortune to ride on the box with him is a happy mixture of deference, conscious possession, and familiarity. His information chiefly lies in the occupancy of houses on the road, prize-fighters, Bow-street runners, and accidents. He concludes that you know Dick Sams, or Old Joey; and proceeds to relate some of the stories that relish his pot and tobacco in the evening. If any of the four-in-hand gentry go by, he shakes his head, and thinks they might find something better to do. His contempt for them is founded on modesty. He tells you that his off-hand horse is as pretty a goer as ever was, but that Kitty—'Yeah now there, Kitty—can't you be still? —Kitty's a devil, sir,—for all you wouldn't think it.' He knows the boys on the road admire him, and gives the horses an indifferent lash with his whip as they go by. If you wish to know what rain and dust can do, you should look at his old hat. There is an indescribably placid and paternal look in the position of his corduroy knees and old top-boots on the foot-board, with their pointed toes and never-cleaned soles. His beau ideal of appearance is a frock-coat with mother-o'-pearl buttons, a striped yellow waistcoat, and a flower in his mouth.

But all our praises why for Charles and Robert?
Rise, honest Mews, and sing the classic Bobart.

Is the quadrijugal virtue of that learned person still extant? That Olympic and Baccalaureated charioteer? —That best-educated and most erudite of coachmen, of whom Dominie Sampson is alone worthy to speak?— That singular punning and driving commentary on the *Sunt quos curriculo collegisse,*—in short, the worthy and agreeable Mr. Bobart, Bachelor of Arts, who drove the Oxford stage some years ago, capped verses and the front of his hat with equal dexterity, and read Horace over his brandy and water of an evening? We once had the pleasure of being beaten by him in that capital art, he having brought up against us an unusual number of those cross-armed letters, as puzzling to verse-cappers as iron-cats unto cavalry, ycleped X's; which said warfare he was pleased to call to mind in after-times unto divers of our comrades. The modest and natural greatness with which he used to say 'Yait' to his horses, and then turn round with his rosy gills, and an eye like a fish, and give out the required verse, can never pass away from us, as long as verses or horses run.

On the Hackney-coach we cannot make as short work, as many persons like to make of it in reality. Perhaps indeed it is partly a sense of the contempt it undergoes, which induces us to endeavour to make the best of it. But it has its merits, as we shall show presently. In the account of its demerits, we have been anticipated by a new, and we are sorry to say a very good poetess, of the name of Lucy V—— L——, who has favoured us with a sight of a manuscript poem, in which they are related with great nicety and sensitiveness.

READER. What, sir, sorry to say that a lady is a good poetess?

INDICATOR. Only inasmuch, madam, as the lady gives such authority to the anti-social view of this subject, and will not agree with us as to the beatitude of the Hackney-coach—But hold:—upon turning to the manuscript again, we find that the objections are put into the mouth of a Dandy Courtier. This makes a great difference. The Hackney resumes all which it had lost in the good graces of the fair authoress. The only

wonder is, how the Courtier could talk so well. Here
is the passage :—

> Eban, untempted by the pastry-cooks
> (Of pastry he got store within the Palace),
> With hasty steps, wrapp'd cloak, and solemn looks,
> Incognito upon his errand sallies,
> His smelling-bottle ready for the allies ;
> He pass'd the hurdy-gurdies with disdain,
> Vowing he'd have them sent on board the gallies :
> Just as he made his vow, it 'gan to rain,
> Therefore he called a coach, and bade it drive amain.

> 'I'll pull the string,' said he, and further said,
> 'Polluted Jarvey ! Ah ! thou filthy hack !
> Whose springs of life are all dried up and dead,
> Whose linsey-woolsey lining hangs all slack,
> Whose rug is straw, whose wholeness is a crack ;
> And evermore thy steps go clatter-clitter ;
> Whose glass once up can never be got back,
> Who prov'st, with jolting arguments and bitter,
> That 'tis of vile no-use to travel in a litter.

> 'Thou inconvenience ! thou hungry crop
> For all corn ! thou snail-creeper to and fro,
> Who while thou goest ever seem'st to stop,
> And fiddle-faddle standest while you go ;
> I' the morning, freighted with a weight of woe,
> Unto some Lazar-house thou journeyest,
> And in the evening tak'st a double row
> Of dowdies, for some dance or party drest,
> Besides the goods meanwhile thou movest east and west.

> 'By thy ungallant bearing and sad mien,
> An inch appears the utmost thou couldst budge ;
> Yet at the slightest nod, or hint, or sign,
> Round to the curb-stone patient dost thou trudge,
> School'd in a beckon, learned in a nudge ;
> A dull-eyed Argus watching for a fare ;
> Quiet and plodding thou dost bear no grudge
> To whisking Tilburies, or Phaetons rare,
> Curricles, or Mail-coaches, swift beyond compare.'

Philosophizing thus, he pull'd the check,
And bade the coachman wheel to such a street,
Who turning much his body, more his neck,
Louted full low, and hoarsely did him greet.

The tact here is so nice, of all the infirmities which are
but too likely to beset our poor old friend, that we should
only spoil it to say more.   To pass then to the merits.
   One of the greatest helps to a sense of merit in other
things is a consciousness of one's own wants.   Do you
despise a hackney-coach ?   Get tired ; get old ; get
young again.   Lay down your own carriage, or make
it less uneasily too easy.   Have to stand up half an
hour, out of a storm, under a gateway.   Be ill, and
wish to visit a friend who is worse.   Fall in love, and
want to sit next your mistress.   Or if all this will not
do, fall in a cellar.
   Ben Jonson, in a fit of indignation at the niggard-
liness of James the First, exclaimed, ' He despises me,
I suppose, because I live in an alley :—tell him, his soul
lives in an alley.'   We think we see a hackney-coach
moved out of its ordinary patience, and hear it say,
' You there, who sit looking so scornfully at me out of
your carriage, you are yourself the thing you take me
for.   Your understanding is a hackney-coach.   It is
lumbering, rickety, and at a stand.   When it moves,
it is drawn by things like itself.   It is at once the most
stationary and the most servile of common-places.   And
when a good thing is put into it, it does not know it.'
   But it is difficult to imagine a hackney-coach under so
irritable an aspect.   It is Hogarth, we think, who has
drawn a set of hats or wigs with countenances of their
own.   We have noticed the same thing in the faces of
houses ; and it sometimes gets in one's way in a land-
scape-painting, with the outlines of the massy trees.   A
friend tells us, that the hackney-coach has its countenance, with gesticulation besides : and now he has
pointed it out we can easily fancy it.   Some of them
looked chucked under the chin, some nodding, some
coming at you sideways.   We shall never find it easy,

however, to fancy the irritable aspect above-mentioned. A hackney-coach always appeared to us the most quiescent of movables. Its horses and it, slumbering on a stand, are an emblem of all the patience in creation, animate and inanimate. The submission with which the coach takes every variety of the weather, dust, rain, and wind, never moving but when some eddying blast makes its old body seem to shiver, is only surpassed by the vital patience of the horses. Can anything better illustrate the poet's line about

> Years that bring the philosophic mind,

than the still-hung head, the dim indifferent eye, the dragged and blunt-cornered mouth, and the gaunt imbecility of body dropping its weight on three tired legs in order to give repose to the lame one ? When it has blinkers on, they seem to be shutting up its eyes for death, like the windows of a house. Fatigue and the habit of suffering have become as natural to the creature as the bit to its mouth. Once in half an hour it moves the position of its leg, or shakes its drooping old ears. The whip makes it go, more from habit than from pain. Its coat has become almost callous to minor stings. The blind and staggering fly in autumn might come to die against its cheek.

Of a pair of hackney-coach horses, one so much resembles the other, that it seems unnecessary for them to compare notes. They have that within which is beyond the comparative. They no longer bend their heads towards each other, as they go. They stand together as if unconscious of one another's company, but they are not. An old horse misses his companion like an old man. The presence of an associate, who has gone through pain and suffering with us, need not say anything. It is talk, and memory, and everything. Something of this it may be to our old friends in harness. What are they thinking of, while they stand motionless in the rain ? Do they remember ? Do they dream ? Do they still, unperplexed as their old blood is by too many foods, receive a pleasure from the elements ; a dull refreshment from the air and sun ? Have they yet a palate for the hay which they pull so feebly ? or for the rarer grain, which induces them to perform their only voluntary gesture of any vivacity, and toss up the bags that are fastened on their mouths, to get at its shallow feast ?

If the old horse were gifted with memory (and who shall say he is not, in one thing as well as another ?) it might be at once the most melancholy and pleasantest feeling he has ; for the commonest hack has very likely been a hunter or racer ; has had his days of lustre and enjoyment ; has darted along the course, and scoured the pasture ; has carried his master proudly, or his lady gently ; has pranced, has galloped, has neighed aloud, has dared, has forded, has spurned at mastery, has graced it and made it proud, has rejoiced the eye, has been crowded to as an actor, has been all instinct with life and quickness, has had its very fear admired as courage, and been sat upon by valour as its chosen seat.

> His ears up prick'd ; his braided hanging mane
> Upon his compassed crest now stands on end ;
> His nostrils drink the air ; and forth again,
> As from a furnace, vapours doth he send ;
> > His eye, which scornfully glistens like fire,
> > Shows his hot courage and his high desire.

> Sometimes he trots as if he told the steps,
> With gentle majesty, and modest pride ;
> Anon he rears upright, curvets and leaps,
> As who would say, lo ! thus my strength is tried ;
> > And thus I do to captivate the eye
> > Of the fair breeder that is standing by.

> What recketh he his rider's angry stir,
> His flattering holla, or his *Stand, I say ?*
> What cares he now for curb, or pricking spur ?
> For rich caparisons, or trappings gay ?
> > He sees his love, and nothing else he sees,
> > For nothing else with his proud sight agrees.

Look, when a painter would surpass the life,
In limning out a well-proportioned steed,
His art with nature's workmanship at strife,
As if the dead the living should exceed :
    So did this horse excel a common one,
    In shape, in courage, colour, pace, and bone.

Round-hoof'd, short-jointed, fetlocks shag and long,
Broad breast, full eyes, small head, and nostril wide ;
High crest, short ears, straight legs, and passing strong,
Thin mane, thick tail, broad buttock, tender hide ;
    Look what a horse should have, he did not lack,
    Save a proud rider on so proud a back.

Alas ! his only riders now are the rain and a sordid harness ! The least utterance of the wretchedest voice makes him stop and become a fixture. His loves were in existence at the time the old sign, fifty miles hence, was first painted. His nostrils drink nothing but what they cannot help,—the water out of an old tub. Not all the hounds in the world could make his ears attain any eminence. His mane is scratchy and lax : his shape an anatomy : his name a mockery. The same great poet who wrote the triumphal verses for him and his loves, has written their living epitaph :—

                The poor jades
Lob down their heads, dropping the hide and hips ;
The gum down roping from their pale dead eyes ;
And in their pale dull mouths the gimmal bit
Lies foul with chew'd grass, still and motionless.
                    K. Henry V, Act iv.

There is a song called 'The High-mettled Racer,' describing the progress of a favourite horse's life, from its time of vigour and glory down to its furnishing food for the dogs. It is not as good as Shakespeare ; but it will do, to those who are half as kind as he. We defy anybody to read that song, or be in the habit of singing it or hearing it sung, and treat horses as they are sometimes treated. So much good may an author do, who is in earnest, and does not go a pedantic way to work.

We will not say that Plutarch's good-natured observation about taking care of one's old horse did more for that class of retired servants than all the graver lessons of philosophy. For it is philosophy which first sets people thinking; and then some of them put it in a more popular shape. But we will venture to say, that Plutarch's observation saved many a steed of antiquity a superfluous thump; and in this respect, the author of 'The High-mettled Racer' (Mr. Dibdin, we believe,—no mean man, after all, in his way) may stand by the side of the illustrious biographer. Next to ancient causes, to the inevitable progress of events, and to the practical part of Christianity (which persons, the most accused of irreligion, have preserved like a glorious infant, through ages of blood and fire) the kindliness of modern philosophy is more immediately owing to the great national writers of Europe, in whose schools we have all been children:—to Voltaire in France, and Shakespeare in England. Shakespeare, in his time, obliquely pleaded the cause of the Jew, and got him set on a common level with humanity. The Jew has since been not only allowed to be human, but some have undertaken to show him as 'the best good Christian though he knows it not.' We shall not dispute the title with him, nor with the other worshippers of Mammon, who force him to the same shrine. We allow, as things go in that quarter, that the Jew is as great a Christian as his neighbour, and his neighbour as great a Jew as he. There is neither love nor money lost between them. But at all events, the Jew is a man; and with Shakespeare's assistance, the time has arrived when we can afford to acknowledge the horse for a fellow creature and treat him as one. We may say for him, upon precisely the same grounds and to the same purpose, as Shakespeare said for the Israelite, 'Hath not a horse organs, dimensions, senses, affections, passions? hurt with the same weapons, subject to the same diseases, healed by the same means, warmed and cooled by the same winter and summer, as a Christian is?' Oh, but some are always at hand to cry out, it would be effeminate to think too much of these things!—Alas! we have no notion of asking the gentlemen to think too much of anything. If they will think at all it will be a great gain. As to effeminacy (if we must use that ungallant and partial word, for want of a better) it is cruelty that is effeminate. It is selfishness that is effeminate. Anything is effeminate, which would get an excitement, or save a proper and manly trouble, at the undue expense of another. How does the case stand then between those who ill-treat their horses and those who spare them?

To return to the coach. Imagine a fine coach and pair, which are standing at the door of a house, in all the pride of their sleek strength and beauty, converted into what they may both really become, a hackney and its old shamblers. Such is one of the meditations of the philosophic eighteen-penny rider. A hackney-coach has often the arms of nobility on it. As we are going to get into it, we catch a glimpse of the faded lustre of an earl's or marquis's coronet, and think how many light or proud hearts have ascended those now rickety steps. In this coach perhaps an elderly lady once rode to her wedding, a blooming and blushing girl. Her mother and sister were on each side of her; the bridegroom opposite in a blossom-coloured coat. They talk of everything in the world, of which they are not thinking. The sister was never prouder of her. The mother with difficulty represses her own pride and tears. The bride, thinking he is looking at her, casts down her eyes, pensive in her joy. The bridegroom is at once the proudest, and the humblest, and the happiest man in the world.—For our parts, we sit in a corner, and are in love with the sister. We dream she is going to speak to us in answer to some indifferent question, when a hoarse voice comes in at the front window and says, 'Whereabouts, sir?'

And grief has consecrated thee, thou reverend dilapidation, as well as joy! Thou hast carried unwilling as well as willing hearts; hearts, that have thought the slowest of thy paces too fast; faces, that have sat back in a corner of thee, to hide their tears from the very thought of being seen. In thee, the destitute have been taken to the poor-house, and the wounded and sick to the hospital and many an arm has been round many an insensible waist. Into thee, the friend or the lover has hurried, in a passion of tears, to lament his loss. In thee, he has hastened to console the dying or the wretched. In thee, the father or mother, or the older kinswoman, more patient in her years, has taken the little child to the grave, like a human jewel that must be parted with.

But joy appears in thee again, like the look-in of the sunshine. If the lover has gone in thee unwillingly, he has also gone willingly. How many friends hast thou not carried to merry meetings! How many young parties to the play! How many children, whose faces thou hast turned in an instant from the extremity of lachrymose weariness to that of staring delight! Thou hast contained as many different passions in thee as a human heart: and for the sake of the human heart, old body, thou art venerable. Thou shalt be as respectable as a reduced old gentleman, whose very slovenliness is pathetic. Thou shalt be made gay, as he is over a younger and richer table, and thou shalt be still more touching for the gaiety.

We wish the hackney-coachman were as interesting a machine as either his coach or horses: but it must be owned, that of all the driving species, he is the least agreeable specimen. This is partly to be attributed to the life which has most probably put him into his situation; partly to his want of outside passengers to cultivate his gentility; and partly, to the disputable nature of his fare, which always leads him to be lying and cheating. The waterman of the stand, who beats him if possible in sordidness of appearance, is more respectable. He is less of a vagabond and cannot cheat you. Nor is the hackney-coachman only disagreeable in himself, but like Falstaff reversed, the cause of disagreeableness in others; for he sets people upon disputing with him in pettiness and ill-temper. He induces the mercenary to be violent, and the violent to seem mercenary. A man whom you took for a pleasant laughing fellow, shall all of a sudden put on an irritable look of calculation, and vow that he will be charged with a constable rather than pay the sixpence. Even fair woman shall waive her all-conquering softness, and sound a shrill trumpet in reprobation of the extortionate charioteer, who, if she were a man, she says, she would expose. Being a woman, then, let her not expose herself. Oh—but it is intolerable to be so imposed upon! Let the lady then get a pocket-book, if she must, with the hackney-coach fares in it ; or a pain in the legs, rather than the temper; or above all, let her get wiser, and have an understanding that can dispense with the good opinion of hackney-coachmen. Does she think that her rosy lips were made to grow pale about two and sixpence ? or that the cut of them will ever be like her cousin Fanny's, if she goes on ?

The stage-coachman likes the boys on the road, because he knows they admire him. The hackney-coachman knows that they cannot admire him, and that they can get up behind his coach ; which makes him very savage. The cry of 'cut behind' from the malicious urchins on the pavement wounds at once his self-love and his interest. He would not mind over-loading his master's horses for another sixpence ; but to do it for nothing is what shocks his humanity. He hates the boy for imposing upon him, and the boys for reminding him that he has been imposed upon ; and he would willingly twinge the cheeks of all nine. The cut of his whip over the coach is very malignant. He has a constant eye to the road behind him. He has also an eye to what may be left in the coach. He will undertake to search the straw for you, and miss the half-crown on purpose. He speculates on what he may get above his fare, according to your manners or company ; and knows how much to ask, for driving faster or slower than usual. He does not like wet weather so much as people suppose ; for he says it rots both his horses and harness, and he takes parties out of town when the weather is fine; which produces good payments in a

lump. Lovers, late supper-eaters, and girls going home
from boarding-school, are his best pay. He has a
rascally air of remonstrance, when you dispute half the
overcharge ; and according to the temper he is in, begs
you to consider his bread, hopes you will not make such
a fuss about a trifle, or tells you you may take his
number, or sit in the coach all night.

LADY. There, sir !

INDICATOR (looking all about him). Where, ma'am ?

LADY. The coachman, sir !

INDICATOR. Oh, pray, madam, don't trouble yourself.
Leave the gentleman alone with him. Do you continue
to be delightful at a little distance.

A great number of ludicrous adventures must have
taken place in which hackney-coaches were concerned.
The story of the celebrated harlequin, Lunn, who secretly
pitched himself out of one into a tavern window, and
when the coachman was about to submit to the loss of
his fare, astonished him by calling out again from the
inside, is too well known for repetition. There is one
of Swift, not perhaps so common. He was going, one
dark evening, to dine with some great man, and was
accompanied with some other clergymen, to whom he
gave their cue. They were all in their canonicals. When
they arrive at the house, the coachman opens the door,
and lets down the steps. Down steps the Dean, very
reverendly in his black robes : after him comes another
personage, equally black and dignified : then another :
then a fourth. The coachman, who recollects taking
up no greater number, is about to put up the steps,
when another clergyman descends. After giving way
to this other, he proceeds with great confidence to toss
them up, when lo ! another comes. Well ; there cannot, he thinks, be well more than six. He is mistaken.
Down comes a seventh ; then an eighth ; then a ninth,
all with decent intervals, the coach in the meantime
rocking as if it were giving birth to so many demons.
The coachman can conclude no less. He cries out, ' The
Devil ! the Devil ! ' and is preparing to run away, when
they all burst into laughter at the success of their joke.

They had gone round as they descended, and got in at the other door.

We remember in our boyhood an edifying comment on the proverb of ' all is not gold that glistens.' The spectacle made such an impression upon us, that we recollect the very spot, which was at the corner of a road in the way from Westminster to Kennington, near a stone-mason's. It was a severe winter; and we were out on a holiday, thinking perhaps of the gallant hardships to which the ancient soldiers used to accustom themselves, when we suddenly beheld a group of hackney-coachmen, not, as Spenser says of his witch,

> Busy, as *seemed*, about some wicked gin,

but pledging each other in what appeared to us to be little glasses of cold water. What temperance! thought we. What extraordinary and noble content! What more than Roman simplicity! There are a set of poor Englishmen, of the homeliest order, in the very depth of winter, quenching their patient and honourable thirst, with modicums of cold water! O true virtue and courage! O sight worthy of the Timoleons and Epaminondases! We know not how long we remained in this error; but the first time we recognized the white devil for what it was,—the first time we saw through the crystal purity of its appearance,—was a great blow to us. We did not then know what the drinkers went through; and this reminds us that we have omitted one great redemption of the hackney-coachman's character,—his being at the mercy of all sorts of chances and weathers. Other drivers have their settled hours and pay. He only is at the mercy of every call and every casualty; he only is dragged, without notice, like the damned in Milton, into the extremities of wet and cold, from his ale-house fire to the freezing rain; he only must go anywhere, at what hour, and to whatever place you choose, his old rheumatic limbs shaking under his weight of rags, and the snow and sleet beating into his puckered face, through streets which the wind scours like a channel.

THE THEATRES

GOING TO THE PLAY

[*Companion*, January 16, 1828]

WITH the exception of Oberon, we have not witnessed
a theatrical performance till the other night for these
six or seven years. Fortune took us another way; and
when we had the opportunity, we did not dare to begin
again, lest our old friends should beguile us. We
mention the circumstance, partly to account for the
notice we shall take of many things which appear to
have gone by; and partly out of a communicativeness
of temper, suitable to a Companion. For the reader
must never lose sight of our claims to that title. On
ordinary occasions, he must remember that we are dis-
cussing morals or mince-pie with him; on political
ones, reading the newspaper with him; and in the
present instance, we are sitting together in the pit (the
ancient seat of criticism), seeing *who* is *who* in the play-
bill, and hearing the delicious discord of the tuning of
instruments,—the precursor of harmony. If our companion is an old gentleman, we take a pinch of his snuff,
and lament the loss of Bannister and Mrs. Jordan.
Toothache and his nephew occupy also a portion of
our remark; and we cough with an air of authority.
If he is a young gentleman, we speak of Vestris and Miss
Foote; wonder whether little Goward will show herself
improving to-night; denounce the absurdity of somebody's boots, or his bad taste in beauty; and are loud
in deprecating the fellows who talk loudly behind us.
Finally, if a lady, we bend with delight to hear the
remarks she is making, ' far above ' criticism; and to
see the finer ones in her eyes. We criticize the ladies
in the boxes; and the more she admires them, the more

we find herself the lovelier. May we add, that ladies in the pit, this cold weather, have still more attractions than usual; and that it is cruel to find ourselves sitting, as we did the other night, behind two of them; when we ought to have been in the middle, partaking of the genial influence of their cloaks, their comfortable sides, and their conversation? We were going to say, that we hope this is not too daring a remark for a Companion:— but far be it from us to apologize for anything so proper. Don't we all go to the theatre to keep up our love of nature and sociality?

It was delightful to see 'the house' again, and to feel ourselves recommencing our old task. How pleasant looked the ceiling, the boxes, the pit, everything! Our friends in the gallery were hardly noisy enough for a beginning; nor on the other hand could we find it in our hearts to be angry with two companions behind us, who were a little noisier than they ought to have been, and who entertained one another with alternate observations on the beauty of the songs, and the loss of a pair of gloves. All is pleasant in these recommencements of a former part of one's life; this new morning, as it were, re-begun with the lustre of chandeliers and a thousand youthful remembrances. Anon, the curtain rises, and we are presented with a view of the lighthouse of Genoa, equally delicious and unlike;—some gunboats, returning from slavery, salute us with meek puffs of gunpowder, about as audible as pats on the cheek,— the most considerate cannon we ever met with:—then follow a crowd and a chorus, with embraces of redeemed captives, meeting their wives and children, at which we are new and uncritical enough to feel the tears come into our eyes; and finally, in comes Mr. 'Atkins,' with a thousand memories on his head,—husband that was of a pretty little singer some twenty years back, now gone, heaven knows where, like a blackbird. It seemed wrong in Atkins to be there, and his wife not with him. Yet we were glad to see him notwithstanding. We knew him the instant we heard him speak.

MANNERS AT THE THEATRE

[*The Town*]

THE whole entertainment of a theatre has been rising in point of accommodation and propriety for the last fifty years. The scenery is better, the music better—we mean the orchestra—and last, not least, the audiences are better. They are better behaved. Garrick put an end to one great nuisance—the occupation, by the audience, of part of the stage. Till his time, people often sat about a stage as at the sides of a room, and the actor had to make his way among them, sometimes with the chance of being insulted; and scuffles took place among themselves. Dr. Johnson, at Lichfield, is said to have pushed a man into the orchestra who had taken possession of his chair. The pit also, from about Garrick's time, seems to have left to the galleries the vulgarity attributed to it by Pope. There still remains, says he—

————to mortify a wit,
The many-headed monster of the pit,
A senseless, worthless, and unhonoured crowd,
Who, to disturb their betters, mighty proud,
Clattering their sticks before ten lines are spoke,
Call for the farce, the bear, or the black-joke.

This would now be hardly a fair description of the galleries; and yet modern audiences are not reckoned to be of quite so high a cast as they used, in point of rank and wealth; so that this is another evidence of the general improvement of manners. Boswell, in an ebullition of vivacity, while sitting one night in the pit by his friend Dr. Blair, gave an extempore imitation of a cow! The house applauded, and he ventured upon some attempts of the same kind which did not succeed. Blair advised him in future to ' stick to the cow.' No gentleman nowadays would think of a freak like this. There is one thing, however, in which the pit have much to

T 2

amend. Their destitution of gallantry is extraordinary, especially for a body so ready to accept the clap-traps of the stage, in praise of their 'manly hearts,' and their 'guardianship of the fair.' Nothing is more common than to see women standing at the sides of the pit benches, while no one thinks of offering them a seat. Room even is not made, though it often might be. Nay, we have heard women rebuked for coming without securing a seat, while the reprover complimented himself on his better wisdom, and the hearers laughed. On the other hand, a considerate gentleman one night, who went out to stretch his legs, told a lady in our hearing that she might occupy his seat 'till he returned!'

A friend of ours knew a lady who remembered Dr. Johnson in the pit taking snuff out of his waistcoat pocket. He used to go into the green-room to his friend Garrick, till he honestly confessed that the actresses excited too much of his admiration. Garrick did not much like to be seen by him when playing any buffoonery. It is said that the actor once complained to his friend that he talked too loud in the stage box, and interrupted his feelings: upon which the doctor said, 'Feelings! Punch has no feelings.' It was Johnson's opinion (speaking of a common cant of critics) that an actor who really 'took himself' for Richard III deserved to be hanged; and it is easy enough to agree with him; except that an actor who did so would be out of his senses. Too great a sensibility seems almost as hurtful to acting as too little. It would soon wear out the performer. There must be a quickness of conception, sufficient to seize the truth of the character, with a coolness of judgement to take all advantages; but as the actor is to represent as well as conceive, and to be the character in his own person, he could not with impunity give way to his emotions in any degree equal to what the spectators suppose. At least, if he did, he would fall into fits, or run his head against the wall. As to the amount of talent requisite to make a great actor, we must not enter upon a discussion which would lead us too far from our main object; but we shall merely express our opinion, that there is a great deal more of it among the community than they are aware.

OLD DRURY

[The Town]

THE existence of a theatre in Drury Lane is as old as the time of Shakespeare. It was then called the Phoenix; was ' a private,' or more select house, like that of Blackfriars ; and had been a cock-pit, by which name it was also designated. Phoenix generally implies that a place has been destroyed by fire, a common fate with the theatres ; but the first occasion on which we hear of the present one is the destruction of it by a Puritan mob. This took place in the year 1617, in the time of James ; and was doubtless caused by the same motives that led to the demolition of certain other houses, which it was thought to resemble in fame. In Howe's Continuation of Stowe it was called a ' new play-house,' so that it had lately been either built or rebuilt. This theatre stood opposite the Castle Tavern. There is still in existence a passage, called Cockpit Alley, into Great Wild Street ; and there is a Phoenix Alley, leading from Long Acre into Hart Street.

The Phoenix was soon rebuilt : and the performances continued till 1648, when they were again stopped by the Puritans, who then swayed England, and who put an end to the play-houses for some time. In the interval some of the most admired of our old dramas were produced there, such as Marlowe's *Jew of Malta ;* Heywood's *Woman killed with Kindness ; The Witch of Edmonton,* by Rowley, Decker, and Ford ; Webster's *White Devil,* or *Victoric Corombona,* Massinger's *New Way to Pay Old Debts,* and indeed many others.[1] It does not appear that Shakespeare or his immediate

---

[1] See Baker's *Biographia Dramatica,* vol. ii.

friends had any pieces performed there. He was a performer in other theatres; and the pressure of court, as well as city, lay almost exclusively in their direction, till the growth of the western part of the metropolis divided it. The Phoenix known in his time was probably nearly as select a house as the Blackfriars. The company had the title of Queen's Servants (James's queen), and the Servants of the Lady Elizabeth (Queen of Bohemia).

A few years before the Restoration, Davenant, supported by some of the less scrupulous authorities, ventured to smuggle back something like the old entertainments, under the pretence of accompanying them with music; a trick understood in our times where a licence is to be encroached upon. In 1656, he removed with them from Aldersgate Street to this house; and, after the fluctuation of different companies hither and thither, the Cockpit finally resumed its rank as a royal theatre, under the direction of the famous Killigrew, whose set of players were called the King's Company, as those under Sir William Davenant had the title of the Duke's. Killigrew, dissatisfied with the old theatre at the Cockpit, built a new one nearly on the site of the present, and opened it in 1663. This may be called the parent of Drury Lane Theatre as it now stands. It was burnt in 1671–2, rebuilt by Sir Christopher Wren, and opened in 1674, with a prologue from the pen of Dryden, from which time it stood till the year 1771. There had been some alterations in the structure of this theatre, which are said to have hurt the effect contemplated by Sir Christopher Wren, and perhaps assisted its destruction; for seventy years is no great age for a public building. Yet Old Drury, as it was called, was said to have died of a ' gradual decline.' It was rebuilt and became Old Drury the second; underwent the usual fate of theatres, in the year 1809; and was succeeded by the one now standing.

It is customary to divide the eras of theatres according to their management; but, as managers become of little consequence to posterity, we shall confine ourselves in this as in other respects to names with which posterity is familiar. In Shakespeare's time, Drury Lane appears to have been celebrated for the best productions of the second-rate order of dramatists, a set of men who would have been first in any other age. We have little to say of the particulars of Drury Lane at this period, no memorandums having come down to us as they did afterwards. All we can imagine is, that—the Phoenix being much out of the way, with fields and country roads in the interval between court and city, and the performances taking place in the day-time—the company probably consisted of the richer orders, the poorer being occupied in their labours. The court and the rich citizens went on horseback; the Duke of Buckingham in his newly-invented sedan. In the time of the Puritans we may fancy the visitors stealing in, as they would into a gambling-house.

The era of the Restoration, or second era of the Stuarts, is that of the popularity of Ben Jonson's and Beaumont and Fletcher's plays, compared with Shakespeare's, though Davenant tried hard to revive him; of the plays of Dryden, Lee, and Otway; and finally of the rise of comedy, strictly so called, in those of Wycherly, Congreve, Farquhar, and Vanbrugh. All these writers had to do with Drury Lane Theatre, some of them almost exclusively. Nineteen out of Dryden's twenty-seven plays were produced there; seven out of Lee's eleven; all the good ones of Wycherly (that is to say, all except *The Gentleman Dancing-Master*); two of Congreve's, *The Old Bachelor* and *Double Dealer*, and all Farquhar's, except *The Beaux Stratagem*. Otway's best pieces came out at the Duke's Theatre; and Vanbrugh's in the Haymarket.[1] This may be called the second era of Drury Lane, or rather the second and third; the former, which is Dryden's and Lee's, having for its principal performers Hart, Mohun, Lacy, Goodman, Nell Gwynn, and others; the latter, which was that of Congreve and Farquhar, presenting us with Cibber, Wilks, Booth, Mrs. Barry, and Mrs. Bracegirdle. The

---

[1] See Baker, *passim*.

two, taken together, began with the Restoration and
ended with George II.

Sir Richard Steele and the sentimental comedy came
in at the close of the third era, and may be said to constitute the fourth ; which, in his person, did not last
long. Steele, admirable as an essayist, and occasionally as humorous as any dramatist in a scene or two,
was hampered in his plays by the new moral ambition
now coming up, which induced him to show, not so
much what people are, as his notions of what they ought
to be. This has never been held a legitimate business
of the stage, which, in fact, is nothing else than what
its favourite metaphor declares it—a glass of men and
manners, in which they are to see themselves as they
actually exist. It is the essence of the wit and dialogue of society brought into a focus. Steele was
manager of Drury Lane Theatre, and made as bad a
one as improvidence and animal spirits could produce.

The sentimental comedy continued into the next or
fifth Drury Lane era, which was that of Garrick, famous
for his great reputation as an actor, and for his triumphant revival of Shakespeare's plays, which have increased in popularity ever since. Not that he revived
them in the strictest sense of the word; for the attempt
was making when he came to town ; but he hastened
and exalted the success of it.

The last era before the present one was that of
Sheridan, who, though he began with Covent Garden,
produced four out of his seven pieces at this theatre ;
where he showed himself a far better dramatist, and a
still worse manager, than Steele.

We shall now endeavour to possess our readers with
such a sense of these different periods, as may enable
them to ' live o'er each scene,' not indeed of the plays,
but of the general epochs of Old Drury ; to go into the
green-room with Hart and Nell Gywnn ; to see Mrs.
Oldfield swim on the stage as Lady Betty Modish ; to
revive the electrical shock of Garrick's leap upon it, as
the lively Lothario ;—in short, to be his grandfather
and great-grandfather before him, and make one of

the successive generations of playgoers, now in his peruke *à la Charles II*, and now in his Ramillie wig, or the bobs of Hogarth. Did we introduce him to all this ourselves, we should speak with less confidence; but we have a succession of playgoers for his acquaintance, who shall make him doubt whether he really is or is not his own ancestor, so surely shall they place him beside them in the pit.

And first, for the immortal and most play-going Pepys. To the society of this jolliest of Government officers we shall consign our reader and ourselves during the reign of Charles II; and if we are not all three equally intimate with Old Drury at that time there is no faith in good company. By Old Drury we understand both the theatres; the Cockpit or Phoenix and the new one built by Killigrew, which took the title of 'King's Theatre.' There was a cockpit at Whitehall, or court theatre, to which Pepys occasionally alludes; but after trying in vain to draw a line between such of his memorandums as might be retained and omitted, we here give up the task as undesirable, the whole harmonizing in one mass of theatrical gossip, and making us acquainted collaterally even with what he is not speaking of. We have not, indeed, retained everything, but we have almost.

We now, therefore, pass Drury House, proceed up the lane by my Lord Craven's garden, and turn into Russell Street amongst a throng of Cavaliers in flowing locks, and ladies with curls *à la Vallière*. Some of them are in masks, but others have not put theirs on. We shall see them masking as the house grows full. It is early in the afternoon. There press a crowd of gallants, who have already got enough wine. Here, as fast as the lumbering coaches of that period can do it, dashes up to the door my lord Duke of Buckingham, bringing with him Buckhurst and Sedley. There comes a greater, though at that time a humbler man, to wit, John Dryden, in a coat of plain drugget, which by and by his fame converted into black velvet. He is somewhat short and stout with a roundish dimpled face and a

sparkling eye ; and, if scandal says true, by his side is
' Madam ' Reeves, a beautiful actress ; for the ladies
of the stage were so entitled at that time.   Horses and
coaches throng the place, with here and there a sedan ;
and, by the pulling off of hats, we find that the king and
his brother James have arrived.   The former nods to
his people as if he anticipated their mutual enjoyment
of the play ; the latter affects a graciousness to match,
but does not do it very well.   As soon as the king passes
in there is a squeeze and a scuffle ; and some blood is
drawn, and more oaths uttered, from which we hasten
to escape.   Another scuffle is silenced on the king's
entrance, which also makes the gods quiet ; otherwise,
at no period were they so loud.   The house is not very
large, nor very well appointed.   Most of the ladies
mask themselves in the pit and boxes, and all parties
prepare for a play that shall render it proper for the
remainder to do so.   The king applauds a new French
tune played by the musicians.   Gallants, not very
sober, are bowing on all sides of us to ladies not very
nice ; or talking to the orange girls, who are ranged in
front of the pit with their backs to the stage.   We hear
criticisms on the last new piece, on the latest panegyric,
libel, or new mode.   Our friend Pepys listens and looks
everywhere, tells all who is who, or asks it ; and his
neighbours think him a most agreeable fat little gentleman.   The curtain rises : enter Mistress Marshall, a
pretty woman, and speaks a prologue which makes all
the ladies hurry on their masks, and convulses the house
with laughter.   Mr. Pepys ' do own ' that he cannot
help laughing too, and calls the actress ' a merry
jade ' ; ' but, lord ! ' he says, ' to see the difference of
the times, and but two years gone.'   And then he utters
something between a sigh and a chuckle, at the recollection of his Presbyterian breeding, compared with the
jollity of his expectations.

RULES FOR THEATRICAL CRITIC

[*Critical Essays on the Performers of the London Theatres*]

In the first place.—Never take any notice whatever of the author of a play, or of the play itself, unless it be a new one : if the author be living, it is most probable you will have no reason to speak of him more than once, and if he be not living you have no reason to speak of him at all, for dead men cannot give dinners.

Secondly.—Indulge an acquaintance with every dramatic writer, and with every actor, and you will have a noble opportunity of showing your fine feelings and your philanthropy, for you will praise every play that is acted, and every actor that plays ; depend upon it, the world will attribute this praise to your undeviating benevolence, which is a great virtue.

Thirdly.—If an audience should not possess this virtue equally with yourselves, but should barbarously hiss a new piece merely because it could not entertain them, say in your next day's criticism, that it would have been infinitely more entertaining if a little had been added, or a little had been taken away, a probability which few will dispute with you. No man of real feeling will thing of damning another merely because the latter cannot succeed in every attempt to please him. If the exclamation *bravo !* will make a man enjoy his supper and put a few pounds into his pocket every winter, who would not cry out *bravo ?* Suppose an ugly, whimsical fellow were to accost you in the streets and to say, ' Sir, I'd thank you to tell me I am handsome, or I shall be miserable for months to come,' you would undoubtedly say, ' Sir, I am enchanted with your appearance, and entreat you to be perfectly happy.' In the same manner it is easy to say to Mr. Reynolds, or Mr. Dibdin, or Mr. Cherry, ' Your play was excellent,' and the poor fellow will be as comfortable as if it were really the case.

Fourthly.—If you do not exactly understand how to conceal your evil opinion of men's writings or performances, but find yourself occasionally apt to indulge in maliciously speaking the truth, always say the direct contrary of what you think. The following little glossary, collected from the most approved critics, may be of service to you in this case ; you will of course make use of the first column :—

A crowded house—a theatre on the night of a performance, when all the back seats and upper boxes are empty.

An amusing author—an author whose very seriousness makes us laugh in spite of himself.

A successful author—an author who has been damned only four times out of five.

A good author—the general term for an author who gives good dinners.

A respectable actor—an insipid actor ; one who in general is neither hissed nor applauded.

A fine actor—one who makes a great noise ; a tatterdemalion of passions ; a clap-trapper : one intended by nature for a town-crier. This appellation may on all occasions be given to Mr. Pope, who has the finest lungs of any man on the stage.

A good actor—the general term for an actor who gives good dinners.

A charming play—a play full of dancing, music, and scenery ; a play in which the less the author has to do the better.

Great applause—applause mixed with the hisses of the gallery and pit.

Unbounded and universal applause—applause mixed with hisses of the pit only. This phrase is frequently to be found at the bottom of the playhouse bills in declaring the reception a new piece has met with. The plays announced in these bills are generally printed in red ink, an emblem, no doubt, of the modesty with which they speak of themselves.

There was once a kind soul of an author who could not bear to use a harsh word, even when speaking of villains ; he used to call highwaymen *tax-gatherers*, pickpockets *collectors*, and ravishers *men of gallantry*. This gentleman would have made an excellent theatrical critic ; he would have called Reynolds Congreve, and Cherry Shakespeare, and everybody would have admired his invention.

Fifthly, and lastly.—When you criticize the performance of an old play, never exceed six or seven lines, but be sure to notice by name the fashionables in the boxes, for such notices are indispensably requisite to sound criticism ; there is a choice collection of sentences which have been in use time immemorial with newspaper critics, and are still used by common consent, just as we universally allow one style for a note of hand or a visiting letter. Your observations, therefore, will generally be such as these :—

DRURY LANE.—Last night the *beautiful* comedy of *The Rivals* was performed with great éclat to an *overflowing* house : Bannister was excellent—Mrs. H. Johnston looked *beautiful*. Among the company we observed the Duchess of Gordon, the Duke of Queensberry, Lady Hamilton, and many other *amiable* and *beautiful* personages. There was a quarrel in the pit.

What can be more concise, more explanatory, more critical, than such a criticism ? Grammarians undertake to teach a language in five months, musicians, the whole theory of music in five weeks, and dancing-masters all sorts of steps in five hours, but by these rules a man may be a profound critic in five minutes. Let Aristotle and Quintilian hide their huge volumes in dismay, and confess the superiority of a criticism, which, like the magic word *Sesame* in the *Arabian Nights*, opens to us a thousand treasures in a breath !

STAGE COSTUME

[Critical Essays on the Performers of the London Theatres]

The majority of an audience were certainly never deluded into a belief that events represented on the stage were realities. The best actors, who are the most likely to produce such a delusion, are always the most applauded; but it is evident they would gain no applause were their assumed character forgotten; for in common life we do not clap any incident that pleases us in the streets, nor cry out 'bravo' at a pathetic circumstance in a room. A rustic, perhaps, who knew nothing of the machinery and trick of the stage, might be momentarily deceived; but the dream would soon be removed by the frequent cessations of the entertainment, and particularly the alteration of scene, so badly managed at the theatre, where you see two men running violently towards each other with half a castle or a garden in their grasp. Though it is impossible, however, and indeed generally considered it would be unpleasant, to maintain this impression of reality, the imitation of life and manners should be as exact as possible, for the same cause that we are pleased with our just resemblance in a glass, though we are convinced that it is a mere resemblance. But the most consummate actor gains but half his effect, if his eloquent imitation is not assisted by the mute imitations of dress and of scenery. A man, for instance, who in his countenance and his action could display to perfection the mind of the great Alfred, would make a singular impression if his dress were made after the fashion of the reign of George the Third, and his room after that of Queen Elizabeth's. Yet the chronological absurdities of the present stage are scarcely less laughable than such a compound. Alexander, indeed, does not rave now in a cocked hat and jack-boots; Timoleon does not frown in a profusion of periwig; nor does Cleopatra wanton in an enormity of hoop-petticoat. But though times and countries are not set at this open defiance, their proprieties are unaccountably neglected.

Perhaps there is not a single performer who knows how to dress with perfect propriety, except Mrs. Siddons, who is excellently classical and just in this respect. Mr. Elliston and Mr. Kemble and his brother Charles are more attentive to their apparel than the generality of actors ; but the second is at all times too fond of a glare of ornament, and we have seen both the brothers, in the parts of modern gentlemen, flaming in court dresses on the most common occasions. As to the other actors, their absurdities in dress are innumerable, and are observable every night of a performance. Old men of the present day are hardly ever without the laced coats and flapped waistcoats of the last century. The ladies wear spangled gowns and ostrich feathers upon all occasions, and the beaux appear in the streets with frogs instead of plain buttons, cocked hats instead of round ones, and swords when nobody wears a sword but at court. Of all beauish dressers, however, Mr. Lewis is the most faulty and the least excusable, because he is an actor of great experience as well as genius ; this gentleman seems to delight in uncouth habiliments, and not unfrequently astonishes the audience by appearing as a beau in a coat chequered with ribs and enlivened with variegated colours : of what age or of what country such coat may be we know not ; all that we can discover is, that it is more like the dress of an ancient French footman than of a modern English gentleman.

ITALIAN DANCING

[Autobiography]

AT Turin was the finest dancer I had ever seen, a girl of the name of De' Martini. She united the agility of the French school with all that you would expect from the Italian. Italian dancers are in general as mediocre as the French are celebrated; but the French dancers in spite of their high notions of the art and the severity of their studies (perhaps that is the reason), have no mind with their bodies. They are busts in barbers' shops, stuck upon legs full of vivacity. You wonder how any lower extremities so lively can leave such an absence of all expression in the upper. De' Martini was a dancer all over. Her countenance partook of the felicity of the limbs. When she came bounding on the stage, in two or three long leaps like a fawn, I should have thought she was a Frenchwoman; but the style undeceived me. She came bounding in front, as if she would have pitched herself into the arms of the pit; then made a sudden drop, and addressed three enthusiastic courtesies to the pit and boxes, with a rapidity and yet a grace, a self-abandonment yet a self-possession, quite extraordinary, and such as, to do justice to it, should be described by a poet combining the western ideas of the sex with eastern licence. She was beautiful, too, both in face and figure, and I thought was a proper dancer to appear before a pit full of those fine fellows I have just mentioned. She seemed as complete in her way as themselves. In short, I never saw anything like it before, and did not wonder that she had the reputation of turning people's heads wherever she went.

MRS. JORDAN

[*Autobiography*]

MRS. JORDAN was inimitable in exemplifying the consequences of too much restraint in ill-educated Country Girls, in Romps, in Hoydens, and in Wards on whom the mercenary have designs. She wore a bib and tucker, and pinafore, with a bouncing propriety, fit to make the boldest spectator alarmed at the idea of bringing such a household responsibility on his shoulders. To see her when thus attired shed blubbering tears for some disappointment, and eat all the while a great thick slice of bread and butter, weeping, and moaning, and munching, and eyeing at every bite the part she meant to bite next, was a lesson against will and appetite worth a hundred sermons of our friends on board the hoy; and, on the other hand, they could assuredly have done and said nothing at all calculated to make such an impression in favour of amiableness as she did, when she acted in gentle, generous, and confiding characters. The way in which she would take a friend by the cheek and kiss her, or make up a quarrel with a lover, or coax a guardian into good-humour, or sing (without accompaniment) the song of 'Since then I'm doom'd,' or ' In the dead of the night,' trusting, as she had a right to do, and as the house wished her to do, to the sole effect of her sweet, mellow, and loving voice—the reader will pardon me, but tears of pleasure and regret come into my eyes at the recollection, as if she personified whatsoever was happy at that period of life, and which has gone like herself. The very sound of the little familiar word *bud* from her lips (the abbreviation of husband), as she packed it closer, as it were, in the utterance, and pouted it up with fondness in the man's face, taking him at the same time by the chin, was a whole concentrated world of the power of loving.

MR. POPE

[*Critical Essays on the Performers of the London Theatres*]

WHEN I place Mr. Pope immediately after Mrs. Siddons, everybody will see I do not criticize the actors according to their rank. But it is for the sake of contrast. If we have just had an example of almost perfect tragedy, we have now an instance of every fault that can make it not only imperfect but disgusting. Mr. Pope has not one requisite to an actor but a good voice, and this he uses so unmercifully on all occasions that its value is lost, and he contrives to turn it into a defect. His face is as hard, as immovable, and as void of meaning as an oak wainscot; his eyes, which should endeavour to throw some meaning into his vociferous declamation, he generally contrives to keep almost shut; and what would make another actor merely serious is enough to put him in a passion. In short, when Shakespeare wrote his description of 'a robustious fellow, who tears a passion to tatters,' one would suppose that he had been shown, by some supernatural means, the future race of actors, as Macbeth had a prophetic view of Banquo's race, and that the robustious phantom was Mr. Pope. Here is an actor, then, without face, expression, or delivery, and yet this complication of negative qualities finds means to be clapped in the theatre and panegyrized in the newspapers. This inconsistency must be explained. As to the newspapers, and their praise of this gentleman, I do not wish to repeat all the prevailing stories. Who does not know their corruptions? There is, however, an infallible method of obtaining a clap from the galleries, and there is an art known at the theatre by the name of *clap-trapping*, which Mr. Pope has shown great wisdom in studying. It consists in nothing more than gradually raising the voice as the speech draws to a conclusion, making an alarming outcry on the last four or five lines, or suddenly dropping them into a tremulous but energetic undertone, and with a vigorous jerk of the right arm rushing off the stage. All this astonishes the galleries; they are persuaded it must be something very fine, because it is so important and so unintelligible, and they clap for the sake of their own reputation.

One might apt to wonder at Mr. Pope's total want of various expression, when his merit as an artist is considered. It should seem that the same imitative observation, which gives so natural an elegance to his portraits on canvas, should enliven and adorn his portraits on the stage: that the same elegant conception which enables him to throw grace into the attitudes and meaning into the eyes of others, should inspire his action with variety and his looks with intelligence.

It is in the acknowledgement of gesture and attitude, but more particularly in the variation of countenance, in the adaption of look to feeling, that the actor is best known. Mr. Pope, in his general style, has but two gestures, which follow each other in monotonous alternation, like the jerks of a toy-shop harlequin: one is a mere extension of the arms, and is used on all occasions of candour, of acknowledgement, of remonstrance, and of explanation; the other, for occasions of vehemence or of grandeur, is an elevation of the arms, like the gesture of Raphael's *St. Paul preaching at Athens,* an action which becomes the more absurd on common occasions, from its real sublimity. If Mr. Pope, however, is confined to two expressions in his gesture, he has but two expressions in his look: a flat indifference, which is used on all sober occasions, and an angry frown, which is used on all impassioned ones. With these two looks he undertakes to represent all the passions, gentle as well as violent; he is like a quack who, with a phial in each hand, undertakes to perform every possible wonder, while the only thing to be wondered at is his cheating the mob. The best character he performs is Othello, because he performs it in a mask: for when an actor's face is not exactly seen, an audience is content to supply by its own imagination the want of expression, just as in reading a book we figure to ourselves the countenance of the persons interested. But when we are presented with the real countenance, we are disappointed if our imagination is not assisted in its turn ; the picture presented to our eyes should animate the picture presented to our mind ; if either of them differ, or if the former is less lively than the latter, a sensation of discord is produced, and destroys the effect of nature, which is always harmonious.

The pain we feel at bad acting seems, indeed, to be entirely the result of a want of harmony. We are pleased when the actor's external action corresponds with the action of his mind, when his eye answers his heart, when all we see is the animated picture of all we feel : we are displeased whenever the passion and the expression are at variance, when the countenance does not become a second language to the dialogue, when moderate tones express vehement emotions and when vehement tones express moderate emotions, when, in short, Mr. Pope is not Rolla [1] or Romeo but Mr. Pope. A musician who tells us that he is going to play a melancholy movement, and then dashes his harp or his piano in a fury, cannot disappoint us more than this actor, when he raises from language merely sorrowful an expression of boisterous passion. The character of Hotspur has been reckoned a proper one for Mr. Pope, because it is loud and violent ; these are good reasons certainly, and we would rather hear him in Hotspur than in Hamlet, for noise, like any other enjoyment, is delightful in its proper season only. But to act Hotspur well is a mark of no great talent ; of all expressions, violence is the most easily affected, because the conception of violence has no sensation of restraint, it has no feelings to hide or to repress, and no niceties of action to study. The gentler passions give us leisure to examine them, we can follow every variation of feeling and every change of expression ; but here we have leisure for nothing ; everything is rapid and confused ; we are in the con-

---

[1] In Sheridan's *Pizarro* (from Kotzebue).

dition of a man who should attempt to count the spokes of a wheel in a chariot-race.

Mr. Pope, in short, may be considered as an example of the little value of a good voice unaccompanied with expression, while Mr. Kemble is a proof how much may be done by an expressive countenance and manner with the worst voice in the world.

But perhaps as I can say nothing of Mr. Pope as a tragic actor, I may be expected to say something of him as a comic one, for he does act in comedy. Any one, however, who examines this double gift, will discover that to act in comedy and to be a comic actor are two very different things. Mr. Kemble performs in comedy, but who will call Mr. Kemble a comic actor? Who will reckon up the comic actors, and say, 'We have Bannister, and Lewis, and Munden, and Kemble'? If Mr. Pope acts in sentimental comedy, what is called sentimental comedy is nothing more than a mixture of tragedy and comedy, or, if Dr. Johnson's definition is to be allowed, it is sometimes entirely tragedy, for he calls tragedy 'a dramatic representation of a serious action.' There may be very often a serious character in humorous comedies, such as a sober merchant, a careful father, or one of those useless useful friends who serve as a kind of foil to a gay hero; but the actor who performs these characters never excites our livelier feelings or our mirth, and therefore cannot be called a comic actor. Lord Townley, for instance, in *The Provoked Husband*, is merely a tragic character who has stepped into comedy: Mr. Kemble represents Lord Townley with much gravity and stateliness; yet nobody in the pit ever said at seeing this character, 'Really that is very comic!' It is necessary to a comic actor that he should be able to excite our laughter, or at least our smiles; but Mr. Pope never excites either, at any rate not designedly. If is for this reason that he has been placed among the tragedians, and that Mr. Charles Kemble, Mr. Henry Johnston, Mr. Murray, and Mr. Siddons will be placed among them too. All these gentlemen might undoubtedly be called comic actors, as Robin

Hood's companion, who was seven feet high, was called Little John ; or we might say such a man was as comic as Mr. Kemble or Mr. Henry Johnston, just as we say such a thing is as smooth as a file. But upon plain subjects I would rather be plain spoken.

HENRY THE FIFTH

[The Tatler]

THE play of *Henry V* was performed here last night [1], but to little purpose. It is a *rifacimento* of Shakespeare's play, partly taken out of *Henry IV*, in order to increase the dramatic effect. But the secret must out. It is not a good acting play—at least not for these times. In every production of Shakespeare's there must be noble passages. There are fine lines in this, ' familiar in our mouths ' (to quote one of them) ' as household words.' But the historical plays of our great poet were written, not merely as dramas, but as chronicles. People in ordinary, in his time, were not so well informed as they are now. They went to the theatre, when one of these plays was performed, not merely to see a play as we do, but to receive an historical lesson, to hear about England and France, and take home the legend to their children, as we carry home a piece of news. Besides, the feeling was not what it is now between the two countries. They affected then (as indeed they did up to a late period) to bully and undervalue one another : Henry V was a popular prince with our ancestors, purely because he went to France, and read the Dauphin's insolence a terrible lesson. But these times are over now : the French (with illustrious reason) are no longer reckoned boasters : those even who conquered them but a little while since may not be popular. The English care little for quarrels between

[1] Drury Lane, November 8, 1830.

kings: audiences at a play want something better than this prince and that stepping out alternately with a flourish of trumpets—then a little huddle of soldiers, which we are to take for an onset—then the English flag running in, and then the French flag—with an occasional speech between, about St. George or St. Denys—and a Welsh captain, who is proud because the King is a Welshman. In a word, the play of *Henry V* was written to please the uninformed subjects of a despotic government two hundred years ago, and as it comprises little of the everlasting humanity that fills most of the plays of Shakespeare, it falls flat on the ears of an audience in these times of popular spirit! Of all the plays that could be selected, it struck us as one of the least fit to be performed on the eve of our present Lord Mayor's Day! and we found it so. Mr. Macready, though too loud in some parts, made a gallant and a gallant prince too (we allude to his courtship of Katharine), and Mr. Webster, in Captain Fluellen, sustained the reputation he acquired as Sir Hugh Evans:—but it would not do. The piece was as flat as the water in Tower Ditch, and about as noisy to no purpose as the beating to arms there.

HENRY THE FOURTH

[*The Tatler*]

LAST night the play of *Henry IV* was performed at this theatre.[1] The historical plays of Shakespeare certainly do not tell as they used to do—no disparagement to his mighty genius. He could not be expected to render kings, and their quarrels and sophistications, as undiminished in interest for ever as the events common to us all. Part of the interest of these plays arose, as we have before observed, from the paucity of books in

[1] Drury Lane, November 19, 1830.

his time. We know history better now, and respect
the performers in it less. Greater matters engage us:
but love is ever interesting, and wit, and domestic pity,
and the struggles of the will with the understanding.
In Shakespeare's time, audiences were contented with
a curtain for a scene, and a few dresses no better than
at a booth: they were content to be absorbed in those
stories of civil wars and royal successions, with the noise
of which their grandfathers' ears had hardly ceased
ringing. At present, we must dress up the historical
plays with plumes, and decorations, and real costume,
in order to amuse the eye, because the other interest
languishes. And we dress it very well, yet it languishes
still. Last night, Mr. Cooper's costume as Henry IV
was a real historical picture. We saw the King himself
before us, with his draperied head; and the performer,
as he rose from his chair, and remained lecturing his son
with his foot planted on the royal stool, displayed the
monarch well—his ermined robe, stretched out by his
elbow, making a back-ground to the portrait. But the
real interest of Henry is gone, when we think so much of
this 'galanty show' of him. For our parts, we confess that we forget all he said, in thinking what sort of a
grand and half-witted wild beast of a man a king was in
those days; and whether the day were far distant, in
which lions and eagles would be thought fit emblems of
national sovereignty.

There is Falstaff, to be sure, in this play; and Mr.
Dowton's Falstaff in *Henry IV* is better than in the
Merry Wives of Windsor. His wit is more exercised
than his enjoyment; and Mr. Dowton lets no fancy pass
without dwelling upon and recommending it in his
acutest manner. But his Falstaff is at no time the
proper rolling tun of a tavern sensualist; he is not fat
enough in the throat, nor festive enough in his general
manner: he takes his graver speeches too literally—
does not let us see the vein of invincible self-complacency running through them: and the other *dramatis
personae* fall into the same error. Vining makes but
a flimsy Prince of Wales, and Wallack but an ordinary

Hotspur. Wallack's best passage of all was the mode in which he died. His fall was excellent, and the posture in which he first clasped the ground, resolute and in good defiance, without exaggeration. Mrs. C. Jones wants humour as Mrs. Quickly—we mean a vein of particularity—of quaint exaggeration. She is natural, and plump, and petulant, and easily placable; but does not add that proper garnish to it all, which makes what we call a character.

THE COUNTRY

COUNTRY LITTLE KNOWN

[Indicator, May 24, 1820]

WE have to inform the public of a remarkable discovery which, though partially disclosed by former travellers, has still remained, for the most part, a strange secret. It is this ;—that there is actually, at this present moment, and in this our own beautiful country of Great Britain, a large tract of territory, which to nine hundred and ninety-nine thousandths of our beloved countrymen is as much an undiscovered land as the other end of New South Wales, or the Pole which they have gone to find out. We have read of places in romance which were more shut out by magic from people's eyes, though close to them, than if a fifty-foot wall encircled them. It would seem as if some such supernatural prohibition existed with regard to the land in question ; for the extremities of it reach to within a short distance from the metropolis, which it surrounds on all sides ; nay, we have heard of persons riding through it, without seeing anything but a signpost or some corn ; and yet it is so beautiful, that it is called emphatically 'The Country.'

It abounds in the finest natural productions. The more majestic parts of it are at a distance ; but the zealous explorer may come upon its gentler beauties in an incredibly short time. Its pastures and cattle are admirable. Deer are to be met with in the course of half a day's journey ; and the traveller is accompanied, wherever he goes, with the music of singing birds. Immediately towards the south is a noble river, which brings you to an upland of the most luxuriant description, looking in the water like a rich-haired beauty in

her glass : yet the place is in general solitary.   Towards
the north, at a less distance, are some other hilly spots
of ground, which partake more of the rudely romantic,
running however into scenes of the like sylvan elegance;
and yet these are still more solitary.   The inhabitants
of these lands, called the Country-People, seem, in truth,
pretty nearly as blind to their merits as those who
never see them ; but their perceptions will doubtless
increase in proportion as their polished neighbours set
the example.   It should be said for them that some
causes, with which we have nothing to do in this place,
have rendered them duller to such impressions than they
appear to have been a century or two ago ; but we
repeat, that they will not live in such scenes to no purpose, if those who know better take an interest in their
improvement.   Their children have an instinct that is
wiser, till domestic cares do it away.   They may be
seen in the fields and green lanes, with their curly locks
and brown faces, gathering the flowers which abound
there, and the names of which are as pretty as the shapes
and colours.   They are called wild roses, primroses,
violets, the rose campion, germander, stellaria, wild
anemone, bird's-eye, daisies and buttercups, lady-
smocks, ground-ivy, harebells or bluebells, wake-robin,
lilies of the valley, &c., &c.   The trees are oaks, elms,
birches, ash, poplar, willow, wild cherry, the flowering
may-bush, &c., &c., all, in short, that we dote upon in
pictures, and wish that we had about us when it is hot in
Cheapside and Bond Street.   It is perfectly transporting, in fine weather, like the present for instance, to
lounge under the hedgerow elms in one of these sylvan
places, and see the light smoke of the cottages fuming up
among the green trees, the cattle grazing or lying about
with a heavy placidity accordant to the time and scene,
' painted jays ' glancing about the glens, the gentle hills
sloping down into the water, the winding embowered
lanes, the leafy and flowery banks, the green oaks against
the blue sky, their ivied trunks, the silver-bodied and
young-haired birches, and the mossy grass treble-car-
peted after the vernal rains.   Transporting is it to see

all this ; and transporting to hear the linnets, thrushes, and blackbirds, the grave gladness of the bee, and the stock-dove ' brooding over her own sweet voice.' And more transporting than all is it to be in such places with a friend that feels like ourselves, in whose heart and eyes (especially if they have fair lids) we may see all our own happiness doubled, as the landscape itself is reflected in the waters.

SOUTHGATE

[Autobiography]

It is a pleasure to me to know that I was even born in so sweet a village as Southgate. I first saw the light there on the 19th of October, 1784. It found me cradled, not only in the lap of the nature which I love, but in the midst of the truly English scenery which I love beyond all other. Middlesex in general, like my noble friend's county of Warwickshire, is a scene of trees and meadows, of ' greenery ' and nestling cottages ; and Southgate is a prime specimen of Middlesex. It is a place lying out of the way of innovation, therefore it has the pure, sweet air of antiquity about it ; and as I am fond of local researches in any quarter, it may be pardoned me if in this instance I would fain know even the meaning of its name. There is no Northgate, Eastgate, or Westgate in Middlesex : what, then, is Southgate ? No topographer tells us ; but an old map of the country twenty-five miles round London, drawn up some years previous to my childhood, is now before me ; and on looking at the boundaries of Enfield Chase, I see that the 'Chase-gate,' the name most likely of the principal entrance, is on the north side of it, by North-Hall and Potter's Bar ; while Southgate, which has also the name of ' South Street,' is on the Chase's opposite border ; so that it seems evident that Southgate meant the southern entrance into the Chase, and that the name became that of a village from the growth of a street. The street, in all probability, was the consequence of a fair held in a wood which ran on the western side of it, and which, in the map, is designated 'Bush Fair.' *Bush*, in old English, meant not only a hedge but a wood; as *Bois* or *Bosco* does in French and Italian. Moses and the 'burning bush' is Moses and the 'burning wood'; which, by the way, presents a much grander idea than the modicum of hedge commonly assigned to the celestial apparition. There is a good deal more wood in the map than is now to be found. I wander in imagination through the spots marked in the neighbourhood, with their pleasant names—Woodside, Wood Green, Palmer Green, Nightingale Hall, &c., and fancy my father and mother listening to the nightingales, and loving the new little baby, who has now lived to see more years than they did.

Southgate lies in a cross-country road, running from Edmonton through Enfield Chase into Hertfordshire. It is in the parish of Edmonton; so that we may fancy the *Merry Devil* of that place still playing his pranks hereabouts, and helping innocent lovers to a wedding, as in the sweet little play attributed to Dryden. For as to any such devils going to a place less harmonious it is not to be thought possible by good Christians. Furthermore, to show what classical ground is round about Southgate, and how it is associated with the best days of English genius, both old and new, Edmonton is the birthplace of Marlowe, the father of our drama, and of my friend Horne, his congenial celebrator. In Edmonton churchyard lies Charles Lamb; in Highgate churchyard, Coleridge; and in Hampstead have resided Shelley and Keats, to say nothing of Akenside before them, and of Steele, Arbuthnot, and others, before Akenside.

But the neighbourhood is dear to me on every account, for near Southgate is Colney Hatch, where my mother became acquainted with some of her dearest friends, whom I shall mention by and by. Near Colney Hatch is Finchley, where our family resided on quitting Southgate; and at no great distance from Finchley is Mill

Hill, where lived excellent Dr. W. M. Trinder, Vicar of Hendon, who presented in his person the rare combination of clergyman and physician. He boasted that he had cured a little child (to wit, myself) of a dropsy in the head. The fact was contested, I believe, by the lay part of the profession; but it was believed in the family, and their love for the good doctor was boundless.

COLOUR

[London Journal, August 29, 1835]

IN this beloved, beautiful, but sometimes foggy, and too often not very brilliant country of ours, we are not fond enough of *colours*,—not fond enough of a beauty, of which Nature herself is evidently *very fond*, and with which, like all the rest of her beauties, it is the business of civilized man to adorn and improve his own well-being. The summer season is a good time for becoming acquainted with them, for it is then we see them best, and may acquire a relish for them against the insipidity of winter. We remember a dyer in Genoa, who used to hang out his silks upon a high wall opposite his shop, where they shone with such lustre under the blue sky (we particularly remember some yellow ones) that it was a treat to pass that way. You hailed them at a distance, like

> another sun
> Risen at noonday;

or as if Nature herself had been making some draperies out of buttercups, and had just presented the world with the phenomenon. It is the blue sky and clear air of their native land which have made the Italian painters so famous for colouring; and Rubens and Watteau, like wise men, saw the good of transferring the beauty to the less fortunate climate of Flanders. One of the first things that attracted our notice in Italy was a red cap on the head of a boatman. In England, where

nobody else wears such a cap, we should have thought
of a butcher ; in Italy the sky set it off to such advantage, that it reminded us of a scarlet bud.

The Puritans, who did us a great deal of good, helped
to do this harm for us.   They degraded material beauty
and gladness, as if essentially hostile to what was
spiritually estimable ; whereas the desirable thing is to
show the compatibility of both, and vindicate the hues
of the creation.   Thus the finest colours in men's
dresses have at last come almost exclusively to livery
footmen and soldiers. A soldier's wife, or a market-
woman, is the only female that ventures to wear a
scarlet cloak ; and we have a favourite epithet of vituperation, *gaudy*, which we bestow upon all colours that
do not suit our melancholy.   It is sheer want of heart
and animal spirits. We were not always so. Puritanism,
and wars, and debts, and the Dutch succession, and
false ideas of utility, have all conspired to take gladness out of our eyesight, as well as jollity out of our
pockets.   We shall recover a better taste, and we trust
exhibit it to better advantage than before ; but we
must begin by having faith in as many good things as
possible, and not think ill of any one of Heaven's means
of making us cheerful, because in itself it is cheerful.
' If a merry meeting is to be wished,' says the man in
Shakespeare, ' may God prohibit it.' So, the more
obviously cheerful and desirable anything is, the more
we seem to beg the question in its disfavour. Reds,
and yellows, and bright blues are ' gaudy ' ; we must
have nothing but browns, and blacks, and drab-colour,
or stone.   Earth is not of this opinion ; nor the heavens
either. Gardens do not think so ; nor the fields, nor
the skies, nor the mountains, nor dawn, nor sunset, nor
light itself, which is made of colours, and holds them
always ready in its crystal quiver, to shoot forth and
divide into loveliness.   The beautiful attracts the beautiful.   Colours find homes of colour.   To red go the red
rays, and to purple the purple.   The rainbow reads
its beauteous lecture in the clouds, showing the sweet
division of the hues ; and the mechanical ' philosopher ',

as he calls himself, smiles with an air of superiority, and thinks he knows all about it, because the division is made.

The little child, like the real philosopher, *knows more*. for his ' heart leaps up,' and he acknowledges a glad mystery. He feels the immensity of what he does *not* know ; and though the purely mechanical-minded man admits that such immensity exists with regard to himself, he does not feel it as the child or the wiser man does, and therefore he does not truly per-ceive—does not thoroughly take it into his con-sciousness. He talks and acts as if he had come to the extent of his knowledge—and he has so. But beyond the dry line of knowledge lies beauty, and all of which is beautiful in hope, and exalting in imagination.

We feel as if there were a moral as well as material beauty in colour,—an inherent gladness,—an intention on the part of Nature to share with us a pleasure felt by herself. Colours are the smiles of Nature. When they are extremely smiling, and break forth into other beauty besides, they are her laughs, as in the flowers. The ' laughing flowers,' says the poet ; and it is the business of the poet to feel truths beyond the proof of the mecha-nician. Nature, at all events, humanly speaking, is manifestly very fond of colour, *for she has made nothing without it*. Her skies are blue ; her fields green ; her waters vary with her skies ; her animals, minerals, vegetables, are all coloured. She paints a great many of them in apparently superfluous hues, as if to show the dullest eye how she loves colour. The pride of the peacock, or some stately exhibition of a quality very like pride, is a singular matter of fact, evidently con-nected with it. Youthful beauty in the human being is partly made up of it. One of the three great arts with which Providence has adorned and humanized the mind—Painting—is founded upon the love and imita-tion of it. And the magnificence of empire can find nothing more precious, either to possess or to be proud of wearing, than

Fiery opals, sapphires, amethysts,
Jacinths, hard topaz, grass-green emeralds,
Beauteous rubies, sparkling diamonds,
And seld-seen costly stones of so great price,
As one of them, indifferently rated,
May serve in peril of calamity
To ransom great kings from captivity.[1]

THE NIGHTINGALE

[A Year of Honeymoons]

But a more wonderful bird comes in April than the swallow—the nightingale. How different from the other! He all so public, so restless, and so given up to his body; this all so hidden, so stationary, so full of soul! We hear him to singular advantage where we live. I verily believe that ours is the last house, near the metropolis, to the garden of which he comes. It is an old practice of mine, taught me by my father, who was a studious cultivator of what he called 'nature's medicine,' to open one of my chamber windows with the dawn of light, and so let in upon my last slumbers the virgin breath of the morning. Never shall I forget the first time I heard the nightingale in company with the dear creature who is the delight of my life. The tears come into my eyes to think of it. Is this from effeminacy? from weakness? Oh, God, no! It is from that secret sense we feel in us of the power of man to perceive and appreciate the wonderful beauty of the universe, mingled with an unconscious regret of our mortality—of the weakness and shortness of our being, compared with the strength of our affections. But far was a tear from my eyes at the time. The fullness of the sweet burthen of beauty was on us, without the weight. Harriet heard the nightingale first. 'Hark!' said she. The sound was not to be mistaken. It was

[1] These are some of Marlowe's 'mighty lines,' as Ben Jonson called them.

one of those passages of his song, not the finest, but still exquisite and peculiar, in which he chucks out a series of his duller notes, as if for the pleasure of showing how rich he is in the common coin of his art, as well as in the more precious. I rose and opened the window. The most divine of all sounds rewarded us—that low, long-drawn, internal, liquid *line of a note,* the deepest and sweetest ever heard, for which it seems as if the bird resorted to the innermost core of his soul, and meditated as he drew it along, over I know not what celestial darkness of delight. It is the meeting with the extreme of pleasure—with the gratitude which melancholy only can express. The sound mingled with our waking dreams, and heaven and earth seemed to enfold us in their blessing.

Mr. Coleridge, in one of those sallies of his genius, in which he has so often startled and instructed one's commonplaces, informed the world some time ago that it was wrong to designate the nightingale by the title 'melancholy,' there being 'in nature nothing melancholy'; and the song of the bird being full of quick, hurried, and lively notes, anything but sorrowful; in short, he concluded, we ought to say, not the melancholy, but the 'merry nightingale.'

I regret that I have not his beautiful lines by me to quote.

The critics, at Mr. Coleridge's direction, inquired into this matter, and pronounced him in the right; and it is now the fashion to say that the talk of the melancholy of the nightingale is an error, and that he is a very gay, laughing, merry fellow, who happens to be out of doors at night like other merry fellows, and is not a whit more given to pensiveness.

Nevertheless, with submission, I think that the new notion is wrong, and that the nightingale of Milton,

Most musical, most melancholy,

is still the real nightingale, and that the old opinion will prevail. Not that the bird is sorrowful, as the ancient legend supposed, though many of his notes, especially

x 2

considering the pauses between them, which give them
an air of reflection, can never be considered as expressing
pleasure by means of gaiety, much less mirth.   There is
no levity in the nightingale.   We know not what complication of feelings may be mixed up in the mystery of
his song ; but we take it for granted, and allow that,
upon the whole, it expresses a very great degree of
pleasure.   I grant that to the full.   But the truth is,
that this pleasure, being not only mixed up with an
extreme of gravity, as I have just been showing, but
bringing with it an idea of loneliness, and coming at
night-time, when the condition of the whole universe
disposes us to meditation, the very pleasure, by the
contrast, forces us more strongly upon the greater idea
of the two ; and hence the effect of the nightingale's
song has been justly pronounced to be melancholy.   It
may be allowed to Mr. Coleridge, that in some very
energetic and comprehensive and final sense of the assertion, there is ' nothing melancholy in nature,' although
to our limited faculties there may seem to be enough
of it to contend with, as the world goes ; but upon the
same principle, melancholy itself is not melancholy, and
so we come round again to the natural opinion.   Shakespeare has made one of his characters in *The Merchant
of Venice* account partly for the reason why music,
generally speaking, produces a serious impression—

' I'm never merry ' (says Jessica to Lorenzo) ' when I
    hear sweet music.'
' The reason is ' (says her lover) ' your spirits are atten-
    tive.
For do but note a wild and wanton herd,
Or race of youthful and unhandled colts,
Fetching mad bounds, bellowing and neighing loud,
Which is the hot condition of their blood :—
If they but hear perchance a trumpet sound,
Or an air of music catch their ears,
You shall perceive them make a mutual stand,
Their savage eyes turn'd to a modest gaze
By the sweet power of music.'

And such, no doubt, is partly the case with all creatures capable of attending to musical sounds. But with the human being the consciousness is mixed up with a thousand unconscious feelings to the effect already mentioned. There falls upon them a shadow of the great mystery of the universe. If a party of glee-singers were to become aware of a nightingale singing near them at one o'clock in the morning, and upon a pause in his song were to strike up a jovial catch by way of answer, they would be thought in bad taste, and a parcel of simpletons. The feeling, in any real lover of music, would be serious—voluptuous, if you please, and enchanting, but still full of the gravity of voluptuousness —serious from its very pleasure.

SHEEP-SHEARING AND HAYMAKING

[*The Months*]

THE rural business of this month [June] is made up of two employments, as beautiful to look at as they are useful,—sheep-shearing and haymaking. Something like a holiday is still made of the former ; and in the south-west of England the custom, we believe, is still kept up of throwing flowers into the streams, an evident relic of paganism ; but altogether, the holiday is but a gleam of the same merry period in the cheap and rural time of our ancestors. Poverty, discontent, the progress of a gloomy fanaticism, and a mechanical and mercenary spirit that cannot see beyond what is falsely called matter-of-fact (for things, with respect to our perception, are just as little or as much as we can make of them), have rendered many people unable to get pleasure, others too sullen for it, others too superstitious, and others ridiculously ashamed of setting about what is graceful and happy ! O wise and unconscious heads, that are ashamed, not of themselves, but of all the best things in the world ! O successful and world-knowing heads, that after they have used their commonplaces and ignorant passions to no real purpose, piously or hopelessly call it a vile world and a vale of tears, having done their utmost, no doubt, to make it so! The sweetest sensation perhaps which even they can get, if they would confess it, is when they 'snatch a fearful joy' now and then, and get out of the clutches of town and its passions :—but 'business must be attended to,' reasonable or unreasonable, already possessing or wanting more ; so must suspicion, scandal, envy, jealousy, self-love, worldliness and other-worldliness of all sorts. The treat is great, but let us get back to our poison ! The happiness is delightful, but then we must go and enable ourselves to complain of the want of it ! The advice is good, nay even pleasant, but then who made the adviser think himself wiser than we !—But, my good friends, he may not think himself very wise after all.—Well, but still he thinks himself wiser than *we*— wiser than *we !*—And so this *we*, in all the shapes of its selfishness, ruins the world.

But the world is *not* ruined ; for is there not hope, and perseverance, and returning imagination ? And are not the smallest things that persevere, stronger than the largest which are fretted away ? And is not June now before us waiting like a sparkling mistress to bless and encourage the lover that journeys to see her ?

Our ancestors took advantage of every natural holiday, to keep it long and gladly. Rural plays, or, as Shakespeare calls them, Whitsun pastorals, succeeded, after a little interval, the games of May ; and now, in June, a feast exclusively rural and popular took place at the time of sheep-shearing. See the *Winter's Tale* ; Drayton's *Pastorals*, eclogue 9 ; and his *Polyolbion*, song 14, where he tells how

The shepherds' king,
Whose flock had chanc'd that year the earliest lamb to
bring,
In his gay baldric sits at his low grassy board,
With flawns, curds, clouted cream, and country dainties
stor'd ;

And whilst the bagpipe plays, each lusty jocund swain
Quaffs sillabubs in cans, to all upon the plain,
And to their country girls, whose nosegays they do wear;
Some roundelays do sing; the rest the burthen bear.

The white fleeces of the sheep on these occasions, the brown hue of the shearers, the blue of the sky, the running silver of the waters, the green of the grass, the various colours of the flowers, and the straw-hatted damsels that wear them, make up a delightful picture to the imagination.

Haymaking is more toilsome, and is performed in modern times by less happy labourers, who chiefly come over from Ireland for that purpose. But they have at least fine weather and a secure pay. The ladies may practise haymaking on a small scale upon lawns and paddocks; and if they are not afraid of giving their fair skins a still finer tinge of the sunny, nothing makes them look better. Allan Ramsay makes his lover become enamoured of the Lass of Patie's Mill, while helping to make hay:—

A tedding of the hay
Bareheaded on the green,
Love 'mid her locks did play,
And wanton'd in her e'en.

Nothing is more lovely than a female head uncovered out of doors. It looks nymph-like, and a part of the fertile landscape.

Theocritus has used it with exquisite grace and nature in a passage imitated by Virgil. A goatherd and shepherd are boasting of their popularity with the village lasses:—

Comatas. βάλλει καὶ μάλοισι τὸν αἰπόλον ἁ Κλεαρίστα
τὰς αἶγας παρελᾶντα καὶ ἁδύ τι ποππυλιάσδει.
Lacon. κἠμὲ γὰρ ὁ Κρατίδας τὸν ποιμένα λεῖος ὑπαντῶν
ἐκμαίνει· λιπαρὰ δὲ παρ' αὐχένα σείετ' ἔθειρα.
Idyl. v. 88–91.

Com. There's Clearista, when my goats go by,
Pelts apples, and then hums me something sly.

Lac. And Cratis meets and maddens me ; her hair
  Shakes at her throat in curls, with such an air.

As to a seat against a hay-cock, on the side farthest
from the sun, with the odour of the new-mown grass
perfuming all the air, and a sense of slumberous beauty
breathing from the warm sky above and the green earth
below,—it is a luxury which has still survived for the
lover of the fields ; and we accordingly nestle to it in
our fancy, and with half-shut eyes rest from our own
pleasant work.

FEBRUARY

[*The Months*]

THE farmer now grapples with earth again, and
renews the friendly contest for her treasures. He
ploughs up his fallows, sows beans, pease, rye, and
spring wheat, sets early potatoes, drains wet lands,
dresses and repairs hedges, lops trees, and plants those
kinds that love a wet soil, such as poplars, alders, and
willows. Here is the noblest putting in of *stock* for a
nation,—the healthiest in its pursuit, and the most truly
rich and returning in its *interest*.

APRIL

[*The Months*]

Next came fresh Aprill, full of lustyhed,
And wanton as a kid whose horne new buds ;
Upon a bull he rode, the same which led
Europa floting through th' Argolick fluds :
His horns were gilden all with golden studs,
And garnishèd with garlonds goodly dight
Of all the fairest flowres and freshest buds

Which th' earth brings forth; and wet he seemed
    in sight
With waves, through which he waded for his love's
    delight.   SPENSER.

APRIL is so called from the Latin *Aprilis*, which is
derived from the word *Aperire*, to *open*. The allusion
is obvious. April is the moist budding month, nourished
with alternate rains and sunshine. Nature, after the less
unequivocal rigour of winter, seems to take delight in
rendering herself more evident in this operation than in
any other. Winter rains and summer suns may appear
to the superficial observer to bring him nothing but
cold and heat; but the watering the vegetation with
light showers, then warming it, and then watering it
again, seem to show to our very eyes her 'own sweet
hand,' divested of its 'cunning.' She dresses her
plants visibly, like a lady at her window.

This is truly the spring and youthfulness of the year.
March was like an honest blustering servant, bringing
home buds and flowers for his young mistress. April is
she herself, issuing forth adorned with them. To these
she adds, of her own rearing, columbines, jonquils, lady-
smocks, 'all silver white,' lilies of the valley, the
lychnis, fumitory, alysson cretan, gentianellas, pulsa-
tillas, moth-mullein, ornithogalum, saxifrage, stocks,
and the large crimson peony, or piony, one of which is
enough to give a glowing light and centre to twenty of
the white vernal flowers. Shakespeare seems to have
observed the singular beauty of this contrast, when he
speaks of

Banks with pionied and lilied brims.

If the season is fine, and the places where they are
planted favourable, and taken care of, the delicate
sprouting green of the trees and shrubs is now inter-
spersed with the blossoms of the barberry, of the cherry-
plum, of the double-flowering cherry, the bird-cherry,
the sweet-scented and sweet-named honeysuckle, hyperi-

cums, the blackthorn or sloe, laburnum or gold-chain
(truly so called), the service or sorb-apple, scorpion-
senna, privet (the ligustrum of Virgil), the apricot,
peach, and nectarine, lilacs, laurustinuses, the laurel vulgarly so called, more properly the lauro-cerasus,[1] and
lastly the real laurel of old, or bay-tree, which the Greeks
associated with every species of victory, which Sophocles and Epaminondas thought of with reverence, which
Caesar wore day by day, and with which Petrarch was
crowned in the capitol.

The swallow, whom the Greeks used to welcome with
a popular song, reappears at the beginning of this
month. The other birds of passage follow by degrees;
and all the singing birds are now in full life, and saturate
the trees with music. The lark, climbing up above
them in the air, with his thrilling heart, seems to be
carrying one of their songs to heaven.

> Hark, hark! The lark
> At heaven's gate sings,
> And Phoebus 'gins arise,
> His steeds to water at those springs
> On chaliced flowers that lies:
> And winking marybuds begin
> To ope their golden eyes:
> With every thing that pretty bin,
> My lady sweet, arise.   SHAKESPEARE.

This is a serenade, and one of exquisite delicacy. What
Shakespeare might have said to the lark, had he
addressed him in the united spirit of modern philosophy and ancient poetry, a living writer has shown
us :—

---

[1] Evelyn says that if the lauro-cerasus, or cherry-laurel,
were not always suffered to run so low and shrubby, it
would make a handsome tree on a stem, with a head
resembling the orange.—Since writing this note we have
seen it so cultivated; and the look was still handsomer and
more diffuse than what we conceive of the orange in our
climate.

All the earth and air
   With thy voice is loud,
As when night is bare,
   From one lonely cloud
The moon rains out her beams, and heaven is overflowed.

What thou art we know not;
   What is most like thee?
From rainbow clouds there flow not
   Drops so bright to see,
As from thy presence showers a rain of melody.

Like a poet hidden
   In the light of thought,
Singing hymns unbidden
   Till the world is wrought
To sympathy with hopes and fears it heeded not.

Like a high-born maiden
   In a palace tower,
Soothing her love-laden
   Soul, in secret hour,
With music sweet as love, which overflows her bower.

. . . .

Sound of vernal showers
   On the twinkling grass,
Rain-awakened flowers,
   All that ever was
Joyous, and clear, and fresh, thy music doth surpass.

Teach us, sprite or bird,
   What sweet thoughts are thine:
I have never heard
   Praise of love or wine
That panted forth a flood of rapture so divine.

. . . .

Better than all measures
   Of delightful sound,
Better than all treasures
   That in books are found,
Thy skill to poet were, thou scorner of the ground.

> Teach me half the gladness
>   That thy brain must know,
> Such harmonious madness
>   From my lips should flow,
> The world should listen then, as I am listening now.[1]

The nightingale, this month, is recognized towards evening, keeping up his inexhaustible song; and, about the middle of the month, the lover of nature, who ventures among the hedges and fields to see how the wild-flowers get forward, is happily startled with the voice of the invisible cuckoo, repeating at intervals its two fluty notes. The Greeks had songs also for the cuckoo; and now that our days of poetry have returned we too have a song for it as genuine as any of theirs:—

> O blithe new-comer! I have heard,
>   I hear thee and rejoice:
> O Cuckoo! shall I call thee bird,
>   Or but a wandering voice?
>
> While I am lying on the grass,
>   Thy loud note smites my ear!
> From hill to hill it seems to pass,
>   At once far off and near!
>
> The same which in my schoolboy days
>   I listened to; that cry
> Which made me look a thousand ways,
>   In bush, and tree, and sky.
>
> And I can listen to thee yet;
>   Can lie upon the plain
> And listen, till I do beget
>   That golden time again.[2]

April, however, is proverbial for its fickleness. All its promises may sometimes be retarded, sometimes blighted, by the return of frosty winds; and the agriculturist,

---

[1] *Prometheus Unbound, with other Poems*, by Percy Bysshe Shelley.
[2] *Poems* by Mr. Wordsworth, vol. i. p. 299.

the more exuberant the season is, thinks with greater
anxiety of the next that depends upon it. The domestic
cultivator of flowers should still take particular care of
them. Hardy annuals may still be planted; anemone,
ranunculus, and hyacinth roots, past flowering, should
be taken up to be preserved; and autumnal flowering
bulbs be taken up and transplanted. Shrubs on very
fine days may now be brought into the balconies, in
order to refresh the eyes with the sight of the spring-
green; but the balconies should be defended from
cutting winds. The more the light is seen through the
leaves of plants, the finer and more vivid they look.
They seem to show the amber sunshine that nourished
them.

JULY

[A Year of Honeymoons]

JULY is a dumb, dreaming, hot, lazy, luxurious, delightful month for those who can do as they please, and
who are pleased with what they do. The birds are
silent; we have no more cuckoo, no more nightingale;
nature is basking in repose; the cattle stand in the
water; shade is loved, and rest after dinner. We
understand, in July, what the Spaniard means by his
siesta. A book and a sofa in the afternoon, near a tree-
shaded window, with a prospect of another room,
seen through folding-doors, in which the hot sun comes
peeping between Venetian blinds, is pleasant to one's
supineness. The sensible thing is to lie on your back,
gently pillowed 'twixt head and shoulders, the head resting on the end of the sofa, and to read—listening at
intervals to the sound of the foliage, or to the passing
visit of the bee. The thing, more sensible, is to have
a companion who loves your book and yourself, and
who reads with you, provided you can let her read.
I must not come, however, to my afternoon before my
morning; though July, being lazy, makes us think of
it first. July and August are afternoon and evening

months; May and June are morning months; September and October are day months; the rest are night months, for firesides, unless we except April, and that is as you can get it. You may experience all the seasons in it, and must catch the sunshine as you can, betwixt the showers.

July, however, though a lazy month, is not lazy from weakness. If nature reposes, it is the repose of affluent power and sovereign beauty. The gardens are in purple, and golden, and white splendour (with the lily); the trees in thickest exuberance; the sky at its bluest; the clouds full, snowy, and mountainous. The genial armies of the rain are collecting against the time when the hot sun shall be too potent. The grandest and at the same time the loveliest of the wild-flowers, the convolvulus, is lording it in the hedges. In the garden, the nasturtium seems a flower born of fire. There is an exquisite flavour of something burning in its taste. The daughter of Linnaeus found out that sparks are emitted from the nasturtium in warm evenings. It was a piece of observation fit for the daughter of the great botanist, and has associated her memory with one of the most agreeable secrets of nature. Female discoveries ought to be in the region of the beautiful and the sprightly. No disparagement to Miss Martineau, who unites poetical and philosophical feeling to a degree hitherto displayed by none of her sex; and whose sphere of the useful, being founded on sympathy, contains in it all the elements of enjoyment. I mention this, because it has been strangely supposed of *me*, Charles Dalton, husband of Harriet D., that I have thrown divers stones, yclept paragraphs, at the head of my wife's namesake; which I should as soon think of doing as being angry with the summer sky.

OF DUMB ANIMALS

ON SEEING A PIGEON MAKE LOVE

[Wishing Cap Papers, *Examiner*, 1824]

Ut albulus columbus, aut Adoneus ?—CATULLUS.

Which is he ? Pigeon, or Adonis ?

THE French have a lazy way, in some of their compositions, of writing prose and verse alternately. The author, whenever it is convenient for him to be inspired, begins dancing away in rhyme. The fit over, he goes on as before, as if nothing had happened. We have essays in prose and verse by Cowley (a delightful book) in which the same piece contains both ; but with one exception, they are rather poems with long prefaces.

If ever this practice is allowable, it is to a periodical writer in love with poetry. He is obliged to write prose ; he is tormented with the desire of venting himself in rhyme ; he rhymes, and has not leisure to go on. Behold me, as a Frenchman would say, with my rhyme and my reason !

The following verses were suggested by a sight of a pigeon making love. The scene took place in a large sitting-room, where a beau might have followed a lady up and down with as bustling a solicitation : he could not have done it with more. The birds had been brought there for sale ; but they knew no more of this than two lovers whom destiny has designs upon. The gentleman was as much at his ease as if he had been a Bond Street lounger pursuing his fair in a solitary street. I must add, as an excuse for the abruptness of the exordium, that the house belonged to a poet of my acquaintance, who was in the room at the same time.[1]

---

[1] Lord Byron. The house was the Casa Saluzzi, at Albaro, near Genoa.

Is not the picture strangely like ?
Doesn't the very bowing strike ?
Can any art of love in fashion
Express a more prevailing passion ?
That air—that sticking to her side—
That deference, ill concealing pride,—
That seeming consciousness of coat,
And repetition of one note,—
Ducking and tossing back his head,
As if at every bow he said,
' Madam, by Heaven,'—or ' Strike me dead.'

And then the lady ! look at her :
What bridling sense of character !
How she declines, and seems to go,
Yet still endures him to and fro ;
Carrying her plumes and pretty clothings,
Blushing stare, and mutter'd nothings,
Body plump, and airy feet,
Like any charmer in a street.

Give him a hat beneath his wing,
And is not he the very thing ?
Give her a parasol or plaything,
And is not she the very she-thing ?

My companion, who had run the round of the great
world, seemed to be rather mortified than otherwise at
this spectacle. It was certainly calculated, at first
blush, to damp the pride of the circles : but upon reflection, it seemed to afford a considerable lift to beaux
and belles in ordinary. It seemed to show how much
of instinct, and of the common unreflecting course of
things, there is even in the gallantries of those who
flatter themselves that they are vicious. Nobody expects wisdom in these persons ; and if they can be found
to be less guilty than is supposed, the gain is much :
for, as to letting the dignity of human nature depend
upon theirs, on the one hand, or expecting to bring about
any change in their conduct by lecturing them on their
faults, on the other, it is a speculation equally hopeless.

If a man of pleasure ' about town ' is swayed by
anything, it is by a fear of becoming ridiculous.   If he
must continue in his old courses, it is pleasant to know
him for what he is, and that pigeons are not confined
to the gaming-table.

I once followed a young man of fashion in and out a
variety of streets at the west end of the town, through
which he was haunting a poor blushing damsel, who
appeared to be at once distressed by him and endan-
gered.   I thought she seemed to be wishing for something to turn the scale in favour of her self-denial ; and
I resolved to furnish it.   Could the consequences of his
success have rested entirely with himself, I saw enough
of the *pigeon* in him not to have been so ill-bred as to
' spoil sport ' ; but considering, as times go, that what
is sport to the gentleman in these cases is very often
death to the lady, I found myself compelled to be rude
and conscientious.   In vain he looked round every now
and then, putting on his best astonishment, and cursing,
no doubt, ' the indelicacy of the fellow.'   There I was,
low and insolent,—sticking to his skirts, wondering
whether he would think me of importance enough for a
challenge, and by what bon-mot or other ingenious
baffling of his resentment I should contrive at once to
save our life and the lady.   At length he turns abruptly
across the street, and I follow the poor girl, till she was
at a safe distance.   I caught but one other glimpse of
her face, which was as red as scarlet.   I fancied, when
all was safe, that some anger against her deliverer might
mingle with her blushes, and was obliged to encourage
myself against a sort of shame for my interference.   I
wished I could have spoken to her ; but this was impossible ; nay, considering the mutual tenderness of
my virtue at that instant, might have been dangerous.
So I made my retreat in the same manner as my gentleman ; and have thought of her face with kindness ever
since.

To return to our pigeons :—the description given in
the verses is true to the letter.   The reader must not think
it a poetical exaggeration.   If he has never witnessed

an exhibition of the kind, he has no conception of the high human hand with which these pigeons carry it. The poets indeed, time out of mind, have taken amatory illustrations from them; but the literal courtship surpasses them all. One sight of a pigeon paying his addresses would be sufficient to unsettle in our minds all those proud conclusions which we draw respecting the difference between reason and instinct. If this is mere instinct as distinguished from reason, if a bird follows another bird up and down by a simple mechanical impulse, giving himself all the airs and graces imaginable, exciting as many in his mistress, and uttering every moment articulate sounds which we are no more bound to suppose deficient in meaning than a pigeon would be warranted in supposing the same of our own speech, then reason itself may be no more than a mechanical impulse. It has nothing better to show for it. Our mechanism may possess a greater variety of movements, and be more adapted to a variety of circumstances; but if there is not variety here, and an adaptation to circumstances, I know not where there is. If it be answered, that pigeons would never make love in any other manner, under any circumstances, we do not know that. Have people observed them sufficiently to know that they always make love equally well? If they have varied at any time, they may vary again. Our own modes of courtship are undoubtedly very numerous; and some of them are as different from others, as the courtship of the pigeon itself from that of the hog. But though we are observers of ourselves, have we yet observed other animals sufficiently to pronounce upon the limits of their capacity? We are apt to suppose that all sheep and oxen resemble one another in the face. The slightest observation convinces us that their countenances are as various as those of men. How are we to know that the shades and modifications of their character and conduct are not as various? A well-drilled nation would hardly look more various in the eyes of a bee, than a swarm of bees does in our own. The minuter differences in our conduct would escape them for want of the habit of observing us, and because their own are of another sort. How are we to say that we do not judge them as ill? Every fresh speculation into the habits and manners of that singular little people produces new and extraordinary discoveries. The bees in *Buffon's time* were in the habit, when they built their hives, of providing for a certain departure from the more obvious rules of architecture, which at a particular part of the construction became necessary. Buffon ingeniously argued, that because they always practised this secret geometry, and never did otherwise, their apparent departure itself was but another piece of instinct; and he concluded that they always had done so, and always would. Possibly they will; but the conclusion is not made out by his argument. A being who knows how to build better than we do might as well assert, that because we have not arrived at certain parts of his knowledge, we never shall. Observe the vast time which it takes us, with all our boasted reason, to attain to improvements in our own arts and sciences: think how little we know after all; what little certainty we have respecting periods which are but as yesterday, compared with the mighty lapse of time; and judge how much right we have to say, This we never did— This we shall never be able to do.

I have read of some beavers, that when they were put into a situation very different from their ordinary one, and incited to build a house, they set about their work in a style as ingeniously adapted as possible to their new circumstances. Buffon might say they had been in this situation before; he might also argue that they were provided with an instinct against the emergency. One argument appears to me as good as the other. But under the circumstances he might tell us that they would probably act with stupidity. And what is done by many human beings? Is our reason as good for us all on one occasion as another? The individuals of the same race of animals are not all equally clever, any more than ourselves. The more they come under our inspection (as in the case of dogs), the more varieties we discern in their characters and understandings. The most philosophical thing hitherto said on the subject appears to be that of Pope.

'I shall be very glad,' said Spence, 'to see Dr. Hales, and always love to see him, he is so worthy and good a man.' POPE. 'Yes, he is a very good man; only I'm sorry he has his hands so much imbrued in blood.' SPENCE. 'What! he cuts up rats?' POPE. 'Aye, and dogs too!' (With what emphasis and concern, cries Spence, he spoke it.) 'Indeed, he commits most of these barbarities with the thought of being of use to man; but how do we know that we have a right to kill creatures that we are so little above as dogs, for our curiosity, or even for some use to us?' SPENCE. 'I used to carry it too far: I thought they had reason as well as we.' POPE. 'So they have, to be sure. All our disputes about that are only disputes about words. Man has reason enough only to know what is necessary for him to know, and dogs have just that too.' SPENCE. 'But then they must have souls too, as imperishable in their nature as ours?' POPE. 'And what harm would that be to us?'

All this passage is admirable, and helps to make us love, as we ought to do, a man who has contributed so much to the entertainment of the world.

That dogs, like men, have 'reason enough only to know what is necessary for them to know,' is, of course, no argument against their acting in a new manner under novel circumstances. It is the same with us. Necessities alter with circumstances. There is a well-authenticated story of a dog, who, having been ill-treated by a larger one, went and brought a still larger dog to avenge his cause, and see justice done him. When does a human necessity reason better than this? The greatest distinction between men and other animals appears to consist in this, that the former make a point of cultivating their reason; and yet it is impossible to say that nothing of the kind has ever been done by the latter. Birds and beasts in general do not take the trouble of going out of their ordinary course: but is the ambition of the common run of human beings any greater? Have not peasants and mechanics, and even those who flourish and grow learned under establishments, an equal tendency to deprecate the necessity of innovation? A farmer would go on with his old plough, a weaver with his old loom, and a placeman with his old opinions, to all eternity, if it were not for the restlessness of individuals; and these are forced to battle their way against a thousand prejudices, even to do the greatest good. An established critic has not always a right to triumph over the learned pig.

We have been told that the 'swinish multitude' are better without books. Now the utmost which the holders of this opinion can say for the superior reason of their species, is, that pigs dispense already with a knowledge which is unfit for men. They tell us, nevertheless (and I receive the text with reverence), that a day shall come when 'the lion will lie down with the lamb'; and yet they will laugh in your face if you suspect that beasts may be improvable creatures, or even that men may deserve to be made wiser. But they will say that this great event is not to be brought about by knowledge. Some of their texts say otherwise. I believe that all which they know of the matter is, that it will not be brought about by themselves.

But we must not be led away from the dignity of our subject by the natural tendencies of these gentlemen. Human means are divine means, if the end be divine. Without controverting the spirit of the text in question, it would be difficult, from what we see already of the power of different animals to associate kindly with each other (such as lions with little dogs, cats and birds in the same cages, &c.), to pronounce upon the limits of improvability in the brute creation, as far as their organs will allow. I would not venture to assert that, in the course of ages, and by the improved action of those causes which give rise to their present state of being, the organs themselves will not undergo alteration. There is a part in the pectoral conformation of the male human being which is a great puzzle to the anatomists, and reminds us of one of Plato's reveries on the original state of mankind. When the Divine Spirit acts, it may act through the medium of human knowledge and will, as well as any other,—as well as through the trunk of a tree in the pushing out of a blossom. New productions are supposed to appear from time to time in the rest of the creatures: old ones are supposed to have become extinct.

Be this as it may, we are not to conclude that the world always was and always will be such as it is, simply because the little space of time during which we know of its existence offers to us no extraordinary novelty. The humility of a philosopher's ignorance (and there is more humility in his very pride than in the 'prostration of intellect' so earnestly recommended by some persons) is sufficient to guard him against this conclusion, setting aside Plato and the mammoth.

With respect to other animals going to heaven, our pride smiles in a sovereign manner at this speculation. We have no objection, somehow, to a mean origin ; but we insist that nothing less dignified than ourselves can be immortal. I wish I could settle the question. I confess (if the reader will allow me to suppose that I shall go to heaven, which does not require much modesty nowadays) I would fain have as much company as possible ; and He was of no different opinion who told us that a time should come when the sucking child should play with the asp. We see that the poet had no more objection to his dog's company in a state of bliss, than the 'poor Indian,' of whom he speaks in his Essay.[1] We think we could name other celebrated authors, who would as lief take their dogs into the next world as a king or a bishop, and yet they have no objection to either. We may conceive much less pleasant additions to our society than a flock of doves, which, indeed, have a certain fitness for an Elysian state. We would confine our argument to one simple question, which the candid reader will allow us to ask him :—

---

[1] Pope's *Essay on Man*, Ep. i. l. 99.—Ed.

' Does not *Tomkins* go to heaven ?' Has not the veriest
bumpkin of a squire, that rides after the hounds, an
immortal soul ? If so, why not the whole pack ? It
may be said, that the pack are too brutal and blood-
thirsty : they would require a great deal of improvement. Well, let them have it, and the squire along
with them. It has been thought by some that the
brutal, or those who are unfit for heaven, will be annihi-
lated. Others conceive that they will be bettered in
other shapes. Whatever be the case, it is difficult to
think that many beasts and birds are not as fit to go
to heaven at once as many human beings,—people who
talk of their seats there with as much confidence as if
they had booked their names for them at a box-office.
To our humble taste, the goodness and kindness in the
countenance of a faithful dog are things that appear
almost as fit for heaven as serenity in a human being.
The prophets of old, in their visions, saw nothing to
hinder them from joining the faces of other animals with
those of men. The spirit that moved the animal was
everything.

It was the opinion of a late writer, that the immortality
of the soul depended on the cultivation of the intellect.
He could not conceive how the sots and fools that
abound on this earth could have any pretensions to
eternity ; or with what feelings they were to enter upon
their new condition. There appears to be too much of
the pride of intellect in this opinion, and too little
allowance for circumstances ; and yet, if the dispensa-
tion that is to take us to heaven is of the exclusive
kind that some would make it, this is surely the more
noble dogma. The other makes it depend on the mere
will of the Divinity, or (to speak plainly) upon a system
of favouritism, that would render a human tyranny
unbearable. I am not here speaking of the mild tenets
inculcated by the spirit of the Church of England, but
of those of certain sects. In neither case would the
majority of us have much better pretensions to go to
heaven than the multitude of other animals ; nor,
perhaps, a jot more, if we knew all their thoughts and

feelings. But I wander out of our subject, and grow more positive than becomes a waking dream.

To conclude with the pleasant animals with whom we commenced, there is a flock of pigeons in the neighbourhood where we are writing,[1] whom I would willingly suppose to be enjoying a sort of heaven on earth. The place is fit to be their paradise. There is plenty of food for them, the dovecots are excellent, the scene full of vines in summer-time, and of olives all the year round. It happens, in short, to be the very spot where Boccaccio is said to have laid the scene of his *Decameron*. He lived there himself. Fiesole is on the height ; the Valley of Ladies in the hollow ; the brooks all poetical and celebrated. As we behold this flock of doves careering about the hamlet, and whitening in and out of the green trees, we cannot help fancying that they are the souls of the gentle company in the *Decameron*, come to enjoy in peace their old neighbourhood. We think, as we look at them, that they are now as free from intrusion and scandal as they are innocent ; and that no falcon would touch them for the sake of the story they told of him.[2]

Ovid, in one of his elegies,[3] tells us that birds have a Paradise near Elysium. Doves, be sure, are not omitted. But peacocks and parrots go there also. The poet was more tolerant in his *orni-theology* than the priests in Delphos, who, in the sacred groves about their temple, admitted doves, and doves only.

---

[1] At Maiano, near Florence.
[2] The well known and beautiful story of the *Decameron*. Mr. Procter has touched it in a high and worthy strain of enthusiasm in his *Dramatic Sketches*.
[3] *Amorum*, lib. ii. eleg. 6.

THE ANXIETIES OF PIG-DRIVING

[*Companion*, March 26, 1828]

FROM the perusal of this article we beg leave to warn off, not any of our Companions (who are doubtless too far-sighted not to see into the merits of it) but vulgar readers of all denominations, whether of the 'great vulgar or the small.' Warn—did we say ? We drive them off ; for Horace tells us that they, as wells as pigs, are to be so treated. *Odi profanum vulgus*, says he, *et arceo.* But do thou lend thine ear, gentle shade of Goldsmith, who didst make thy bear-leader denounce 'everything as is low' ; and thou, Bickerstaff, who didst humanize upon public-houses and puppet-shows ; and Fielding thou, whom the great Richardson, less in that matter (and some others) than thyself, did accuse of vulgarity, because thou didst discern natural gentility in a footman, and yet wast not to be taken in by the airs of Pamela and my Lady G.

The title is a little startling ; but 'style and sentiment,' as a lady said, ' can do anything.' Remember then, gentle reader, that talents are not to be despised in the humblest walks of life. We will add, nor in the muddiest. The other day we were among a set of spectators, who could not help stopping to admire the patience and address with which a pig-driver huddled and cherished onward his drove of unaccommodating *élèves* down a street in the suburbs. He was a born genius for a manœuvre. Had he originated in a higher sphere, he would have been a general, or a stage-manager, or at least the head of a set of monks. Conflicting interests were his forte ; pig-headed wills, and proceedings hopeless. To see the *hand* with which he did it ! How hovering, yet firm ; how encouraging, yet compelling ; how indicative of the space on each side of him, and yet of the line before him ; how general, how particular, how perfect ! No barber's could quiver about a head with more lightness of apprehension ;

no cook's pat up and proportion the side of a pasty with
a more final eye. The whales, quoth old Chapman,
speaking of Neptune

> The whales exulted under him, and knew their mighty
>   king.

The pigs did not exult, but they knew their king.
Unwilling was their subjection, but 'more in sorrow
than in anger.' They were too far gone for rage.
Their case was hopeless. They did not see why they
should proceed, but they felt themselves bound to do
so; forced, conglomerated, crowded onwards, irresistibly compelled by fate and Jenkins. Often would they
have bolted under any other master. They squeaked
and grunted as in ordinary; they sidled, they shuffled,
they half stopped; they turned an eye to all the little
outlets of escape; but in vain. There they stuck (for
their very progress was a sort of sticking), charmed into
the centre of the sphere of his action, laying their heads
together, but to no purpose; looking all as if they were
shrugging their shoulders, and eschewing the tip-end of
the whip of office. Much eye had they to their left leg;
shrewd backward glances; not a little anticipative
squeak, and sudden rush of avoidance. It was a superfluous clutter, and they felt it; but a pig finds it more
difficult than any other animal to accommodate himself
to circumstances. Being out of his pale, he is in the
highest state of wonderment and inaptitude. He is
sluggish, obstinate, opinionate, not very social; has no
desire of seeing foreign parts. Think of him in a multitude, forced to travel, and wondering what the devil it
is that drives him. Judge by this of the talents of his
driver.

We beheld a man once, an inferior genius, inducting
a pig into the other end of Long Lane, Smithfield. He
had got him thus far towards the market. It was
much. His air announced success in nine parts out of
ten, and hope for the remainder. It had been a happy
morning's work: he had only to look for the termination of it; and he looked (as a critic of an exalted turn

of mind would say in brightness and in joy. Then
would he go to the public house, and indulge in porter
and a pleasing security. Perhaps he would not say much
at first, being oppressed with the greatness of his
success ; but by degrees, especially if interrogated, he
would open, like Aeneas, into all the circumstances of
his journey and the perils that beset him. Profound
would be his set out ; full of tremor his middle course ;
high and skilful his progress ; glorious, though with a
quickened pulse, his triumphant entry. Delicate had
been his situation in Ducking Pond Row : masterly his
turn at Bell Alley. We saw him with the radiance of
some such thought on his countenance. He was just
entering Long Lane. A gravity came upon him, as he
steered his touchy convoy into this his last thorough-
fare. A dog moved him into a little agitation, darting
along ; but he resumed his course, not without a happy
trepidation, hovering as he was on the borders of
triumph. The pig still required care. It was evidently
a pig with all the peculiar turn of mind of his species ;
a fellow that would not move faster than he could help ;
irritable ; retrospective ; picking objections, and prone
to boggle ; a chap with a tendency to take every path
but the proper one, and with a sidelong tact for the
allies.

He bolts !

He's off !—*Evasit, erupit.*

' Oh, Ch—st ! ' exclaimed the man, dashing his hand
against his head, lifting his knee in an agony, and
screaming with all the weight of a prophecy which the
spectators felt to be too true,—' *he'll go up all manner
of streets !* '

Poor fellow ! we think of him now sometimes, driving
up Duke Street, and not to be comforted in Barbican.

ELEPHANT AND GIRAFFE

[From 'A Visit to the Zoological Gardens,' *New Monthly Magazine*, August, 1836]

THE elephant would seem to be more comfortably situated than most. He has water to bathe in, mud to stick in, and an area many times bigger than himself for his circuit. Very interesting is it to see him throw bits of mud over himself, and to see, and *hear* him, suck the water up in his trunk and then discharge it into his great red throat ; in which he also receives, with sage amenity, the biscuits of the ladies. Certainly, the more one considers an elephant, the more he makes good his claim to be considered the Doctor Johnson of the brute creation. He is huge, potent, sapient, susceptible of tender impressions ; is a good fellow ; likes as much water as the other did tea ; gets on at a great uncouth rate when he walks ; and though perhaps less irritable and melancholy, can take a witty revenge ; as witness the famous story of the tailor that pricked him, and whom he drenched with ditch-water. If he were suddenly gifted with speech, and we asked him whether he liked his imprisonment, the first words he would utter would unquestionably be—' Why, no, sir.' Nor is it to be doubted, when going to dinner, that he would echo the bland sentiment of our illustrious countryman on a like occasion, 'Sir, I like to dine.' If asked his opinion of his keeper he would say, ' Why, sir, Hipkins is, upon the whole, " a good fellow,"—like myself, sir (*smiling*),—but not quite so considerate ; he knows I love him, and presumes a little too much upon my forbearance. He teases me for the amusement of the bystanders. Sir, Hipkins takes the display of allowance for the merit of ascendancy.'

This is what the elephant manifestly thought on the present occasion ; for the keeper set a little dog at him, less to the amusement of the bystanders than he fancied; and the noble beast, after butting the cur out of the way, and taking care to spare him as he advanced (for one tread of his foot would have smashed the little pertinacious wretch as flat as a pancake), suddenly made a stop and, in rebuke of both of them, uttered a high indignant scream, much resembling a score of cracked trumpets.

Enter the three lady-like and most curious giraffes, probably called forth by the noise; which they took, however, with great calmness. On inspection, their faces express insipidity and indifference more than anything else—at least the one that we looked at did; but they are interesting from their novelty, and from a singular look of cleanliness, delicacy, and refinement, mixed with a certain *gaucherie*, arising from their long, poking necks, and the disparity of length between their fore and hind legs. They look like young ladies of animals, naturally not ungraceful, but with bad habits. Their necks are not on a line with their fore legs, perpendicular and held up; nor yet arched like horses' necks; but made a feeble-looking, obtuse angle, completely answering to the word 'poking.' The legs come up so close to the necks, that in front they appear to have no bodies; the back slopes like a hill, producing the singular disparity between the legs; and the whole animal, being slender, light-coloured, and very gentle, gives you an idea of delicacy amounting to the fragile. The legs look as if a stick would break them in two, like glass. Add to this, a slow and uncouth lifting of the legs, as they walk, as if stepping over gutters; and the effect is just such as has been described,—the strangest mixture in the world of elegance and uncouthness. The people in charge of them seemed to be constantly curry-combing them after a gentle fashion, for extreme cleanliness is necessary to their health; and the novelty of the spectacle is completed by the appearance of M. Thibaut in his Arab dress and beard,—the Frenchman who brought them over. The one we spoke of, moving its lips, but not the expression of its countenance, helped itself to a mouthful of feathers out of a lady's bonnet, as it stooped over the rails.

BEARS

[Table-Talk]

IT is natural in bear-hunters, who have witnessed the creature's ravages, and felt the peril of his approach, to call him a ferocious animal, and gift him at times with other epithets of objection ; but we who sit in our closets, far removed from the danger, may be allowed to vindicate the character of the bear, and to think that Bruin, who is only labouring in his vocation, and is not more ferocious than hunger and necessity make him, might, with at least equal reason, have advanced some objections against his invader. He might have said, if he possessed a little Aesopean knowledge of mankind, ' Here, now, is a fellow coming to kill me for getting my dinner, who eats slaughtered sheep and lobsters boiled alive ; who, with the word " ferocity " in his mouth, puts a ball into my poor head, just as the highwayman vindicates himself by abusing the man he shoots ; and who then writes an account of his humane achievement with a quill plucked from the body of a bleeding and screaming goose.'

Or, knowing nothing of mankind, he might say, ' Here comes that horrid strange animal to murder us, who sometimes has one sort of head and sometimes another (hat and cap), and who carries another terrible animal in his paw—a kind of stiff snake—which sends out thunder and lightning ; and so he points his snake at us, and in an instant we are filled with burning wounds, and die in agonies of horror and desperation.'

There is much resemblance to humanity in the bear. I would not make invidious comparisons ; but travellers as well as poets have given us beautiful accounts of the maternal affections of the bear ; and furthermore, the animal resembles many respectable gentlemen whom we could name. When he wishes to attack anybody he rises on his hind legs, as men do in the House of Commons. He dances, as aldermen do, with great solemnity

and weight ; and his general appearance, when you see
him walking about the streets with his keeper, is surely
like that of many a gentleman in a great-coat, whose
enormity of appetite and the recklessness with which he
indulges it, entitle him to have a keeper also.

TURKEYS

[Table-Talk]

It is amusing to see the turkey strutting and gobbling
about the homestead. He looks like a burlesque on the
peacock. Good old Admiral S. ! How sorry he was to
hear the simile ; and what good things he had to say
on the worth of turkeys in general, and of a foreign
species of the race in particular. But is it not true ?
Look at the animal's attempt to get up a sensation with
his ' tail,' or what is called such. Look at the short-
coming size of it, the uncouth heaviness of his body, the
sombre tawdriness of his colours, and, above all, that
ineffable drawing back of the head and throat into an
intensity of the arrogant and self-satisfied ! He looks
like a corpulent fop in a paroxysm of conceit. John
Reeve was not greater in the character of Marmaduke
Magog the beadle, when he stamped the ground in a
rapture of pomp and vanity. Bubb Doddington might
have looked so, when he first put on his peer's robes,
and practised dignity before a looking-glass. The name
of Bubb is very turkey-like. The bird's familiar name
in Scotland, admirably expressive of its appearance, is
Bubbly Jock. Goethe says that Nature has a lurking
sense of comedy in her, and sometimes intends to be
jocose ; and it is not difficult to imagine it when one
considers that she includes art, and comedy itself, and
is the inventress of turkeys.

The turkey is a native of America, and Franklin
recommended it for the national symbol !

THE WEATHER

A NOW. OF A HOT DAY

[Indicator, June 28, 1820]

Now the rosy- (and lazy-) fingered Aurora, issuing from her saffron house, calls up the moist vapours to surround her, and goes veiled with them as long as she can ; till Phoebus, coming forth in his power, looks everything out of the sky, and holds sharp uninterrupted empire from his throne of beams. Now the mower begins to make his sweeping cuts more slowly, and resorts oftener to the beer. Now the carter sleeps a-top of his load of hay, or plods with double slouch of shoulder, looking out with eyes winking under his shading hat, and with a hitch upward of one side of his mouth. Now the little girl at her grandmother's cottage door watches the coaches that go by, with her hand held up over her sunny forehead. Now labourers look well resting in their white shirts at the doors of rural alehouses. Now an elm is fine there, with a seat under it ; and horses drink out of the trough, stretching their yearning necks with loosened collars ; and the traveller calls for his glass of ale, having been without one for more than ten minutes ; and his horse stands wincing at the flies, giving sharp shivers of his skin, and moving to and fro his ineffectual docked tail ; and now Miss Betty Wilson, the host's daughter, comes streaming forth in a flowered gown and earrings, carrying with four of her beautiful fingers the foaming glass, for which, after the traveller has drank it, she receives with an indifferent eye, looking another way, the lawful twopence : that is to say, unless the traveller, nodding his ruddy face, pays some gallant compliment to her before he drinks, such as ' I'd rather kiss you, my dear, than the tumbler,'—or ' I'll wait for you, my love, if you'll marry me ' ; upon which, if the man is good-looking and the lady in good-humour, she smiles and bites her lips, and says, ' Ah—men can talk fast enough'; upon which the old stage-coachman, who is buckling something near her, before he sets off, says in a hoarse voice, ' So can women too for that matter,' and John Boots grins through his ragged red locks, and dotes on the repartee all the day after. Now grasshoppers ' fry,' as Dryden says. Now cattle stand in water, and ducks are envied. Now boots and shoes, and trees by the roadside, are thick with dust; and dogs, rolling in it, after issuing out of the water, into which they have been thrown to fetch sticks, come scattering horror among the legs of the spectators. Now a fellow who finds he has three miles further to go in a pair of tight shoes is in a pretty situation. Now rooms with the sun upon them become intolerable; and the apothecary's apprentice, with a bitterness beyond aloes, thinks of the pond he used to bathe in at school. Now men with powdered heads (especially if thick) envy those that are unpowdered, and stop to wipe them up hill, with countenances that seem to expostulate with destiny. Now boys assemble round the village pump with a ladle to it, and delight to make a forbidden splash and get wet through the shoes. Now also they make suckers of leather, and bathe all day long in rivers and ponds, and follow the fish into their cool corners, and say millions of ' My eyes!' at ' tittlebats.' Now the bee, as he hums along, seems to be talking heavily of the heat. Now doors and brick walls are burning to the hand; and a walled lane, with dust and broken bottles in it, near a brick-field, is a thing not to be thought of. Now a green lane, on the contrary, thick-set with hedgerow elms, and having the noise of a brook ' rumbling in pebble-stones,' is one of the pleasantest things in the world. Now youths and damsels walk through hay-fields, by chance; and the latter say, ' Ha' done then, William'; and the overseer in the next field calls out to ' let thic thear hay thear bide'; and the girls persist, merely to plague ' such a frumpish old fellow.'

Now, in town, gossips talk more than ever to one
another, in rooms, in doorways, and out of window,
always beginning the conversation with saying that the
heat is overpowering. Now blinds are let down, and
doors thrown open, and flannel waistcoats left off, and
cold meat preferred to hot, and wonder expressed why
tea continues so refreshing, and people delight to sliver
lettuces into bowls, and apprentices water doorways
with tin-canisters that lay several atoms of dust. Now
the water-cart, jumbling along the middle of the street,
and jolting the showers out of its box of water, really
does something. Now boys delight to have a water-
pipe let out, and see it bubbling away in a tall and frothy
volume. Now fruiterers' shops and dairies look pleasant,
and ices are the only things to those who can get them.
Now ladies loiter in baths; and people make presents
of flowers; and wine is put into ice; and the after-
dinner lounger recreates his head with applications of
perfumed water out of long-necked bottles. Now the
lounger, who cannot resist riding his new horse, feels
his boots burn him. Now buck-skins are not the lawn
of Cos. Now jockeys, walking in great-coats to lose
flesh, curse inwardly. Now five fat people in a stage
coach hate the sixth fat one who is coming in, and think
he has no right to be so large. Now clerks in offices do
nothing, but drink soda-water and spruce-beer, and
read the newspaper. Now the old-clothes man drops
his solitary cry more deeply into the areas on the hot
and forsaken side of the street; and bakers look vicious;
and cooks are aggravated; and the steam of a tavern
kitchen catches hold of one like the breath of Tartarus.
Now delicate skins are beset with gnats: and boys make
their sleeping companion start up, with playing a burning-
glass on his hand; and blacksmiths are super-carbon-
ated; and cobblers in their stalls almost feel a wish to
be transplanted; and butter is too easy to spread; and
the dragoons wonder whether the Romans liked their
helmets; and old ladies, with their lappets unpinned,
walk along in a state of dilapidation; and the servant-
maids are afraid they look vulgarly hot; and the author,

who has a plate of strawberries brought him, finds that he has come to the end of his writing.

We cannot conclude this article, however, without returning thanks, both on our own account and on that of our numerous predecessors who have left so large a debt of gratitude unpaid, to this very useful and ready monosyllable—'Now.' We are sure that there is not a didactic poet, ancient or modern, who, if he possessed a decent share of candour, would not be happy to own his acknowledgements to that masterly conjunction, which possesses the very essence of wit, for it has the talent of bringing the most remote things together. And its generosity is in due proportion to its talent, for it always is most profuse of its aid where it is most wanted.

We must enjoy a pleasant passage with the reader on the subject of this 'eternal Now' in Beaumont and Fletcher's play of *The Woman Hater*.—Upon turning to it, we perceive that our illustrious particle does not make quite so great a figure as we imagined ; but the whole passage is in so analogous a taste, and affords such an agreeable specimen of the wit and humour with which fine poets could rally the commonplaces of their art, that we cannot help proceeding with it. Lazarello, a foolish table-hunter, has requested an introduction to the Duke of Milan, who has had a fine lamprey presented him. Before the introduction takes place, he finds that the Duke has given the fish away ; so that his wish to be known to him goes with it ; and part of the drollery of the passage arises from his uneasiness at being detained by the consequences of his own request, and his fear lest he should be too late for the lamprey elsewhere.

COUNT. (*Aside to the Duke.*) Let me entreat your Grace
    to stay a little,
To know a gentleman, to whom yourself
Is much beholding. He hath made the sport
For your whole court these eight years, on my know-
    ledge.
DUKE. His name ?

COUNT. Lazarello.

DUKE. I heard of him this morning :—which is he ?

COUNT. (*Aside to Laz.*) Lazarello, pluck up thy spirits. Thy fortune is now raising. The Duke calls for thee, and thou shalt be acquainted with him.

LAZ. He 's going away, and I must of necessity stay here upon business.

COUNT. 'Tis all one : thou shalt know him first.

LAZ. Stay a little. If he should offer to take me with him, and by that means I should lose that I seek for ! But if he should, I will not go with him.

COUNT. Lazarello, the Duke stays. Wilt thou lose this opportunity ?

LAZ. How must I speak to him ?

COUNT. 'Twas well thought of. You must not talk to him as you do to an ordinary man, honest plain sense ; but you must wind about him. For example, if he should ask you what o'clock it is, you must not say, ' If it please your Grace, 'tis nine ' ; —but thus : ' Thrice three o'clock, so please my sovereign ' :—or thus :

' Look how many Muses there doth dwell
Upon the sweet banks of the learned well,
And just so many strokes the clock hath struck ' ;

and so forth. And you must now and then enter into a description.

LAZ. I hope I shall do it.

COUNT. Come.—May it please your Grace to take note of a gentleman, well seen, deeply read, and thoroughly grounded in the hidden knowledge of all sallets and pot-herbs whatsoever ?

DUKE. I shall desire to know him more inwardly.

LAZ. I kiss the ox-hide of your Grace's foot.

COUNT. (*Aside to Laz.*) Very well.—Will your Grace question him a little ?

DUKE. How old are you ?

LAZ. Full eight-and-twenty several almanacs
Have been compiled, all for several years,
Since first I drew this breath. Four prenticeships
Have I most truly served in this world :

And eight-and-twenty times hath Phoebus' car
Run out his yearly course, since——

    DUKE. I understand you, sir.

    LUCIO. How like an ignorant poet he talks!

    DUKE. You are eight-and-twenty years old? What time of the day do you hold it to be?

    LAZ. About the time that mortals whet their knives
On thresholds, on their shoe-soles, and on stairs.
Now bread is grating, and the testy cook
Hath much to do now : now the tables all——

    DUKE. 'Tis almost dinner-time?

    LAZ. Your Grace doth apprehend me very rightly.

A NOW. OF A COLD DAY

[London Journal, Dec. 3, 1834]

A FRIEND tells us, that having written a ' Now,' descriptive of a hot day, we ought to write another, descriptive of a cold one; and accordingly we do so. It happens that we are, at this minute, in a state at once fit and unfit for the task, being in the condition of the little boy at school, who, when asked the Latin for ' cold,' said he had it ' at his fingers' ends '; but this helps us to set off with a right taste of our subject, and the fire, which is clicking in our ear, shall soon enable us to handle it comfortably in other respects.

Now, then, to commence.—But first, the reader who is good-natured enough to have a regard for these papers may choose to be told of the origin of the use of this word Now, in case he is not already acquainted with it. It was suggested to us by the striking convenience it affords to descriptive writers, such as Thomson and others, who are fond of beginning their paragraphs with it, thereby saving themselves a world of trouble in bringing about a nicer conjunction of the various parts of their subject.

Now when the first foul torrent of the brooks—

Now flaming up to heaven, the potent sun—
Now when the cheerless empire of the sky—
But now—
When now—
Where now—
For now—, &c.

We say nothing of similar words among other nations,
or of a certain *But* of the Greeks, which was as useful
to them on all occasions as the *And so* of the little
children's stories. Our business is with our old indi-
genous friend. No other *Now* can be so present, so
instantaneous, so extremely *Now* as our own Now. The
Now of the Latins,—*Nunc*, or *Jam*, as he sometimes
calls himself,—is a fellow of past ages. He is no Now.
And the *Nun* of the Greek is older. How can there be
a *Now* which was *Then* ? a ' *Now-then*,' as we sometimes barbarously phrase it. ' Now *and* then ' is intelligible ; but ' Now-then ' is an extravagance, fit
only for the delicious moments of a gentleman about to
crack his bottle, or to run away with a lady, or to open
a dance, or to carve a turkey and chine, or to pelt snowballs, or to commit some other piece of ultra-vivacity,
such as excuses a man from the nicer proprieties of
language.

But to begin.

Now, the moment people wake in the morning, they
perceive the coldness with their faces, though they are
warm with their bodies, and exclaim, ' Here's a day ! '
and pity the poor little sweep, and the boy with the
water-cresses. How anybody can go to a cold ditch,
and gather water-cresses, seems marvellous. Perhaps
we hear great lumps in the street of something falling ;
and, looking through the window, perceive the roofs of
the neighbouring houses thick with snow. The breath is
visible, issuing from the mouth as we lie. Now we hate
getting up, and hate shaving, and hate the empty grate
in one's bedroom, and water freezes in ewers, and you
must set the towel upright on its own hardness, and the
window-panes are frost-whitened, or it is foggy, and
the sun sends a dull, brazen beam into one's room ; or,

if it is fine, the windows outside are stuck with icicles; or a detestable thaw has begun, and they drip; but, at all events, it is horribly cold, and delicate shavers fidget about their chambers, looking distressed, and cherish their hard-hearted enemy, the razor, in their bosoms, to warm him a little, and coax him into a consideration of their chins. Savage is a cut, and makes them think destiny really too hard.

Now breakfast is fine; and the fire seems to laugh at us as we enter the breakfast-room, and say, ' Ha! ha! here's a better room than the bed-chamber!' and we always poke it before we do anything else; and people grow selfish about seats near it; and little boys think their elders tyrannical for saying, ' Oh, *you* don't want the fire; your blood is young.' And truly that is not the way of stating the case, albeit young blood is warmer than old. Now the butter is too hard to spread; and the rolls and toast are at their maximum; and the former look glorious as they issue, smoking, out of the flannel in which they come from the baker's; and people who come with single knocks at the door are pitied; and the voices of boys are loud in the street, sliding, or throwing snowballs; and the dustman's bell sounds cold; and we wonder how anybody can go about selling fish, especially with that hoarse voice; and schoolboys hate their slates, and blow their fingers, and detest infinitely the no-fire at school; and the parish-beadle's nose is redder than ever.

Now sounds in general are dull, and smoke out of chimneys looks warm and rich, and birds are pitied, hopping about for crumbs, and the trees look wiry and cheerless, albeit they are still beautiful to imaginative eyes, especially the evergreens, and the birch with boughs like dishevelled hair. Now mud in roads is stiff, and the kennel ices over, and boys make illegal slides in the pathways, and ashes are strewed before doors; or you crunch the snow as you tread, or kick mud-flakes before you, or are horribly muddy in cities. But if it is a hard frost, all the world is buttoned up and great-coated, except ostentatious elderly gentlemen, and pre-

tended beggars with naked feet; and the delicious
sound of 'All hot' is heard from roasted apple and
potato-stalls, the vendor himself being cold, in spite
of his 'hot,' and stamping up and down to warm his
feet; and the little boys are astonished to think how
he can eat bread and cold meat for his dinner, instead
of the smoking apples.

Now skaters are on the alert; the cutlers' shop-
windows abound with their swift shoes; and as you
approach the scene of action (pond or canal) you can hear
the dull grinding noise of the skates to and fro, and see
tumbles, and Banbury-cake men and blackguard boys
playing 'hockey,' and ladies standing shivering on the
banks, admiring anybody but their brother, especially
the gentleman who is cutting figures of eight, who,
for his part, is admiring his own figure. Beginners
affect to laugh at their tumbles, but are terribly angry,
and long to thump the bystanders. On thawing days,
idlers persist to the last in skating or sliding amidst the
slush and bending ice, making the Humane-Society
man ferocious. He feels as if he could give them the
deaths from which it is his business to save them.
When you have done skating, you come away feeling
at once warm and numb in the feet, from the tight
effect of the skates; and you carry them with an
ostentatious air of indifference, as if you had done
wonders; whereas you have fairly had three slips, and
can barely achieve the inside edge.

Now riders look sharp, and horses seem brittle in the
legs, and old gentlemen feel so; and coachmen, cabmen,
and others, stand swinging their arms across at their
sides to warm themselves; and blacksmiths' shops
look pleasant, and potato shops detestable; the fish-
mongers' still more so. We wonder how he can live
in that plash of wet and cold fish, without even a window.
Now clerks in offices envy the one next the fireplace;
and men from behind counters hardly think themselves
repaid by being called out to speak to a Countess in her
chariot; and the wheezy and effeminate pastry-cook,
hatless and aproned, and with his hands in his breeches-

pockets (as the graphic Cruikshank noticeth in his almanac) stands outside his door, chilling his household warmth with attending to the ice which is brought him, and seeing it unloaded into his cellar like coals. Comfortable look the Miss Joneses, coming this way with their muffs and furs; and the baker pities the maidservant cleaning the steps, who, for her part, says, she is not cold, which he finds it difficult to believe.

Now dinner rejoiceth the gatherers together, and cold meat is despised, and the gout defieth the morrow, thinking it but reasonable, on such a day, to inflame itself with ' t'other bottle '; and the sofa is wheeled round to the fire after dinner, and people proceed to burn their legs in their boots, and little boys their faces ; and young ladies are tormented between the cold and their complexions, and their fingers freeze at the pianoforte, but they must not say so, because it will vex their poor comfortable grand-aunt, who is sitting with her knees in the fire, and who is so anxious that they should not be spoilt.

Now the muffin-bell soundeth sweetly in the streets, reminding us, not of the man, but his muffins, and of twilight, and evening, and curtains, and the fireside. Now playgoers get cold feet, and invalids stop up every crevice in their rooms, and make themselves worse ; and the streets are comparatively silent : and the wind rises and falls in moanings ; and fires burn blue and crackle ; and an easy chair with your feet by it on a stool, the lamp or candles a little behind you, and an interesting book just opened where you left off, is a bit of heaven upon earth. People in cottages crowd close into the chimney, and tell stories of ghosts and murders, the blue flame affording something like evidence of the facts.

The owl, with all her feathers, is a-cold,[1]

---

[1] Keats, in *The Eve of St. Agnes*. Mr. Keats gave us some touches in our account of the ' Hot Day ' (first published in *The Indicator*) as we sat writing it in his company thirteen or fourteen years back. We have here made

or you think her so. The whole country feels like a petrifaction of slate and stillness, cut across by the wind; and nobody in the mail-coach is warm but the horses, who steam pitifully when they stop. The 'oldest man' makes a point of never having 'seen such weather.' People have a painful doubt whether they have any chins or not; ears ache with the wind; and the waggoner goes puckering up his teeth, and thinking the time will never arrive when he shall get to the Five Bells.

At night, people get sleepy with the fireside, and long to go to bed, yet fear it on account of the different temperature of the bedroom; which is furthermore apt to wake them up. Warming-pans and hot-water bottles are in request; and naughty boys eschew their night-shirts, and go to bed in their socks.

'Yes,' quoth a little boy, to whom we read this passage, 'and make their younger brother go to bed first.'

A RAINY DAY. I

[*Indicator*, June 21, 1820]

THE day that we speak of is a complete one of its kind, beginning with a dark wet morning and ending in a drenching night. When you come downstairs from your chamber, you find the breakfast-room looking dark, the rain-spout pouring away, and unless you live in a street of traffic, no sound out of doors but a clack of pattens and an occasional clang of milk-pails. (Do you see the rogue of a milkman? He is leaving them open to catch the rain.)

We never see a person going to the window on such a morning, to take a melancholy look at the washed houses and pavement, but we think of a reanimation which we once beheld of old Tate Wilkinson. But

him contribute to our 'Cold Day.' This it is to have immortal friends, whose company never forsakes us.

observe how sour things may run into pleasant tastes
at last. We are by no means certain that the said
mimetic antique, Tate Wilkinson, was not patentee of
the York Theatre, wore a melancholy hat tied the wrong
way, and cast looks of unutterable dissatisfaction at a
rainy morning, purely to let his worthy successor and
surpasser in mimicry, Mr. Charles Mathews, hand down
his aspect and countenance for the benefit of posterity.
We once fell into company with that ingenious person
at a bachelor's house, where he woke us in the morning
with the suspicious sound of a child crying in another
room. It was having its faced washed ; and had we
been of a scandalizing turn, or envied our host for his
hospitality, we should certainly have gone and said that
there was a child in his house who inherited a sorrowful
disposition from somebody, and who might be heard
(for all the nurse's efforts of a morning) whining and
blubbering in the intervals of the wash-towel ;—now
bursting into open-mouthed complaint as it left him to
dip in the water ; and anon, as it came over his face
again, screwing up its snubbed features and eyes, and
making half-stifled obstinate moan with his tight mouth.
The mystery was explained at breakfast ; and as it happened to be a rainy morning, we were entertained with
the reanimation of that 'living dead man' poor Tate
aforesaid,—who had been a merry fellow too in his day.
Imagine a tall, thin, withered, desponding-looking old
gentleman, entering his breakfast-room with an old hat
on tied under his chin the wrong way of the flap,—a
beaver somewhat of the epicene order, so that you do
not know whether it is his wife's or his own. He
hobbles and shrinks up to the window, grunting gently
with a sort of preparatory despair ; and having cast up
his eyes at the air, and seen the weathercock due east
and the rain set in besides, drops the corners of his
mouth and eyes into an expression of double despon-
dency, not unmixed (if we may speak unprofanely) with
a sort of scornful resentment ; and turns off with one
solitary, brief, comprehensive, and groaning ejaculation
of 'Eh—Christ !'—We never see anybody go to the

window of a rainy morning, but we think of this poor old barometer of a patentee, whose face, we trust, will be handed down in successive facsimiles to posterity, for their edification as well as amusement ; for Tate had cultivated much hypochondriacal knowledge in his time, and been a sad fellow in a merry sense before he took to it in its melancholy one.

The preparation for a rainy day in town is certainly not the pleasantest thing in the world, especially for those who have neither health nor imagination to make their own sunshine. The comparative silence in the streets, which is made dull by our knowing the cause of it,—the window-panes drenched and ever-streaming, like so many helpless cheeks,—the darkened rooms,—and at this season of the year, the having left off fires ;—all fall like a chill shade upon the spirits. But we know not how much pleasantry can be made out of un-pleasantness, till we bestir ourselves. The exercise of our bodies will make us bear the weather better, even mentally ; and the exercise of our minds will enable us to bear it with patient bodies indoors, if we cannot go out. Above all, some people seem to think that they cannot have a fire made in a chill day, because it is summer-time, —a notion which, under the guise of being seasonable, is quite the reverse, and one against which we protest. A fire is a thing to warm us when we are cold ; not to go out because the name of the month begins with J. Besides, the sound of it helps to dissipate that of the rain. It is justly called a companion. It looks glad in our faces ; it talks to us ; it is vivified at our touch ; it vivifies in return ; it puts life, and warmth, and comfort in the room. A good fellow is bound to see that he leaves this substitute for his company when he goes out, especially to a lady ; whose solitary work-table in a chill room on such a day is a very melancholy refuge. We exhort her, if she can afford it, to take a book and a footstool, and plant herself before a good fire. We know of few baulks more complete than coming down of a chill morning to breakfast, turning one's chair as usual to the fireside, planting one's feet on the fender and one's eyes on a book, and suddenly discovering that there is no fire in the grate. A grate that ought to have a fire in it, and gapes in one's face with none is like a cold grinning empty rascal.

There is something, we think, not disagreeable in issuing forth during a good honest summer rain, with a coat well buttoned up and an umbrella over our heads. The first flash open of the umbrella seems a defiance to the shower, and the sound of it afterwards over our dry heads corroborates the triumph. If we are in this humour, it does not matter how drenching the day is. We despise the expensive effeminacy of a coach; have an agreeable malice of self-content at the sight of crowded gateways; and see nothing in the furious little rain-spouts but a lively emblem of critical opposition, —weak, low, washy, and dirty, gabbling away with a perfect impotence of splutter.

Speaking of malice, there are even some kinds of legs which afford us a lively pleasure in beholding them splashed.

LADY. Lord, you cruel man!

INDICATOR. Nay, I was not speaking of yours, madam. How could I wish ill to any such very touching stockings? And yet, now I think of it, there are very gentle and sensitive legs (I say nothing of beautiful ones, because all gentle ones are beautiful to me) which it is possible to behold in a very earthy plight;—at least the feet and ankles.

LADY. And pray, sir, what are the very agreeable circumstances under which we are to be muddied?

INDICATOR. Fancy, madam, a walk with some particular friend, between the showers, in a green lane; the sun shining, the hay sweet-smelling, the glossy leaves sparkling like children's cheeks after tears. Suppose this lane not to be got into, but over a bank and a brook, and a good savage assortment of wagon-ruts. Yet the sunny green so takes you, and you are so resolved to oblige your friend with a walk, that you hazard a descent down the slippery bank, a jump over the brook, a leap (that will certainly be too short) over the ploughed

mud. Do you think that a good thick-mudded shoe
and a splashed instep would not have a merit in his
barbarous eyes, beyond even the neat outline of the
Spanish leather and the symbolical whiteness of the
stocking ? Ask him.

LADY. Go to your subject, do.

INDICATOR. Well, I will. You may always know
whether a person wishes you a pleasant or unpleasant
adventure, by the pleasure or pain he has in your company. If he would be with you himself (and I should
like to know the pleasant situation, or even the painful
one, if a share of it can be made pleasant, in which we
would not have a woman with us), you may rest assured
that all the mischief he wishes you is very harmless.—
At the same time, if there are situations in which one
could wish ill even to a lady's leg, there are legs and
stockings which it is possible to fancy well-splashed
upon a very different principle.

GENTLEMAN. Pray, sir, whose may they be ?

INDICATOR. Not yours, sir, with that delicate flow of
trouser, and that careless yet genteel stretch out of toe.
There is a humanity in the air of it,—a graceful but
at the same time manly sympathy with the drapery
beside it. I allude, sir, to one of those portentous legs,
which belong to an over-fed money-getter, or to a bulky
methodist parson who has doting dinners got up for
him by his hearers. You know the leg I mean. It is
'like unto the sign of the leg,' only larger. Observe,
I do not mean every kind of large leg. The same thing
is not the same thing in every one,—if you understand
that profound apophthegm. As a leg, indifferent in
itself, may become very charming, if it belongs to a
charming owner ; so even when it is of the cast we speak
of in a man, it becomes more or less unpleasant according to his nature and treatment of it. I am not carping
at the leg of an ordinary jolly fellow, which good temper
as well as good living helps to plump out, and which he
is, after all, not proud of exhibiting ; keeping it modestly
in a boot or trousers, and despising the starched ostentation of the other : but at a regular, dull, uninformed,

hebetudinous, ' gross, open, and palpable' leg, whose calf glares upon you like the ground-glass of a post-chaise lamp. In the parson it is somewhat obscured by a black stocking. A white one is requisite to display it in all its glory. It has a large balustrade calf, an ankle that would be monstrous in any other man, but looks small from the contrast, a tight knee well buttoned, and a seam inexorably in the middle. It is a leg at once gross and symbolical. Its size is made up of plethora and superfluity ; its white cotton stocking affects a propriety ; its inflexible seam and side announce the man of clock-work. A dozen hard-worked dependents go at least to the making up of that leg. If in black, it is the essence of infinite hams at old ladies' Sunday dinners. Now we like to see a couple of legs of this sort, in white, kicking their way through a muddy street, and splashed unavoidably as they go, till their horrid glare is subdued into spottiness. A lamplighter's ladder is of use, to give them a passing spurn : upon which the proprietor, turning round to swear, is run against in front by a wheelbarrow ; upon which, turning round again, to swear worse, he thrusts his heel upon the beginning of a loose stone in the pavement, and receives his final baptism from a fount of mud.

Our limits compel us to bring this article to a speedier conclusion than we thought ; and to say the truth, we are not sorry for it ; for we happened to break off here in order to write the one following, and it has not left us in a humour to return to our jokes.

We must therefore say little of a world of things we intended to descant on,—of pattens,—and eaves,—and hackney-coaches,—and waiting in vain to go out on a party of pleasure, while the youngest of us insists every minute that ' it is going to hold up,'—and umbrellas dripping on one's shoulder,—and the abomination of soaked gloves,—and standing up in gateways, when you hear now and then the passing roar of rain on an umbrella,—and glimpses of the green country at the end of streets,—and the foot-marked earth of the country roads —and clouds eternally following each other from

the west,—and the scent of the luckless new-mown hay,
—and the rainbow,—and the glorious thunder and
lightning,—and a party waiting to go home at night,—
and last of all, the delicious moment of taking off your
wet things, and resting in the dry and warm content of
your gown and slippers.

A RAINY DAY. II

[London Journal, Aug. 1, 1835]

'POUR! pour! pour! There is no hope of its *leaving
off*,'—says a lady, turning away from the window;
'you must make up your mind, Louisa, to stay at home,
and lose your romps, and have a whole frock to sit in
at dinner, and be very unhappy with mamma.'

'No, mamma, not that; but don't you think it will
hold up? Look—the kennels are not quite so bad;
and those clouds—they are not so heavy as they were.
It is getting quite light in the sky.'

'I am afraid not,' says the lady, at once grave and
smiling; 'but you are a good girl, Louisa; give me a
kiss. We will make the day as happy as we can at
home. I am not a very bad playfellow, you know, for
all I am so much bigger and older.'

'Oh, mamma, you know I never enjoy my cousin's
company half so much, if you don't go with me; but'
(here two or three kisses are given and taken, the lady's
hands holding the little girl's cheeks, and her eyes
looking fondly into hers, which are a little wet)—'but—
but don't you think we *really* shall be able to go—don't
you think it will *hold up?*' And here the child returns
to the window.

'No, my darling; it is *set in* for a rainy day. It has
been raining all the morning; it is now afternoon, and
we have, I fear, no chance whatever.'

'The puddles don't dance quite as fast as they did,'
says the little girl.

'But hark!' says the lady; '*there's* a furious dash of water against the panes.'

'*T l t l*' quoth the little girl against her teeth; 'dear me! It's very bad indeed; I wonder what Charles and Mary are thinking of it.'

'Why, they are thinking just as you are, I dare say; and doing just as you are, very likely,—making their noses flat and numb against the glass.'

The little girl laughs, with a tear in her eye, and mamma laughs and kisses her, and says, 'Come; as you cannot go to see your cousins, you shall have a visitor yourself. You shall invite *me* and Miss Nayler to dinner, and sit at the head of the table in the little room, and we will have your favourite pudding, and no servant to wait on us. We will wait on ourselves; and I will try to be a very great, good, big little child, and behave well; and you shall tell papa, when he comes home, what a nice girl I was.'

'Oh, dear mamma, that will be very pleasant. What a nice, kind mamma you are, and how afraid I am to vex you, though you do play and romp with me.'

'Good girl! But—Ah, you need not look at the window any more, my poor Louisa. Go, and tell cook about the pudding, and we will get you to give us a glass of wine after it, and drink the health of your cousins, so as to fancy them partaking it with us; and Miss Nayler and I will make fine speeches, and return you their thanks; and then you can tell them about it, when you go next time.'

'Oh, dear, dear, *dear* mamma, so I can; and how very nice that will be; and I'll go this instant about the pudding; and I don't think we could go as far as Welland's now, if the rain did hold up; and the puddles are worse than ever.'

And so, off runs little fond-heart and bright-eyes, happy at dining in fancy with her mother and cousins all at once, and almost feeling as if she had but exchanged one holiday for another.

The sight of mother and daughter has made us forget our rainy day.—Alas! the lady was right, and the little child wrong, for there is no chance of to-day's clearing up. The long-watched and interesting puddles are not indeed 'worse than ever'—not suddenly hurried and exasperated, as if dancing with rage at the flogging given them: they are worse even than that, for they are everlastingly the same:—the same full, twittering, dancing, circle-making overflowings of gutter, which they have been ever since five in the morning, and which they mean to be, apparently, till five to-morrow.

Wash! wash! wash! The window-panes, weltering, and dreary, and rapid, and misty with the rain, are like the face of a crying child who is afraid to make a noise, but who is resolved to be as 'aggravating' as possible with the piteous ostentation of his wet cheeks,—weeping with all his might, and breathing, with wide-open mouth, a sort of huge, wilful, everlasting sigh, by way of accompaniment. Occasionally, he puts his hand over to his ear,—hollow,—as though he feared to touch it, his master having given him a gentle pinch: and at the same moment, he stoops with bent head and shrugged shoulders, and one lifted knee, as if in the endurance of a writhing anguish.

You involuntarily rub one of the panes, thinking to see the better into the street, and forgetting that the mist is made by the rain on the other side.—On goes the wet as ever, rushing, streaming, running down, mingling its soft and washy channels; and now and then comes a clutter of drops against the glass, made by a gust of wind.

Clack, meantime, goes the sound of pattens; and when you do see, you see the street almost deserted, —a sort of lay Sunday. The rare carriages drive as fast as they can; the hackney-coaches lumber along, glossy (on such occasions only) with the wet, and looking as old and rheumatic as the poor coachmen, whose hat and legs are bound with straw;—the rain-spouts are sputtering torrents; messengers dart along in oil-skin capes; the cry of the old shrimp-seller is hoarse; the postman's knock is ferocious.

If you are out of doors, woe betide you should you

have gone out unprepared, or relying on a coach. Your shoes and stockings are wet through, the latter almost as muddy as the dog that ran by just now without an owner; the rain washes your face, gets into the nape of your neck, makes a spout of your hat. Close by your ears comes roaring an umbrella, the face underneath it looking astonished at you. A butcher's boy dashes along, and contrives to come with his heel plump upon the exact spot of a loose piece of pavement, requisite for giving you a splash that shall embrace the whole of your left leg. To stand up under a gateway is impossible, because in the state you are in, you will catch your 'death o' cold'; and the people underneath it look at you amazed, to think how you could have come out 'such a day, in such a state.' Many of those who *are* standing up, have umbrellas; but the very umbrellas are wet through. Those who pass by the spot, with their oil or silk-skins roaring, as above (a sound particularly distressing to the non-possessors), show that they have not been out of doors so long. Nobody puts his hand out from under the gateway, to feel whether it is still raining. There can be no question of it. The only voluntary person visible in the street is a little errand-boy, who, because his mother has told him to make great haste, and not get wet feet, is amusing himself with double zest, by kicking something along through the gutter.

In private streets the pavement is washed clean; and so it is, for the moment, in public: but horrible will be the mud to-morrow. Horses are splashed up to the mane; the legs of the rider's overalls are as if he had been sitting in a ditch; poor girls with bandboxes trip patiently along, with their wet curls over their eyes, and a weight of skirt. A carriage is coming down a narrow street; there is a plenitude of mud between you and the wheels, not to be eschewed; on dash they, and give you three beauty spots, one right on the nose.

Swift has described such a day as this, in lines which first appeared in the *Tatler*, and which hearty, unenvying Steele introduces as written by one 'who

treats of every subject after a manner that no other
author has done, and better than any one can do.'
[In transcribing such words, one's pen seems to partake
the pleasure of the writer.] Swift, availing himself of
the licence of a different age, is apt to bring less pleasant
images among his pleasant ones than suit everybody
now ; but here follows the greater part of his verses :—

Careful observers may foretell the hour,
By sure prognostics, when to dread a shower :
While rain depends, the pensive cat gives o'er
Her frolics, and pursues her tail no more.
If you be wise, then go not far to dine,
You'll spend in coach-hire more than save in wine,
A coming shower your shooting corns presage,
Old aches will throb, your hollow tooth will rage.
Sauntering in coffee-house is Dulman seen ;
He damns the climate, and complains of spleen.

Meanwhile the south, rising with dabbled wings,
A sable cloud athwart the welkin flings.

Brisk Susan *whips her linen from the rope,*
While the first drizzling shower is borne aslope ;
Such is that sprinkling which some careless quean
Flirts on you from her mop, but not so clean.
You fly, invoke the gods ; then, turning, stop
To rail ; *she, singing, still whirls on her mop.*
Not yet the dust had shunned the unequal strife,
But, aided by the wind, fought still for life ;
And, wafted with its foe by violent gust,
'Twas doubtful which was rain and which was dust.
Ah ! where must needy poet seek for aid,
When dust and rain at once his coat invade ?—
His only coat,—where dust confused with rain,
Roughens the nap, and leaves a mingled stain ?

Now in contiguous drops the flood comes down,
Threatening with deluge this devoted town.
To shops in crowds the draggled females fly,
Pretend to cheapen goods, but nothing buy.

The Templar spruce, with every spout abroach,
Stays till 'tis fair, *yet seems to call a coach.*
The tucked-up sempstress walks with hasty strides,
While streams run down her oil'd umbrella's sides.
There various kinds, by various fortunes led,
Commence acquaintance underneath a shed.
Triumphant Tories and desponding Whigs
Forget their feuds, *and join to save their wigs.*
Box'd in a chair,[1] the beau impatient sits,
While spouts run clattering o'er the roof by fits;
And ever-and-anon with frightful din,
The leather sounds ; *he* trembles from within.

So when Troy chairmen bore the wooden steed,
Pregnant with Greeks, impatient to be freed
(Those bully Greeks, who, as the moderns do,
Instead of paying chairmen ran them through),
Laocoon struck the outside with his spear,
And each imprisoned hero quaked for fear.

The description concludes with a triumphant account
of a gutter, more civic than urbane.

How to make the best of a bad day has been taught by
implication in various pages throughout our Journal,
especially in those where we have studied the art of
making everything out of nothing, and have delivered
immense observations on raindrops. It may be learnt
in the remarks which appeared a few weeks ago on
a ' Dusty Day.' The secret is short and comprehensive, and fit for trying occasions of all sorts. *Think
of something superior to it* ;—make it yield entertaining
and useful reflection, as the rain itself brings out the
flowers. Think of it as a benignant enemy, who keeps
you indoors, or otherwise puts your philosophy to a
trial, for the best of purposes,—to fertilize your fields,
to purify your streets against contagion,—to freshen
your air, and put sweets upon your table,—to furnish
life with variety, your light with a shadow that sets it
off, your poets with similes and descriptions. When

---

[1] A sedan.

the summer rains, Heaven is watering your plants.
Fancy an insect growling at it under his umbrella of
rose-leaf. No wiser is the man who grumbles under his
gateway; much less over his port wine. Very high-
bred ladies would be startled to learn that they are doing
a very vulgar thing (and hurting their tempers to boot)
when they stand at a window, peevishly objecting to
the rain with such phrases as 'Dear me! how tiresome!'—My lady's maid is not a bit less polite, when
she vows and 'purtests' that it is '*quite contráry*';
—as if Heaven had sent in on purpose to thwart her
ladyship and her waiting-woman! By complaint we
dwindle and subject ourselves, make ourselves little-
minded, and the slaves of circumstance. By rising
above an evil, we set it at a distance from us, render it
a small object, and live in a nobler air.

A wit, not unworthy to be named in the same page
with the Dean of St. Patrick's, has given a good lesson
on the subject.—Green, in his poem on the 'Spleen,'—
a teacher the fittest in the world to be heard upon it,
because he was subject to what he writes about, and
overcame it by the cultivation of sense and good-temper.
Some bookseller with a taste,—Mr. Pickering, or Mr.
Van Voorst,—should give us a new edition of this
poem, with engravings. Mr. Wilkie, Mr. Mulready,
and others might find subjects enough to furnish a
design to every page.

> In rainy days keep double guard,
> Or spleen will surely be too hard;
> *Which, like those fish by sailors met,*
> *Fly highest when their wings are wet,*
> In such dull weather so unfit
> To enterprise a work of wit,
> When clouds one yard of azure sky
> That's fit for simile deny,
> I dress my face with studious looks,
> And shorten tedious hours with books;
> But if dull fogs invade the head,
> That mem'ry minds not what is read,

I sit in windows dry as ark,
And on the drowning world remark:
Or to some coffee-house I stray
For news, *the manna of the day*,
And from the hipp'd discourses gather,
That politics go by the weather;
Then seek good-humoured tavern-chums,
And play at cards, but for small sums;
Or with the merry fellows quaff,
And laugh aloud with them that laugh;
Or drink a joco-serious cup
With souls who've took their freedom up,
And let my mind, beguiled by talk,
In Epicurus' garden walk,
Who thought it heaven to be serene;
Pain, hell; and purgatory, spleen.

A DUSTY DAY

[London Journal, July 11, 1835]

AMONG the 'Miseries of Human Life,' as a wit
pleasantly entitled them, there are few, while the rascal
is about it, worse than a Great Cloud of Dust, coming
upon you in street or road, you having no means of
escape, and the carriages, or flock of sheep, evidently being
bent on imparting to you a full share of their besetting
horror. The road is too narrow to leave you a choice,
even if it had two pathways; which it has not:—the
day is hot; the wind is whisking; you have come out in
stockings instead of boots, not being aware that you were
occasionally to have two feet depth of dust to walk in:—
now, NOW the dust is on you,—you are enveloped,—you
are blind; you have to hold your hat on against the
wind; the carriages grind by, or the sheep go pattering
along, baaing through all the notes of their poor gamut;
perhaps carriages and sheep are together, the latter
eschewing the horses' legs, and the shepherd's dog
driving against your own, and careering over the woolly

backs:—Whew! what a dusting! What a blinding!
What a whirl! The noise decreases; you stop; you
look about you; gathering up your hat, coat, and
faculties, after apologizing to the gentleman against
whom you have 'bumped,' and who does not look a bit
the happier for your apology. The dust is in your eyes,
in your hair, in your shoes and stockings, in your neckcloth, in your mouth. You grind your teeth in dismay,
and find them gritty.

Perhaps another carriage is coming; and you, finding
yourself in the middle of the road, and being resolved
to be master of, at least, this inferior horror, turn about
towards the wall or paling, and propose to make your
way accordingly, and have the dust behind your back
instead of in front; when lo! you begin sneezing, and
cannot see. You have taken involuntary snuff.

Or you suddenly discern a street, down which you
can turn, which you do with rapture, thinking to get
out of wind and dust at once; when, unfortunately,
you discover that the wind is veering to all points of the
compass, and that instead of avoiding the dust, there
is a ready-made and intense collection of it, then in the
act of being swept into your eyes by the attendants on
a——dust cart!

The reader knows what sort of a day we speak of. It
is all dusty;—the windows are dusty; the people are
dusty; the hedges in the roads are horribly dusty,—
pitiably,—you think they must feel it; shoes and boots
are like a baker's; men on horseback eat and drink
dust; coachmen sit screwing up their eyes; the gar-
dener finds his spade slip into the ground, fetching up
smooth portions of earth, all made of dust. What is
the poor pedestrian to do?

To think of something *superior* to the dust,—whether
grave or gay. This is the secret of being master of any
ordinary, and of much extraordinary, trouble:—bring
a better idea upon it, and it is hard if the greater thought
does not do something against the less. When we meet
with any very unpleasant person, to whose ways we
cannot suddenly reconcile ourselves, we think of some

delightful friend, perhaps two hundred miles off,—in Northumberland, or in Wales. When dust threatens to blind us, we shut our eyes to the disaster, and contrive to philosophize a bit, even then.

'Oh, but it is not worth while doing that.'

Good. If so, there is nothing to do but to be as jovial as the dust itself, and take all gaily. Indeed, this is the philosophy we speak of.

'And yet the dust is annoying too.'

Well—take then just as much good sense as you require for the occasion. Think of a jest ; think of a bit of verse ; think of the dog you saw just now, coming out of the pond, and frightening the dandy in his new trousers. But at all events don't let your temper be mastered by such a thing as a cloud of dust. It will show, either that you have a very infirm temper indeed, or no ideas in your head.

On all occasions in life, great or small, you may be the worse for them, or the better. You may be made the weaker or the stronger by them ; aye, even by so small a thing as a little dust.

When the famous Arbuthnot was getting into his carriage one day, he was beset with dust. What did he do ? Damn the dust, or the coachman ? No ; that was not his fashion. He was a wit, and a good-natured man ; so he fell to making an epigram, which he sent to his friends. It was founded on scientific knowledge, and consisted of the following pleasant exaggeration :—

ON A DUSTY DAY.

The dust in smaller particles arose,
Than those which fluid bodies do compose.
Contraries in extremes do often meet ;
It was so dry, that you might call it wet.

Dust at a distance sometimes takes a burnished or tawny aspect in the sun, almost as handsome as the great yellow smoke out of breweries ; and you may amuse your fancy with thinking of the clouds that pre-ceded armies in the old books of poetry,—the spears gleaming out,—the noise of the throng growing on the ear,—and, at length, horses emerging, and helmets, and flags,—the Lion of King Richard, or the Lilies of France.

Or you may think of some better and more harmless palm of victory, 'not without dust' (*palma non sine pulvere*); dust, such as Horace says the horsemen of antiquity liked to kick up at the Olympic games, or as he more elegantly phrases it, 'collect' (*collegisse juvat*, —which a punster of our acquaintance translated, 'kicking up a dust at college'); or if you are in a very philosophic vein indeed, you may think of man's derivation from dust, and his return to it, redeeming your thoughts from gloom by the hopes beyond dust, and by the graces which poetry and the affections have shed upon it in this life, like flowers upon graves,—lamenting with the tender Petrarch, that 'those eyes of which he spoke so warmly,' and that golden hair, and 'the lightning of that angel smile,' and all those other beauties which made him a lover 'marked out from among men,' —a being abstracted 'from the rest of his species,'— are now 'a little dust, without a feeling'—

> *Poca polvere son che nulla sente*—

or repeating that beautiful lyric of the last of the Shakespearean men, Shirley, which, they say, touched even the thoughtless bosom of Charles the Second :—

DEATH'S FINAL CONQUEST.

The glories of our blood and state
    Are shadows, not substantial things:
There is no armour against fate;
    Death lays his icy hand on kings:
        Sceptre and crown
        Must tumble down,
And in the dust be equal made
With the poor crooked scythe and spade.

Some men with swords may reap the field
    And plant fresh laurels where they kill;
But their strong nerves at last must yield,
    They tame but one another still.

> Early or late
> They stoop to fate,
> And must give up their murmuring breath,
> *When they, pale captives, creep to death.*
>
> The garlands wither on your brow,
> 　Then boast no more your mighty deeds ;
> Upon death's purple altar now
> 　See where the *victor-victim* bleeds :
> 　　All heads must come
> 　　To the cold tomb :
> *Only the actions of the just*
> *Smell sweet, and blossom in the dust.*[1]

Most true ;—but with the leave of the fine poet (which
he would gladly have conceded to us), Death's conquest
is not 'final' ; for Heaven triumphs over him, and Love
too, and Poetry ; and thus we can get through the cloud
even of his dust, and shake it, in aspiration, from our
wings. Besides, we know not, with any exactitude,
what, or who, Death is, or whether there is any such
personage, even in his negative sense, except inasmuch
as he is a gentle voice, calling upon us to go some
journey ; for the very dust that he is supposed to deal
in, is alive ; is the cradle of other beings and vegetation ;
nay, its least particle belongs to a mighty life ;—is
planetary,—is part of our star,—is the stuff of which the
worlds are made, that roll and rejoice round the sun.

Of these or the like reflections, serious or otherwise,
are the cogitations of the true pedestrian composed ;—
such are the weapons with which he triumphs over the

---

[1] See p. 76 of the first volume of *Songs of England and
Scotland*, edited by Mr. Cunningham, jun., a welcome book,
and of hereditary promise. But it might have been much
improved. We ought to have had more of Sedley, Suckling,
Herrick, and others, and a great deal more of Beaumont and
Fletcher (the truest lyrists in the language), and other old
dramatists ; also more of Dibdin, Barry Cornwall, and
various writers ' about town ' in the last century. There
is even no O'Keefe,—a great omission in a song-book.
His muse was as fresh as a dairymaid.

most hostile of his clouds, whether material or meta-
phorical ; and, at the end of his dusty walk, he beholdeth
in beautiful perspective, the towel and the basin of
water, with which he will render his eyes, cheeks, and
faculties as cool and fresh as if no dust had touched
them ; nay, more so, *for the contrast.*   Never forget that
secret of the reconcilements of this life ; to sit down,
newly washed and dressed, after a dusty journey, and
hear that dinner is to be ready ' in ten minutes,' is a
satisfaction—a crowning and ' measureless content '—
which we hope no one will enjoy who does not allow fair
play between the harmless lights and shadows of existence, and treat his dust with respect.   We defy him to
enjoy it, at any rate, like those who do.   His ill-temper,
somehow or other, will rise in retribution against him,
and find dust on his saddle of mutton.

FINE DAYS IN JANUARY AND FEBRUARY

[Companion, Jan. 30, 1828]

WE speak of those days, unexpected, sunshiny, cheerful, even vernal, which come towards the end of January,
and are too apt to come alone.   They are often set in
the midst of a series of rainy ones, like a patch of blue
in the sky.   Fine weather is much at any time, after or
before the end of the year ; but, in the latter case, the
days are still winter days ; whereas, in the former, the
year being turned, and March and April before us, we
seem to feel the coming of spring.   In the streets and
squares, the ladies are abroad, with their colours and
glowing cheeks.   If you can hear anything but noise,
you hear the sparrows.   People anticipate at breakfast
the pleasure they shall have in ' getting out.'   The
solitary poplar in a corner looks green against the sky ;
and the brick wall has a warmth in it.   Then in the
noisier streets, what a multitude and a new life !   What
horseback !   What promenading !   What shopping,
and giving good day !   Bonnets encounter bonnets :—

all the Miss Williamses meet all the Miss Joneses ; and
everybody wonders, particularly at nothing. The shop
windows, putting forward their best, may be said to be
in blossom.   The yellow carriages flash in the sunshine ;
footmen rejoice in their white calves, not dabbed upon,
as usual, with rain ; the gossips look out of their three
pair-of-stairs windows ; other windows are thrown
open ; fruiterers' shops look well, swelling with full
baskets ; pavements are found to be dry ; lap-dogs
frisk under their asthmas ; and old gentlemen issue
forth, peering up at the region of the north-east.

Then in the country, how emerald the green, how
open-looking the prospect ! Honeysuckles (a name
alone with a garden in it) are detected in blossom ; the
hazel follows ; the snowdrop hangs its white perfection,
exquisite with green ; we fancy the trees are already
thicker ; voices of winter birds are taken for new ones ;
and in February new ones come—the thrush, the chaf-
finch, and the wood-lark. Then rooks begin to pair ;
and the wagtail dances in the lane. As we write this
article, the sun is on our paper, and chanticleer (the
same, we trust, that we heard the other day) seems to
crow in a very different style, lord of the ascendant, and
as willing to be with his wives abroad as at home. We
think we see him, as in Chaucer's homestead :

> He looketh, as it were a grim leoùn ;
> And on his toes he roameth up and down ;
> Him deigneth not to set his foot to ground ;
> He clucketh when he hath a corn yfound,
> And to him runnen then his wives all.

Will the reader have the rest of the picture, as Chaucer
gave it ? It is as bright and strong as the day itself,
and as suited to it as a falcon to a knight's fist. Hear
how the old poet throws forth his strenuous music ;
as fine, considered as mere music and versification, as
the description is pleasant and noble.

> His comb was redder than the fine coràll,
> Embatteled, as it were a castle wall.

His bill was black, and as the jet it shone ;
Like azure were his leggès and his tone ;
His nailès, whiter than the lilly flower,
And like the burnèd gold was his colòur.

Hardly one pause like the other throughout, and yet
all wingèd and sweet.   The pause on the third syllable in
the last line but one, and that on the sixth in the last,
together with the deep variety of vowels, make a beautiful concluding couplet ; and indeed the whole is a study
for versification.   So little were those old poets unaware
of their task, as some are apt to suppose them : and
so little have others dreamt, that they surpassed
them in their own pretensions.   The accent, it is to be
observed, in those concluding words, as *coral* and *colour*,
is to be thrown on the last syllable, as it is in Italian.
Colòr, *colòre*, and Chaucer's old Anglo-Gallican word,
is a much nobler one than our modern *còlour*.   We have
injured many such words by throwing back the accent.
We should beg pardon for this digression, if it had
not been part of our understood agreement with the
reader to be as desultory as we please, and as befits
Companions.   Our very enjoyment of the day we are
describing would not let us do otherwise.   It is also an
old fancy of ours to associate the ideas of Chaucer with
that of any early and vigorous manifestation of light and
pleasure.   He is not only the ' morning-star ' of our
poetry, as Denham called him, but the morning itself,
and a good bit of the noon ; and we could as soon help
quoting him at the beginning of the year, as we could
help wishing to hear the cry of primroses, and thinking
of the sweet faces that buy them.

TO ANY ONE WHOM BAD WEATHER DEPRESSES

[Indicator, Nov. 10, 1819]

IF you are melancholy for the first time, you will find upon a little inquiry, that others have been melancholy many times, and yet are cheerful now. If you have been melancholy many times, recollect that you have got over all those times ; and try if you cannot find out new means of getting over them better.

Do not imagine that mind alone is concerned in your bad spirits. The body has a great deal to do with these matters. The mind may undoubtedly affect the body ; but the body also affects the mind. There is a mutual reaction between them ; and by lessening it on either side, you diminish the pain on both.

If you are melancholy, and know not why, be assured it must arise entirely from some physical weakness ; and do your best to strengthen yourself. The blood of a melancholy man is thick and slow. The blood of a lively man is clear and thick. Endeavour therefore to put your blood in motion. Exercise is the best way to do it ; but you may also help yourself, in moderation, with wine, or other excitements. Only you must take care so to proportion the use of any artificial stimulus, that it may not render the blood languid by over-exciting it at first ; and that you may be able to keep up, by the natural stimulus only, the help you have given yourself by the artificial.

Regard the bad weather, as somebody has advised us to handle the nettle. In proportion as you are delicate with it, it will make you feel ; but

> Grasp it like a man of mettle,
> And the rogue obeys you well.

Do not the less, however, on that account, take all reasonable precaution and arms against it,—your boots, &c., against wet feet, and your great coat or umbrella against the rain. It is timidity and flight which are to be deprecated, not proper armour for the battle. The first will lay you open to defeat, on the least attack. A proper use of the latter will only keep you strong for it. Plato had such a high opinion of exercise, that he said it was a cure even for a wounded conscience. Nor is this opinion a dangerous one. For there is no system, even of superstition, however severe or cruel in other matters, that does not allow a wounded conscience to be curable by some means. Nature will work out its rights and its kindness some way or other, through the worst sophistications ; and this is one of the instances in which she seems to raise herself above all contingencies. The conscience may have been wounded by artificial or by real guilt ; but then she will tell it in those extremities, that even the real guilt may have been produced by circumstances. It is her kindness alone, which nothing can pull down from its predominance.

See fair play between cares and pastimes. Diminish your mere wants as much as possible, whether you are rich or poor : for the rich man's wants, increasing by indulgence, are apt to outweigh even the abundance of his means ; and the poor man's diminution of them renders his means the greater. Do not want money, for instance, for money's sake. There is excitement in the pursuit ; but it is dashed with more troubles than most others, and gets less happiness at last. On the other hand, increase all your natural and healthy enjoyments. Cultivate your afternoon fireside, the society of your friends, the company of agreeable children, music, theatres, amusing books, an urbane and generous gallantry. He who thinks any innocent pastime foolish, has either yet to grow wiser or is past it. In the one case, his notion of being childish is itself a childish notion. In the other, his importance is of so feeble and hollow a cast, that it dare not move for fear of tumbling to pieces.

A friend of ours, who knows as well as any man how to unite industry with enjoyment, has set an excellent example to those who can afford the leisure, by taking two Sabbaths every week instead of one ;—not Methodistical Sabbaths, but days of rest which pay true homage to the Supreme Being by enjoying his creation. He will be gratified at reading this paragraph on his second Sunday morning.

One of the best pieces of advice for an ailing spirit is to go to no sudden extremes,—to adopt no great and extreme changes in diet or other habits. They may make a man look very great and philosophic to his own mind ; but they are not fit for a nature to which custom has been truly said to be a second nature. Dr. Cheyne (as we remember reading on a stall) may tell us that a drowning man cannot too quickly get himself out of the water : but the analogy is not good. If the water has become a second habit, he might almost as well say that a fish could not get too quickly out of it.

Upon this point, Bacon says that we should discontinue what we think hurtful by little and little. And he quotes with admiration the advice of Celsus,—that ' a man do vary and interchange contraries, but rather with an inclination to the more benign extreme.' ' Use fasting,' he says, ' and full eating, but *rather* full eating ; watching and sleep, but rather sleep ; sitting and exercise, but rather exercise, and the like ; so shall nature be cherished, and yet taught masteries.'

We cannot do better than conclude with one or two other passages out of the same Essay, full of his usual calm wisdom. ' If you fly physic in health altogether, it will be too strange for your body when you need it.' (He means that a general state of health should not make us over-confident and contemptuous of physic ; but that we should use it moderately if required, that it may not be too strange to us when required most.) ' If you make it too familiar, it will have no extraordinary effect when sickness cometh. I commend rather some diet for certain seasons, than frequent use of physic, except it be grown into a custom : for those diets alter the body more, and trouble it less.'

' As for the passions and studies of the mind,' says

he, 'avoid envy, anxious fears, anger fretting inwards, subtle and knotty inquisitions, joys and exhilarations in excess, sadness not communicated' (for as he says finely somewhere else, They who keep their griefs to themselves, are 'cannibals of their own hearts'). 'Entertain hopes; mirth rather than joy' (that is to say, cheerfulness rather than what we call boisterous merriment); 'variety of delights rather than surfeit of them; wonder and admiration, and therefore novelties; studies that fill the mind with splendid and illustrious objects, as histories, fables, and contemplations of nature.'

THE SUN

[Table-Talk]

No mystery in creation need sadden us, as long as we believe nothing of the invisible world inferior to what the visible proclaims. Life and geniality predominate; death is brief; pain fugitive; beauty universal; order paramount and everlasting. What a shame, to know that the sun, the great visible object in our universe, combines equal gentleness with power, and does us nothing but good, and at the same time to dare to think worse of its Maker!

AT HOME

A CAT BY THE FIRE.

[*London Journal*, Nov. 26, 1834]

A BLAZING fire, a warm rug, candles lit and curtains drawn, the kettle on for tea (if rich, you may have a silver kettle, and so partake the pleasures of the poor), and finally, the cat before you, attracting your attention,—it is a scene which everybody likes unless he has a morbid aversion to cats ; which is not common. There are some nice inquirers, it is true, who are apt to make uneasy comparisons of cats with dogs,—to say they are not so loving, that they prefer the house to the man, &c. But agreeably to the good old maxim, that ' comparisons are odious,' our readers, we hope, will continue to like what is likeable in anything, for its own sake, without trying to render it unlikeable from its inferiority to something else,—a process by which we might ingeniously contrive to put soot into every dish that is set before us, and to reject one thing after another, till we were pleased with nothing. Here is a good fireside, and a cat to it ; and it would be our own fault, if, in removing to another house and another fireside, we did not take care that the cat removed with us. Cats cannot look to the moving of goods, as men do. If we would have creatures considerate towards us, we must be so towards them. It is not to be expected of everybody, quadruped or biped, that they should stick to us in spite of our want of merit, like a dog or a benevolent sage. Besides, stories have been told of cats very much to the credit of their benignity ; such as their following a master about like a dog, waiting at a gentleman's door to thank him for some

obligation over-night, &c. And our readers may remember the history of the famous Arabian Godolphin,
upon whose grave a cat that had lived with him in the
stable, went and stretched itself, and died.

The cat purrs, as if it applauded our consideration,
—and gently moves its tail. What an odd expression
of the power to be irritable and the will to be pleased
there is in its face, as it looks up at us. We must own,
that we do not prefer a cat in the act of purring, or of
looking in that manner. It reminds us of the sort of
smile, or *simmer* (*simper* is too weak and fleeting a word)
that is apt to be in the faces of irritable people, when
they are pleased to be in a state of satisfaction. We
prefer, for a general expression, the cat in a quiet unpretending state, and the human countenance with a
look indicative of habitual grace and composure, as if it
were not necessary to take any violent steps to prove
its amiability,—the ' smile without a smile,' as the poet
beautifully calls it.[1]

Furthermore (in order to get rid at once of all that
may be objected to poor Pussy, as boys at school get
down their bad dumpling as fast as possible, before the
meat comes) we own we have an objection to the way
in which a cat sports with a mouse before she kills it,
tossing and jerking it about like a ball, and letting it go,
in order to pounce upon it with the greater relish. And
yet what right have we to apply human measures of
cruelty to the inferior reflectability of a cat ? Perhaps
she has no idea of the mouse's being alive, in the sense
that we have,—most likely she looks upon it as a
pleasant movable toy, made to be eaten,—a sort of
lively pudding, that oddly jumps hither and thither.
It would be hard to beat into the head of a country
squire, of the old class, that there is any cruelty in hunt-
ing a hare ; and most assuredly it would be still harder
to beat mouse-sparing into the head of a cat. You
might read the most pungent essay on the subject into
her ear, and she would only sneeze at it.

[1] Knowles, in *The Beggar of Bethnal Green*.

As to the unnatural cruelties, which we sometimes read of, committed by cats upon their offspring, they are exceptions to the common and beautiful rules of nature, and accordingly we have nothing to do with them. They are traceable to some unnatural circumstances of breeding or position. Enormities as monstrous are to be found among human beings, and argue nothing against the general character of the species. Even dogs are not always immaculate; and sages have made slips. Dr. Franklin cut off his son with a shilling, for differing with him in politics,

But cats resemble tigers? They are tigers in miniature? Well,—and very pretty miniatures they are. And what has the tiger himself done, that he has not a right to his dinner, as well as Jones? A tiger treats a man much as a cat does a mouse;—granted; but we have no reason to suppose that he is aware of the man's sufferings, or means anything but to satisfy his hunger; and what have the butcher and poulterer been about meanwhile? The tiger it is true, lays about him a little superfluously sometimes, when he gets into a sheepfold, and kills more than he eats; but does not the Squire or the Marquis do pretty much like him in the month of September? Nay, do we not hear of venerable judges, that would not hurt a fly, going about in that refreshing month, seeking whom they may lame? See the effect of habit and education! And you can educate the tiger in no other way than by attending to his stomach. Fill that, and he will want no men to eat, probably not even to lame. On the other hand, deprive Jones of his dinner for a day or two, and see what a state he will be in, especially if he is by nature irascible. Nay, keep him from it for half an hour, and observe the tiger propensities of his stomach and fingers,—how worthy of killing he thinks the cook, and what boxes of the ear he feels inclined to give the footboy.

Animals, by the nature of things, in their present state, dispose of one another into their respective stomachs, without any ill-will on any side. They keep down the several populations of their neighbours, till the time may come when superfluous population of any kind need not exist, and predatory appearances may vanish from the earth, as the wolves have done from England. But whether they may or not, is not a question by a hundred times so important to moral inquirers as into the possibilities of human education and the nonsense of ill-will. Show the nonsensity of that, and we may all get our dinners as jovially as we can, sure of these three undoubted facts,—that life is long, death short, and the world beautiful. And so we bring our thoughts back again to the fireside, and look at the cat.

Poor Pussy! she looks up at us again, as if she thanked us for those vindications of dinner; and symbolically gives a twist of a yawn, and a lick to her whiskers. Now she proceeds to clean herself all over, having a just sense of the demands of her elegant person,—beginning judiciously with her paws, and fetching amazing tongues at her hind-hips. Anon, she scratches her neck with a foot of rapid delight, leaning her head towards it, and shutting her eyes, half to accommodate the action of the skin, and half to enjoy the luxury. She then rewards her paws with a few more touches;—look at the action of her head and neck, how pleasing it is, the ears pointed forward, and the neck gently arching to and fro. Finally she gives a sneeze, and another twist of mouth and whiskers, and then, curling her tail towards her front claws, settles herself on her hind quarters, in an attitude of bland meditation.

What does she think of?—Of her saucer of milk at breakfast? or of the thump she got yesterday in the kitchen, for stealing the meat? or of her own meat, the Tartar's dish, noble horse-flesh? or of her friend the cat next door, the most impassioned of serenaders? or of her little ones, some of whom are now large, and all of them gone? Is *that* among her recollections when she looks pensive? Does she taste of the noble prerogative sorrows of man?

She is a sprightly cat, hardly past her youth; so happening to move the fringe of the rug a little with our foot, she darts out a paw, and begins plucking it and inquiring into the matter, as if it were a challenge to play, or something lively enough to be eaten. What a graceful action of that foot of hers, between delicacy and petulance,—combining something of a thrust out, a beat, and a scratch. There seems even something of a little bit of fear in it, as if just enough to provoke her courage, and give her the excitement of a sense of hazard. We remember being much amused with seeing a kitten manifestly making a series of experiments upon the patience of its mother,—trying how far the latter would put up with positive bites and thumps. The kitten ran at her every moment, gave her a knock or a bite of the tail; and then ran back again, to recommence the assault. The mother sat looking at her, as if betwixt tolerance and admiration, to see how far the spirit of the family was inherited or improved by her sprightly offspring. At length, however, the 'little Pickle' presumed too far, and the mother, lifting up her paw, and meeting her at the very nick of the moment, gave her one of the most unsophisticated boxes of the ear we ever beheld. It sent her rolling half over the room, and made her come to a most ludicrous pause, with the oddest little look of premature and wincing meditation.

That lapping of the milk out of the saucer is what one's human thirst cannot sympathize with. It seems as if there could be no satisfaction in such a series of atoms of drink. Yet the saucer is soon emptied; and there is a refreshment to one's ears in that sound of plashing with which the action is accompanied, and which seems indicative of a like comfort to Pussy's mouth. Her tongue is thin, and can make a spoon of itself. This, however, is common to other quadrupeds with the cat, and does not, therefore, more particularly belong to our feline consideration. Not so the electricity of its coat which gives out sparks under the hand; its passion for the herb valerian (did the reader ever see one roll in it? it is a mad sight) and other singular delicacies of nature, among which perhaps is to be reckoned its taste for fish, a creature with whose element it has so little to do, that it is supposed even to abhor it; though lately we read somewhere of a swimming cat, that used to fish for itself. And this reminds us of an exquisite anecdote of dear, dogmatic, diseased, thoughtful, surly, charitable Johnson, who would go out of doors himself, and buy oysters for his cat, because his black servant was too proud to do it! Not that we condemn the black, in those enslaving, unliberating days. He had a right to the mistake, though we should have thought better of him had he seen farther, and subjected his pride to affection for such a master. But Johnson's true practical delicacy in the matter is beautiful. Be assured that he thought nothing of 'condescension' in it, or of being eccentric. He was singular in some things, because he could not help it. But he hated eccentricity. No: in his best moments he felt himself simply to be a man, and a good man too, though a frail,—one that in virtue as well as humility, and in a knowledge of his ignorance as well as his wisdom, was desirous of being a Christian philosopher; and accordingly he went out, and bought food for his hungry cat, because his poor negro was too proud to do it, and there was nobody else in the way whom he had a right to ask. What must anybody that saw him thought, as he turned up Bolt Court! But doubtless he went as secretly as possible,—that is to say if he considered the thing at all. His friend Garrick could not have done as much! He was too grand, on the great 'stage' of life. Goldsmith could; but he would hardly have thought of it. Beauclerc might; but he would have thought it necessary to excuse it with a jest or a wager, or some such thing. Sir Joshua Reynolds, with his fashionable, fine-lady-painting hand, would certainly have shrunk from it. Burke would have reasoned himself into its propriety, but he would have reasoned himself out again. Gibbon! Imagine its being put into the head of Gibbon!! He and his bag-wig would have started with all the horror of a gentleman-usher; and he would have rung the bell for the cook's-deputy's-under-assistant-errand-boy.

Cats at firesides live luxuriously, and are the picture of comfort ; but lest they should not bear their portion of trouble in this world, they have the drawbacks of being liable to be shut out of doors on cold nights, beatings from the 'aggravated' cooks, over-pettings of children (how should we like to be squeezed and pulled about in that manner by some great patronizing giants ?), and last, not least, horrible, merciless tramples of unconscious human feet and unfeeling legs of chairs. Elegance, comfort, and security seem the order of the day on all sides, and you are going to sit down to dinner, or to music, or to take tea, when all of a sudden the cat gives a squall as if she was mashed ; and you are not sure that the fact is otherwise. Yet she gets in the way again, as before ; and dares all the feet and mahogany in the room. Beautiful present sufficingness of a cat's imagination ! Confined to the snug circle of her own sides, and the two next inches of rug or carpet.

TEA-DRINKING

[From essays on 'Breakfasts,' *London Journal,* July 9, 1834]

WE allude to China and the Chinese. The very word *tea,* so petty, so infantine, so winking-eyed, so expressive somehow or other of something inexpressibly minute, and satisfied with a little (*tee !*), resembles the idea one has (perhaps a very mistaken one) of that extraordinary people, of whom Europeans know little or nothing, except that they sell us this preparation, bow back again our ambassadors, have a language consisting only of a few hundred words, gave us *China*-ware and the strange pictures on our tea-cups, made a certain progress in civilization long before we did, mysteriously stopped at it and would go no further, and if numbers, and the customs of 'venerable ancestors' are to carry the day, are at once the most populous and the most respectable nation on the face of the earth. As a population they certainly are a most enormous and wonderful body; but as individuals, their ceremonies, their trifling edicts, their jealousy of foreigners, and their tea-cup representations of themselves (which are the only ones popularly known) impress us irresistibly with a fancy, that they are a people all toddling, little-eyed, little-footed, little-bearded, little-minded, quaint, overweening, pig-tailed, bald-headed, cone-capped or pagoda-hatted, having childish houses and temples with bells at every corner and story, and shuffling about in blue landscapes, over 'nine-inch bridges,' with little mysteries of bell-hung whips in their hands,—a boat, or a house, or a tree made of a pattern, being over their heads or underneath them (as the case may happen), and a bird, as large as the boat, always having a circular white space to fly in. Such are the Chinese of the tea-cups and the grocers' windows, and partly of their own novels too, in which everything seems as little as their eyes,—little odes, little wine-parties, and a series of little satisfactions. However, it must be owned, that from these novels one gradually acquires a notion that there is a great deal more good sense and even good poetry among them, than one had fancied from the accounts of embassies and the autobiographical paintings on the China-ware; and this is the most probable supposition. An ancient and great nation, as civilized as they, is not likely to be so much behindhand with us in the art of living as our self-complacency leads us to imagine. If their contempt of us amounts to the barbarous, perhaps there is a greater share of barbarism than we suspect in our scorn of them.

SLEEP

[Indicator, Jan. 12, 1820]

THIS is an article for the reader to think of, when he
or she is warm in bed a little before he goes to sleep,
the clothes at his ear, and the wind moaning in some
distant crevice.

'Blessings,' exclaimed Sancho, ' on him that first
invented sleep ! It wraps a man all round like a cloak.'
It is a delicious moment certainly,—that of being well
nestled in bed,—and feeling that you shall drop gently to
sleep. The good is to come, not past : the limbs have
been just tired enough to render the remaining in one
posture delightful : the labour of the day is done. A
gentle failure of the perceptions comes creeping over
one :—the spirit of consciousness disengages itself more
and more, with slow and hushing degrees, like a mother
detaching her hand from that of her sleeping child ;—
the mind seems to have a balmy lid closing over it, like
the eye :—'tis closing ;—'tis more closing ;—'tis closed.
The mysterious spirit has gone to take its airy rounds.

It is said that sleep is best before midnight : and
Nature herself, with her darkness and chilling dews,
informs us so. There is another reason for going to bed
betimes : for it is universally acknowledged that lying
late in the morning is a great shortener of life. At
least, it is never found in company with longevity. It
also tends to make people corpulent. But these
matters belong rather to the subject of early rising,
than of sleep.

Sleep at a late hour in the morning is not half so
pleasant as the more timely one. It is sometimes, however, excusable, especially to a watchful or over-
worked head ; neither can we deny the seducing merits
of ' t' other doze,'—the pleasing wilfulness of nestling
in a new posture, when you know you ought to be up,
like the rest of the house. But then you cut up the
day and your sleep the next night.

In the course of the day, few people think of sleeping, except after dinner; and then it is often rather a hovering and nodding on the borders of sleep, than a sleep itself. This is a privilege allowable, we think, to none but the old, or the sickly, or the very tired and careworn; and it should be well understood, before it is exercised in company. To escape into slumber from an argument; or to take it as an affair of course, only between you and your biliary duct; or to assent with involuntary nods to all that you have just been disputing; is not so well: much less, to sit nodding and tottering beside a lady; or to be in danger of dropping your head into the fruit-plate or your host's face; or of waking up and saying ' Just so ' to the bark of a dog, or ' Yes, madam ' to the black at your elbow.

Careworn people, however, might refresh themselves oftener with day-sleep than they do; if their bodily state is such as to dispose them to it. It is a mistake to suppose that all care is wakeful. People sometimes sleep, as well as wake, by reason of their sorrow. The difference seems to depend upon the nature of their temperament; though in the *most* excessive cases, sleep is perhaps Nature's never-failing remedy, as swooning is upon the rack. A person with jaundice in his blood shall lie down and go to sleep at noon-day, when another of a different complexion shall find his eyes as uncloseable as a statue's, though he has had no sleep for nights together. Without meaning to lessen the dignity of suffering, which has quite enough to do with its waking hours, it is this that may often account for the profound sleeps enjoyed the night before hazardous battles, executions, and other demands upon an over-excited spirit.

The most complete and healthy sleep that can be taken in the day, is in summer-time, out in a field. There is perhaps no solitary sensation so exquisite as that of slumbering on the grass or hay, shaded from the hot sun by a tree, with the consciousness of a fresh but light air running through the wide atmosphere, and the sky stretching far overhead upon all sides. Earth, and heaven, and a placid humanity, seem to have the creation to themselves. There is nothing between the slumberer and the naked and glad innocence of Nature.

Next to this, but at a long interval, the most relishing snatch of slumber out of bed is the one which a tired person takes before he retires for the night, while lingering in his sitting-room. The consciousness of being very sleepy and of having the power to go to bed immediately, gives great zest to the unwillingness to move. Sometimes he sits nodding in his chair; but the sudden and leaden jerks of the head to which a state of great sleepiness renders him liable, are generally too painful for so luxurious a moment; and he gets into a more legitimate posture, sitting sideways with his head on the chair-back, or throwing his legs up at once on another chair, and half reclining. It is curious however to find how long an inconvenient posture will be borne for the sake of this foretaste of repose. The worst of it is, that on going to bed the charm sometimes vanishes; perhaps from the colder temperature of the chamber; for a fireside is a great opiate.

Speaking of the painful positions into which a sleepy lounger will get himself, it is amusing to think of the more fantastic attitudes that so often take place in bed. If we could add anything to the numberless things that have been said about sleep by the poets, it would be upon this point. Sleep never shows himself a greater leveller. A man in his waking moments may look as proud and self-possessed as he pleases. He may walk proudly, he may sit proudly, he may eat his dinner proudly; he may shave himself with an air of infinite superiority; in a word, he may show himself grand and absurd upon the most trifling occasions. But Sleep plays the petrifying magician. He arrests the proudest lord as well as the humblest clown in the most ridiculous postures: so that if you could draw a grandee from his bed without waking him, no limb-twisting fool in a pantomime should create wilder laughter. The toy with the string between its legs is hardly a posture-master more extravagant. Imagine a despot lifted up

to the gaze of his valets, with his eyes shut, his mouth
open, his left hand under his right ear, his other twisted
and hanging helplessly before him like an idiot's, one
knee lifted up, and the other leg stretched out, or both
knees huddled up together ; what a scarecrow to lodge
majestic power in !

But Sleep is kindly, even in his tricks ; and the poets
have treated him with proper reverence. According
to the ancient mythologists, he had even one of the
Graces to wife. He had a thousand sons, of whom
the chief were Morpheus, or the Shaper ; Icelos, or the
Likely ; Phantasus, the Fancy ; and Phobetor, the
Terror. His dwelling some writers place in a dull and
darkling part of the earth ; others, with greater compliment, in heaven ; and others, with another kind of
propriety, by the sea-shore. There is a good description of it in Ovid ; but in these abstracted tasks of
poetry the moderns outvie the ancients ; and there is
nobody who has built his bower for him so finely as
Spenser. Archimago in the first book of the *Faery
Queene* (Canto 1, st. 39) sends a little spirit down to
Morpheus to fetch him a dream.

> He, making speedy way through spersed ayre,
> And through the world of waters, wide and deepe,
> To Morpheus' house doth hastily repaire.
> Amid the bowels of the earth full steepe,
> And low, where dawning day doth never peepe,
> His dwelling is. There, Tethys his wet bed
> Doth ever wash ; and Cynthia still doth steepe
> In silver dew his ever-drouping hed,
> Whiles sad Night over him her mantle black doth
>   spred.
>
> And more to lulle him in his slumber soft
> A trickling streame from high rocke tumbling downe,
> And ever-dringling raine upon the loft,
> Mixt with a murmuring winde, much like the soune
> Of swarming bees, did cast him in a swoune.
> No other noise, nor people's troublous cryes,

As still are wont to annoy the walled towne,
Might there be heard, but carelesse Quiet lyes,
Wrapt in eternall silence, farre from enimyes.

Chaucer has drawn the cave of the same god with
greater simplicity ; but nothing can have a more deep
and sullen effect than his cliffs and cold-running waters. It
seems as real as an actual solitude, or some quaint old
picture in a book of travels in Tartary. He is telling
the story of Ceyx and Alcyone in the poem called his
Dream.   Juno tells a messenger to go to Morpheus and
' bid him creep into the body' of the drowned king,
to let his wife know the fatal event by his apparition.

This messenger tooke leave, and went
Upon his way ; and never he stent
Till he came to the dark valley,
That stant betweene rockes twey.
There never yet grew corne, ne gras,
Ne tree, ne nought that aught was,
Beast, ne man, ne naught else ;
Save that there were a few wells
Came running fro the cliffs adowne,
That made a deadly sleeping soune,
And runnen downe right by a cave,
That was under a rocke ygrave,
Amid the valley, wonder-deepe.
There these goddis lay asleepe,
Morpheus and Eclympasteire,
That was the god of Sleepis heire,
That slept and did none other worke.

Where the credentials of this new son and heir, Eclympasteire, are to be found, we know not ; but he acts
very much, it must be allowed, like an heir presumptive,
in sleeping, and doing 'none other work.'

We dare not trust ourselves with many quotations
upon sleep from the poets ; they are so numerous as well
as beautiful. We must content ourselves with men-
tioning that our two most favourite passages are one in
the *Philoctetes* of Sophocles, admirable for its contrast to

a scene of terrible agony, which it closes; and the
other the following address in Beaumont and Fletcher's
tragedy of *Valentinian*, the hero of which is also a
sufferer under bodily torment. He is in a chair,
slumbering; and these most exquisite lines are gently
sung with music.

> Care-charming Sleep, thou easer of all woes,
> Brother to Death, sweetly thyself dispose
> On this afflicted prince. Fall like a cloud
> In gentle showers: give nothing that is loud
> Or painful to his slumbers: easy, light,
> And as a purling stream, thou son of Night,
> Pass by his troubled senses: sing his pain
> Like hollow murmuring wind, or silver rain
> Into this prince, gently, oh gently slide;
> And kiss him into slumbers, like a bride.

How earnest and prayer-like are these pauses! How
lightly sprinkled, and yet how deeply settling, like rain,
the fancy! How quiet, affectionate, and perfect the
conclusion!

Sleep is most graceful in an infant; soundest, in
one who has been tired in the open air; completest,
to the seaman after a hard voyage; most welcome, to
the mind haunted with one idea; most touching to
look at, in the parent that has wept; lightest, in the
playful child; proudest, in the bride adored.

GETTING UP ON COLD MORNINGS

[*Indicator*, Jan. 19, 1820]

An Italian author,—Giulio Cordara, a Jesuit,—has written a poem upon insects, which he begins by insisting, that those troublesome and abominable little animals were created for our annoyance, and that they were certainly not inhabitants of Paradise. We of the North may dispute this piece of theology; but on the other hand, it is as clear as the snow on the house-tops, that Adam was not under the necessity of shaving; and that when Eve walked out of her delicious bower, she did not step upon ice three inches thick.

Some people say it is a very easy thing to get up of a cold morning. You have only, they tell you, to take the resolution; and the thing is done. This may be very true; just as a boy at school has only to take a flogging, and the thing is over. But we have not at all made up our minds upon it; and we find it a very pleasant exercise to discuss the matter, candidly, before we get up. This at least is not idling, though it may be lying. It affords an excellent answer to those who ask how lying in bed can be indulged in by a reasoning being,—a rational creature. How? Why with the argument calmly at work in one's head, and the clothes over one's shoulder. Oh—it is a fine way of spending a sensible, impartial half-hour.

If these people would be more charitable, they would get on with their argument better. But they are apt to reason so ill, and to assert so dogmatically, that one could wish to have them stand round one's bed of a bitter morning, and lie before their faces. They ought to hear both sides of the bed, the inside and out. If they cannot entertain themselves with their own thoughts for half an hour or so, it is not the fault of those who can. If their will is never pulled aside by the enticing arms of imagination, so much the luckier for the stage-coachman.

Candid inquirers into one's recumbency, besides the
greater or less privileges to be allowed a man in proportion to his ability of keeping early hours, the work given
his faculties, &c., will at least concede their due merits
to such representations as the following. In the first
place, says the injured but calm appealer, I have been
warm all night, and find my system in a state perfectly
suitable to a warm-blooded animal. To get out of this
state into the cold, besides the inharmonious and uncritical abruptness of the transition, is so unnatural to
such a creature, that the poets, refining upon the tortures of the damned, make one of their greatest agonies
consist in being suddenly transported from heat to
cold,—from fire to ice. They are ' haled ' out of their
' beds,' says Milton, by ' harpy-footed furies,'—fellows
who come to call them.—On my first movement towards
the anticipation of getting up, I find that such parts of
the sheets and bolster as are exposed to the air of the
room are stone cold. On opening my eyes, the first
thing that meets them is my own breath rolling forth,
as if in the open air, like smoke out of a cottage-
chimney. Think of this symptom. Then I turn my
eyes sideways and see the windows all frozen over.
Think of that. Then the servant comes in. ' It is
very cold this morning, is it not ?'—'Very cold, sir.'—
' Very cold indeed, isn't it ? '—' Very cold indeed,
sir.'—' More than usually so, isn't it, even for this
weather ?' (Here the servant's wit and good nature
are put to a considerable test, and the inquirer lies on
thorns for the answer.) ' Why, sir——I think it is.'
(Good creature ! There is not a better or more truth-
telling servant going.) ' I must rise, however—Get me
some warm water.'—Here comes a fine interval between the departure of the servant and the arrival of
the hot water ; during which, of course, it is of ' no
use ' to get up. The hot water comes. ' Is it quite
hot ? '—' Yes, sir.'—' Perhaps too hot for shaving : I
must wait a little ? '—' No, sir ; it will just do.'
(There is an over-nice propriety sometimes, an officious
zeal of virtue, a little troublesome.) ' Oh—the shirt—

you must air my clean shirt:—linen gets very damp this weather.'—'Yes, sir.' Here another delicious five minutes. A knock at the door. 'Oh, the shirt—very well. My stockings—I think the stockings had better be aired too.'—'Very well, sir.'—Here another interval. At length everything is ready, except myself. I now, continues our incumbent (a happy word, by the by, for a country vicar)—I now cannot help thinking a good deal—who can?—upon the unnecessary and villainous custom of shaving: it is a thing so unmanly (here I nestle closer)—so effeminate (here I recoil from an unlucky step into the colder part of the bed).— No wonder that the Queen of France took part with the rebels against that degenerate King, her husband, who first affronted her smooth visage with a face like her own. The Emperor Julian never showed the luxuriance of his genius to better advantage than in reviving the flowing beard. Look at Cardinal Bembo's picture—at Michael Angelo's—at Titian's—at Shakespeare's—at Fletcher's —at Spenser's—at Chaucer's—at Alfred's—at Plato's. I could name a great man for every tick of my watch. Look at the Turks, a grave and otiose people.— Think of Haroun Al Raschid and Bed-ridden Hassan.— Think of Wortley Montague, the worthy son of his mother, a man above the prejudice of his time.—Look at the Persian gentlemen, whom one is ashamed of meeting about the suburbs, their dress and appearance are so much finer than our own.—Lastly, think of the razor itself—how totally opposed to every sensation of bed—how cold, how edgy, how hard! how utterly different from anything like the warm and circling amplitude, which

> Sweetly recommends itself
> Unto our gentle senses.

Add to this, benumbed fingers, which may help you to cut yourself, a quivering body, a frozen towel, and an ewer full of ice; and he that says there is nothing to oppose in all this, only shows, at any rate, that he has no merit in opposing it.

Thomson, the poet, who exclaims in his *Seasons*—

Falsely luxurious! Will not man awake?

used to lie in bed till noon, because he said he had no
motive in getting up. He could imagine the good of
rising; but then he could also imagine the good of lying
still; and his exclamation, it must be allowed, was
made upon summer-time, not winter. We must proportion the argument to the individual character. A
money-getter may be drawn out of his bed by three
and fourpence; but this will not suffice for a student.
A proud man may say 'What shall I think of myself,
it I don't get up?' but the more humble one will be
content to waive this prodigious notion of himself, out
of respect to his kindly bed. The mechanical man
shall get up without any ado at all; and so shall the
barometer. An ingenious lier in bed will find hard
matter of discussion even on the score of health and
longevity. He will ask us for our proofs and precedents
of the ill effects of lying later in cold weather; and
sophisticate much on the advantages of an even temperature of body; of the natural propensity (pretty
universal) to have one's way; and of the animals that
roll themselves up, and sleep all the winter. As to
longevity, he will ask whether the longest life is of
necessity the best; and whether Holborn is the handsomest street in London.

We only know of one confounding, not to say confounded argument, fit to overturn the huge luxury,
the 'enormous bliss'—of the vice in question. A lier
in bed may be allowed to profess a disinterested indifference for his health or longevity; but while he is
showing the reasonableness of consulting his own, or
one person's comfort, he must admit the proportionate
claim of more than one; and the best way to deal with
him is this, especially for a lady; for we earnestly
recommend the use of that sex on such occasions, if not
somewhat *over*-persuasive; since extremes have an
awkward knack of meeting. First then, admit all the
ingeniousness of what he says, telling him that the bar

has been deprived of an excellent lawyer. Then look at him in the most good-natured manner in the world, with a mixture of assent and appeal in your countenance, and tell him that you are waiting breakfast for him; that you never like to breakfast without him; that you really want it too; that the servants want theirs; that you shall not know how to get the house into order, unless he rises; and that you are sure he would do things twenty times worse, even than getting out of his warm bed, to put them all into good humour and a state of comfort. Then, after having said this, throw in the comparatively indifferent matter, to *him*, about his health; but tell him that it is no indifferent matter to you; that the sight of his illness makes more people suffer than one; but that if nevertheless he really does feel so very sleepy and so very much refreshed by——Yet stay; we hardly know whether the frailty of a——Yes, yes; say that too, especially if you say it with sincerity; for if the weakness of human nature on the one hand, and the *vis inertiæ* on the other, should lead him to take advantage of it once or twice, good-humour and sincerity form an irresistible junction at last; and are still better and warmer things than pillows and blankets.

Other little helps of appeal may be thrown in, as occasion requires. You may tell a lover, for instance, that lying in bed makes people corpulent; a father, that you wish him to complete the fine manly example he sets his children; a lady, that she will injure her bloom or her shape, which M. or W. admires so much; and a student or artist, that he is always so glad to have done a good day's work in his best manner.

READER. And pray, Mr. Indicator, how do *you* behave yourself in this respect?

INDICATOR. Oh, madam, perfectly, of course; like all advisers.

READER. Nay, I allow that your mode of argument does not look quite so suspicious as the old way of sermonizing and severity, but I have my doubts, especially from that laugh of yours. If I should look in to-morrow morning——

INDICATOR. Ah, madam, the look in of a face like yours does anything with me. It shall fetch me up at nine, if you please——*six*, I meant to say.

CHRISTMAS

[*Monthly Repository*, December, 1837]

So many things have been said of late years about Christmas, that it is supposed by some there is no saying more. Oh they of little faith ! What ? do they suppose that everything has been said that *can* be said, about any one Christmas thing ?

About beef, for instance ?

About plum-pudding ?

About mince-pie ?

About holly ?

About ivy ?

About rosemary ?

About mistletoe ? (Good God ! what an immense number of things remain to be said about mistletoe ?)

About Christmas-eve ?

About hunt-the-slipper ?

About hot-cockles ?

About blind-man's-buff ?

About shoeing the wild mare ?

About thread-the-needle ?

About he-can-do-little-that-can't-do-this ?

About puss-in-the-corner ?

About snapdragon ?

About forfeits ?

About Miss Smith ?

About the bellman ?

About the waits ?

About chilblains ?

About carols ?

About the fire ?

About the block on it ?
About schoolboys ?
About their mothers ?
About Christmas-boxes ?
About turkeys ?
About Hogmanay ?
About goose-pie ?
About mumming ?
About saluting the apple-trees ?
About brawn ?
About plum-porridge ?
About hobby-horse ?
About hoppings ?
About wakes ?
About 'Feed-the-dove' ?
About hackins ?
About yule-doughs ?
About going-a-gooding ?
About loaf-stealing ?
About *julklaps* ? (Who has exhausted that subject, we should like to know ?)
About wad-shooting ?
About elder-wine ?
About pantomimes ?
About cards ?
About New-Year's day ?
About gifts ?
About wassail ?
About twelfth-cake ?
About king and queen ?
About characters ?
About eating too much ?
About aldermen ?
About the doctor ?
About all being in the wrong ?
About Charity ?
About all being in the right ?
About Faith, Hope, and Endeavour ?
About the Greatest Plum-pudding for the Greatest Number ?

Esto perpetua ; that is, Faith, Hope, and Charity, and Endeavour ; and plum-pudding enough, by and by, all the year round, for everybody that likes it. Why that should not be the case, we cannot see,—seeing that the earth is big, and human kind teachable, and God very good, and inciting us to do it. Meantime, gravity apart, we ask anybody whether any of the above subjects are exhausted ; and we inform everybody, that all the above customs still exist in some parts of our beloved country, however unintelligible they may have become in others.—But to give a specimen of the non-exhaustion of any one of their topics.

Beef, for example. Now we should like to know who has exhausted the subject of the fine old roast Christmas piece of beef,—from its original appearance in the meadows as part of the noble sultan of the herd, glorious old Taurus, the lord of the sturdy brow and ponderous agility, a sort of thunderbolt of a beast, well chosen by Jove to disguise in, one of Nature's most striking compounds of apparent heaviness and unencumbered activity,—up to its contribution to the noble Christmas dinner, smoking from the spit, and flanked by the outposts of Bacchus. John Bull (cannibalism apart) hails it like a sort of relation. He makes it part of his flesh and blood ; glories in it ; was named after it ; has it served up, on solemn occasions, with music and a hymn, as it was the other day at the royal city dinner :—

> Oh ! the roast beef of old England ;
> And oh ! the old English roast beef.

' *And* oh ! ' observe ; not merely ' oh ! ' again ; but ' and ' with it ; as if, though the same piece of beef, it were also another ;—another and the same ;—cut, and come again ;—making two of one, in order to express intensity and reduplication of satisfaction :—

> Oh ! the roast beef of old England ;
> *And* oh ! the old English roast beef.

We beg to assure the reader, that a whole essay might be written on this single point of the Christmas dinner ;

and 'shall we be told' (as orators exclaim) 'and this
too in a British land,' that the subject is '*exhausted*'!

Then plum-pudding! What a word is that! how
plump, and plump again! How round, and repeated, and
plenipotential! (There are two *p's*, observe, in plenipotential, and so there are in plum-pudding. We love
an exquisite fitness,—a might and wealth of adaptation.)
Why, the whole round cheek of universal childhood
is in the idea of plum-pudding; aye, and the weight of
manhood, and the plenitude of the majesty of city
dames. Wealth itself is symbolized by the least of its
fruity particles. 'A plum' is a city fortune,—a
million of money. He (the old boy, who has earned it)

> Puts in his thumb,

videlicet, into his pocket,

> And pulls out a plum,
> And says what a '*good man*' am I.

Observe a little boy at a Christmas dinner, and his
grandfather opposite him. What a world of secret
similarity there is between them. How hope in one,
and retrospection in the other, and appetite in both,
meet over the same ground of pudding, and understand
it to a nicety. How the senior banters the little boy
on his third slice; and how the little boy thinks within
himself that he dines that day as well as the senior.
How both look hot, and red, and smiling, and juvenile.
How the little boy is conscious of the Christmas-box
in his pocket (of which indeed the grandfather jocosely
puts him in mind); and how the grandfather is quite
as conscious of the plum, or part of a plum, or whatever fraction it may be, in his own. How he incites
the little boy to love money and good dinners all his
life; and how determined the little boy is to abide by
his advice,—with a secret addition in favour of holidays
and marbles,—to which there is an analogy, in the
senior's mind, on the side of trips to Hastings, and a
game at whist. Finally, the old gentleman sees his
own face in the pretty smooth one of the child; and if

the child is not best pleased at his proclamation of the likeness (in truth, is horrified at it, and thinks it a sort of madness), yet nice observers, who have lived long enough to see the wonderful changes in people's faces from youth to age, probably discern the thing well enough; and feel a movement of pathos at their hearts, in considering the world of trouble and emotion that is the causer of the changes. *That* old man's face was once like that little boy's! *That* little boy's will be one day like that old man's! What a thought to make us all love and respect one another, if not for our fine qualities, yet, at least, for the trouble and sorrow which we all go through!

Aye, and joy too! for all people have their joys as well as troubles, at one time or another; most likely both together, or in constant alternation; and the greater part of troubles are not the worst things in the world, but only graver forms of the requisite motion of the universe, or workings towards a better condition of things, the greater or less violent according as we give them violence for violence, or respect them like awful but not ill-meaning gods, and entertain them with a rewarded patience.—Grave thoughts, you will say, for Christmas. But no season has a greater right to grave thoughts, in passing; and for that very reason, no season has a greater right to let them pass, and recur to more light ones.

So a noble and merry season to you, my masters; and may we meet, thick and threefold, many a time and oft in blithe yet most thoughtful pages. Fail not to call to mind, in the course of the 25th of this month, that the Divinest Heart that ever walked the earth was born on that day, and then smile and enjoy yourselves for the rest of it, for mirth is also of Heaven's making, and wondrous was the wine-drinking at Galilee.

OF DRESS AND MANNERS

HATS, ANCIENT AND MODERN

[*Indicator*, March 8, 1820]

WE know not what will be thought of our taste in so important a matter, but we must confess we are not fond of a new hat. There is a certain insolence about it : it seems to value itself upon its finished appearance, and to presume upon our liking before we are acquainted with it. In the first place, it comes home more like a marmot or some other living creature, than a manufacture. It is boxed up, and wrapt in silver paper, and brought delicately. It is as sleek as a lap-dog. Then we are to take it out as nicely, and people are to wonder how we shall look in it. Maria twitches one this way, and Sophia that, and Caroline that, and Catharine t'other. We have the difficult task, all the while, of looking easy, till the approving votes are pronounced : our only resource (which is also difficult) is to say good things to all four ; or to clap the hat upon each of their heads, and see what pretty milk-women they make. At last the approving votes are pronounced ; and (provided it is fine) we may go forth. But how uneasy the sensation about the head ! How unlike the old hat, to which we had become used, and which must now make way for this fop of a stranger ! We might do what we liked with the former. Dust, rain, a gale of wind, a fall, a squeeze,—nothing affected it. It was a true friend, a friend for all weathers. Its appearance only was against it : in everything else it was the better for wear. But if the roads or the streets are too dry, the new hat is afraid of getting dusty : if there is wind, and it is not tight, it may be blown off into the dirt : we may have to scramble after it through dust or mud ; just reaching it with our fingers, only to see it blown away

again. And if rain comes on! Oh, ye gallant
apprentices, who have issued forth on a Sunday
morning, with Jane or Susan, careless either of storms
at nightfall, or toils and scoldings next day! Ye, who
have received your new hat and boots but an hour
before ye set out; and then issue forth triumphantly,
the charmer by your side! She, with arm in yours, and
handkerchief in hand, blushing, or eating gingerbread,
trips on: ye, admiring, trudge: we ask ye, whether
love itself has prevented ye from feeling a certain fearful
consciousness of that crowning glory, the new and glossy
hat, when the first drops of rain announce the coming
of a shower? Ah, hasten, while yet it is of use to haste;
ere yet the spotty horror fixes on the nap! Out with
the protecting handkerchief, which tied round the hat,
and flowing off in a corner behind, shall gleam through
the thickening night like a suburb comet! Trust not
the tempting yawn of stable-yard or gateway, or the
impossible notion of a coach! The rain will continue;
and alas! ye are not so rich as in the morning. Hasten!
or think of a new hat's becoming a rainspout! Think
of its well-built crown, its graceful and well-measured
fit, the curved-up elegance of its rim, its shadowing
gentility when seen in front, its arching grace over the
ear when beheld sideways! Think of it also the next
day! How altered, how dejected!

How changed from him
That life of measure, and that soul of rim!

Think of the paper-like change of its consistence; of
its limp sadness,—its confused and flattened nap, and
of that polished and perfect circle, which neither brush
nor hot iron shall restore!

We have here spoken of the beauties of a new hat;
but, abstractedly considered, they are very proble-
matical. Fashion makes beauty for a time. Our ancestors found a grace in the cocked hats now confined
to beadles, Chelsea Pensioners, and coachmen. They
would have laughed at our chimney-tops with a border;
though upon the whole we do think them the more

graceful of the two. The best modern covering for the
head was the imitation of the broad Spanish hat in use
about thirty years back, when Mr. Stothard made his
designs for the *Novelist's Magazine*. But in proportion
as Society has been put into a bustle, our hats seem
to have narrowed their dimensions: the flaps were
clipped off more and more till they became a rim; and
now the rim has contracted to a mere nothing; so that
what with our close heads and our tight succinct mode
of dress, we look as if we were intended for nothing but
to dart backwards and forwards on matters of business,
with as little hindrance to each other as possible.

This may give us a greater distaste to the hat than
it deserves; but good-looking or not, we know of no
situation in which a new one can be said to be useful.
We have seen how the case is during bad weather: but
if the weather is in the finest condition possible, with
neither rain nor dust, there may be a hot sunshine; and
then the hat is too narrow to shade us: no great evil,
it is true! but we must have our pique out against the
knave, and turn him to the only account in our power:
—we must write upon him. For every other purpose,
we hold him as naught. The only place a new hat can
be carried into with safety, is a church; for there is
plenty of room there. There also takes place its only
union of the ornamental with the useful, if so it is to
be called:—we allude to the preparatory ejaculation
whispered into it by the genteel worshipper, before he
turns round and makes a bow to Mr. and Mrs. Jones and
the Miss Thompsons. There is a formula for this occasion; and doubtless it is often used, to say nothing of
extempore effusions:—but there are wicked imaginations, who suspect that instead of devouter whisperings,
the communer with his lining sometimes ejaculates no
more than Swallow, St. James's Street; or, Augarde and
Spain, Hatters, No. 51, Oxford Street, London:—after
which he draws up his head with infinite gravity and
preparation, and makes the gentle recognition aforesaid.

But wherever there is a crowd, the new hat is worse
than useless. It is a pity that the general retrenchment

of people's finances did away with the flat opera hat,
which was a very sensible thing. The round one is only
in the way. The matting over the floor of the Opera
does not hinder it from getting dusty; not to mention
its chance of a kick from the inconsiderate. But from
the pit of the other theatres, you may bring it away
covered with sawdust, or rubbed up all the wrong way
of the nap, or monstrously squeezed into a shapeless
lump. The least thing to be expected in a pressure is
a great poke in its side like a sunken cheek.

Boating is a mortal enemy to new hats. A shower
has you fast in a common boat; or a sail-line, or an
inexperienced oar, may knock the hat off; and then
fancy it tilting over the water with the tide, soaked all
the while beyond redemption, and escaping from the
tips of your outstretched fingers, while you ought all
to be pulling the contrary way home.

But of all wrong boxes for a new hat, avoid a mail-
coach. If you kept it on, you will begin nodding perhaps at midnight, and then it goes jamming against the
side of the coach, to the equal misery of its nap and your
own. If you take it off, where is its refuge? Will the
clergyman take the least heed of it, who is snoring comfortably in one corner in his nightcap? Or will the
farmer, jolting about inexorably? Or the regular traveller, who in his fur-cap and infinite knowledge of
highway conveniences, has already beheld it with contempt? Or the old market-woman, whom it is in
vain to request to be tender? Or the young damsel,
who wonders how you can think of sleeping in such a
thing? In the morning, you suddenly miss your hat,
and ask after it with trepidation. The traveller smiles.
They all move their legs, but know nothing of it; till
the market-woman exclaims, 'Deary me! Well—
lord, only think! A hat, is it, sir? Why I do believe,
—but I'm sure I never thought o' such a thing more
than the child unborn—that it must be a hat then
which I took for a pan I've been a buying; and so I've
had my warm foot in it, Lord bless us, ever since five
o'clock this blessed morning!'

It is but fair to add that we happen to have an educated antipathy to the hat.   At our school no hats were worn, and the cap was too small to be a substitute.   Its only use is to astonish the old ladies in the street, who wonder how so small a thing can be kept on ; and to this end, it used to be rubbed into the back or side of the head, where it hung like a worsted wonder.   It is after the fashion of Katharina's cap in the play: it seems as if

> Moulded on a porringer ;
> Why, 'tis a cockle, or a walnut-shell,
> A knack, a toy, a trick, a baby's cap,
> A custard coffin, a bauble.

But we may not add :

> I love thee well, in that thou lik'st it not.

Ill befall us, if we ever dislike anything about thee, old nurse of our childhood ! How independent of the weather used we to feel in our old friar's dress,—our thick shoes, yellow worsted stockings, and coarse long coat or gown ! Our cap was oftener in our hand than on our head, let the weather be what it would. We felt a pride as well as pleasure, when everybody else was hurrying through the streets, in receiving the full summer showers with uncovered poll, sleeking our glad hair like the feathers of a bird.

It must be said for hats in general, that they are a very ancient part of dress, perhaps the most ancient ; for a negro who has nothing else upon him, sometimes finds it necessary to guard off the sun with a hat of leaves or straw. The Chinese, who carry their records farther back than any other people, are a hatted race, both narrow-brimmed and broad. We are apt to think of the Greeks as a bare-headed people ; and they liked to be so ; but they had hats for journeying in, such as may be seen on the statues of Mercury, who was the god of travellers. They were large and flapped, and were sometimes fastened round under the chin like a lady's straw-bonnet. The Eastern nations generally wore turbans, and do still, with the exception of the Persians, who have exchanged them for large conical caps of felt. The Romans copied the Greeks in their dress, as in everything else ; but the poorer orders wore a cap like their boasted Phrygian ancestors, resembling the one which the reader may now see about the streets upon the busts of Canova's Paris. The others would put their robes about their heads upon occasion,—a custom which probably gave rise to the hoods of the middle ages, and to the cloth head-dresses which we see in the portraits of Dante and Petrarch. From these were taken the draperies on the heads of our old Plantagenet kings and of Chaucer. The velvet cap which succeeded, appears also to have come from Italy, as in the portraits of Raphael and Titian : and it would probably have continued till the French times of Charles the Second, for our ancestors up to that period were always great admirers of Italy, had not Philip the Second of Spain come over to marry our Queen Mary. The extreme heats of Spain had forced the natives upon taking to that ingenious union of the hat and umbrella, still known by the name of the Spanish hat. We know not whether Philip himself wore it. His father, Charles the Fifth, who was at the top of the world, is represented as delighting in a little humble-looking cap. But we conceive it was either from Philip, or some gentleman in his train, that the hat and feather succeeded among us to the cap and jewels of Henry the Eighth. The ascendancy of Spain in these times carried it into other parts of Europe. The French, not requiring so much shade from the sun, and always playing with and altering their dress, like a child with his toy, first covered the brim with feathers, then gave them a pinch in front ; then came pinches up at the side ; and at last appeared the fierce and triple-daring cocked hat. This disappeared in our childhood, or only survived among the military, the old, and the reverend, who could not willingly part with their habitual dignity. An old beau or so would also retain it, in memory of its victories when young. We remember its going away from the heads of the foot-guards. The heavy dragoons retained it till very lately. It is now almost sunk into the mock-heroic, and confined, as we before observed, to beadles and coachmen, &c. The modern clerical beaver, agreeably to the deliberation with which our establishments depart from old custom, is a cocked hat with the hind flap let down, and only a slight pinch remaining in front. This is what is worn also by the judges, the lawyers being of clerical extraction. Still, however, the true cocked hat lingers here and there with a solitary old gentleman; and wherever it appears in such company, begets a certain retrospective reverence. There was a something in its connexion with the high-bred drawing-room times of the seventeenth century, in the gallant though quaint ardour of its look, and in its being lifted up in salutations with that deliberate loftiness, the arm arching up in front and slowly raising it by the front angle with finger and thumb,—that could not easily die. We remember, when our steward at school, remarkable for his inflexible air of precision and dignity, left off his cocked hat for a round one, there was, undoubtedly, though we dared only half confess it to our minds, a sort of diminished majesty about him. His infinite self-possession began to look remotely finite. His Crown-Imperial was a little blighted. It was like divesting a column of its capital. But the native stateliness was there, informing the new hat. He

> Had not yet lost
> *All* his original beaver; nor appeared
> Less than arch-steward ruined, and the excess
> Of glory obscured.

The late Emperor Paul had conceived such a sense of the dignity of the cocked hat, aggravated by its having given way to the round one of the French republicans, that he ordered all persons in his dominions never to dare be seen in public with round hats, upon pain of being knouted and sent to Siberia.

Hats, being the easiest part of the European dress to be taken off, are doffed among us out of reverence. The

Orientals, on the same account, put off their slippers instead of turbans; which is the reason why the Jews still keep their heads covered during worship. The Spanish grandees have the privilege of wearing their hats in the royal presence, probably in commemoration of the free spirit in which the Cortes used to crown the sovereign; telling him (we suppose in their corporate capacity) that they were better men than he, but chose him of their own free will for their master. The grandees only claim to be as good men, unless their families are older. There is a well-known story of a picture, in which the Virgin Mary is represented with a label coming out of her mouth, saying to a Spanish gentleman, who has politely taken off his hat, 'Cousin, be covered.' But the most interesting anecdote connected with a hat, belongs to the family of the De Courcys, Lords Kinsale. One of their ancestors, at an old period of our history, having overthrown a huge and insolent champion, who had challenged the whole court, was desired by the king to ask him some special favour. He requested that his descendants should have the privilege of keeping their heads covered in the royal presence, and they do so to this day. The new lord, we believe, always comes to court on purpose to vindicate his right. We have heard that on the last occasion, probably after a long interval, some of the courtiers thought it might as well have been dispensed with; which was a foolish as well as a jealous thing: for these exceptions only prove the royal rule. The Spanish grandees originally took their privilege instead of receiving it; but when the spirit of it had gone, their covered heads were only so many intense recognitions of the king's dignity, which it was thought such a mighty thing to resemble. A Quaker's hat is a more formidable thing than a grandee's.

FASHIONS—THE HOOP

[*Old Court Suburb*]

THE reader must fancy the Kensington Garden pro-
menaders, during this long lapse of time, waxing and
waning through almost all the vicissitudes of wigs, coats,
cocked-hats, and hoop-petticoats; for, with the exception of the full-bottomed peruke of the second Charles
and James, this was the great period of the reign of
those habiliments. The gentlemen began with the full-
bottomed peruke in the time of George the First; went
into the various modes of bag-wigs, and bobs, and
cocked-hats; and changed their coats from ugly to
uglier, but all of the same stiff race, with narrow shoulders, and broad hips and skirts, their swords being
retained to show that the narrow shoulders belonged
to men. The short-tailed coat that was in ascendancy
not long ago, with its wretched snipped horse-collar,
was the worst and most degenerate offspring of these
coats; for it was made as spare as possible, and had
not even colour to speak of; whereas its predecessors
were at least ample in the skirts and sleeves, and the
whole suit of clothes blazed out, whether in good taste
or otherwise, in silks and velvets, in reds, greens, and
gold lace. Colour was, at all events, respected, and
dress not grudged its proper dimensions.

The ladies, of course, during all this half century, and
these Kensington promenades, outdid the gentlemen
in the variety and novelty of their fashions. Their
head-dresses rose and fell in all the fluctuations of
piled-up and flowing hair; of ringlets, plain and powdered; of lappets, laces, ribbons, feathers, commodes,
hoods, bonnets, and mob-caps. Their colours were of
the brightest and most blooming kind. The fan was
in constant requisition; and muffs increased from small
to great. Morning dresses, indoors, might look a little
too careless to modern eyes, as the names of sacks and
negligées survive to testify. They might seem too
much like bed-gowns; or, at least, gowns unlaced.

And the bosom, in general, would be thought too much exposed. But the walking-dress, besides being more careful in that respect, showed an opposite extreme of tightness in the stays, while its skirts carried a weight of flounce and furbelow. Tory and Whig ladies, during the disputes about the Hanover succession, patched at one another in beauty-spots, differently arranged; and the white rose of the Pretender was sometimes ventured in public, on the bosom of the fair partisan. But the great glory of the whole period, with the exception of a brief interval, was the hoop. This Spanish invention (for such it is supposed to have been, and which originated perhaps in some royal dropsy, or other reason, best known to the inventor) is said to have been first copied by the court of France, in the time of Francis the First. It began there with the fardingales, which gradually swelled into the 'wheel,' 'big drum,' or sort of 'go-cart'; but in England it seems to have burst forth at once into all its bloom about the year 1708, during the reign of Anne; and it waxed and waned afterwards, in proportion as general adoption rendered the vicissitude necessary to the exclusives. The *Tatler* immediately took notice of it, in papers full of pleasant astonishment; and Pope assigned its 'important charge,' and 'wide circumference,' to twenty of his guardian spirits in the *Rape of the Lock*; who, besides the circumventions of the designing, were to save it from the aspersions of tea and coffee—

Trembling, and conscious of the rich brocade.

The hoop is considered the most monstrous enormity that ever made its appearance in the world of fashion. We confess we cannot think so. We think the notion originates in a mistake;—in a confusion of ideas; and that the monstrosity was confined to its minor phases; —to the drum, the go-cart, and the pair of panniers; which last was the form of it that prevailed towards the close of the reign of George the Third; and, under which, it finally went out in that of his son (for the hoop lasted a good hundred years in England): and even the

panniers, we think, were by no means at their worst,
when they were at their biggest. For the philosophy
of the matter (to use a fine modern phrase) we take to
be this. The hoop, like any other habiliment, was only
ugly inasmuch as it interfered with the mind's idea of
the body's shape. It was ugly, when it made the hips
appear dislocated, the body swollen, the gait unnatural ;
in other words, as long as it suggested the idea of some
actual deformity, and might have been considered as
made to suit it.

But when it was large, and the swell of it hung at a
proper distance from the person, it became, not an
habiliment, but an enclosure. The person stood aloof
from it, and was imagined to do so. The lady, like a
goddess, was half concealed in a hemisphere ; out of
which the rest of her person rose, like Venus out of the
billows. When she moved, and the hoop was of
proper length as well as breadth, she did not walk ;—
her steps were not visible ;—she was borne along ; she
was wafted ; came gliding. So issued the Wortley
Montagues, the Coventrys, and the Harveys, out of
their sedans ; and came radiant with admirations of
beholders, through avenues of them at palace doors.
Thus, poor Marie Antoinette came, during the height
of her bloom and ascendancy, through arrays, on either
side, of guards and adorers ; and swept along with her
the eyes and the reformations of Mr. Burke.

Therefore, we do not at all wonder at the enthusiasm
of Thomson in his juvenile days, when he wrote the
verses on Beauty :—

> One thing I mind—a spreading hoop she wore,
> Than nothing which adorns a lady more.
> With equal rage could I its beauties sing,
> I'd, with the hoop, make all Parnassus ring.
>
> With ladies there my ravish'd eyes did meet,
> That oft I've seen grace fair Edina's street,
> When their broad hoops cut through the willing air,
> Pleased to give place unto the lovely fair.

He thought High Street, Edinburgh, heaven itself, while the hoops were thus ethereally making their way :—

> Sure this is like those blissful seats above,
> Where all is peace, transporting joy, and love.

And again, in some verses written expressly ' On the Hoop.' Its appearance, it seems, in the Scottish capital, was not equally welcome to all parties. There were grave elders, whose imaginations beheld more danger in it than was conceivable by the juvenile poet. He grows angry, calls them hypocrites, and vindicates the innocence of the beloved enormity in a pleasant strain of mingled indignation, humour, and weak versification. There is one capital line, however, about the Quakers :—

> The hoop, the darling, justly, of the fair,
> Of every generous swain deserves the care.
> It is unmanly to desert the weak ;
> 'Twould urge a stone, if possible, to speak,
> To hear staunch hypocrites bawl out, and cry
> ' This hoop 's a (wanton) garb ; fie, ladies, fie ? '
> O cruel and audacious man, to blast
> The fame of ladies more than vestals chaste !
> Should you go search the globe throughout,[1]
> None will you find so pious and devout,
> So modest, chaste, so handsome, and so fair,
> As our dear Caledonian ladies are.
> When awful beauty puts on all her charms,
> Nought gives our sex such terrible alarms,
> As when the hoop and tartan both combine
> To make a virgin like a goddess shine.
> Let Quakers cut their clothes unto the quick,
> And with severities themselves afflict,
> But may the hoop adorn Edina's Street,
> Till the South Pole shall with the Northern meet.

Thomson's countryman, Allan Ramsay, was equally

---

[1] A foot has been dropped out of this verse.

zealous in behalf of hoops and tartans. He has even a
good word to say for patches :—

> In your opinion, nothing matches,
> O horrid sin ! the crime of patches !
> 'Tis false, ye clowns. I'll make 't appear,
> The glorious sun does patches wear ;
> Yea, run through every frame of nature,
> You'll find a patch for every creature ;
> E'en you yourselves, ye blacken'd wretches,
> To Heliconians are the patches.

Milton likens Dalila full dressed to a ship in full
sail :—

> With all her bravery on, and tackle trim,
> Sails fill'd, and streamers waving.

But Dalila must have been dressed after Eastern
fashion, which was rather draped than swelling ; more
turbaned or hooded, than topped with ribbons. What
could he have said, had he seen his image of the ship
enlarged and made out after true naval fashion, by the
swelling hoop, the air-catching fan, the solid, mast-like
stomacher, re-ascending in the pillar of the throat, and
the 'streamers waving in the wind,' of ribbons *à la
Fontange* ?

Imagine a squadron of them,—a dozen sail of the
line (of beauty),—headed by Admiral the Lady Mary,
or my Lady Hervey, supported by Captains Mrs.
Hewet and Mrs. Murray, or Commanders the Demoi-
selles Bellenden and Lepell. They are all coming up
the great high roadstead of Kensington Gardens,
between Bayswater and the town ; the gentlemen-
beholders dying by hundreds in their swords and periwigs, with their hats under their arms ; and the ladies
who have not been to court that day feeling envious
of the slaughter. Their sails are not mere white or
brown : they are of all the colours of the rainbow,
varied with gold and silver ; and Pope, who is looking
from one of the Palace windows with Dr. Mead, sees the
spirits of his *Rape of the Lock* filliping the jewels in
their ears, to make them tremble in the sun.

FACES, ABROAD

[Autobiography]

AT Paris we could stop but two days, and I had but two thoughts in my head ; one of the Revolution, the other of the times of Molière and Boileau. Accordingly I looked about for the Sorbonne, and went to see the place where the guillotine stood ;—the place where thousands of spirits underwent the last pang of mortality ; many guilty, many innocent, but all the victims of a reaction against tyranny, such as will never let tyranny be what it was, unless a convulsion of nature should swallow up knowledge, and make the world begin over again. These are the thoughts that enable us to bear such sights, and that serve to secure what we hope for.

Paris, besides being a beautiful city in the quarter that strangers most look to, the Tuileries, Quai de Voltaire, &c., delights the eye of a man of letters by the multitude of its bookstalls. There seemed to be a want of old books ; but the new were better than the shoal of *Missals* and *Lives of the Saints* that disappoint the lover of duodecimos on the stalls of Italy ; and the Rousseaus and Voltaires were endless. I thought, if I were a bachelor, not an Englishman, and had no love for old friends and fields, and no decided religious opinions, I could live very well, for the rest of my life, in a lodging above one of the bookseller's shops on the Quai de Voltaire, where I should look over the water to the Tuileries, and have the Elysian fields in my eye for my evening walk.

I liked much what little I saw of the French people. They are accused of vanity, and doubtless they have it, and after a more obvious fashion than other nations ; but their vanity, at least, includes the wish to please ; other people are necessary to them ; they are not wrapped up in themselves ; not sulky ; not too vain even to tolerate vanity. Their vanity is too much confounded with self-satisfaction. There is a good deal of touchiness, I suspect, among them—a good deal of ready-made heat, prepared to fire up in case the little commerce of flattery and sweetness is not properly carried on. But this is better than ill-temper, or than such egotism as is not to be appeased by anything short of subjection. On the other hand, there is more melancholy than one could expect, especially in old faces. Consciences in the south are frightened in their old age, perhaps for nothing. In the north, I suspect, they are frightened earlier, perhaps from equal want of knowledge. The worst in France is (at least, from all that I saw), that *fine* old faces are rare. There are multitudes of pretty girls; but the faces of both sexes fall off deplorably as they advance in life; which is not a good symptom. Nor do the pretty faces, while they last, appear to contain much depth, or sentiment, or firmness of purpose. They seem made like their toys, not to last, but to break up.

Fine faces in Italy are as abundant as cypresses. However, in both countries, the inhabitants appeared to us amiable, as well as intelligent; and without disparagement to the angel faces which you meet with in England, and some of which are perhaps finer than any you see anywhere else, I could not help thinking, that, as a race of females, the countenances both of the French and Italian women announced more pleasantness and reasonableness of intercourse, than those of my fair and serious countrywomen. The Frenchwoman looked as if she wished to please you at any rate, and to be pleased herself. She is too conscious; and her coquetry is said, and I believe with truth, to promise more than an Englishman would easily find her to perform: but at any rate she thinks of you somehow, and is smiling and good-humoured. An Italian woman appears to think of nothing, not even of herself. Existence seems enough for her. But she also is easy of intercourse, smiling when you speak to her, and very unaffected. Now, in simplicity of character the Italian appears to me to have the advantage of the English women, and in pleasantness of intercourse both Italian and French. When I came to England, after a residence of four years abroad, I was grieved at the succession of fair sulky faces which I met in the streets of London. They all appeared to come out of unhappy homes. In truth, our virtues, or our climate, or whatever it is, sit so uneasily upon us, that it is surely worth while for our philosophy to inquire whether, in some points of moral and political economy, we are not a little mistaken. Gipsies will hardly allow us to lay it to the climate.

It was a blessed moment, nevertheless, when we found ourselves among those dear sulky faces, the country-women of dearer ones, not sulky. We set out from Calais in the steamboat, which carried us to London, energetically trembling all the way under us, as if its burning body partook of the fervour of our desire. Here (thought we), in the neighbourhood of London, we are ; and may we never be without our old fields again in this world, or the old ' familiar faces ' in this world or in the next.

SHAKING HANDS

[*Indicator*, July 12, 1820]

AMONG the first things which we remember noticing in the manners of people, were two errors in the custom of shaking hands. Some, we observed, grasped every-body's hand alike,—with an equal fervour of grip. You would have thought that Jenkins was the best friend they had in the world ; but on succeeding to the squeeze, though a slight acquaintance, you found it equally flattering to yourself ; and on the appearance of some-body else (whose name, it turned out, the operator had forgotten) the crush was no less complimentary :—the face was as earnest and beaming, the ' glad to see you ' as syllabical and sincere, and the shake as close, as long, and as rejoicing, as if the semi-unknown was a friend come home from the Desarts.

On the other hand, there would be a gentleman now

and then as coy of his hand as if he were a prude, or
had a whitlow. It was in vain that your pretensions
did not go beyond the 'civil salute' of the ordinary
shake; or that being introduced to him in a friendly
manner and expected to shake hands with the rest of the
company, you could not in decency omit his. His
fingers, half coming out, and half retreating, seemed
to think that you were going to do them a mischief;
and when you got hold of them, the whole shake was
on your side: the other hand did but proudly or pen-
sively acquiesce,—there was no knowing which: you
had to sustain it, as you might a lady's in handing her
to a seat: and it was an equal perplexity to know
how to shake or to let it go. The one seemed a violence
done to the patient; the other an awkward responsibility brought upon yourself. You did not know, all
the evening, whether you were not an object of dislike
to the person; till on the party's breaking up, you saw
him behave like an equally ill-used gentleman, to all
who practised the same unthinking civility.

Both these errors, we think, might as well be avoided:
but of the two we must say we prefer the former. If
it does not look so much like particular sincerity, it
looks more like general kindness; and if those two
virtues are to be separated (which they assuredly need
not be, if considered without spleen) the world can
better afford to dispense with an unpleasant truth than
a gratuitous humanity. Besides, it is more difficult to
make sure of the one, than to practise the other; and
kindness itself is the best of all truths. As long as we
are sure of that, we are sure of something, and of something pleasant. It is always the best end, if not in
every instance the most logical means.

This manual shyness is sometimes attributed to
modesty, but never, we suspect, with justice, unless it
be that sort of modesty, whose fear of committing itself
is grounded in pride. Want of address is a better reason,
but this particular instance of it would be grounded in
the same feeling. It always implies a habit either of
pride or distrust. We have met with two really kind

men, who evinced this soreness of hand. Neither of them perhaps thought himself inferior to anybody about him, and both had good reason to think highly of themselves; but both had been sanguine men contradicted in their early hopes. There was a plot to meet the hand of one of them with a fish-slice, in order to show him the disadvantage to which he put his friends by that flat mode of salutation; but the conspirator had not the courage to do it. Whether he heard of the intention, we know not; but shortly afterwards he took very kindly to a shake. The other was the only man of a warm set of politicians who remained true to his first love of mankind. He was impatient at the change of his companions and at the folly and inattention of the rest; but though his manner became cold, his consistency still remained warm; and this gave him a right to be as strange as he pleased.

GALLANTRY

[A Year of Honeymoons]

When I had finished this lovely passage, Harriet, who had been loud and profuse in her expressions of delight at the others, said simply at this, in a low voice, 'How *very* sweet!' and stooping down on my hand, kissed it. It was to thank me for all the thoughts which she knew had passed between us on the subject, though we had not spoken, and for the relief I had afforded her by means of the poet. She is exquisite at this kind of *womanly gallantry*, if I may so call it, without degrading the feeling by the word. She never would allow from the first (indeed I never contested the point with her), that all the manifestation of courtesy, and deference, and gratitude should be on the man's side; and she says there are moments of exceeding fullness of heart, understood on both sides, when it is a grace in a woman to be foremost in manifesting her feelings. I know that, from a person of her exquisite taste, it is a very exquisite compliment.

CICISBEISM

[*Autobiography*]

THE famous order of things called *Cicisbeism* is the consequence of a state of society more inconsistent than itself, though less startling to the habits of the world; but it was managed in a foolish manner; and, strange to say, it was almost as gross, more formal, and quite as hypocritical as what it displaced. It is a stupid system. The poorer the people, the less, of course, it takes place among them; but as the husband, in all cases, has the most to do for his family, and is the person least cared for, he is resolved to get what he can before marriage; so a vile custom prevails among the poorest, by which no girl can get married unless she brings a certain dowry. Unmarried females are also watched with exceeding strictness; and in order to obtain at once a husband and freedom, every nerve is strained to get this important dowry. Daughters scrape up, servants pilfer for it. If they were not obliged to ornament themselves, as a help towards their object, I do not know whether even the natural vanity of youth would not be sacrificed, and girls hang out rags as a proof of their hoard, instead of the ' outward and visible sign' of crosses and earrings. Dress, however, disputes the palm with saving; and as a certain consciousness of their fine eyes and their natural graces survives everything else among southern womankind, English people have no conception of the high hand with which the humblest females in Italy carry it at a dance or an evening party. Hair dressed up, white gowns, satins, flowers, fans, and gold ornaments, all form a part of the glitter of the evening, and all, too, amidst as great, and perhaps as graceful a profusion of compliments and love-making as takes place in the most privileged ball-rooms. Yet it is twenty to one that nine out of ten persons in the room have dirty stockings on, and shoes out at heel. Nobody thinks of saving up articles of that description ; and they are too useful, and not showy enough, to be cared for *en passant*. Therefore Italian girls may often enough be well compared to flowers ; with head and bodies all ornament, their feet are in the earth ; and thus they go nodding forth for sale, 'growing, blowing, and all alive.' A foolish English servant whom we brought out with us, fell into an absolute rage of jealousy at seeing my wife give a crown of flowers to a young Italian servant, who was going to a dance. The latter, who was of the most respectable sort, and looked as lady-like as you please when dressed, received the flowers with gratitude, though without surprise ; but English and Italian both were struck speechless when, in addition to the crown, my wife presented the latter with a pair of her own shoes and stockings. Doubtless, they were the triumph of the evening. Next day we heard accounts of the beautiful dancing ;—of Signor F., the English valet, opening the ball with the handsome chandler's-shopkeeper, &c., and our poor countrywoman was ready to expire.

RESPECTABILITY

[*Table-Talk*]

' WHEN the question was put to one of the witnesses on the trial of Thurtell, " What sort of a person was Mr. Weare ? " the answer was, " Mr. Weare was *re-spectable*." On being pressed by the examining counsel as to what he meant by respectability, the definition the witness was, that " *he kept a gig* " ! '

' A person,' says the *York Courant*, on this incident, ' was annoying a whole company in a public room, and one of them reproving him sharply for his indecorum, an apologist whispered, ' Pray, do not offend the gentleman ; I assure you he is a *respectable* man. He is worth *two hundred a year independent property*.'

There is no getting at the root of these matters, unless we come to etymology. People mean something when they say a man is respectable—they mean something different from despicable or intolerable. What is it they do mean? Why, they mean that the gentleman is worth *twice looking at*—he is respectable, *re-spectabilis*; that is to say, literally, one who is to be looked at *again*; you must not pass him as though he were a common man; you must turn round and observe him well; a second look is necessary if you have the least respect for him: if you have more, you look at him again and again: and if he is very respectable indeed, and you have the soul of a footman, you look at him till he is out of sight, and turn away with an air as if you could black his shoes for him,

But what *is* 'respectable'? What is the virtue that makes a man worth twice looking at? We have intimated it in what has been said. The *York Courant* has told us—*he keeps a gig*. Gig is virtue. A buggy announces moral worth. *Curriculus evehit ad deos.*

But you must be sure that he does keep it. He may come in a gig, and yet the gig not be his own; in which case it behoves you to be cautious. You must not be taken in by appearances. He may look like a gentleman; he may be decently dressed; you may have seen him perform a charitable action; he may be a soldier covered with scars, a patriot, a poet, a great philosopher; but for all this, beware how you are in too much haste to look twice at him—the gig may have been borrowed.

On the other hand, appearances must not condemn a man. A fellow (as you may feel inclined to call him) drives up to the door of an inn; his face (to your thinking) is equally destitute of sense and goodness; he is dressed in a slang manner, calls for his twentieth glass of gin, has flogged his horse till it is raw, and *condemns*, with energetic impartiality, the eyes of all present, his horse's, the bystanders', and his own. Now, before you pronounce this man a blackguard, or think him rather to be turned away from with loathing, than looked at twice out of respect, behave you as impartially as he: take the ostler aside, or the red-faced fellow whom he has brought in the gig with him, and ask,

'Is the gig his own?' The man, for aught you know, may reply, 'His own! Lord love you, he has a mint of money. He could ride in his coach if he pleased. He has kept a gig and Moll Fist these two years.' Thus you see, without knowing it, you might have loathed a respectable man. 'He keeps his gig.'

But this respectable gentleman not only keeps his gig—he might keep his coach. He is respectable *in esse; in posse* he is as respectable as a sheriff—you may look twice at him; nay, many times. Let us see. We have here a clue to the degrees of a man's respectability. To keep a gig is to be simply respectable; you may look twice at the gig-man. A curricle, having two horses, and costing more, is, of course, more respectable. You may look at the possessor of a curricle at least twice and a half. A chariot renders him fit to be regarded over and over again: a whole carriage demands that you should many times turn your neck to look at him; if you learn that he drives a coach and four, the neck may go backwards and forwards for three minutes; and if the gentleman abounds in coaches, his own carriage for himself, and another for his wife, together with gig, buggy, and dog-cart, you are bound to stand watching him all the way up Pall Mall, your head going like a fellow's jaws over a pan-pipe, and your neck becoming stiff with admiration.

The story of 'the two hundred a year independent property' is a good appendage to that of the gig-keeping worthy. The possessor of this virtue was annoying a whole company in a public room, and one of them reproving him for his indecorum, somebody whispered, 'Do not offend the gentleman; he is a respectable man, I assure you. He is worth two hundred a year independent property.' The meaning of this is, 'I am a slave, and believe you to be a slave: think what strutting fellows *we* should be if we possessed two hundred a year; and let us respect ourselves in the person of this bully.'

If people of this description could translate the feelings they have towards the rich, such is the language their version would present to them, and it might teach them something which they are ignorant of at present. The pretence of some of them is, that money is a great means of good as well as evil, and that of course they should secure the good and avoid the evil. But this is not the real ground of their zeal; otherwise they would be zealous in behalf of health, temperance, and honesty, good-humour, fair dealing, generosity, sincerity, public virtue, and everything else that advances the good of mankind. No; it is the pure, blind love of power, and the craving of weakness to be filled with it. Allowance should be made for much of it, as it is the natural abuse in a country where the most obvious power is commercial; and the blindest love of power, after all (let them be told this secret for the comfort of human nature), is an instinct of sympathy—is founded on what others will think of us, and what means we shall find in our hands for adding to our importance. It is this value for one another's opinion which keeps abuses so long in existence; but it is in the same corner of the human heart, now that reform has begun, that the salvation of the world will be found.

The World's Classics

THE best recommendation of The World's Classics is the books themselves, which have earned unstinted praise from critics and all classes of the public. Some two million copies have been sold, and of the volumes already published nearly one-half have gone into a second, third, fourth, fifth, sixth, seventh, eighth, ninth, or tenth impression. It is only possible to give so much for the money when large sales are certain. The clearness of the type, the quality of the paper, the size of the page, the printing, and the binding—from the cheapest to the best—cannot fail to commend themselves to all who love good literature presented in worthy form. That a high standard is insisted upon is proved by the list of books already published and of those on the eve of publication. A great feature is the brief critical introductions written by leading authorities of the day. The volumes of The World's Classics are obtainable, bound in cloth and leather, as given on page 1; and special attention is directed to the sultan-red limp leather style for presentation.

The Pocket Edition is printed on thin opaque paper, by means of which the bulk is greatly reduced.

January, 1918.

LIST OF THE SERIES

The figures in parentheses denote the number of the book in the series

List of the Series—*continued*

List of the Series—*continued*

List of the Series—*continued*

List of the Series—*continued*

List of the Series—*continued*

HUMPHREY MILFORD
OXFORD UNIVERSITY PRESS
LONDON, EDINBURGH, GLASGOW
NEW YORK, TORONTO, MELBOURNE, BOMBAY
CAPE TOWN, & SHANGHAI